THE SKETCH, THE TALE, AND THE
BEGINNINGS OF AMERICAN LITERATURE

The Sketch, the Tale, and the Beginnings of American Literature

Lydia G. Fash

UNIVERSITY OF VIRGINIA PRESS

Charlottesville and London

University of Virginia Press
© 2020 by the Rector and Visitors of the University of Virginia
All rights reserved

First published 2020

9 8 7 6 5 4 3 2 1

Library of Congress Cataloging-in-Publication Data

Names: Fash, Lydia G., 1981– author.
Title: The sketch, the tale, and the beginnings of American literature /
    Lydia G. Fash.
Description: Charlottesville ; London : University of Virginia Press, 2020. |
    Includes bibliographical references and index.
Identifiers: LCCN 2019045163 (print) | LCCN 2019045164 (ebook) |
    ISBN 9780813943978 (hardcover) | ISBN 9780813943985 (paperback) |
    ISBN 9780813943992 (epub)
Subjects: LCSH: Short stories, American—History and criticism. | American
    fiction—19th century—History and criticism. | Literature and society—
    United States—History—19th century. | Literary form—History—19th
    century. | Books and reading—United States—History—19th century.
Classification: LCC PS374.S5 F37 2020 (print) | LCC PS374.S5 (ebook) |
    DDC 823/.010908—dc23
LC record available at https://lccn.loc.gov/2019045163
LC ebook record available at https://lccn.loc.gov/2019045164

Cover art: Shutterstock/Abstractor; Shutterstock/Cold Berry; Shutterstock/
Elovich; Shutterstock/Flas100; Shutterstock/locote; Shutterstock/Sailorr;
Shutterstock/Lukasz Szwaj

For Leo and Nico, who both had their beginnings while I wrote this book, and for Nate. Obviously.

❖ CONTENTS ❖

❖ ACKNOWLEDGMENTS ❖

I have incurred many debts over the long years I have been working on this book, and it is a pleasure to thank those who have helped me compose and complete it. First, it seems fitting to acknowledge that this manuscript started as a dissertation and benefited from the guidance and feedback of both Michael T. Gilmore and Susan S. Lanser at Brandeis University. I remember the certain cock of Timo's head and his probing questions when I pointed out that Irving's *Sketch Book* was composed of sketches and tales: "You could do something with that," he said. I owe a particular debt to Sue not just for her scholarly critique but also for championing me as I tried to balance writing and motherhood. I remain unendingly grateful for her reassurance that I would be able to continue *after I recovered* as I struggled to heal from giving birth as well as her later care for me and mine. I am grateful too to John Plotz and John Burt, who mentored me both when and after I was at Brandeis by writing letters on my behalf, giving generous advice, and providing examples of admirable scholarship. Thank you to Aliyyah Abdur-Rahman, who remains a model of the socially conscious, intellectually challenging, pedagogically innovative, and effortlessly graceful academic.

I am also happy to thank Cory Elizabeth Nelson, Lisa Rourke, and Njelle Hamilton, whose companionship and humor buoyed me through graduate school. Lisa's ongoing friendship, as our cohort moved away for work, is a joy. Cory read every single word of my dissertation multiple times, caught innumerable mistakes, and made all of my arguments better. In addition to all the feedback she gave during graduate school, Njelle shared everything she learned about publishing monographs with me as she herself went through the publication process. Her cheerleading and pointed questions kept me trekking—sometimes trudging—along toward this final manuscript.

I am overjoyed to have found an intellectual home at Simmons University among colleagues—Renée Bergland, Pam Bromberg, Sheldon George, Audrey Golden, Suzanne Leonard, Lowry Pei, and Richard Wollman—committed to excellence in the classroom and on the page. I am grateful for the comradery of all of these scholar-teachers. My thanks in particular to Suzanne, whose critical eye greatly improved my prospectus and whose encouragement pushed me to send it to presses, and to Renée, who gave me advice on how to think about the different offers that I received. Thank you too to Leanne Doherty for supporting the completion of this book by means of a course release.

I am thrilled that this manuscript found a home with the University of Virginia Press, and I am indebted to Eric Brandt, Helen Chandler, George Roupe, and the other talented folks at the Press.

I have the deepest appreciation and love for my parents, whose unflagging belief in me and my abilities has been a grounding rod throughout my life. Their support has taken innumerable forms over the years, from moving help to babysitting and copy-editing. All of this has helped this monograph—and all that is wonderful about my life—come to be. Thank you.

Finally, to Nate, my love and my partner, without whom I would never have written a book or stuck it out in academia. Life, even the ugly parts, is wonderful with you. Thank goodness Jumbo went to Diesel that day once long ago. (I was hoping for one of those before we left.) And to Leo and Nico, my beautiful brilliant sons, for making me want to finish this book and for reminding me why I should take a break from working on it. ¡Ah, Mambru, esto es la gloria! Los quiero mucho mucho.

Two anonymous reviewers from the University of Virginia Press offered trenchant feedback in two rounds of review that made this a much better project; similarly, some earlier reviewers who read parts of this project in article form helped with the clarification and evolution of my ideas. My thanks to all these busy scholars for their insights. Portions of this work are reprinted with permission from the following sources: a version of chapter 1 first appeared in *Symbiosis: A Journal of Transatlantic and Literary Cultural Relations*, 20, no. 2 (2016): 147–69. Parts of chapter 4 first appeared in *Narrative* 21, no. 2 (2013): 221–42. And sections about *The Scarlet Letter, Uncle Tom's Cabin,* and *Moby-Dick* from chapter 6 first appeared the *New England Quarterly* 89, no. 2 (2016): 167–91. I am grateful to these publications for allowing me to reprint my arguments here in expanded and altered form.

THE SKETCH, THE TALE, AND THE
BEGINNINGS OF AMERICAN LITERATURE

Narrative and Historical Beginnings

In 1776, when Thomas Jefferson, John Adams, and Benjamin Franklin were tasked with choosing a motto for the Great Seal of the United States, they turned to the London-based *Gentleman's Magazine* and borrowed *E Pluribus Unum*, Latin for "out of many, one," from the title page of a year of bound issues. Selected by the magazine's founder Edward Cave, this phrase expressed that disparate texts formed a single literary product, an idea reinforced by an engraving of a hand holding a bouquet of flowers. As Jefferson, Adams, and Franklin imagined it, the United States was similar, a single country constituted of many states and many individuals with distinct identities and voices. And yet, just as not all people were represented equally within the United States, not all genres were represented equally within a miscellany. Short prose forms (written by white authors) dominated the *Gentleman's Magazine,* and as the years passed and these turned into sketches and tales, they came to dominate American periodicals. Such short fiction offered succinct but entertaining literary transport. Through brevity, they assured variety and interest and, when compiled, created a shaggy coherence symbolic of a national unity. Hence, the popular gift book the *Atlantic Souvenir* (1827) featured *E Pluribus Unum* on its cover and contained within its pages both tales and sketches, including Lydia Maria Child's "The Rival Brothers: A *Tale* of the Revolution" and an anonymously authored "Biographical *Sketch* of the Life of Alexander Wilson, Ornithologist." (The volume also contained tales by James Kirke Paulding and Catharine Maria Sedgwick and a sketch by Washington Irving.) Both because of their miscellaneous structure and because of the included short

Title page for the 1775 volume of the *Gentleman's Magazine or, Monthly Intelligencer*, showing a bouquet of flowers accompanied by the phrase *e pluribus unum*. (Courtesy American Antiquarian Society)

fiction about and by Americans, *Atlantic Souvenirs* became "national works of so much merit" and, like the *Gentleman's Magazine*, felt representative of the United States and its people.[1]

Mapping the literary collection onto the United States goes against decades of received critical wisdom that privilege a connection between novel and nation. Cathy Davidson pointed out in her magisterial *Revolution and the Word* (1986) that both the United States and the novel burst onto the world stage together in the late eighteenth century. But as Davidson notes,

Paper board cover of the *Atlantic Souvenir* of 1827
with patriotic imagery and the phrase *e pluribus unum.*
Gift books and collections, and the short fiction they
contained, were marked as American through their
subject matter and because they formed one collection out of many parts, or *e pluribus unum.* (Courtesy
American Antiquarian Society)

early American novels are rarely over three hundred pages, and sometimes
less than one hundred, a fact that indicates that the genre is not consol-
idated as the "novel," even though Davidson relies on the term.[2] On the
theoretical side, Mikhail Bakhtin's belief that, like the democratic nation,
the novel is "a phenomenon multiform in style and variform in speech," per-
mitting a "multiplicity of social voices and a wide variety of their links and

interrelationships (always more or less dialogized)" has had huge influence.[3] And yet, in privileging the singular story world of the novel under the guise of celebrating its multiform contents, Bakhtin implies that nations are fully cohered and their people unproblematically unified. *E pluribus unum* suggests that Jefferson, Adams, Franklin, and their fellows did not project this same flattening, single-story world onto the nascent republic. Instead, like Ralph Waldo Emerson, they saw the country as a storehouse of all sorts of written objects lying side by side and joined together by a cover.[4] The metaphor of the miscellany recognizes the regional affiliations and local characteristics that, as Trish Loughran has argued, informed earlier US literary production and self-identities while simultaneously celebrating the narrative links and social bonds that made these distinct pieces into a riotous, uneven whole.[5]

That is to say, the miscellany, a term that includes gift books, magazines, literary newspapers, and collections, works well as a metaphor for the nation precisely because it is a fractious object whose coherence is produced through bindings, collocations (the placement of items next to each other), and paratexts (Gerard Genette's term for items like prefaces and book jacket copy that surround and frame the main text). Moreover, while I focus on short fiction in this book, the nation as miscellany foregrounds the presence of other cultural forces and modes of writing that contribute to the idea of the nation. Through the metaphor of the miscellany, therefore, I reject the idea that a single genre creates and reflects all processes of national formation. Incorporating different treatments of time, different levels of diction, and different formats, the miscellany is unpredictable and imperfect. But because it contains tensions and contradictions, because it is artificial and manufactured, it provides a vehicle for a more nuanced and complicated view of the varied literary evocation of our more perfect union. Embracing this messiness, I examine what short fiction, which was a mainstay of collections and periodicals in the nineteenth century, can tell us about ideas of the United States before 1845. In its brevity, short fiction expresses the miscellany's aesthetic of fragmentation and reflects efforts to represent the United States at a moment when it too was disjunctive.

In form and in content, US short fiction was a critical vehicle for forming the "people," that political conception of oneself as part of a larger national community. This ideological phenomenon is both a projection and creator of the nation, since the nation only exists insofar as it represents a group of people, but these individuals come into being as a national *people* only through the existence of the nation. Hence, the Constitution, which outlines the structure of the government, opens with "We, the people" and then indicates that the people are those who "insure domestic tranquility, provide for the common defense," and so on. The appositive that restates "we" with "the people" incorporates the "I" into a collective "we" that then becomes symbolic of the political and ideological nation. In that grammatical move, normal citizens are elevated and transformed into something larger and grander.

Appearing in all types of publications, American short fiction helped readers make this same imaginative jump as its quotidian nature—that is, its frequent appearance and its comfortable claim of portraying US citizens—incorporated and reincorporated regular readers into the *people*. For forming the people was and is not a one-time act. It is a process of continual renewal, negotiation, and interpolation that makes individuals feel that they are part of a social grouping that is distinct and unique. Short fiction was suited for this task in part because it aesthetically reflected contemporary ideas about the United States. In *Democracy in America* (1835), Alexis de Tocqueville mused that democratic literature was necessarily various, even vulgar, and irregular, while aristocratic literature was long, erudite, and structured into recognizable and strict forms. The latter caters to those with learning and leisure, and its rigid formal qualities mirror an ossified social hierarchy. The former privileges life over refinement and practical brevity over length. Concision answers to the time constraints of self-reliant Americans, who have little ability to devote hours to belles lettres and want to make the most of the minutes they can use to read. In a truly democratic country where literature reflects the people and caters to them, de Tocqueville believed, "small productions will be more common than bulky books."[6] Surrounded by the sketches and tales of the 1830s United States, this national observer concluded that short fiction—direct, exciting, vital, and accessible—was the form that fit the United States and its people. It was the form that told readers who was American and what it meant to be so.

Despite its enormous cultural importance, short fiction has long gotten critical short shrift. Indeed, even with copious evidence to the contrary, most modern critics treat the sketch and the tale, the two major forms of nineteenth-century short fiction, as indistinguishable. And critics frequently rely on the anachronistic label "short story," which only came into usage in the third quarter of the nineteenth century.[7] For example, Robert F. Marler, who uses "tale" as a critical category in his article "From Tale to Short Story" (1974), argues that "the terms 'tale,' 'story,' 'short story,' and 'sketch' were interchangeable."[8] More recently, in *American Enchantment* (2017), Michelle Sizemore treats the terms as synonymous when she calls "Rip Van Winkle" both a "tale" and a "sketch," and refers to Hawthorne's "The May-Pole of Merry Mount" as a "short story."[9] Likewise, Tim Killick asserts, "It is worth re-iterating here that terms such as 'sketch,' 'scene,' 'tale,' and 'story' were often used interchangeably," although his book title, *British Short Fiction in the Early Nineteenth Century: The Rise of the Tale* (2008), positions "tale" as central to his argument.[10] It is true that the sketch and the tale have some overlap and that some pieces of short fiction are hard to classify.[11] But the sketch and the tale are nonetheless real, distinguishable, and important genres in nineteenth-century English-language literature.[12] After Washington Irving offered different narrators and national associations for the sketches and for the tales in his best-selling *Sketch Book* (1819–20), Sarah Josepha Hale penned "Sketches of American Character," Nathaniel Hawthorne wrote "Tales from the Province House," and Edgar Allan Poe lauded his own "tales of ratiocination."[13] Acknowledging the popularity of both genres, Catharine Maria Sedgwick collected her previously published short fiction into *Tales and Sketches* (1835). She was in good company titling her collection with these genre names. Between 1819 and 1845, William Leete Stone, Chandler Robbins Gilman, Benjamin Smith, Drake Benjamin, Nathaniel Greene, James Lawson, and a number of anonymous authors all also penned volumes with *Tales and Sketches* in their titles or subtitles. This recognition of tales and sketches was not limited to the eastern United States. Across the Atlantic, Charles Dickens similarly labeled pieces tales and sketches, as in the table of contents and prefatory note of *Sketches by Boz* (1836). So too Mary Mitford's celebrated collection *Our Village* (1824) was originally entitled "Village Sketches," and James Hogg wrote both *Altrive Tales, Collected among the Peasantry of Scotland* (1832) and a collection of Scottish short fiction called *Tales and Sketches, by the Ettrick Shepherd* (1837).[14] Even as the tale and the sketch were found cheek by jowl, British and American authors used them as distinct and identifying genre terms, especially after the spectacular success of Irving's collection made the genres legible and meaningful to US readers.

In both a thematic and a narrative sense, this book traces the figuration of American beginnings in those early nineteenth-century sketches and tales. As Edward Said would remind us and as nineteenth-century US authors well knew, beginnings are "the first step in the intentional production of meaning."[15] Said's comment highlights both the artificiality and the necessity of beginnings like the one I have supplied at the start of this book. It also points to the ideological weight that beginnings hold in national stories—that we celebrate the Fourth of July as "America's birthday" illustrates the point. Because beginnings have such resonance, they were powerful, even dangerous, narrative tools. In an 1835 magazine tale, Nathaniel Hawthorne depicted the enraged Oberon (a fictive alter ego who has Hawthorne's college nickname) burning a manuscript about a Puritan "fiend."[16] Rejected over and over by publishers because this devil did not fit with accounts of Puritans as protodemocrats, the manuscript does not just burn itself. It sets a boardinghouse's roof on fire. The tale's moral is that an unrepentantly evil Puritan is incompatible with the accepted understanding of Puritans as national founders, and although a delirious Oberon laughs that his "brain has set the town on fire," his life and that of his fellow townspeople are in mortal danger from his risky depiction.[17] That this Hawthorne story appeared in a magazine in 1835 under a pseudonym ("Ashley A. Royce") and was never subsequently republished—although Hawthorne brought out three volumes of previously printed tales—suggests that Hawthorne saw the Puritan fiend as truly dangerous despite Oberon's tale-end bravado.

In the narration of the nation, beginnings help define a people by highlighting important themes or characteristics of that group. By mapping the point from which the people sprang, origin stories give the people what Etienne Balibar calls a "fictive ethnicity," a projected "natural community, possessing of itself an identity of origins, culture, and interests which transcend individuals and social conditions."[18] As they resonate with the idea of "American," beginning stories give individuals origins that are often not personally accurate: nineteenth-century Americans could, like contemporary Americans often do, claim Puritans as their past even if their relatives came from elsewhere a hundred years after the Puritans arrived. My example here is purposeful, for through focus on the Puritans, on the Founding Fathers, and on Jamestown, beginning stories fashioned the fictive ethnicity of the United States as indisputably *white* before the 1840s. In a period when slavery was legal and before whiteness became fractured through increasing immigration, many European immigrants were unproblematically enfolded into this shared imagined white people. Published short fiction reflects this history not just in the whiteness it projects but also in the fact that it was white authors who wrote it. Someone like Jane Johnston Schoolcraft, the first known female Native American writer, writes items, not clearly sketches or tales, in a manuscript magazine the *Literary Voyageur or Muzzeniegun* (1826–27), passed between friends in Sault Ste. Marie, Michigan. Her work is shut out of broadly distributed printed periodicals and volumes. Back in New York, the *Anglo-African Magazine,* home of the first published short story by an African American (Frances Ellen Watkins Harper's "The Two Offers"), does not start publication until 1859, by which point the dynamics of literary production that encourage both beginning celebrations and short fiction have altered. Only with the increasing circulation of slave narratives and abolitionist screeds in the 1840s was there wider public challenge to the racial exclusion conjured in short fiction.

Focusing on the sketches and tales of seven white and one black writer—Washington Irving, Sarah Hale, Catharine Sedgwick, Nathaniel Hawthorne, Edgar Allan Poe, Herman Melville, Harriet Beecher Stowe, and William Wells Brown—*The Sketch, the Tale, and the Beginnings of American Literature* recognizes the fictive ethnicity of the people and the critical role that short fiction beginning stories played in creating and maintaining it before 1845, a time of improving infrastructure, increasing literacy, and greater stability in the book industry. By attending to both the aesthetics and the functions of sketches and tales, I argue that the formal dimensions of short fiction made it a particularly compelling mode of writing about US beginnings for the three decades between the War of 1812 and the Mexican-American War, a period of time I call the culture of beginnings.[19] To understand this moment, I accept an author's stated intentions and use their invocations of the national to decode the social networks and communities formed by reading and writing. For during these years short fiction enabled an *e pluribus unum* of white people, both through myriad celebrations of American history and through formal means.[20] Because of their brevity, sketches and tales were almost always a smaller part of another publication, be it newspaper, magazine, or volume. This double framing of story proper and larger collection meant that while individual narratives evoked powerful somatic responses, part of their utility lay in the expectation that there was more outside that particular story world. Tales and sketches thereby allowed nineteenth-century white US readers to imagine themselves as part of a larger national community. Operating under the assumption that "formal features of a text, matters of style, can be indices to large intellectual and cultural matters," I rescue early nineteenth-century short fiction from long-standing neglect and position it prominently and properly in accounts of US letters, while fully highlighting the racial exclusion consciously built into that literary tradition.[21]

The Time of Beginnings

Through attention to genre and narrative technique, this project joins the growing field of what have been called time studies, characterized by the recent notable contributions of scholars including Michelle Sizemore, Matthew P. Brown, Lloyd Pratt, Rita Felski, Wai Che Dimock, and Elizabeth Freeman. While their critical stances and objects of study differ, these and other scholars seek to complicate the presumption of a single, shared, homogenous empty time, as popularized by Benedict Anderson in *Imagined Communities* (1983). Anderson posited that the realist novel and the newspaper are the dominant textual genres of modern nation formation. Both formats allowed geographically distant readers with little in common to imagine themselves invested in the same stories at what they perceived to be the same time. Someone in New York reads about a train crash and imagines someone in Boston doing the same. That projected simultaneity makes the readers feel that they share an empty, uncomplicated, even chronology, one critical, according to Anderson, for producing the "imagined community" that is the nation. For Anderson this empty time is partly the result of changes in timekeeping: as the nineteenth century wore on, individual communities moved from local time, as reckoned by the sun's behavior in that particular location, to standardized time, as dictated by railroad timetables, factory bells, and new clocks and as eventually codified in the time zones that exist today.[22] In other words, because of industrialization, people were forced away from their local social and temporal communities into imagined relationships with far-flung others in their nation. In turn, they came to believe that they shared ideals and values with their compatriots. Starting with Homi Bhabha and Partha Chatterjee, more recent critics have disputed this account of the modern condition and the foundation of the modern nation-state, for nineteenth-century peoples across the globe had a much more sophisticated experience of temporality than the idea of "empty time" represents. I join this expansion of our understanding of time in the chapters that follow by articulating how US readers were aware of and invested in local temporalities and specific reading networks that presented them with circular, suspended, and backward story time. That is not to say, however, that there were not also representations of the single straight temporal arrow of progress presumed in accounts of modernity. Tales and sketches most certainly grappled with this figuration of time and country, even as they explored new narrative techniques that bent and reshaped time. I show that the negotiation between these two positions—temporal innovation and temporal linearity—displays calculated attempts to form readerly communities that could lay claim to national status. The temporal strategies developed and deployed in these tales and sketches are about making space in a culture of beginnings, a culture vocally invested in defining the United States.

Between the War of 1812 and the Compromise of 1850, many believed that American beginnings were what made the country one of a kind. In 1776, no other colony had asserted its independence, and no European country had such a clearly defined moment of birth. While England's history stretched back into foggy myths and imprecise dates, Americans could, to use Jeremy Belknap's phrasing in the *History of New Hampshire* (1794–98), "fix the beginning of this great American Empire" on July 4, 1776, when the Declaration of Independence announced independent statehood.[23] "Perhaps no people on the globe," agreed John Lendrum in A *Concise and Impartial History of the American Revolution* (1795), "can trace the history of their origin and progress with so much precision."[24] In his *American Annals, or, A Chronological History of America* (1805), Abiel Holmes similarly gushed about the United States, "That remarkable discovery, those events and actions, can now be accurately ascertained without recourse to such legends, as have darkened and disfigured the early annals of most nations."[25] Homi Bhabha opened his *Nation and Narration* with the observation that "nations, like narratives, lose their origins in the myths of time," but Americans felt exceptional and proud precisely because they did not believe this to be true about their country.[26] Being able to identify a certain origin gave and gives Americans a perceived cosmological relation to their history: the story of American genesis becomes a version of Genesis. Yet obviously, no beginning is actually so clear. Indeed, July 4 is not the date on which Congress voted for independence but the date on which the delegates *approved* the Declaration of Independence and ordered that it be sent to the printer. It would thus be as valid—or more valid—to have July 2 be America's birthday rather than that which we currently celebrate. Or perhaps a better starting day might be April 19, 1775, when the Battle of Lexington and Concord occurred. Or even March 5, 1770, when British regulars opened fire on Bostonians, killing five in what would later be known as the Boston Massacre. Or maybe October 1768, when Redcoats first began occupying Boston and inadvertently fanning the flames of revolution. Just as proper might be November 11, 1620, when the Mayflower Compact, which has come to be read as the first assertion of self-governance by European colonists in the Americas, was signed, or May 13, 1607, when Jamestown was founded. Or we might point to 1507, when German cartographer Martin Waldseemüller drew the world map that first used the term "America" for North and South America. (In 2003 the Library of Congress purchased the only surviving copy of this wall map, which it called "America's birth certificate," for $10 million.)[27] And then of course there is October 12, 1492, when Christopher Columbus sighted land in the Americas, unleashing a tide of European migration and conquest. We would also be right to acknowledge that groups like the Powhatan, integral to the survival of the early English colonists and Americans in their own right, lived in what is now the United States for ages before Columbus. Each of these dates—as well as a host of others—is some sort of American beginning. Each is also an obvious continuation of ideas and actions both prior and subsequent, for beginnings are as false as they are useful.

As such, whether or not the sketches and tales that I discuss were historically accurate is all but immaterial. Despite being treated as a proto–Declaration of Independence, the Mayflower Compact was no attempt to assert freedom from the king. Rather, in the opening line of the short document, the signers acknowledge themselves "the loyal subjects of our dread Sovereigne Lord, King James, by the grace of God, of Great Britaine, France and Ireland king, defender of the faith, etc." The Mayflower Compact works as a proto–Declaration of Independence only because the Declaration of Independence later comes to pass. What follows determines what is chosen as the beginning, and in turn the beginning determines what follows. Oedipus's natal prophecy, for example, explains and predestines his later parricide and incest but is only relevant and interesting because of those subsequent events. Put another way, when critics like Perry Miller and Sacvan Bercovitch see the Puritans as moral modern figures, they are affirming their beliefs that they and those like them are too. The power of sketches and tales about Revolutionary soldiers, Puritan theologians, dissenting Quakers, Old Dutch farmers, and homesteading women was precisely that they imagined social relations and naturalized them enough for readers to accept as a version of history that explained their present.

Literature is just one way in which beginnings were enacted for nineteenth-century citizens, for between 1815 and 1845, a plethora of festivals, statues, and orations depicted the United States as unique, noble, and history-rich—qualities Europeans mocked Americans for not being. Having started in Massachusetts where the Pilgrims had landed, Forefathers' Day celebrations swept through the country during the early nineteenth century. In Pennsylvania, Georgia, Kentucky, South Carolina, Kansas, Louisiana, Illinois, Michigan, Ohio, California, and Oregon, partygoers celebrated the Pilgrims on December 22, with food (often succotash and clams), drink, speeches, and sometimes dancing or parades.[28] In 1820, at a bicentennial celebration of the Pilgrims' landing at Plymouth Rock, Daniel Webster gave a more than two-hour patriotic oration that became an instant classic school children were forced to memorize for decades afterward.[29] The actual granite rock, part of which was moved to the front lawn of Pilgrim Hall Museum at the institution's opening in 1834, experienced a frenzy of souvenir hunters who chipped off bits and pieces to take home, and many Puritan texts were published or republished in the early nineteenth century.[30] The appearance of these primary sources indicated the wide interest in Puritans, but the expense of such volumes meant that the average reader could not buy them. Instead, they subscribed to magazines, annuals, newspapers, and collections in which short fiction about Puritans helped form their ideas of history. Hawthorne and Sedgwick, both of whom wrote about Puritans, interpreted history in a calculated way to make it fresh, new, and relevant for their specific readers.

While the New England Pilgrims were nationally recognized as forefathers, they were not the only significant American progenitors. In 1837, Congress commissioned a number of huge paintings for the new US Capitol building—twelve feet by eighteen feet—of various American beginnings: the *Embarkation of the Pilgrims*, the *Baptism of Pocahontas*, *Daniel Boone's*

Cabin in Kentucky, and the *Landing of Columbus.*[31] The Wild West, James-town, and Columbus were US origins because nationalism was built both around the land the United States controlled and that which it desired. The American Revolution and the Declaration of Independence were simi-larly important beginnings, of course, and images of the Revolution and Declaration had been enshrined on the Capitol walls years earlier, in four twelve-by-eighteen-foot paintings that were commissioned by Congress in 1817 and installed during the 1820s. In fact, the signing of the Declaration of Independence (the image on our two-dollar bill), the surrender of Gen-eral Burgoyne, the surrender of Lord Cornwallis, and George Washington's resigning his commission flank the west front door of the rotunda. These eight events literally encircle the heart of Washington, DC, the point from which the city's four quadrants are drawn, and they offer a mythic, predes-tined, even divine account of US history. In this way, these paintings reveal what type of nation the United States is in the present day.

Directly below the rotunda lies the Capitol crypt, completed in 1827 and intended as a final resting place for George Washington. Washington's heir stymied that intention, but that did not stop the statues and monu-ments to revolutionary heroes. In 1836 Ralph Waldo Emerson famously indicted the "age" for being "retrospective" and "build[ing] the sepulchers of the fathers."[32] But on July 4, 1837, the town of Concord, Massachusetts, dedicated an obelisk at the site of the Battle of Concord and Lexington, and Emerson read a now-familiar poem that he had composed for the occasion: "By the rude bridge that arched the flood / Their flag to April's breeze unfurled / Here once the embattled farmers stood / And fired the shot heard round the world." Twelve years earlier, General Lafayette him-self had helped lay the cornerstone for the Bunker Hill Monument, a huge granite obelisk in Charlestown, Massachusetts. Other early cultural institu-tions, like the Franklin Institute (founded in 1824) took their names from Founding Fathers or, like the Connecticut Historical Society (founded in 1825), which holds Mayflower passenger William Brewster's chest and revolutionary general Israel Putnam's painted sign, wanted to preserve their memory. Further south, some twenty-five hundred people had cele-brated the 1807 bicentennial of Jamestown's founding in what was dubbed the "Grand National Jubilee."[33] The James River filled with vessels, Col-lege of William and Mary students gave patriotic orations, and a barn was converted into a temporary theater for dramatic performances. There was also parading, feasting, and dancing. A similar two-day celebration took place in May of 1822, when Jamestown hosted the "Virginiad," and participants cavorted, gambled, danced, and ate. Yet another took place in 1834. Though historically strange, revelers at these Virginiads were called "pilgrims," because the first two successful English colonies, Jamestown and Plymouth, were in direct competition for being seen as the great national beginning—a grand national jubilee, as it were. This celebration indicates some of the temporal complexities of the culture of beginnings. Not only did the Virginiad conflate two distinct moments—1607 and 1620—through use of the term "pilgrims," but it also invited participants to enact the past in the present, crafting a sort of temporal suspension that belied linear time. Through their bodies, the festivalgoers ritually recalled history, conjuring the founding of Jamestown into a sacred time, a form of constant present distinct from the logic of human chronology.

So too nostalgia, which is perhaps best seen in the incorporation of Native Americans in the culture of beginnings, disrupts progressive time wherein each temporal unit is measurable, equal, and continually passing. As the tribes that had not been exterminated or dispersed were violently removed from east of the Mississippi, romanticizing the "noble savage" became popular with a swath of liberal coastal whites. Between 1821 and 1842, Charles Bird King, a former student of history painter Benjamin West, was commissioned by the federal government to paint some 140 images of Native Americans who came to Washington, DC, on diplomatic trips.[34] In 1832 George Catlin set out on his first journey to paint Native Americans in their own lands. He had spent time with forty-eight tribes by 1840 and displayed his portraits in Boston, New York, Philadelphia, and Washington.[35] For voyeuristic whites safely separated from frontier battles, these indigenous people provided an exciting past that clearly differentiated the United States from Europe. Indeed, Washington Irving included two Native American sketches for the British version of his *Sketch Book* to play to European preconceptions and stereotypes. For most, claiming indigenous people as an American past hinged on belief in the tribes' near extinction (whether or not the conviction was based in reality). Some whites could thus feel sympathy without any corresponding call to action, and many others could support Andrew Jackson's ethnic cleansing through removal. Nostalgia allowed for positive feelings about a past that did not exist but rather read as an alternative and separated temporal moment. Native Americans thereby became an American beginning that was simultaneously displayed and erased. Both James Fenimore Cooper's *The Last of the Mohicans* (1826), which builds to the death of the last young Mohican warrior, and the Capitol rotunda painting of Pocahontas's baptism, which shows Pocahontas as she becomes the Christian Rebecca, enact the phenomenon.[36]

That cultural critics called for authors to manufacture a collective national history through historical fiction filled with American details supported the proliferation of stories about the past. In 1825 in the pages of *Blackwood's Edinburgh Monthly Magazine*, John Neal, an early American literary man, passionately advocated for such prose. When the call was put out for fictionalizing the Puritan forefathers, Neal wrote, "We did hope that some native, bold writers of the woods; a powerful, huge barbarian, without fear, and without reproach, would rise up to the call; come forth in his might; and, with a great regard for historical truth, give out a volume or two, worthy, in some degree, of the stout, strange, noble characters."[37] Historical fiction had the ability to elevate American literature precisely because it allowed Americans to narrate what they knew, bringing emancipation from European chauvinism, "emancipation," Neal wrote, "from that unworthy prejudice, (made up of a stupid apathy, self-distrust, and childish deference, God knows wherefore,) which degrades a people."[38] In 1833 Rufus Choate urged American writers to fictionalize the American past, starting with the Puritans who foretold the American Revolution and the democratic republic of the United States. "Every lover of his country, and every lover of literature . . . would wish," he said, "the tones of a ravishing national minstrelsy."[39] Such stories would "fix" the historic United States "deep in the general mind and memory of the whole people," thereby portraying this glorious history for a present readership.[40] Because history was understood as on a spectrum with, rather than opposite to, fiction, these stories would validate the nineteenth-century United States.[41] As Choate argued, "The Grand natural outline and features of the country were indeed the same then as now, and are so yesterday, to-day, and always."[42] Choate and Neal subscribed to the notion that beginnings were predictive, determinative, and powerful, and their ideas encouraged authors interested in cultivating reading communities and literary careers to invoke the national, not because such writing created a consistent, coherent, unified imagined community, but because speaking of "America" and "Americans" had calculated literary effects.

Of course, one of the great ironies of the literary nationalism described above is that Choate and Neal were asking American writers to craft unique American literature by copying a Scotsman's formula. In fact, Choate unapologetically titled his speech "The Importance of Illustrating New-England History by a Series of Romances like the Waverly Novels" in the hopes of spurring mimicry of Walter Scott's hugely successful series. *Waverley, or 'Tis Sixty Years Since* (1814) and Scott's many subsequent novels do provide valuable models for how fiction can portray a location—Scotland in Scott's case—as culturally and nationally distinct. But they also illustrate how all these American beginnings, even as they put forth a guise of being distinctly *American,* are in conversation with European writers, thinkers, and readers. Like Jefferson, Adams, and Franklin, who borrowed the motto for the Great Seal from a London magazine, US writers were involved in constant exchange with Europe. Their work was printed in Britain and reviewed by British critics, and their stories directly competed with European texts in the domestic market. They also read European literature and carried on friendships with European literati. Washington Irving was Walter Scott's admirer and friend; Sarah Josepha Hale regularly recommended London books to her readers; Catharine Maria Sedgwick dedicated her *Tales and Sketches* to the British social theorist Harriet Martineau; Nathaniel Hawthorne's sketch collection was reprinted (without permission) by a press in Halifax, England; and Edgar Allan Poe read about himself in a French newspaper. Knowing how their writing could and did cross terrestrial boundaries meant that while these authors invoked ideas of America, they retained an awareness of the artificiality of that construction. What I am elucidating, then, are articulations of American character defined with and against Europe through the selective invocation of past events in which both the efforts and the events were regional in their manifestations. The Capitol building sought to weave together Plymouth and Jamestown and the dramatically different European colonists who founded them, but both New Englanders and Virginians would have identified more with one group of settlers than with the other. So, too, communities were divided on the basis of sex, race, and other identity categories, so when Sarah Hale and Catharine Sedgwick write, they target not all Americans, but middle- and upper-class white women readers. Studies of beginning figures in short fiction reveal an incipient and provisional national literary culture that was not monolithic, inevitable, or fully domestic. Acknowledging that Boston, New York, and Philadelphia are the major nineteenth-century publishing centers in the United States, I focus on authors with strong ties—personal and professional—to these cities and particularly to New England. But I also illuminate stories that range across the United States, the Caribbean, and Europe in their settings as these East Coast authors invite their readers to imagine spaces that have connections to the developing national story. That Irving, Hale, Sedgwick, Hawthorne, and Poe—with the addition of Harriet Beecher Stowe, Herman Melville, and William Wells Brown in the final chapter—do not fully represent, in geography, class, race, sexuality, or beliefs, everyone in the country is obvious. Yet that they advertised their writing as somehow American—with all the presumption and inaccuracy of that term—allows me to plumb national character as prominent and prolific short fiction writers were constituting it, often in contradictory and transnational ways.

Given the obvious importance of beginnings to the nation and to all forms of narration, it is surprising more scholarly work has not been done on them. Besides Aristotle's definition of a beginning in the *Poetics*—"that which does not itself follow anything by causal necessity, but after which something naturally is or comes to be"—and Horace's instruction for storytellers to begin in media res, almost nothing was said about narrative beginnings until the late twentieth century.[43] In 1976, Edward Said's *Beginnings: Intention and Method*, which I have already referenced, offered a wide-ranging and ruminative structuralist exploration of the simultaneous multiplicity and impossibility of beginnings. Questioning the ability of beginnings to exist, since they require a radical discontinuity that is artificial and impossible, Said challenges the project of literary criticism itself. How can one interpret a text if that text has no borders and if the author, an origin, cannot be located? Throughout his work, Said is interested in questions of power: how structures are started and maintained, how authority is created, and what obligations are baked into human relationships.[44] Hence, though he cites beginnings as artificial, he acknowledges them as necessary to the placement of ideas "in some sort of telling order, sequential, moral, or logical."[45] In 2008 Brian Richardson edited a collection called *Narrative Beginnings* that probes the question of beginnings in a variety of ways. Included essays focus on writing by Laurence Sterne, Salman Rushdie, Virginia Woolf, James Joyce, Samuel Beckett, and Vladimir Nabokov, as well as beginnings in World War II, modern theater and film, and the World

Wide Web. Catherine Romagnolo, whose work on recessive origins in Julia Alvarez's *How the Garcia Girls Lost Their Accents* had appeared in Richardson's *Narrative Beginnings*, published *Opening Acts* (2015), investigating how beginnings in twentieth-century novels are used by historically marginalized groups to establish authority. As these summaries show, the little work on narrative beginnings has focused almost exclusively on modern or postmodern writers, implying that, save *Tristram Shandy* (1759), nothing written before the twentieth century shows sufficient narrative innovation to be interesting. Of course, though, as this project shows, this is not true. Short fiction authors including Irving, Hale, Sedgwick, Hawthorne, and Poe twisted and shifted time to stretch and shape the relatively short history of a young nation for nineteenth-century purposes. This allowed authors who felt pressure to write about figures from the American past to consider what historical legacy had been gifted them and how it could be used to professionalize US literature.

The currents of short story criticism—what criticism exists—have focused largely on epiphanies and closure. The presumption is that because of their concision, short stories have a relentless teleology toward the end and that ending with catharsis or surprise is its ultimate artistic achievement. As Sarah Hardy summarized the state of short story criticism in the 1990s, "The complexity of closure in the shorter form continues to inform treatments of the fictional moment."[46] Too little has changed. Although some individual pieces have tried to deemphasize these features of the form, the body of short story criticism is still dominated by the concepts. And yet endings are in the eye of the beholder. Read in a single sitting, readers are able to hold the entirety of a sketch or tale in their mind, thus allowing the beginning to more fully inform the reader's perception of the ending. Critics have long assumed that effect was intimately connected to the tale's finale. In chapter 4, I argue that it is actually part of the story's beginning. The concision of short fiction assures that beginnings do not recede, which allowed nineteenth-century sketch and tale writers to theorize different ways of fictionalizing the US past and conjuring an American people. The brevity of sketches and tales became critical to the narrative play authors brought to the form. Attending to the temporal innovations in short fiction allows me to advance our understandings of narrative beginnings and of short fiction, both important but understudied areas of literary inquiry.

The Sketch and the Tale

In this book, I am interested in what Homi Bhabha calls "the nation *as it is written*," the many competing and noisy printed discussions of what the United States meant at a particular moment in history.[47] I am also interested in a correlative of Bhabha's formulation, the nation *as it was read*, and, as well as they can be recovered, the exchanges that got a printed page to a reader. While I will sometimes use the term "print culture," I must underscore that there was no even, consistent national system of print distribution in the first half of the nineteenth century. In this reality, short fiction was printed and reprinted.[48] It appeared in magazines and newspapers and volumes. It was bought, sold, borrowed, and gifted. Because of its portability and ubiquity, short fiction was more likely to reach something closer to national circulation than copyrighted volumes. Still that does not mean that short fiction was exactly lucrative. Only after editors had expended considerable effort preparing audiences to expect literature by native-born Americans could US authors, and then only the famous ones like Sedgwick, demand a reasonable fee per page for a periodical contribution. Even when there was some traction in the magazine market, volumes remained risky because reprinted European works, which were not protected by US copyright, were so inexpensive. Before 1850, then, US authors, with the exception of James Fenimore Cooper, were more likely to find financial success with shorter works.[49] Sales figures support this conclusion. Between 1810 and 1819, Frank Luther Mott identifies eight best-selling fictional works, and all but one, Washington Irving's *The Sketch Book*, is British.[50] Four of the others are by Sir Walter Scott. The trend continues until midcentury. Between 1820 and 1849, there are forty-two best-selling fictional works, twenty-six of which are by Europeans and one by a Canadian.[51] Before 1850, Americans are buying and reading Hans Christian Andersen, Jane Austen, Charlotte Brontë, Emily Brontë, Edward Bulwer-Lytton, Charles Dickens, Alexandre Dumas, Victor Hugo, Eugene Sue, Alfred Tennyson, and William Thackeray in large numbers. But when not buying European novels, American readers buy a lot of US short fiction, including Nathaniel Hawthorne's *Twice-Told Tales* (1837) and Edgar Allan Poe's *Tales of the Grotesque and Arabesque* (1840), both best sellers. Excluding such things as literary annuals (gift book miscellanies issued in the fall on a yearly basis for Christmas and New Year's presents), Mott's numbers actually discount an entire segment of publishing dominated by sketches and tales. When such works are included, numbers show that short fiction and compilations made up almost 60 percent of US bound volume sales between 1820 and 1846 and are the dominant prose form in nonbound texts. In contrast, longer novellas and novels composed just a third of published books and did not appear in serialized form in periodicals until the middle of the century.[52] Until the later 1840s, short fiction is the king of literary prose forms.

There are systemic reasons for the popularity of short fiction in the first half of the nineteenth-century United States. The high cost of materials (especially type and paper), poor infrastructure (leading to difficulties with distribution), inconsistent banking systems, and even a depression (following the Panic of 1837) made printing a risky business. Although magazines frequently went under, periodicals and collections of shorter works simply seemed like safer bets than novels, which needed to succeed on their own merits rather than relying on subscriber network and internal variety. As Irving noted in a conclusion to his *Sketch Book*, a miscellany was more likely to provide "something to suit each reader" than a single story.[53] Even when publishing collections, printers tried to hedge their bets, often requiring authors to insure them against losses. Unbeknownst to him, Nathaniel Hawthorne's friend Horatio Bridge fronted $250 to limit the risk of printing *Twice-Told Tales*, although the stories had proven their popularity when printed in magazines and annuals. Such financial realities meant that authors found short fiction as useful as printers. If one magazine rejected it, the author could send it somewhere else—a newspaper, a literary annual, or another magazine. And the entire work represented less time commitment than a novel did, a real consideration in a fractured and uncertain literary landscape.[54] For these reasons, writers were actively using short fiction to further their literary careers qua literary careers—to improve their name recognition and to make money.

Short fiction before 1850 took multiple forms, some more firmly defined than others. As I have said above, the two most commonly used genre names for short fiction were the "sketch" and the "tale."[55] I should pause here to say that the point of genre is not to create and police borders between narrative forms but rather, as Wai Che Dimock argues, to provide a "provisional set [representing the genre] that will always be bent and pulled and stretched by its many subsets."[56] Following Wittgenstein, I rely on the notion of "family resemblance" to craft my definitions of genre, acknowledging that not every sketch and every tale looks exactly like every other sketch and every other tale.[57] Nonetheless, when boiled down to its essence, the tale emphasizes plot and movement through time, and the tale's fictional world often relies on interpretive play. The reader may supply multiple explanations for a story event, making the story a compelling object of contemplation. Nathaniel Hawthorne's tales are, of course, famous for their ambiguity, but Washington Irving's and Edgar Allan Poe's tales usually also leave multiple possibilities open. Turn the tale one way and see one story; turn it another way and see another. Tales also tend to evoke temporal distance (a "once upon a time") and foreground the mechanics of their story production, often by highlighting an oral genealogy. Irving's "Rip Van Winkle," as we learn, is widely told among the descendants of Old Dutch New York, and Catharine Sedgwick's tales are often told to an audience by a character in the story world. (Noah Webster makes note of the oral associations of tales in his 1828 dictionary.) Foregrounding the transmission of the story allowed tales to evoke intimacy and invite credulity. These (sometimes tall) tales were stories that would be and maybe had been told around the hearth, validated by generations of belief and extended by plenty of embellishment. Even as they transported readers to a story world, they felt rooted in the community that they sprang from.

In contrast, following the visual metaphor inherent in its name, the sketch seeks to describe space more than time through the close examination of a single moment, landscape, or idea that the narrator, even when he is a character in the sketch, frames in protodocumentary and "true" manner. The sketcher thus offers a mix of proximity, distance, objectivity, and insight. For example, though British writer Mary Mitford was lauded for the democratic approach of her best-selling sketch collection *Our Village*, the narrator who travels among and with these rural English inhabitants retains her superiority. She describes the town "scholar," a little boy whose "sheet of flourishing writing," is "something between a valentine and a sampler" in a light mocking tone, and she notes, when watching a man skating on the pond, that he must find relief in knowing that she, having seen ice-skating before, is able to appreciate his display more fully than others.[58] Class-inflected city knowledge validates her as the rural observer.[59] While varied in their realization, American sketches descended from the *Spectator* and *Tatler*, in which Joseph Addison and Richard Steele used journalistic personas, two gentleman named Isaac Bickerstaff and Mr. Spectator, to develop a style that was clear and straightforward, almost reporting, while also friendly and perceptive. Washington Irving's Geoffrey Crayon in particular owes much to these figures, but more generally Addison and Steele influenced the sketch's association with speaking from a place of observation and learning. Details and essence, rather than florid prose and sentimentality, communicated truth. Lydia Child, Catharine Sedgwick, and other female sketch writers like the British evangelical Hannah More associate the truth of the sketch with a reflection of propriety, hence their didactic texts that foreground proper social behavior. Alternatively, truth could be construed as sincerity: with fewer lines and less description, the sketch offers the unvarnished impression of an observer who prefers essence to polish.[60] Thus, Launcelot Temple (actually John Armstrong), author of the first English-language volume with sketch in its title, *Sketches, or, Essays on Various Subjects* (1758), "dreads the danger of writing too well."[61] Truth also takes the form of essence in sketches that delineate a type, like Sedgwick's "Old Maids" or Hale's "The Belle and the Bleu," or a place, like Irving's "The Country Church." In the decades when writers and readers were formulating stories that claimed to be national, the sketch, perfect for articulating types and regions, offered a shrewd conduit for metonymically labeling the local world and its people (those fragments of a larger whole) as American. In its projection of a small community as broadly significant, the tale similarly proposed a link between the regional and national.

While the sketch had truth baked into it and often presented a protodocumentary stance toward its subject, both the tale and the sketch acquired links with authenticity from being printed alongside political articles, editorials, and other news pieces in early nineteenth-century periodicals.[62] Journals, which often did not distinguish between factual and fictional contributions, implied that both forms of writing spoke directly to concerns and events of the moment. When sketches and tales appeared in literary journals like Sarah Hale's *Ladies' Magazine*, they also had a feeling of currency, underscored by reviews of just-published volumes, essays on recent events, and a dated header. So too when Sedgwick and Hawthorne published in the *Token*, a literary annual intended to be gifted for Christmas, their tales felt of the moment because they were explicitly mementos of the year listed on the title page, and they were customarily kept on the parlor table during the year they were gifted. If the original publishing conditions of short fiction created currency, traditions of reprinting whole stories in reviews and for filler could keep short fiction freshly in front of the public. Poe's "The Fall of the House of Usher," for example, first appeared in Burton's *Gentleman's Magazine* (September 1839), but was legally reprinted in the London magazine *Bentley's Miscellany* (August 1840). The entirety of *Bentley's* was then repirated for sale in the United States.[63] After Irving's success, American stories also more frequently appeared in British volumes. In 1830, for example, Mary Mitford edited *Stories of American Life, by American Writers*, which included three of Sedgwick's tales as well as stories by James Kirke Paulding, John Neal, and N. P. Willis. Two years later, Mitford edited a sequel, *Lights and Shadows of American Life*, which included another one of Sedgwick's tales. And in January of 1831, the *Lady's Book*, the periodical owned by Louis Godey, reprinted Sedgwick's "A Story of Shay's War" with a casual note about taking it from a popular literary annual. Sedgwick and Poe would not have seen any money from these reprintings, but these publications would have helped their tales stand as valid and current "stories of American life" (to borrow Mitford's title). Their printing and reprinting made short fiction, much more than US novels, feel like common property, owned by authors and readers alike as they articulated what it meant to be American in the first half of the nineteenth century.

Sometimes explicitly in series, like Hale's "Sketches of American Character," and sometimes more implicitly through the serialization of periodicals, short fiction about the past also promised a shared future for readers. Something like Benjamin Franklin's *Autobiography* had to come to an end, but Hale could always have another installment in her "Sketches of American Character" that would further articulate to all her readers what made the nation distinct. The promise of repetition and variation provided by series is stabilizing, assuring that the American past will maintain its explanatory power even as each generation shifts its understanding of national ideals. As part of a vast universe of stories about American beginnings, then, Puritans, revolutionary soldiers, and George Washingtons can undergo endless change and still be understood as the same characters. This change in constancy—a new literary annual for each year with different material but the same brand of annual, for example—has immense appeal. It provides comfort in newness and familiarity in difference, and it encourages feedback. Between issues or installments, readers can show their displeasure or enjoyment with the series by purchasing or not purchasing an installment—a magazine, newspaper, or literary annual—or otherwise giving the author feedback and thereby influencing the content of subsequent installments. Hence, when Hale ceased her sketches of American character after twelve sketches, readers clamored for more, and Hale started writing them again. As dynamic and inclusive story worlds, series encourage affective bonds. While the culture of beginnings cannot be called a series proper, the ubiquity of often unsigned or pseudonymous stories about the US past combined with the portability of those stories made these sketches and tales feel part of the kind of proliferating world created by series—the world of American beginnings.

In these ways, short fiction was a much more flexible form than nineteenth-century poetry. Read, snipped, traded, and memorized, poetry did hold an important position in interpersonal relationships, as Michael Cohen has shown. Volumes of poetry by Lord Byron, Walter Scott, Henry Wadsworth Longfellow, and Alfred Tennyson sold well in the first half of the century, and poetry appeared in miscellanies. Joel Barlow even tried his hand at writing a national epic in verse with *The Columbiad* (1807). Yet the obviously constructed nature of the metered, rhyming poetry popular during the first half of the nineteenth century assured that this medium foregrounded its manufacture. It advertised itself as carefully ordered, and reviewers pointed out any perceived failures of diction, meter, or rhyme. In 1828, for example, a reviewer for the *Yankee and Boston Literary Gazette* criticized the word choice of Grenville Mellen's poem "The Bridal" by altering the vocabulary. "Here I have altered three words for the better," notes the reviewer, adding, "I hope that Mellen will substitute some other word for *iron* hereafter. *Iron* years—*iron* nature—both very good words in their way: but very hard stuff to make a poem of."[64] Because of formal conventions in the years that this project focuses on, poetry conjured studied emotion and invited attention to individual words and, correspondingly, poetic faults. (Walt Whitman and Emily Dickinson are obvious exceptions to such poetic constraint, but Whitman's first *Leaves of Grass* appears in 1855, after the publication of all the works I treat in depth, and, save a scant handful of poems, Dickinson's work is not published until 1890.) It did not offer authentic, spontaneous, and protodocumentary accounts that knit swaths of people together under the title American. Unlike poetry, short fiction felt natural and unobtrusive, like a newspaper story or a familiar yarn from the town storyteller.

William Austin's popular "Peter Rugg, the Missing Man" nicely shows the genre features that I have been describing. Published in three installments in the *New-England Galaxy,* a Boston newspaper, between 1824 and 1827, "Peter Rugg, the Missing Man" tells a story of a mysterious ghost-man who leaves Boston in 1770 on a journey with his daughter. On the way home, Rugg stops in Concord, Massachusetts, where he defies an impending storm and tries to race his open carriage back to Boston. This hubristic act curses him, and he spends the next fifty years traveling up and down the Eastern Seaboard, lost but believing that he can arrive home before nightfall. As Rugg rides along, a vicious thunderstorm follows him, frequently dousing his horse, his daughter, and himself. Poor Rugg serves as a potent and obvious metaphor for the overwhelming desire to return to the beginning in the decades after the War of 1812. Though written by the lawyer William Austin, the sketch was published under the name Jonathan Dunwell, a fictional Boston business man who in 1820 goes down to Providence, Rhode Island, sees Peter Rugg, and writes a letter to Mr. Herman Kruff, which then is somehow forwarded to the *Galaxy's* editor. While the sketch begins with a "Dear Sir," it proceeds more like an informal investigative report. Dunwell stakes his own credibility on the truth of what he has seen and discovered, assuring his correspondent—and thus the readers—that he will "now relate to you all the particulars of the lost man and child which [he has] been able to collect."[65] Dunwell is as good as his word, carefully describing the dress, horse, chaise, speed, and demeanor of the mysterious traveler like a good sketch writer. And yet Rugg is no ordinary object of observation. Whereas Rugg seems ghostly and fantastic in parts of the story, at other moments he is flesh and blood. Thus Rugg is able to catapult over or ride straight through (it is never clear which) a turnpike gate as if he were supernatural, and he never stops to eat, drink, or sleep. But in the sketch's final installment, Dunwell manages to interview Rugg and establish that Rugg, despite being unaged for the last fifty years, is somehow *real.* Both the supposed everyman author and the personal exchange of epistolary format frame the account as true and reliable, even as it is unbelievable and extraordinary.

The article's collocation encouraged its association with authenticity and reporting. The original story, which appeared on September 10, 1824, is immediately preceded by an account of the prior week's festivities during General Lafayette's visit to Boston, and otherwise surrounded by death notices, a write-up of Masonic ceremonies, and political speeches—in other words, by the news. The second installment (printed on September 1, 1826) and final installment of "Peter Rugg" (printed January 9, 1827) were similarly placed near marriage announcements, a summary of beet sugar production in France, news on the inaction of the Massachusetts State Legislature, and a write-up of the recent commencement at Harvard College. Notices about current theater productions ran down the right side of the page with the third installment of "Peter Rugg," next to an ad for "Cream of Amber: For removing PIMPLES, SPOTS, FRECKLES, and all eruptions of the skin."[66] These blocks of text—ad, notice, and article—mark the everyday cares and concerns of Bostonians. Through placement in this busy, five-column, four-page newspaper, Peter Rugg became part of the world and stayed that way throughout the century: the story gained enough currency to be published as part of a volume, name-checked in many other stories, and even have a poetic adaptation.[67] The editor of the *Galaxy*, Joseph Buckingham, claimed that it "was reprinted in other papers and books, and read more than any newspaper communication that has fallen within [his] knowledge."[68] Peter Rugg even took on an extratextual life within the pages of the *New-England Galaxy* when in 1826 he was mentioned in a letter to the editor of the *Galaxy*, and in 1831 a "Peter Rugg" authored an absurdist column there.[69]

That is not to say, despite what critics like Bernard Terramorsi have claimed, that readers were fooled into believing that someone really had been riding the same horse and carriage for fifty years.[70] Rather, I am arguing that the story's flirtation with truth made it believable in its unbelievability. The *Galaxy* editor illustrated this conundrum by including a small note with the first installment: "A considerable space is occupied this day with a sketch (*Fancy's Sketch*, it is presumed) which may amuse some of our readers. We know not that it has any reference to matters of fact. . . . We should be glad to confer with Mr. Dunwell."[71] The editor *presumes* that Rugg is fiction but finds himself asserting that idea through a tortured construction that highlights the sketch's feeling of authenticity. That this editorial admission comes two articles after "Peter Rugg"—and is thus removed from the story by a full column of text—makes it an uneasy afterthought. Did the printer set the type for two more articles while the editor ruminated about Peter Rugg and decided some comment was needed? Was the comment only entered because there was space to fill?

The story's popularity surely hinged not just on its projected authenticity but also on how it captured the zeitgeist, for "Peter Rugg" dramatizes the possibilities and the limitations of revivifying the past for nineteenth-century desires. Indeed Peter Rugg's curse is to search for his beginning and the American beginning, which are one and the same, the "Boston massacre—1770."[72] Although Michelle Sizemore contends that Rugg has disappeared only to reappear in 1824, Austin depicts Rugg as having spent some fifty years trying to return to the cradle of the Revolution from whence he started his journey.[73] That these fifty years pass for others without seeming to pass at all for Rugg shows the irregularity of time for those who would reanimate the American past. Because the experience of time is specific to a community, time conjures social groups. Rugg experiences time with the child in his carriage, and readers are joined together by the elongated serialization of the sketch that prolonged poor Rugg's ill-fated journey. For neither group is this Benedict Anderson's empty time. Rather it is an uneven progression with moments of activity and development separated by suspense and suspension.

Despite the nineteenth-century reverence for beginnings, Rugg's hope to return to the past is not achievable. The story's end finds Rugg present in nineteenth-century, not eighteenth-century, Boston. Rugg's home, near the Old North Church in whose steeple the sexton placed the lanterns that spur Paul Revere's famous ride, has gone, and Rugg's family has died. Even as Rugg can recognize some of the crowd as descendants of his dead friends, he cannot understand that he is seeing the auctioning of his North End home to a nineteenth-century crowd. Rugg's property and story literally show the commodification of American origins and how incomprehensible such would be to the figures of the past. Those who crowd around the auctioneer want to buy Rugg's land not just because it lies in a valuable part of the city of Boston but also because it connects directly to the story of the Revolution—and thus to the story of the United States. Indeed, given that Rugg's address is Middle Street, now called Hanover Street, the parcel of land could even be where Paul Revere lived. (Peter Rugg shares Revere's initials and is similarly famous for riding through the countryside.) Rugg's story allows us to embrace what Jeffrey Insko calls "the pastness in the present," which has long been ignored or underplayed by literary historicism.[74] Yes, Peter Rugg drove into the nineteenth-century present, but he was also brought there by the readerly interest that encouraged subsequent installations and drew Rugg out of his damned carriage. While critics treat "Peter Rugg, the Missing Man" as a single story, its printing shows a negotiation between readers, editor, and writer that pushed fleeting contacts between past and present to a final meeting. Only when we look at how the story was written and how it was read do we understand the temporal and social complexities the story—and short fiction—represent in the first half of the nineteenth century.

When Beginnings Come to an End

Let me now detail the many parts that make up this one book. Washington Irving, who must figure large in any story about nineteenth-century short fiction in the United States and Britain, is the subject of chapter 1. His *Sketch Book of Geoffrey Crayon, Gent.* (1819–20), the first transatlantic best seller written by a native-born American, illustrates how deep transatlantic ties were, even after two wars had frayed the Anglo-American relationship. I argue that the composition of Irving's *Sketch Book*—its British sketches and Old Dutch New York tales, its print history, and the temporal coding of its tales and sketches—created a Janus-faced collection that was paradoxically claimed by both British and US readers. In turn, Irving's massive sales offered a paradigm for other US writers looking to US beginnings for literary success. I theorize the sketch and the tale as Irving uses them, establish how Irving's collection became so unexpectedly popular, and demonstrate what influence Irving's success had in the United States, on the nineteenth-century use of short fiction, the later twentieth-century ideas about the Americanness of the short story, and the ability of more US authors to write professionally. I thereby recover Irving not just as the author of "Rip Van Winkle" and "The Legend of Sleepy Hollow" but as a savvy tale *and* sketch writer whose strategic use of genre and time summoned a tradition of nineteenth-century short fiction.

Into this ascendant culture of beginnings came Sarah Josepha Hale and her *Ladies' Magazine,* the first successful magazine for women and the focus of my second chapter. Within twelve "Sketches of American Character," one for each number of the *Ladies' Magazine's* initial volume (1828), Sarah Josepha Hale elongates the beginnings of her sketches to stretch story time into real time and genders waiting and beginnings as female. As both literary theme and narrative strategy, waiting fashions a conservative but productive space for the white women who figured in traditional origin stories as the mothers, daughters, or lovers of Founding Fathers. Foretelling the wide geographical success of *Godey's Lady's Book*, which Hale went on to edit for decades and which has received what little critical attention has been paid to her writing, Hale portrays the patient reception and edifying perusal of a women's periodical as the ultimate national act. In so doing, she encourages her female readers to think of themselves as American. So too in the name of her women readers, Hale champions domestic literature by paying her authors, crediting them with consistent bylines, and publishing only original work. These three choices set standards that transformed American magazine writing and broadly impacted the American literary scene.

Miscellaneous like the *Ladies' Magazine*, literary annuals, which have been all but ignored by scholars, became popular ritualized gifts that men gave to women at Christmas and New Year's in the 1820s and 1830s. Chapter 3 elucidates how Catharine Sedgwick, the single most popular contributor to US literary annuals, activated this exchange economy with her submissions to ten years' worth of literary annuals starting with the first US literary annual (the *Atlantic Souvenir* for 1826). Peppered with historical characters, from the Quaker Mary Dyre to revolutionary veterans, Sedgwick's tales and sketches foregrounded the multivocality and orality that groups of women used to discover and affirm new truths. The male gift givers, intentionally or not, helped circulate and validate this women-centered short fiction, making Sedgwick's stories authorized and communal accounts of history. Shifting a form—the literary annual—that was borrowed from Europe, Sedgwick carved out a nonsynchronous synchronicity for her readers and characters. While their stories exist in different moments, together they are joined in a layered time and space, what I call (building on Mikhail Bakhtin's idea of the chronotope as a literary figuration of time-space) a chronotopic palimpsest.

In chapter 4, I theorize two narrative temporalities: the *chronicle*, a forward-moving arrow of events, and the *reckoning*, a story's end or a revelation of predestination that forces readers to reconsider previous happenings. Using this new understanding of narrative time, I reveal how Hawthorne's *Twice-Told Tales* (1837), a collection of short fiction previously published in literary annuals and magazines, indicts the reckoning of the Pilgrims as Founding Fathers even as it celebrates them. Referencing the many other temporal conceptions that have governed New England life, Hawthorne makes a larger argument about the challenges and rewards of writing historical fiction in which authors are limited less by facts than by readerly expectations. The temporal paradox of chronicle and reckoning explains much of what appealed to nineteenth-century US critics, much of what ruffled nineteenth-century British readers, and much of what still fascinates us today about Hawthorne's Puritan tales. This treatment of Hawthorne, like the chapters that precede it, widens our understanding of the varied sense of time in the nineteenth century. It also leads us to a moment when the dynamics that created the culture of beginnings shift.

With the arrival of the Mexican-American War and the threat of slavery expanding into formerly Mexican territory, writers began to use beginnings figures and symbols to stake a political position about the pressing issues of the moment. Famously, Henry David Thoreau refashioned celebrations of the Declaration of Independence by beginning his American experiment on July 4, 1846. Something was inadequate and unsatisfactory about American life, and his sojourn at Walden was intended to prove that an alternative model existed. Three years later, Elizabeth Peabody, Hawthorne's sister-in-law, would publish Thoreau's account of civil disobedience, a treatise spurred by the Mexican-American War, its resulting land acquisition, and the inevitable spread of American slavery. As Thoreau says, "When a sixth of the population of a nation which has undertaken to be the refuge of liberty are slaves, and a whole country [Mexico] is unjustly overrun and conquered by a foreign army, and subjected to military law, I think that it is not too soon for honest men to rebel and revolutionize."[75] For Thoreau, revolutions are not the stuff of the heroic past. They are present techniques necessitated by political realities. National celebrations and historical fiction could no longer unify the country with a story of liberty, democracy, and providence, and the decrease in fiction about the glorious past revealed a growing anxiety about the gap between American ideals and American reality. Chapter 5, focusing on Poe's cynical take on how beginnings are endings, speaks to this shift in the culture of beginnings. After explaining how the invention of the whodunit, which relocates the story's origin (a murder) to the tale's ending (when the detective reveals how the crime was committed), is reliant on the opposition of white logic and black brutality, I argue that Poe's second detective tale, "The Mystery of Marie Rogêt" (1842–43), wherein the actual mysterious death of American Mary Rogers is restaged in France, enacts a despair over American social order. That this story, the second ever whodunit, fails the genre rules that Poe invented and policed indicates that identifying beginnings had a direct relationship to presumptions of a white fictive ethnicity under threat from imperialism, immigration, and abolition.

Although some, like William Apess, spoke out against the hypocrisy and racism of the United States before 1845, the Mexican-American War and the Compromise of 1850 made the literary currents of anger and disillusionment wider and stronger. Hence, Harriet Beecher Stowe, who had written *The Mayflower, or Sketches of Scenes and Characters among the Descendants of the Pilgrims* (1843 but written earlier), cites her fury as the reason for authoring *Uncle Tom's Cabin* (1851–52), which includes a slave owner's thin justification for slavery through reference to Thomas Jefferson. More and more those who continued to write about historical figures shifted how they did so both in tone and genre, using the Founding Fathers to stake a position over slavery. Poets like John Pierpont and Elizabeth Barrett Browning retooled the Pilgrim into an abolitionist symbol in, respectively, "Plymouth Rock" and "The Runaway Slave at Pilgrim Point." And Henry Wadsworth Longfellow wrote a historically inaccurate "Paul Revere's Ride" (January 1861) not because he was ignorant but because he wanted Revere to stand as a model of individual power in a crisis, encouraging readers in anticipation of the coming brutal civil war. Like Thoreau before him, Frederick Douglass also chose America's birthday to highlight the failure of the US experiment, asking on July 5, 1852, "What to the Slave is the Fourth of July?" Two years after a nationally enacted and nationally enforced Fugitive Slave Law, Douglass queried, "What have I, or those I represent, to do with your national independence? Are the great principles of political freedom and of natural justice, embodied in that Declaration of Independence, extended to us?"[76] The answer was no. Douglass's black body prevented recognition of his equality under American law. In the 1850s, African Americans were enslaved or at risk of being so, and it seemed to a number of African Americans and their allies that liberty could only come through an armed revolution like that led by John Brown in 1858. In the decade and a half before the Civil War, the Fourth of July was increasingly a time to challenge—not celebrate—the US nation and its imagined community.

In some ways, Daniel Webster, that white Massachusetts senator, best exemplifies the historical arc that I have been tracing from celebration of the American past to involvement with the sectional politics of the midcentury. In 1820, he had headlined the bicentennial celebration of the landing of the Plymouth Pilgrims. By 1850, however, the politician symbolized to New England abolitionists the abandonment of principle and the conciliation of the slaveholding South. In supporting the controversial Compromise of 1850, Webster's motive was simple—preservation of the United States. Tracing the national troubles back to the admission of Texas as a slave state and the subsequent war with Mexico, Webster refashioned his praise for New England history into shared blame for a fracturing country. Rather than glorifying Puritan resistance of tyrannical laws as he had in 1820, Webster found that "slavery did exist in the States before the adoption of this Constitution" and that the North has "in their legislative capacity or any other capacity" no right "at all; none at all" to "endeavor to get round this Constitution or to embarrass the free exercise of the rights secured by the Constitution to the persons whose slaves escape from them."[77] Precisely because the Puritans had been established as fonts of democratic liberty, Webster sought to undercut the use of Pilgrim history in arguments against slavery. Even though he had not supported Texas's admission as a state, Webster would take Texas, slavery, and the Fugitive Slave Law over the dissolution of the Union. As he said to the US Senate: "Our ancestors, our fathers and our grandfathers, those of them that are yet living amongst us with prolonged lives, would rebuke and reproach us; and our children and our grandchildren would cry out shame upon us, if we of this generation should dishonor these ensigns of the power of the government and the harmony of that Union which is everyday felt among us with so much joy and gratitude."[78] Instead of fostering connections, these forefathers are chastising listeners, drawing sharp lines between "ancestors . . . fathers . . . grandfathers" and nineteenth-century whites. The Civil War would not come until 1861, but short fiction beginning stories and their reverence for Founding Fathers were anachronistic by the late 1840s. In the book's final chapter, I thus turn to the afterlife of sketch and tale. After illuminating how historical changes in US infrastructure, publisher finances, and printing technologies made the publication of longer works appealing, I demonstrate that four American novels—three of them canonized—Nathaniel Hawthorne's *The Scarlet Letter* (1850), Herman Melville's *Moby-Dick* (1851), Harriet Beecher Stowe's *Uncle Tom's Cabin* (1851–52), and William Wells Brown's *Clotel; or, The President's Daughter* (1853) are beholden to the sketch and tale. Short fiction, as it had developed during the early nineteenth century, offered a particularly effective vehicle for fashioning authentic fiction when the celebration of beginnings had lost its allure. While Hawthorne's, Melville's, and Stowe's novels all indict slavish reverence for the past, Brown's story co-opts the sketch and tale in a way that exposes their established utility for the project of whiteness. By 1850, the genres Irving had vaulted into the literary world were regressive, but when turned into novels, they could and did form some of our most celebrated works of American literature.

The turn away from the national in literary criticism has helpfully decentered the nation as a monolithic and inadequately interrogated concept. And yet, just because planetary and global studies have gained currency does not mean that we should disregard the category of American. It *is* arbitrary and hard to define (not to mention a reference to both a country and to two continents), but accepting that truth and foregrounding the complexity with which the idea was deployed in the nineteenth century gives us ways to read the literature of that moment. If we jettison the national frame entirely, we lose the ability to meet the authors on their own terms—which very obviously include "American"—and understand what they are telling us. Foregrounding the inconsistent, developing, exclusionary, and transnational ideas of Americanness, I embrace the cultural work of the often plotless sketch (which stilled time) and the "once upon a time" of the tale (which merged reality with the fantastic). I articulate how and why short fiction is a site of innovation about narrative beginnings, and I do so in works that themselves have claims to being beginnings: the first transatlantic best seller by an American (Irving's *The Sketch Book*); the first attributed volume published by a notable author (Hawthorne's *Twice-Told Tales*); the first example of a literary genre (Hale's, the first successful US ladies' magazine; Sedgwick's, part of the first US literary annual; and Poe's, the invention of the whodunit); the first candidates for the title of great American novel (*The Scarlet Letter, Moby-Dick,* and *Uncle Tom's Cabin*), and the first novel by an African American author (*Clotel*). As these many firsts testify, defining the American people and their literature through narrative innovation felt both possible and imperative in these thirty-odd years. American beginnings, with their fixation on primacy and their embrace of the national, were central to how short fiction sketched whiteness as the core of the American character. Recognizing this truth by reveling in the disaggregating power of sketches and tales offers a new account of American literature, one in which *e pluribus unum* shows its contradictions and complexities.

❖ 1 ❖

Dueling Temporalities in Irving's Best-Selling *Sketch Book*

On March 1, 1819, Washington Irving sent a packet from England to his friend Henry Brevoort in New York. These manuscripts, including "Rip Van Winkle," made up the first number of *The Sketch Book of Geoffrey Crayon, Gent.*, which was published by the felicitously named Cornelius S. Van Winkle. Numbers 2, 3, and 4 of *The Sketch Book* followed upon the tail of the first. The fifth number was in print on New Year's Day 1820. Eight months later, before the final two numbers appeared in the United States, the eminent London publisher John Murray registered copyright on a British version of *The Sketch Book*.[1] Even though Irving was living in England, he was an American citizen and thus ostensibly not protected by English copyright. Yet, that Murray *did* pay Irving for the copyright (albeit a small sum) demonstrates a fascinating fact about this collection: at the moment of its publication, both the United States and England claimed *The Sketch Book* and its author. These competing claims helped make the collection the first transatlantic best seller written by a native-born American and set a model for conjuring the American people through short fiction about the US past.

Because of the frayed relationship between the United States and United Kingdom in the first decades of the nineteenth century, no one thought an American author could win a domestic and international audience. During the Napoleonic Wars (1803–15), both France and England seized American vessels, but England earned the particular ire of the US government by taking American goods *and* impressing any suspected Britons into the Royal Navy. In so doing, they conscripted many unwilling American sailors and raised a vital question: How could one tell the difference between a Briton and an American, especially when British captains denied the ability to relinquish the status of British subject for that of American citizen?[2] American resentment over this thorny issue helped catalyze the War of 1812—the war that was, depending on one's vantage, either "the Second War of Independence" or "the third English Civil War." Fights between the United States and United Kingdom were often figured as family quarrels, those of an insubordinate child and wronged parent or of a tyrannical parent and a liberty-loving child. Given that reality, it is unsurprising that the American and British literary markets—and American and British literature—were similarly deeply connected and deeply opposed. In the first half of the nineteenth century, Americans read and reprinted British novels, poetry, magazines, and reviews.[3] So, too, they adopted British narrative forms, styles, and subjects. After all, many American colonists had been British: their cultural history and patrimony were shared with their former rulers and recent enemies. And yet in January 1820, the *Edinburgh Review,* a publication with considerable circulation in the United States, printed Sydney Smith's infamous taunt: "In the four quarters of the globe, who reads an American book? or goes to an American play? or looks at an American picture or statute?"[4] The young United States and its cultural products were easily dismissed.[5] In line with these truths, Paul Giles argues that British literature and American literature developed "not so much in opposition but rather as heretical alternatives to each other."[6] In other words, British and American authors produced funhouse mirror images of each other—distorted and warped but still recognizable—because both countries understood themselves in relation to each other. When the United States severed itself from its cultural past, Britain lost its most precious colony.

Nowhere is this funhouse mirror phenomenon more evident than in Irving's *Sketch Book.* As Giles explains, Irving's project can be understood as one of burlesque, an attempt to lower both the American and the British to the level of the fool while allowing the two nations—which had so recently been a single country—to view each other and thus also themselves as a wishful and warped projection. Building on Giles's description of Irving's use of burlesque, I illuminate how composition—both the contents of the collection and the collection's print history—helped create such a double sensibility. With the use of contemporary reviews and sales figures, I also demonstrate the practical result of such a squinting text; namely, I show how in being claimed by England and the United States, *The Sketch Book* became the first transatlantic best seller written by a native-born American. Irving's luck and savvy enabled him to publish two slightly different, if identically named, collections simultaneously in New York and London. Although no other critic has remarked on the fact, both collections juxtaposed two genres, two temporalities, and two nationalities: staid *sketches* predominantly about Britain, composed by the fictional Geoffrey Crayon, and the lively American *tales* told by Irving's previously established Dutch historian persona, Diedrich Knickerbocker.[7] (The British first edition included two additional American *sketches* designed to appeal to British readers, a fact to which I will return.) Like the double genre format, the assorted tales and sketches are Janus-faced, allowing readers to pick out the narrative lines that flatter their own national sensibilities. Irving's stories thus illustrate both the greatness and the stasis of English culture, both the absurdity and the vitality of American stories. It is this duality that explains the competing national claims over *The Sketch Book* and creates a riot of temporalities that displaces rather than counters ideas of American cultural primitivity. As I show below, *The Sketch Book* offers a window into the complicated structures of feelings that composed the Anglo-American relationship and provides a model for successful and authentic-feeling stories that claimed to be nationally representative. This chapter, then, starts the story of *The Sketch, the Tale, and the Beginnings of American Literature* by describing the first massive success of the tale and the sketch, exposing its temporal flexibility, and illuminating the cultural associations it grants short fiction.

English and American, Sketches and Tales

Upon reading *The Sketch Book*, British reviewers boldly proclaimed that Irving was English. As the *Edinburgh Monthly* asked, "Who is there of us that would not hail as a brother, the man that could entertain and express such sentiments?"[8] So too the *Retrospective Review* declared Washington Irving "not *national*, but English."[9] The *Edinburgh Monthly* lauded Crayon for being "part and portion of the English commonwealth," while Briton Christopher North praised how Irving "has engrafted himself matter and style, on English literature, and must be contented to be among the crowd of good English writers."[10] A *Blackwood's* article similarly meant a high compliment when it said that Irving's collection was "very graceful—infinitely more so than any piece of American writing that ever came from any other hand, and well entitled to be classed with the best English writings of our day."[11] Reviewers were eager to induct Irving into the pantheon of British authors in large part because, as one reviewer said, Crayon's sketches brought to mind "some of the best papers in the Tatler and Spectator."[12] American critics praised in similarly national terms. In 1822 the *Columbian Star* agreed with an enthusiastic French review that "An American, Mr. Washington Irving, *has raised himself by a single work,* to the level of the purest and most elegant writers produced by England."[13] Likewise the *New-England Galaxy*, where "Peter Rugg" would later be printed, gushed: "Those who feel an interest in the literary reputation of America, and are willing to be pleased with the productions of American scholars, will read with no common emotions 'the Sketch Book of Geoffrey Crayon.'"[14] These warm reviews reflect the generous reception given to Irving's work on both sides of the Atlantic. Frank Luther Mott concludes that when newly published *The Sketch Book* sold at least seventy-five thousand American copies, a significant number for the time.[15] On the English side, *The Sketch Book* quickly became John Murray's best-selling item, and Murray went through three editions—the second of which had two printings—in two years.[16] The American *Sketch Book* was on its fourth edition by 1824. The public, as far away as India, was aware of the book's immense success. The *Calcutta Journal* conjectured that by November of 1822 "excepting Scott's Novels," *The Sketch Book* was "the most popular book in England."[17]

Although twentieth-century critics came to see Irving as not sufficiently national, both the United States and England continued for decades to try to claim him. In 1849, John Murray III, the son of Irving's original British publisher and then head of the House of Murray, took to court Henry George Bohn, a printer who was making cheap editions of Irving's work. Along with explaining that Irving published in London before New York, Murray contended that Irving was legally equivalent to a Briton: he pointed out that Irving's parents, born in the United Kingdom before the American Revolution, were British, and Irving had lived and written in England for many years. To assist the House of Murray, Irving happily certified his father's Scottish and mother's English births, though he could not keep himself from underlining his father's allegiance to the American cause both before and after the Revolution.[18] As Irving wrote in a memorandum designed to aid the House of Murray, he would "take all proper steps to protect" Murray's "pecuniary interest" while not "compromising" his own "character as a native born and thoroughly loyal American citizen."[19] Murray wanted Irving and *The Sketch Book* to be British; Irving wanted to help Murray argue that—as long as Irving could maintain that he was *also* first and foremost American. This lawsuit, like the critical response that was divided along national lines, parallels bifurcations within *The Sketch Book*. Most obviously, the collection's doubleness comes from its two genres and two temporalities, each with a different national association, but it also, as I show below, was encouraged by the double valence of the collection's individual pieces, both sketches and tales.[20]

In the nineteenth century, the sketch was a flexible genre that held associations with truth, sincerity, and fragmentation. As Kristie Hamilton has shown, a wide variety of authors, from the enslaved (like Harriet Jacobs and Harriet Wilson) to the cosmopolitan (like N. P. Willis and Nathaniel Hawthorne) used the genre.[21] As varied as their writers, sketches could take the form of character descriptions, regional accounts, or reflective essays. Unlike the tale, they were often plotless or loosely plotted. Instead of unfolding over time, they offered a close examination of a limited moment, landscape, or idea, demonstrating the genre's relationship to *space* and highlighting the visual metaphor inherent in the genre's name. Seemingly jotted down in haste, the sketch gave the sensation of being an accurate, though incomplete, impression of a moment, place, or idea.[22] Given its aesthetic of fragmentation, the sketch was particularly suited to documenting a rapidly changing modern world. According to Hamilton, the sketch "brought into the open, and made thinkable, the disruptions within modernization that the novel smoothed over with coherence and closure."[23] The genre's acceptance of the incomplete provided a way for readers and writers to consider both the massive technological change of the nineteenth century and the dizzying variation of a geographically and demographically expanding nation.[24] The tale, in contrast, hinged on the development of a planned plot; it recorded change over time and, in *The Sketch Book*, offered narrative ambiguity in which the central story event had two possible explanations.

With these two genres, Irving set up a collection that, like early nineteenth-century British and American cultural narratives more broadly, offers a grotesque and uncomfortable twinning centered on whiteness.

The Sketch Book of Geoffrey Crayon, Gent. begins with an epigraph that introduces Crayon as an unencumbered observer. He "has no wife nor children, good or bad, to provide for. A mere spectator of other men's fortunes and adventures" (Van Winkle *SB* 1:i).[25] Crayon's nonattachment, the epigraph implies, allows for a certain objective distance. It is because of his bachelorhood that Crayon can be a "mere spectator," a word recalling the famous eighteenth-century English periodical the *Spectator.*[26] Based as he was on English models, Crayon was the epitome of the gentleman sketcher, a fact his name underlines and his stated project makes explicit. ("Crayon" was a term for a hasty visual sketch.) The essays feel accurate because of their protodocumentary stance, an impression Irving cultivated by listing Crayon as the author, not just narrator, of the book. The London *Literary Gazette,* the magazine whose unauthorized (but legal) reprintings of *The Sketch Book* encouraged Irving to publish in England, praised Crayon as displaying "an amiable and cultivated mind, free from violent prejudices, and endued with very considerable talent."[27] Crayon was reliable—even to a British audience—and his subjects were apt. He goes to Westminster Abbey, Liverpool, Stratford-on-Avon, Windsor Castle, and London. He describes "the good-hearted, good-tempered" John Bull (Van Winkle *SB* 4:11) and the "amiable but unfortunate" James I of Scotland (Van Winkle *SB* 3:177) with discernment and interest. His light humor and pleasing tone encourage his British readers to see him as the ideal American, one who appreciated Britain as much as the British. In fact, although Crayon calls himself a "stranger," his understanding frequently proves greater than the natives'. For example, when Crayon goes to Liverpool to visit the birthplace of William Roscoe, author of a well-regarded history of Lorenzo de' Medici, he learns that the "good people of the vicinity thronged like wreckers" when the scholar's library was sold at auction (Van Winkle *SB* 1:34). Only Crayon has the proper empathy to comprehend Roscoe's loss and the refinement to see the crassness of the public means by which the books were dispersed. In short, Crayon serves as the upper-class English projection of a like-minded American and a lost brother. He allows British critics to claim him and thus to reclaim their imagined America, which, of course, was an extension of England.

But I am not accusing Irving of being Anglophilic, a label that many twentieth-century US literary critics pasted onto *The Sketch Book* with derision. For even while credentialing himself as British, Crayon often winks at his intended US audience. To take a case in point, in the second number, when Crayon praises the effect of rural life "upon the national character," he is talking about both English yeomen and their American cousins who exhibit "a robustness of frame and freshness of complexation" from "their living so much in the open air" (Van Winkle *SB* 2:130). (It is worth remembering that the first four numbers were written for publication in New York and only later published in London.) The squinting nature of Crayon's sketches—an integral part of a genre grounded in suggestion and incompletion—allowed even nationalistic American reviewers to see themselves in the English vignettes. As the *New-England Galaxy* asked about one of Crayon's more sentimental sketches, "Who, that has endured the vicissitudes of life to old or even to middle age, will not find an echo in his heart responding to such language?"[28] While Crayon detailed foreign ways, Americans saw shared structures of feelings. They also saw attractively familiar and exotically odd history and manners, which confirmed how similar—and different—the United Kingdom and United States were. Biographically, Irving embodied this Gordian knot of familiarity and difference. Irving's parents had emigrated from the United Kingdom, Irving was part of his family's transatlantic shipping business, and Irving wanted the copyright protections of an English author. Still, even when he spent seventeen years living abroad, Irving, who had served in the War of 1812 as an aide-de-camp, remained insistent that he was an American patriot. In his later years, he even displayed in his house a watercolor of the (possibly imagined) moment when General Washington had blessed his namesake after liberating New York from the British.[29] Britain was, for Irving, the past: his family's origin, and by the time *The Sketch Book* was in print, the gravesite of the family shipping business, P. & E. Irving and Company.

The Sketch Book similarly links Britain with death, stasis, and the replication of moribund tradition and idea. For example, when Crayon goes to the country for a series of five sketches on Christmas festivities, he stays with Squire Bracebridge, "a bigoted devotee of the old school," who is intent on reviving long-dead Christmas customs (Van Winkle *SB* 5:371–72). The squire's house is chockablock with "obsolete finery in all its original state," and the squire encourages his servants to learn and play a series of ancient country games (Van Winkle *SB* 5:378). Though he immensely enjoys the outing, Crayon makes clear that the squire's "strenuous advoca[cy] for the revival of the old rural games and holyday observances" serves neither convenience nor progress (Van Winkle *SB* 5:372). For Crayon has to "ring repeatedly" to summon the servants who are busy playing these old games (Van Winkle *SB* 5:379). Believing this harkening to the past to be the duty of the landed English gentry, the squire encourages poor reanimations of history. As Eliza Tamarkin has noted, the appeal of England for nineteenth-century Americans "is always historically . . . regressive"—even when one had business or literary interests there.[30] Irving codes this regression into the sketch genre.

Crayon presents other more direct connections between death, stasis, and Britain. "Rural Funerals" describes Arcadian funerary traditions. Among them, the sketch details a "most delicate and beautiful rite observed in some of the remote villages of the south" of England (Van Winkle *SB* 4:274). When a young unmarried girl dies, another girl "nearest in age, size, and resemblance" carries a "chaplet of white flowers" and walks ahead of the body during the funeral (Van Winkle *SB* 4:274). Praising the beauty of the rite, Crayon reveals a necrophiliac fascination with how the British dead coexist with the living. The chaplet, which the dead girl's stand-in carries, is even hung in the church over the dead girl's usual seat. In a later sketch Crayon himself experiences a similar merging of death and life when the countryside "perpetuates[s] the memory of a dead friend" (Van Winkle *SB* 4:283). In Britain, those who have passed never really pass, a governing logic that would push early nineteenth-century British critics to consider the United States an extension of Britain. The United States can never be truly separate or distinct because the United Kingdom and the United States share the same past—and the past and the present coexist. At most, the United States is a version of Britain.

Irving seems to understand the different valence of death and decay in the United States and Britain. In the London volume, Crayon advertises this theme as a display of his admiration for the Old World. He acknowledges in the final paragraph of the English *Sketch Book*, a passage not in the American *Sketch Book*, that he "has been accustomed, from childhood, to regard with the highest feelings of awe and reverence" the English public and, by extension, Britain (Van Winkle *SB* 2:418–19). While the English sketches testify to his admiration in Britain, they work differently for an

American audience. No early nineteenth-century American critic that I have found explicitly comments on the sketches' connection to death, but Irving's contemporaries do acknowledge the different feelings of the English sketches and American tales. Richard Henry Dana Sr. explains these divergent sensations as the difference between lively and languorous—between vital and moribund. Unlike the Knickerbocker tales, Crayon's sketches lack "strength, quickness, and life of thoughts and feelings."[31] Dana believes that the lively *is* American in style, topic, and fact. In contrast, for Crayon and Dana, British writing was much like the British physical world: moribund, old, and timeworn. In "Rural Funerals," for example, Crayon cites death-focused quotations from famous English authors, including William Shakespeare and Robert Herrick. Then in "The Art of Bookmaking," Crayon reveals that "extreme fecundity of the [nineteenth-century British] press" is a result of thievery, not imagination (Van Winkle *SB* 2:155). As he watches, old men reassemble excerpts from dusty old tomes into newly published books until the portraits of dead men on the walls of the British Museum Reading Room come to life and shout, "thieves! thieves!" (Van Winkle *SB* 2:167). Britain is constrained by its backward-looking gaze, and Britain is, for the United States, a backward look. The sketch freezes these moments in time, compounding their feeling of pastness: these dusty tomes and death-centered quotations are emotionally authentic but temporally remote. Crayon's bemused proto-objectivity and fixation on the moribund assures that is the case.

In contrast, Crayon made clear that he saw the United States as moving forward—and he connected that movement to American writing. In "English Writers on America," after chastising British travelers who "forget their usual probity and candour, in the indulgence of spleen, and an illiberal spirit of ridicule" when talking about the United States, Crayon goes on to issue a warning (Van Winkle *SB* 2:102). "We are a young people," he says, and "the tissue of misrepresentation attempted to be woven round us, are like cobwebs woven round the limbs of an infant giant" (Van Winkle *SB* 2:118, 108). The burgeoning United States will grow and break these webs, and then ancient England, subject to the fall of all empires, will regret its ignorant, prejudicial accounts. The United States is forward-looking and present tense, while the United Kingdom is still and past. The sketch's fragmentation and objectivity make this temporal coding attractive to both Britons and Americans. Indeed, these three sketches critical of British writing—"Rural

Funerals," "English Writers on America," and "The Art of Bookmaking"—all appeared in the second number of the American *Sketch Book* months before a London *Sketch Book* was in the works. (Irving wrote to his friend Henry Brevoort that he "had not made any determination about publishing" in England in a letter dated almost a month after the second number was published in the United States.)[32] They were national boosterism from a writer intent on making money by his pen, and American publications like the *North American Review,* the *Western Review and Literary Cabinet,* and the *Ladies' Literary Cabinet* singled out "English Writers on America" for its patriotism.[33] Yet despite their obvious criticism of England, these essays worked for a British audience too. When Irving republished his *Sketch Book* in London, although he did make some other changes, he did not pull any of the pieces.[34] Reviewers read the sketches through their cisatlantic preconceptions of the United States and of honor, objectivity, and authorship. Thus British publications, including *Blackwood's,* the *Edinburgh Monthly Review,* the *British Critic,* the *Investigator,* the *Quarterly Review,* and the *New Monthly Magazine,* praised Irving's evenhanded treatment of English travel accounts of the United States.[35]

British critics enjoyed Crayon's careful criticism of British writers in part because *The Sketch Book* gave a calculated experience of temporal and aesthetic variety. In the afterword ("L'Envoy") of the first London *Sketch Book*—a piece that only appeared in the English edition—Crayon writes that he was unsure how to compose the volume until he realized "that his work being miscellaneous, and written for different humors, it could not be expected that any one would be pleased with the whole; but that if it should contain something to suit each reader, his end would be completely answered" (Miller-Murray *SB* 2:417). The heterogeneity of the collection—its *e pluribus unum* structure—forces the reader to piece bits together to create meaning. As a result, the reader can excuse any political or aesthetic component he dislikes as incongruous, unimportant, or, Irving suggests in a line only given to British readers, suited for those who are less sophisticated—perhaps for Americans. If the reader "should find here and there something to please him, to rest assured that it was written expressly for intelligent readers like himself; but entreating him, should he find any thing to dislike, to tolerate it, as some of those articles which the author has been obliged to write for readers of a less refined taste" (Miller-Murray *SB* 2:418). As he moved from publishing just in the United

States to publishing transatlantically, the genre of the sketch helped Irving modify and thus achieve his original intention—as he said in a "Prospectus" only found in the American volume, to "have a secure and cherished, though humble, corner in the good opinions and kind feelings of his countrymen" (Van Winkle *SB* 1:iv). For through his success in England, Irving increased his readership at home and supplied a model for the sketches and tales that articulated the temporal experience of being an American looking over his shoulder at Europe.

American Tales of Change and Vitality

As I have argued, the nature of the two short fiction genres in *The Sketch Book*—just as much as the transatlantic printing—were central to encouraging readers to see both themselves and their transatlantic siblings in a nexus of competing identification and renunciation. The incompletion inherent in the sketch and the double-plotting of the tale meant such double readings were baked into Irving's prose. Surely the characters of Rip Van Winkle, who absurdly sleeps through the American Revolution, and Ichabod Crane, who is frightened by a pumpkin, allowed English readers to laugh at Americans, their quondam compatriots. But these two tales also supplied vital American narratives that showed characters remaking their worlds through words about the past, for both Rip Van Winkle, who becomes the town historian, and Ichabod Crane, who loves to recount tales of Massachusetts witches, are storytellers. In this way, the characters share much with their narrator, Diedrich Knickerbocker, the funny Old Dutch historian-persona who whiles the hours swapping tales with his research subjects (the Old Dutch New Yorkers), and with Washington Irving, who was a calculated exploiter of the American past. Knickerbocker(-Irving)'s earlier satirical history of New Netherlands, *A History of New York, from the Beginning of the World to the End of the Dutch Dynasty*, embraced American beginnings even as it mocked them. Indeed, Irving arranged to publish the volume on December 6, 1809, the feast day of Saint Nicholas, the patron saint of New Netherlands, in the bicentenary year of Henry Hudson's discovery of New York. Although it came before the War of 1812, the volume made the past seem alive and relevant; after all, many read within its pages an allegory of contemporary politics.[36] That the successful *History of New York* was Irving's first book and that he returned to it and revised it no fewer than five times shows that he was a long-standing savvy participant in the culture of beginnings, one who knew how to leverage interest in the US past. Irving gave that same skill to Diedrich Knickerbocker, Rip Van Winkle, and Ichabod Crane, for both "Rip Van Winkle" and "The Legend of Sleepy Hollow" provide models for lively American beginnings that speak to nineteenth-century readers and invite them to imagine themselves as American.

Let us start with "Rip Van Winkle," the first of the two Knickerbocker tales. Despite widespread readerly acceptance of Hudson's ghost, exactly what happens during Rip's long absence is unclear. Yes, Rip may well have gone into the woods, met Henry Hudson, drunk from a magic keg, and fallen asleep for twenty years. But the story suggests, fed up with his wife, Rip may instead have stolen away from his domestic responsibilities, not to return until his wife is dead and his children grown. Knickerbocker gives plenty of motivation for such an act: Dame Van Winkle constantly berates her husband, for as a result of Rip's laziness, his children wander about in rags, his fields grow weeds, and his house needs repairs. Moreover, Dame Van Winkle's behavior gets worse as the years wear on. As Knickerbocker says, a "tart temper never mellows with age, and a sharp tongue is the only edged tool that grows keener with constant use" (Van Winkle SB 1:66–67). In the early years of their marriage, Rip visits the local inn when his wife is angry. Eventually, though, "from even this strong-hold the unlucky Rip" is "routed by his termagant wife" (Van Winkle SB 1:68, 69). By the time Rip goes up the mountain, his "only alternative to escape from the labour of the farm and the clamour of his wife, [is] to take gun in hand, and stroll away into the woods" (Van Winkle SB 1:69). In short, to continue to shirk his duties, Rip must leave. While critics have normally accepted the existence of Hudson's ghost, many, like Judith Fetterley and Leslie Fiedler, have acknowledged the misogyny of the tale and thus underlined the logic of Rip's fashioning a story about Henry Hudson as a blind for his escape from the "terrible virago" (Van Winkle SB 1:69).[37] Supporting this reading is that Rip waits to identify himself until after he is sure his wife is dead, and he is "observed, at first, to vary on some points every time he told" his story about the ghostly Dutchman (Van Winkle SB 1:92–93).

Like "Rip Van Winkle," "The Legend of Sleepy Hollow" offers narrative dynamism through an alternative explanation for the major plot happening. Either Ichabod Crane, the persecuted Connecticut pedagogue, met an actual headless horseman, or Brom Bones, seeking to eliminate a rival for Katrina's affections, pretended to be a decapitated Hessian. Surely, just as "Rip" lends more weight to Rip's (less plausible) magical sleep, "Sleepy Hollow" favors the explanation of Brom's trickery. Still, the story takes pains to leave the two options open. Knickerbocker presents Ichabod's post-horseman corporeal existence as secondhand, possibly unreliable intelligence from an "old farmer" (Van Winkle *SB* 6:115). As Knickerbocker reminds us, "The old country wives . . . maintain to this day, that Ichabod was spirited away by supernatural means" (Van Winkle *SB* 6:116–17). Moreover, Knickerbocker ends the tale with the eerie psalm tunes, those that Ichabod used to whistle, being heard among the trees; the reports of the ghosts in Ichabod's old schoolhouse; and the relocation, to a less thoroughly haunted area, of the road that poor Ichabod rode. In sum, locals—and perhaps Knickerbocker—believe that the headless horseman is still upon his steed. My point is less that one plot explanation is superior to another and more that the suggestion built into these Knickerbocker tales appoints the reader as a fellow interpreter of Ichabod's and Rip's fates. It interpolates the reader into the complex double plot and into Sleepy Hollow where the uncertain past is present and future. In "Rip Van Winkle" the inn sign is both George Washington and the underpainted King George. In "Sleepy Hollow," Cotton Mather's history of witches is a historical account, Ichabod's source for ghost stories, and a possible explanation for the town's strange ongoing happenings. I agree with recent scholars that Knickerbocker's stories are, to borrow Jeffery Insko's language about "Rip Van Winkle," "thick with layers of past and present" and that in them "time passes irregularly, alternately slowing and accelerating."[38] But I think this more nuanced understanding of time in Knickerbocker's tales requires an examination of genre in *The Sketch Book,* for Irving grants the tale a double-plotting that he himself enacts in the collection. He marks this winking narration as American and as a necessary strategy for US authors hoping to succeed. Readings that isolate "Rip Van Winkle" and "Sleepy Hollow" miss how this bending and twisting depiction of time offers a larger aesthetic argument.

For nineteenth-century readers, these tales would have made meaning in part through juxtaposition with British sketches, and the serialization of *The Sketch Book* markedly heightened the importance of these two tales within the American collection. "Rip Van Winkle" ended the first number, which Irving put out as a feeler; if the number did well—and of course it did—he promised to publish more. Similarly, "The Legend of Sleepy Hollow" ended the sixth number of the American *Sketch Book*, which was the final group of sketches and tales published in the United States before the English *Sketch Book* was fully in print. Whereas they had waited about two months between each of the first six serialized segments, American readers had to wait a full six months before receiving number 7. These two tales of American beginnings thus had pride of place at the ending of what were arguably the two most significant numbers. With the forced temporal gaps between numbers, *The Sketch Book*'s serialization made the tales linger like the final guest at a party. In turn, their presence made these serialized segments feel more relevant, more important, and more American to US readers. The quality of the physical book reinforced this sensation. Printed in octavo with twelve-point type that had a half of a line of space between each line of type and on good quality paper with big margins, *The Sketch Book* stood out. According to James Green, "No fictional work, whether native or reprinted, had ever been produced in such large type on such large paper." Indeed, Green concludes, "*The Sketch Book* was the first American work of fiction that looked like an original, not a reprint."[39] The physical object communicated the signifigance of American writing and elevated the importance of the American tales. In so doing, it underscored the value in donning the label of "American" as a reader and a writer.

The situation was radically different across the Atlantic. In the English volumes, the two New York tales were squished between British sketches: "Rip" was fifth of seventeen sketches in the first volume, while "Sleepy Hollow," the penultimate piece in volume 2, was followed by "L'Envoy," an afterword written expressly to argue for English critical leniency and generosity. Instead of closing with "Rip Van Winkle" as does the first American number, the first volume of the English *Sketch Book* pivoted decidedly away from the United States and finished with a German tale, "The Spectre Bridegroom." The only *Sketch Book* tale not set in New York and told by Knickerbocker, "The Spectre Bridegroom" tells of a young bridegroom who dies on the way to his wedding and his friend who, after being mistaken as the bridegroom's ghost, falls in love with the bride. Along with being set in Europe rather than the United States, this tale lacks the narrative ambiguity of "Rip" and "Sleepy." Yes, initially the bride's family thinks the friend is a specter, but by the end of the tale all realize that he is "substantial flesh and blood" (Van Winkle SB 4:335). There is no true double-plotting or narrative vitality. Instead, what the tale offers is a story of age and decay. The bride's father, Baron Von Landshort, is "a dry branch of the great family of Katzenellenbogen" with a single child and a large castle (Van Winkle *SB* 6: 304). The family is so withered, it seems only fitting that his daughter will marry someone who playacts being dead. While the American tales—and by extension the US story—leave open multiple narrative possibilities, the European story is fixed. The German tale's teleology dictates that the bereaved friend must marry his friend's intended; the young bridegroom's dying plea assures that outcome. This story takes on outside importance in the English volumes because Irving's finances made the appearance of the second English volume unsure, and he did not initially make clear that more sketches would be forthcoming. Hence, many British reviewers commented on the first volume as a whole piece.[40] That fact meant that this German tale was, for a time, the capstone to the English *Sketch Book*. Called "the last, and perhaps the best, chapter" by John Murray's *Quarterly Review,* "The Spectre Bridegroom" provides an appropriately morbid ending to a collection rife with considerations of death and decay.[41]

I am arguing here that the temporality of the publication and the arrangement of materials within the various installments helped to form an impression of the collection as a whole. For Americans, that impression was of dynamic American stories that brought them into the story world through double-plotting and serialization. For Britons, the two-volume publication submerged the American tales and reinforced ideas of the provincialism and absurdity of their former colonists. The calm pastness of the British sketches and European tale reigned. Critics on both sides of the Atlantic aided these impressions by emphasizing different material within *The Sketch Book:* Americans spoke most about the tales, while Britons wrote most about the sketches. In a thirty-five-page consideration of Irving within the *North American Review* (1819), Richard Henry Dana Sr. declared that Irving's Knickerbocker voice "was masculine—good bone and muscle" but Crayon's writing was "feminine, *dressy,* elegant." In fact, Dana said, Crayon's prose was "as if his mother English had been sent abroad to be improved, and in attempting to be accomplished, had lost too many of her home qualities."[42] The charges of Crayon's effeminacy and betrayal convey Dana's marked preference for the American tales over the English sketches. Three years later in the same magazine, Edward Everett called the collection an "agreeable work" but condemned Irving's subject—England—as "less original," a phrase that means insufficiently American. Everett continued: "Our complaint is . . . that Mr. Irving has endeavored to graft himself, manner and matter, onto the English stock" and thus produced a product "inferior to the author's earlier" *History of New York*.[43] These reviews show that *The Sketch Book* won over many American critics almost entirely on the merits of "Rip Van Winkle" and "The Legend of Sleepy Hollow"—just two of the twenty-eight pieces in the American *Sketch Book*. These pieces are the ones that helped Americans see their past as energetic, relevant, and distinctive, and thus helped them see themselves as that way too. In contrast, many British critics disregarded the presence of the American tales, and others directly criticized their placement in Crayon's *Sketch Book*. An 1820 piece from the London *Eclectic Review* acknowledges that "Rip Van Winkle" was "well-told" and "entertaining enough; but one would have thought that the observant Geoffrey Crayon, *Gent.* might, with Europe fresh before him, have found other matter wherewith to fill his Sketch Book." In other words, observational pieces (about Britain) were most appropriate for a sketcher and a sketch book. True to this logic, the London paper praised the contents of the second American number—one containing four sketches that the reviewer had received from New York—as "more of what we expect from a traveller."[44] Whether, like the London *Examiner* and the *Edinburgh Monthly,* the magazine notes the presence of New York tales, or, like the *Literary Gazette,* the *British Literary Chronicle* and the *Monthly Review,* the magazine ignores them, these British critics gush over Crayon's treatment of British themes. As Americans did, British critics looked into *The Sketch Book* and saw themselves and their world.

Native American Sketches and Vital American Stories

Like they had of the American tales, few British reviewers made note of the two sketches about Native Americans that Irving had revised and included in the British *Sketch Book*.[45] Although "Philip of Pokanoket" and "Traits of Indian Character" did not receive much critical ink, it is likely that, as Laura Murray and Joseph Rezek have argued, Irving was trying to credential himself as exotically American for a British audience.[46] The additions did allow Irving to claim that the English *Sketch Book* was revised and expanded, and altering something previously written was surely the most expedient way to enlarge the collection. Yet the two Native American sketches, which were not published in the original American *Sketch Book,* not only muddled the neat division between British sketches and American tales, but they also implied that there was little difference between the American and the English—the United States, like its former colonizer, had a dead past.[47] As the biggest difference between the original American and English *Sketch Books*, these sketches show Irving's interest in enabling the funhouse mirror images of self and other held by two distinct national readerships.

When composed for the *Analectic Magazine* in 1814, "Traits of Indian Character" and "Philip of Pokanoket" had clear and contemporary political purpose: they indicted the violent policies of an American government at war with the Creek Indians in the southeastern United States. Originally Irving had hoped "if possible to mitigate the fury of passion and prejudice, and to turn aside the bloody hand of violence" perpetrated by US soldiers under the command of Andrew Jackson.[48] Yet, by the 1820 version of "Traits of Indian Character," the United States government had become benevolent: "The American government, too, has wisely and humanely exerted itself to inculcate a friendly and forbearing spirit towards them, and to protect them from fraud and injustice" (Miller-Murray *SB* 2:215–16). To emphasize the point, Irving included a footnote praising the government's "indefatigable . . . exertions to ameliorate the situation of the Indians"—exertions that would later include the infamous Trail of Tears (Miller-Murray *SB* 2:216). For his British audience, Irving transformed political critique into romantic musing. Like the manuscripts that Crayon sees authors assembling in the Reading Room of the British Museum, these reworked Native American sketches lack vitality. They communicate death and stasis. The last lines of "Traits of Indian Character" put it this way: "'We are driven back,' said an old warrior, 'until we can retreat no further—our hatchets are broken, our bows are snapped, our fires are nearly extinguished—a little longer and the white man will cease to persecute us—for we shall cease to exist!'" (Miller-Murray *SB* 2: 236). Like Chingachgook of Cooper's *The Last of the Mohicans*, Irving's noble warrior represents a doomed race. He voices his own and his people's end, becoming, to borrow Laura Murray's formulation, "simultaneously visible and invisible."[49] Even as he appears as a sympathetic figure in the sketch, he disappears as a live one. So too in "Philip of Pokanoket" does Irving recount the bloody excesses of the Pequot War (originally meant to be analogous to the Creek War) and leave all his Native American characters dead by sketch end. Betrayed by his confederates, King Philip himself is captured and killed by the Puritans. In the 1820 English *Sketch Book*, Irving locks such unfortunate violence in a precivilized past calculated to appeal to British readers, who were fascinated by the exotic savagery of North America, rather than Americans, who might be uncomfortable with considering their own complicity in such extermination. These Native American sketches—the only *American* sketches within the volume and the only sketches not voiced by creative Geoffrey Crayon—depict the United States as formally related and beholden to England. They are examples of a genre that *The Sketch Book* associates with England, and they mobilize the leitmotif of death that is similarly marked as British. That Irving intended the version of *The Sketch Book* that contained two Native American sketches for a British audience furthers my point that he catered to national and racial prejudices. Without the political criticism of the 1814 versions, the pieces provide an unthreatening account of an "authentic" American past for a transatlantic audience, one as fading and poetic as that which Crayon records in Britain. That this British *Sketch Book* with its American sketches became the definitive version of *The Sketch Book* in 1824, after three serialized American editions, reinforces *The Sketch Book's* projection of a white America. For while Irving's sympathy is with the Native Americans in these two sketches, his distant tone and the marked pastness of the sketches make clear that readers should recognize figures like Rip and Ichabod as the present and future United States. By the time they are incorporated into the American *Sketch Book*, Irving's Native Americans count as history, not compatriots.

I do not wish to suggest, however, that these two sketches—the only parts of *The Sketch Book* written in the United States—undo Irving's belief in vital American stories. Despite the fact that Irving includes just three of them in *The Sketch Book*, he makes it clear that tales are more powerful than sketches. "The Voyage," the second sketch within *The Sketch Book*, contains an embedded tale about a tragic midocean collision during a heavy fog. Unable to see, the captain, who recounts the story to Crayon during their Atlantic crossing, sails straight into an unlighted vessel ahead. The watch had sounded the alarm, but before any action could be taken, they crash. By the time the crew turns the ship around, no survivors can be found, though the captain looks for several hours. The tale is shocking and potent, and Crayon must "confess [that] these stories, for a time, put an end to all my fine fancies." Later, when Crayon resumes sketching the chiaroscuro of sky and the sea, the captain's tale, which makes an accordion of time with its fast collision and slow search, haunts his images. As if his boat has also been run over, Crayon sees "the ship staggering and plunging among these roaring caverns" and thinks it "miraculous that she regained her balance, or preserved her buoyancy" (Van Winkle *SB* 1:19). "It seemed," Crayon acknowledges, "as if death were raging round this floating prison, seeking for his prey" (Van Winkle *SB* 1:20). This tale upsets Crayon, overlaying past happenings onto his present crossing, like an image of George Washington painted over King George, and with its somber plot, it prepares us for the coming death and decay of the British sketches. Moving from the United States to England, "The Voyage," more than any other piece in *The Sketch Book,* is geographically placed to evaluate the relative power of the two genres in the collection. In this contest, Crayon, the consummate gentleman sketcher, favors the American tale. The captain's story (with its suggestively oppressive white fog) affects Crayon much more than the boiling sea in front of him, and as Richard Henry Dana Sr. acknowledges, "the plain story told by the captain leaves a deeper impression" than do Crayon's reflections.[50] In the end, then, *The Sketch Book* offers a cheek-by-jowl presentation of English and American which launches the sketch and the tale and their racial exclusion. Even as it curried favor with British readers, the collection advocated for dynamic American stories where past and present coexisted. It coded short fiction as a vital genre for temporal mediation, temporal innovation, nation building, and literary success. Richard McLamore has accused *The Sketch Book* of being "neither American nor English enough," and Harriet Martineau sighed that Irving was "a mixture of the American of the present day and of the Englishman of the last century."[51] But indeed, *The Sketch Book*'s great nineteenth-century success was its ability to juggle temporalities and genres in order to pass as a national product in both places. It could be read as *both* English *and* American. In creating such a successful American book, Irving permanently changed US letters and the future of short fiction. It was an American beginning that inspired many subsequent authors, making its true and lasting legacy the importance of the sketch and the tale in the culture of beginnings.[52]

Coda: The Impact of Irving's Double Thesis on Short Story Critics

The Sketch Book's success was hugely influential to early nineteenth-century authors who emulated Geoffrey Crayon's poise, the collection's mix of sketches and tales, and Knickerbocker's lively beginning stories. But Irving's best seller has had even more influence on twentieth-century and contemporary national biases in short story theory, for it is Irving's collection that first links the tale—and thus the related form of the short story—with the United States and the sketch with Britain. Short fiction critics have long identified the short story as the most American genre. For one, in 1885, Brander Matthews asserted: "Almost as soon as America began to have any literature at all it had good Short-stories. . . . For fifty years the American Short-story has had a supremacy which any competent critic could not but acknowledge."[53] Likewise, in 1957 Walter A. Reichart argued that "short stories [are] a genre acknowledged as an American contribution to literature."[54] As if his subtitle were not clear enough, the second sentence of William Peden's *The American Short Story: Front Line in the National Defense of Literature* (1964) declares the same idea: the short story "is the only major literary form of essentially American origin and the only one in which American writers have always tended to excel."[55] In *The Lonely Voice* (1962), Frank O'Connor adds, "The Americans have handled the short story so wonderfully that one can say that it is a national art form."[56] More explicitly comparing England and the United States, Barbara Korte understands that the "short story in Britain appears a stepchild of literary criticism and history when compared to its counterpart 'across the pond,'" while W. Somerset Maugham admits, "English writers on the whole have not taken kindly to the art of the short story."[57]

Critics give multiple reasons for the strong correlation between the United States and the short story, a genre widely accepted as growing out of or, for those who apply the term anachronistically, as equivalent to the early nineteenth-century tale.[58] The most popular explanations are two. First, as I discuss more in a later chapter, Edgar Allan Poe's review of Nathaniel Hawthorne's tales is accepted as the origin of short story theory. The stature of these two American masters—Poe and Hawthorne—thus gives a national association to the genre. Second, American printers offered and offer more opportunities for publishing short fiction.[59] Hence, the argument goes, American authors are encouraged to write shorter works. Without doubt, these explanations have some merit. Yet the still influential critical correlation between the short story and the United States (and, though less strongly, between Britain and the sketch) started with the massive success of *The Sketch Book*. Many nineteenth- and early twentieth-century critics credited Irving with single-handedly developing the American short story. For example, in 1881, Charles Dudley Warner cited Knickerbocker as he declared "our national indebtedness" to Irving for "investing a crude and new land with the enduring charms of romance and tradition."[60] In 1900 Barrett Wendell made Irving's formal contributions explicit: "Perhaps his [Irving's] most noteworthy feat . . . is that he made prominent in English literature a literary form in which for a long time to come Americans excelled native Englishmen,—the short story."[61] Similarly convinced that Irving was the progenitor of the short story, in 1923 Fred Lewis Pattee listed "nine distinctive services" Irving performed for the genre and concluded that "he endowed the short story with a style that was finished and beautiful, one that threw its influence over large areas of the later product. To many critics this was Irving's chief contribution to American literature."[62] For half of the twentieth century, scholars acknowledged that Irving marked the short story—although the more accurate term would be the tale—as a distinct form with a link to the United States. Even when, in 1973, Arthur Voss adjudged Irving a "classic, if minor, American author," he recognized Irving's position at, as Voss's chapter title indicates, the "beginnings of the American short story."[63] The first transatlantic best seller written by an American thus provided a number of important beginnings. It heralded the international arrival of the native-born American author. It made space, through formal differentiation and temporal theorization, for the construction of dynamic stories about American beginnings, and it served as a potent origin for ongoing assumptions about the American nature of the short story, a descendant of the nineteenth-century tale. Providing a model for Americans who saw rupture and continuance with a British past, Irving's *Sketch Book* established the utility of short fiction for conjuring an American people and supporting American literary professionalism.

2

Biding Time in Hale's *Ladies' Magazine*

Turning from Geoffrey Crayon's bachelor travels to Sarah Josepha Hale's character sketches, I want to foreground the gendered dynamics of American beginnings. Most obviously, the culture of beginnings was patriarchal in its subject matter. Puritan divines, early colonists, revolutionary generals, and daring statesmen were the customary heroes of origin stories. When present, which was not often, nonwhite women (and men) were mostly slaves or savages.[1] White women were also rarely depicted as anything but asides. According to Theodore Gottlieb, Betsy Ross, that maker of the first American flag, was completely unknown in the early nineteenth century. In fact, Gottlieb traces the legend's start to an 1870 paper William J. Canby gave at the Historical Society of Pennsylvania, a paper "now generally discredited as to alleged facts, historical statements and inferences, very faulty and not reliable."[2] Abigail Adams, another inspiring revolutionary American, was similarly not marked as such during the nineteenth century. Her grandson Charles Francis Adams did publish a collection of her letters in 1840, and that collection was prefaced by a "Memoir" that gave biographical information on both John and Abigail. Nonetheless, no full-length biography of Abigail Adams existed until the mid-twentieth century, and most scholarly attention to her life and thought has come since 1980. Her famous epistolary admonition to "remember the ladies"—to which I will return below—was publicized by modern feminists, not celebrated by Sarah Hale's contemporaries. Exchanging letters with the likes of Abigail Adams and Hannah Winthrop (wife of a Harvard professor and descendant of the first Massachusetts governor), the politically active

Mercy Otis Warren wrote propaganda for the American Revolution as well as one of the earliest histories of that war. Still, it was not until 1896 that a biography of her appeared, and, even now, Warren does not serve as a paragon of the American past for many, if any, Americans. In short, women who contributed to the American Revolution by making symbols and by writing letters and tracts were not the subjects of the origin tales that Rufus Choate and others earnestly requested. Yet, of course, women—both white and of color—were important figures in the American Revolution and American history.

Recognizing the previously unacknowledged importance of American women to US national myths and the US national community, Hale advocates for various types of female action and female writing. Indeed, if Washington Irving pushed American literary professionalism forward by penning the first transatlantic best seller by a native-born American, Sarah Hale was hugely responsible for creating the conditions by which US authors, particularly white women authors, could more broadly achieve a professional status. With her *Ladies' Magazine,* the first successful American periodical that targeted an all-female readership and thus an important beginning, Hale, as Patricia Okker has shown, eschewed the British reprints used by so many other scissor editors; encouraged attribution from her authors, which allowed them to build reputations; and supported the fair compensation of writers for their writing.[3] With these three acts, Hale single-handedly attempted to shift US authorship models, again placing the sketch and the tale at the center of efforts to secure a robust American literary tradition. While both short fiction forms were important within the *Ladies' Magazine,* this chapter shows how Hale found the sketch particularly useful for inserting women as active participants in the American past and centering them as the heart of the American character.

Productive Waiting

Sarah Josepha Hale (born 1788) expected to live life as a wife and mother who did a bit of writing on the side. Although she learned all she could from first her mother, then her college-educated brother, Horatio, and finally from her lawyer husband, David, this education happened in fits and starts. Unable to go to university because she was a woman, Hale had to wait for her brother to return from Dartmouth at term end and share his coursework. Likewise, Hale had to wade through the many tasks of a mother and wife before she could sit with her husband to complete evening lessons.[4] In the in-between times, Hale remained active, writing compositions that would later be corrected by David and pursuing her amateur interests in French and botany.[5] When David, unexpectedly died just four days before Hale gave birth to their fifth child, however, she was forced into supporting her family. Through the modest success of her early novel *Northwood* (1827), Hale came to the attention of the Reverend John L. Blake, a Boston-based publisher seeking an editor for his *Ladies' Magazine.* Under Hale's leadership the magazine would become the first successful US periodical for women, and when Hale sold the magazine and transferred her editorial duties, the basis for the first US periodical with a national readership, Louis A. Godey's *Lady's Book.*[6] Throughout her years of editing she published numerous volumes, poems, stories, and reviews, but she never stopped wearing widow's weeds or expressing longing, in poetry and prose, for her dead husband. In a very real way, she spent her productive life waiting to rejoin him.

Despite her prodigious output and nineteenth-century stature, Hale has not been a favorite with scholars. Ruth E. Finley's dated *Lady of Godey's* (1931), Isabelle Webb Entrikin's sometimes dismissive 1946 dissertation, and Olive Burt's trade biography *First Woman Editor* remain the only full-length works about Sarah Josepha Buell Hale.[7] Patricia Okker's *Our Sister Editors* (1995) and Nicole Tonkovich's *Domesticity with a Difference* (1997), which cast wider nets, do both feature Hale prominently.[8] Yet even these excellent studies, like the handful of articles that exist about Hale, focus most on Hale's forty-one-year tenure at *Godey's Lady's Book.* They thus give relatively little attention to the *Ladies' Magazine,* which started it all. All this raises the question of why, despite recognition of the cultural importance of the *Lady's Book,* as Godey's magazine was called, and despite Hale's being cited as one of the most influential women in the nineteenth-century United States, have scholars spent so little time thinking about her. Part of the answer is that in the early twentieth century, critics mostly dismissed Hale's literary merit.[9] The eminent scholar of American periodicals, Frank Luther Mott, for example, declared that "sentimentality, which infected the literature of the time pretty generally anyway, was fulsome in the *Lady's Book.*"[10] Hale, of course, was held responsible for such aesthetic failures.

Along with suffering from the denigration of domestic fiction, Hale has likely been neglected because she was on the wrong side of history on two critical issues: slavery and women's suffrage. When not avoiding the topic of slavery because of its incendiary nature as she did after 1853, Hale worked for colonization efforts and believed that it was part of a grand Christian plan that slavery should end by sending freed Protestant African Americans back to Africa to convert the continent to Christianity; as she wrote, the "African . . . among us has no home, no position, and no future."[11] More than that, as Beverly Peterson has noted, between 1852 (the year *Uncle Tom's Cabin* came out in volume form and was reviewed everywhere) and 1854, Hale published seventeen or more notices of books with proslavery or antiabolitionist positions.[12] Furthermore, Hale's version of domesticity postulated a material difference between men and women (and she would have been thinking of white men and women of the middle and upper classes). An antisuffragette, Hale believed that women should cultivate their untainted status and moral superiority by escaping sullying contact with markets and politics, ideas that appear even in the earliest issues of the *Ladies' Magazine*.[13] While there are ways to explain Hale's convictions, including that they sold well, there is little that can justify Hale's beliefs. Yet, perhaps precisely because of the nineteenth-century popularity of these unpalatable stances on suffrage and slavery, Hale can tell us much about how many middle- and upper-class white women attempted to access more social power while reaffirming the limitations of their sex and embracing a projection of an all-white American people.

As editor, or *editress* as Hale would have said, of the *Ladies' Magazine*, Hale produced a morally steady, cohesive, and patriotic magazine that distinguished itself from competitors.[14] In the January 1828 introduction to the *Ladies' Magazine*, Hale proclaimed that her periodical would be "national—be American;—and [full of] well written communications, whether poems, letters, sketches, tales, or essays, descriptive of American scenery, character, and manners." This patriotism was supposed to be both motivating and comforting. Indeed, she elicited the help of fathers, brothers, and lovers in taking the magazine for the women in their lives, who would, in turn, become better daughters, sisters, and wives. "Systematic and thorough education," Hale wrote, will "qualify woman to be a rational companion, an instructive as well as agreeable friend" and will "be compatible with the cheerful discharge of her domestic duties, and the delicacy of feeling, and love of retirement, which nature obviously imposed on the sex."[15] Hale linked the improvement of women's minds with strengthened gender roles. In her hand and in her magazine, women's advancements were nonthreatening, patriotic, and passive. Instead of dramatizing women who seized opportunity and grabbed power, Hale offered female characters who practiced productive waiting. In a twelve-part series called "Sketches of American Character" that ran in the inaugural volume of the *Ladies' Magazine,* Hale genders both waiting and beginnings as female as a means of coding white women as American. Through character, Hale was determined to show, women influenced the destiny and idea of the nation. As George Forgie has argued, "It was taken for granted from the start that the survival of the Republic for any length of time would depend heavily on the virtue of its citizens. Character was perceived to be the point of contact between individual lives and national fate."[16] Placed one per magazine issue throughout 1828, these sketches stake this claim from the first installment, "Walter Wilson," which focuses on the haughty son of a Revolutionary War veteran and the dutiful daughter of an old-time Puritan. Yet because Hale's interest is in the female characters who could not be veterans or Pilgrims themselves, she constantly foregrounds the waiting that happens when a lover, father, or brother is absent—like her college-going brother had been and like her husband, after death, was. She forces her readers to wade through long prefaces and even, in one case, wait six months before the second part of a sketch was serialized. For Hale's characters *and* for Hale's readers (as it had for Hale herself), biding time provides educational opportunities or self-knowledge. The sketches teach and enact a productive waiting that makes the projected white female reader part of the US past and the US present.

Energizing the waiting inherent in women's condition and emphasizing its productive possibilities allowed Hale to advocate for white women's opportunities without disrupting nineteenth-century gender norms. After all, productive waiting is an integral part of making a child, and, in an age before reliable contraception, it was a definitional part of almost all married women's lives.[17] Hale herself carried five children to term, and she relied on that experience and her concomitant status as mother and widow to frame her magazine and its contents as decorous, proper, and appropriate. Over the course of her long career, she evoked her position as widow and mother to champion increased legal rights for women; to normalize women working as schoolteachers; to encourage and advertise labor-saving and leisure-giving devices like the sewing machine; and to espouse the importance of female education, supporting the efforts of her friend Catherine Beecher and helping to found Vassar College. Embracing female subscribers and female characters as the essence of the country, Hale fashions the patient reception and careful reading of a women's periodical as the ultimate national act. Hale's program within the *Ladies' Magazine,* while severely limited in its scope and inclusiveness, was progressive: it made space for white women in the culture of beginnings and cast their lot—of being left behind during war or being helpmate during colonization—as a fruitful one. In this way Hale's project in the *Ladies' Magazine* is in fact aligned with many of the goals of feminism, even as Hale herself opposed suffrage. Hale may have praised women who fulfilled appropriate female roles, but under the banner of patriotism, she worked hard to expand the contours of those roles so that women were more learned, more self-sufficient, and better included in the national imaginary. Because of Hale's editorship, short fiction in ladies' magazines became integral to the development of American literary professionalism and the story of the United States.

Delayed Beginnings

In her series of twelve "Sketches of American Character," Hale invites and mandates waiting for her readers and her characters in a strategy that is overtly patriotic and slyly didactic. Mentions of forefathers, often the uncles or fathers of the main characters, as well as references to historic past events and famous US documents are sprinkled through Hale's magazine, but they are never more obvious than in "The Soldier of the Revolution" (the April sketch of American character), which takes place during the Revolutionary War.[18] Here Hale articulates the ideology of the culture of beginnings, namely, that American character is intimately connected to and made distinct by American history. As she says in extensive and dry introductory comments, "The causes which roused the Americans to take up arms were most favorable to the development of the virtuous energies of men," and their "generous devotedness of the American soldiery to the principles of liberty and equal rights, and their prompt obedience to civil government, have no parallel in history."[19] On the basis of this widely accepted and seemingly inoffensive logic, Hale wants to obviate women's inclusion in the culture of beginnings, for "the ladies of America are indebted to the free institutions established by the war of the Revolution, for their inestimable privileges of education, and that elevation of character and sentiment they now possess."[20] The prosy start of "The Soldier of the Revolution" connects education with the American Revolution to declare female learning is patriotic. Moreover, this introduction, with its more plodding sentences and content, denies readers narrative absorption, pushing them instead toward careful consideration and slow reading; it directs females to ponder woman's place in the nation, rather than read for the plot. By telling stories that mobilize the US past, Hale can affirm female education and position women as a central part of the body politic. In turn, women, seen as equal members of the country, gain rights—not the suffrage that Hale opposed, but such things as the ability to sign contracts and to own property (both of which were denied married women in most states until the 1850s) and, if single and working, to receive better social and political support. At a time when, as Arthur Shaffer has argued, many Americans formed their understanding of history through newspapers and magazines, the *Ladies Magazine* could and did become a potent tool in the construction of a sense of "nationness."[21]

The slow introduction to "The Soldier of the Revolution"—by which I mean a narrative style that resists quick reading—as well as the actions within Hale's sketches, argue that productive waiting is how a woman can imagine herself as fully part of the American people. After Walter's grandfather sends Walter to board with a farmer in "Walter Wilson," the first sketch of American character, Hale cautions against hasty judgment and encourages patience: "No doubt the reader, if a young lady, thinks his destination very vulgar—wonders why he was not sent to college, or at least, placed behind some counter; and all interest in the hero at an end, prepares to turn to some amusing article. If she does, she will lose the description of as fair a girl as herself, besides one or two love scenes."[22] The warning sets up Hale's point that (American) character matters more than riches, the message Walter's veteran grandfather (that literal connection to the founding of the United States) articulates at story's end. But Hale is also here encouraging tenacity in the readers who are tempted to abandon a story at its beginning. While Walter, originally resentful of farm life, interrogates his own preconceptions and comes to value diligence and honesty over showy markers of class, Hale's lady reader learns the value of endurance, both in Walter and in herself. Fanny, the major female character and Walter's love interest, experiences this same growth. When Fanny's father sends Walter away for a year to prove he can be "steady and industrious" before claiming his bride, Fanny must turn the waiting into skill building at home; she must become "more steady" and mind how to bake, to brew, and to season pies.[23] Hale seeks an immersed reader who self-reflexively applies the story to her own life and character. For reading is potentially an act of self-recognition and thus of increased self-knowledge. As a contributor—likely Hale—wrote in an 1833 *Ladies' Magazine* essay, "I have come to the considerate but decided conclusion that mankind read too much, and reason and reflect too little."[24] The solution to this problem is for readers to "weigh and consider things as they ought" rather than zooming through novels and stories.[25] Hale's sketches attempt to inculcate this practice by slowing down narrative progression and temporally representing everyday domestic work.

Like the plot of "Walter Wilson," the plot of "The Soldier of the Revolution" involves waiting, which it marks as deeply patriotic and quintessentially female. When the revolutionary veteran Captain Blake recalls his military service and courtship for his listening granddaughter (the stand-in for the magazine reader), he declares that "'tis the anticipation of the combat that makes cowards, and sometimes brave men tremble." In other words, the easy part is fighting the British; the hard part is *waiting* for the fight to begin. More startlingly, Captain Blake describes "the most painful moment of a soldier's life, at least of those who have a dear home and kind friends" as the moment "when they part from them."[26] Like Walter Wilson before them, these paragons of American service become feminized by the misery of departure and of waiting. With Captain Blake's admission, waiting, gendered female as it is, becomes an essential and patriotic wartime act, for despite the pain of separation, Blake and his fellows do leave home, and their womenfolk, afflicted by the same ache, remain behind. This recognition of shared experience reveals that through women and family, soldiers form their emotional bonds to the nation. If a man has no home to protect, he has little reason to fight for his country, and he ceases, in some sense, to identify as fully American. Constructing women's role as nation building, Hale aligns her sketches with sentimentalism, which, in Shirley Samuel's words, is "a project about imagining the nation's bodies and the national body" through the forging of emotional bonds between reader and character.[27] By being left at home and tending to the necessary domestic duties, women do critically important national work—they form and maintain the identity of the United States. When Hale's readers identify with the female characters who wait, then, they endorse an idea of America and include themselves within it.

Women's work has occasionally been recognized as central to national self-concepts. In fact, revolutionary newspapers made the link between women's waiting and national identity in their coverage of the homespun movement. In the mid-1760s while the Sons of Liberty were out drinking toasts, roasting pigs, and causing trouble, the Daughters of Liberty were calmly spinning fibers into homespun cloth. A reaction to the taxes levied on items coming into the colonies, the nonimportation agreements transformed the making of cloth into a matter of colonial pride and political will. (Previously, textiles were made in England and shipped over.) Celebrating this productive waiting in national terms, newspaper reports about the homespun movement in the *Boston Evening Post* and the *Essex Gazette* tied spinning to the "intolerable Burdens now Laid upon us" and the need to fight for "our rights, properties and privileges."[28] They praised women for their diligence and closely followed spinning bees and local outputs. Women and their women's work became symbols for addressing the crisis and claiming a self-reliant, powerful local identity. Biding their time as their men caroused, these women produced more than just linen, however. As John Cleaveland, a minister, observed about their spinning, "Women might recover to this country the full and free enjoyment of all our rights, properties and privileges (which is more than the men have been able to do): And so have the honour of building not only for their own, but the houses of so many thousand."[29] Performing domestic chores while the men were away allowed women to work toward a national victory and to consider the free enjoyment of rights, property, and privileges that are owed them. Weaving gave a woman time to think *for* herself and thus to think *of* herself as a full member of the American people, with the political and symbolic resonance that category implies.

That is not to say that Hale's idea of productive waiting is unquestionably radical. Assuring that women wait for men is part of a heteronormative social project invested in the purity and regulation of offspring. Women wait so that men can assure the sanctity of their bloodlines and the security of passing property to the next generation. While it holds possibility, then, waiting is a women's duty. Mary Saunders, the heroine of "The Soldier of the Revolution," waits first while her lover's (Captain Blake's) father prohibits her seeing her Captain Blake, and then while her lover is off boldly fighting in the American Revolution. In the first six months of waiting, Mary seems to solidify her political opinions, pro-independence and opposed to her father's rabidly Tory stance. While she waits two and a half years more for Captain Blake to return from war, she cares for her father and their isolated farm (isolated because of her father's outspoken defense of the British). Aligned with a project of white nation building, her actions do prove her fidelity and virtue to lover and country—assuring the (racial) purity of the nation. Yet through both periods of waiting, though not detailed in the sketch, Mary also works and develops. (Work, Elaine Scarry has noted, is hard to depict because it is "perpetual, repetitive, habitual," an ongoing rather than "discrete action" that makes it resist narrative representation.)[30] She lives for herself in a way that she will not be able to once married. Doing her duty can thus hold powerful possibilities if the time is mobilized for self-growth. Many of Hale's own readers would have identified with Mary, having themselves awaited menfolk during the War of 1812 or having had mothers and grandmothers who bided time during the Revolutionary War. Accepting the truth of women's waiting and activating this waiting means that women can find agency without overtly challenging social norms. They can claim a position as waiting warriors, integral to the national effort and the culture of beginnings. In this way, Mary's actions read as significant personally and nationally. They assure Mary's future happiness, *and* they secure the United States: political society, to quote Hannah Arendt, is a "curiously hybrid realm where private interests assume public significance."[31] Mary's story reveals that the hidden heart of the nation is feminine and that women do and have always influenced the political realm.

As it is in "A Story of the Revolution," the beginnings of other sketches in the series are slow or elongated. Most particularly in "The Apparition," the tenth sketch of American character, Hale spends two and a half close-spaced pages leisurely describing a town called Harmony and discoursing on the tax beliefs and worship practices of its townspeople. Aware of the likely reception of this long nonplotted section, Hale defends herself: "These remarks are not foreign to my subject, though they may *seem* misplaced, and actually be uninteresting or dull."[32] Similarly, in "The Village Schoolmistress," the fifth sketch, Hale discusses the importance of female education at length. Part way through she acknowledges that she "may not dwell on the subject" anymore because her "preface is already too long" and concedes that "readers soon tire of prefaces, and skip them, and so the labor of writing them is lost."[33] Yet she continues for another page. While Hale seems to know that, as Teresa De Lauretis has argued, the progression of a plot is fueled by the desire to know what happens next, Hale purposefully attenuates the action to the point where she might—and likely did—lose readers.[34] At least one contemporary reviewer thought Hale should make her magazine snappier to maintain interest.[35] Hale even acknowledged such charges in the seventh sketch of American character: "Public taste demands, in a periodical, change and variety, more than has as yet been afforded them in the Ladies' Magazine." Nonetheless Hale eschews this re-sponsibility in her own sketches, saying she relies "on the 'good and gifted' contributors" for "interest to the pages."[36] These contributors are both other authors who send in literary material *and* the sketch readers who make the stories come alive in their mind. Indeed, Hale begins her twelfth sketch of American character, "A Winter in the Country," with a question directly to the reader: "Did you ever live in the country?"[37] This query reflects a concern throughout the series with drawing the readers into the story and magazine community. "Let it be remembered," Hale cautions in her ninth sketch of American character, "that though *we* may be excessively annoyed by the prejudices of others, *we* shall never be quite wretched if *we* do not yield ourselves to the guidance of our own."[38] Hale's engaging narrative style—her direct addresses to and invocation of the reader—encourages the reader to see herself as part of the story, similarly learning with the charac-ters and forging links to the US past.

I am arguing that these slow beginnings are calculated efforts to teach the reader certain skills, and rather than dismissing these sketches as poorly written, we should try to understand how the narrative pacing creates pur-poseful effects. Women readers, like women characters, must learn to wait, sublimating whatever frustration arises to make the space of time produc-tive and meaningful. Hale's elongated passages are the formal version of the courtship interruptions that Mary experiences, or the manner in which a wedding is delayed pending a father's approval. In their dilation of story to allow women characters to realize what they do and do not know, they might also be considered prescient of, to borrow Heather Schor's descrip-tion, the "particularly and pointedly gendered," baggy, overlong middles of

Victorian novels.[39] The attempt to represent the lives of women in those English novels leads to attenuated narrative momentum and, for critics like Franco Moretti who see banality, a failure of story action.[40] Hale similarly slows down temporal movement to represent her women characters and women readers. Like her story events, Hale's prosy introductions control desire by separating lovers, both the characters in the story from each other and the story reader from the story action. In this space where women are left behind, they can practice holding and developing an idea rather than receiving it already fully formulated. Hale's poetics, in other words, challenge the common belief that, as an 1821 article advocating female education put it, woman's "mental, like her physical constitution" is "less vigorous" than man's and her "stretch of thought is not quite so extended."[41] When the men are absent and when desire is frustrated, readers can cultivate a patience critical to self-improvement. Fracturing the reading experience made a periodical targeted at a female audience less threatening, more didactic, and ultimately more successful—and provided a decorous logic for presenting characters whose modesty required their actions to refuse the spotlight. It mirrored the life experiences of and the cultural expectations for white women so that it could reach those women readers and teach them to activate moments of involuntary waiting. Hale's short fiction shifts the absorptive experience of fiction reading into an imaginative collaboration between sketcher, character, and reader. All three proceed through the story at a considered pace that allows for intellectual work and advancement, a pace that makes the form reinforce the contents.

Hale used an aesthetic of waiting both because she saw it as judicious and because it reflected her own experience. In 1827, a Boston magazine noted that Hale had written her novel *Northwood* while "surrounded by her children, and constantly suffering interruption from business of a very anti-literary nature."[42] Hale herself said that she wrote "with a baby in my arms."[43] This process of composition was nothing like the Romantic ideal of authorship wherein one writes, cloistered away, in an inspired frenzy. Instead, women authors like Hale had to wait through the interruptions of family duties, nursing their ideas and their children until they could return to the composition. Indeed, Fanny Fern (Sarah Payson Willis), the prolific and popular midcentury columnist and sketch writer, saw waiting as inherent to female storytelling. In 1869, Fern sighed: "I see parenthesis in Uncle Tom's Cabin and Jane Eyre and Shirley, where the authors stated, that here they stopped to . . . make bread or put kindling in the oven prepatory to it, while the celestial spark stood in abeyance. Sometimes 'stopped to wash baby' might have been inserted on the margin opposite some interrupted pathetic passage."[44] Women like Sarah Hale, Harriet Beecher Stowe, Elizabeth Ellet, and Fanny Fern turned to authorship because of a need to support children. (And women like Charlotte Brontë, who took charge of her younger siblings after her mother's death, helped raise brothers and sisters.) Whereas this reason—supporting one's family—made a woman's writing more socially acceptable, it most certainly did not make the task easier. As Virginia Woolf would say a century after Hale's magazine launched, a writer needs a "room of one's own." Woolf's point was that women habitually are not granted this private space to think and work. Hale well knew this, and while she did not conjure a physical room for each of her readers, she did offer them in-tellectual space within her "Sketches of American Character," which found a home in a magazine marked out for women. With elongated beginnings and revolutionary heroes, Hale's stories combine structure and theme to activate women's position in the culture of beginnings. Her characters use the absence of their menfolk to develop valuable skills, to grow their sense of self, and to seize a critical place within the category of American. Hale practiced what she preached, working diligently as an editor for fifty years, and becoming known as someone who was calm and productive. One Professor Hart commended Hale's *Woman's Record* (1854), a nine-hundred-page work with biographical sketches of distinguished women from Eve to the moment of publication, for "the high aims, the indefatigable industry, the varied reading, and the just discrimination of its ever-to-be-honored author."[45] Similarly in 1855 Rev. D. W. Clark pointed to Hale's patience and endurance: "It is evident that Mrs. Hale is a hard student, and that her pro-ductions are the result of laborious, persevering effort. She did not flash out upon the world as with a meteor glare and as rapidly pass away. But her lit-erary reputation has been of gradual growth, and consequently rests upon a firmer basis."[46] Both her convictions and her condition mandated patient and persistent effort. Hale's quiet achievement is the result of productive waiting—and that productive waiting provides an explanation for why Hale has so long gone unappreciated.

Story Time Meets Reference Time

Hale places each sketch of American character near but not at the beginning of the magazine. By delaying each sketch of American character with a short prose piece and a few lines of poetry, she seems to be enacting one more mode of elongating beginnings, obstructing action, and teaching her readers to wait. Still the most striking example of stretching a narrative beginning comes with the fifth and eleventh sketches, which turn out to be two halves of the same story serialized six months apart. That Hale, even though she swapped the order of other pieces, kept "The Village Schoolmistress" and "William Forbes" separated by five other sketches when she published the series in volume form (*Sketches of American Character,* 1829) illustrates how very important the intermediary pause was. This gap creates the most overt elongation of a story's beginning in the magazine's first volume and thus the most significant space for the female character's and the female readers' productive waiting. As she would not be able to do if married, the heroine schoolmistress is able to grow as a teacher, mastering her craft and her subject matter and becoming beloved by countless students and their families. This waiting prepares her to be a mother, educating the little ones who will cling to her apron strings, but it also offers a fail-safe, a means for self-support, if her lover proves faithless. Indeed, such does happen. The two linked sketches concern Elizabeth Brooks and William Forbes, who have been affianced before William "depart[s] for New-York, where he intend[s] to study law, select a place of residence, and then return and claim his bride." Only William does not return. Instead, he marries a beautiful New York socialite, who turns out to be brainless. (In contrast, William and Elizabeth have first fallen in love over intellectual communion—sharing books, writing scholarly letters, and otherwise learning about literature, language, and philosophy.) Although she is devastated by news of William's marriage, Elizabeth is not defeated. For while William is in New York, Elizabeth has "evinced the goodness of her heart and temper by good works, by usefulness" and become a talented schoolmistress.[47] The productivity of her waiting saves her from William's inconstancy and has an autobiographical note for Hale. Starting in 1806, Hale herself had been a schoolteacher for seven tumultuous years, during which her mother and sister died, one brother (Horatio) went to college, one brother (Charles) disappeared at sea, and her father opened a tavern, which quickly failed.

Left behind by the males who departed and the females who died, Hale put her learning and abilities to use, only leaving her teaching post when she married David Hale.[48] Hale's social agenda, then, is to equip women to be able to support themselves and, if necessary, their families until the men return.

Within this relentlessly heteronormative mold, there are some who have no male protector for whom to wait. Hale understood this condition as arising because the father, brother, or husband would no longer come home. Either he had abandoned his duty or, as for Hale, he had died. These poor women (and often their children) "who, when left without support, are the most forlorn and destitute of any class of people in the world" are stuck in a sort of perpetual waiting that could be made productive when women banded with women.[49] From the first issue of the Ladies' Magazine, Hale championed the Boston-based Fatherless and Widows' Society for destitute women, and then in 1833 she formed the Seaman's Aid Society for the widows and abandoned wives of seafarers. Both were designed to provide succor and material aid to women without male providers. Hale had bolder aims than charitable handouts, however. Under her guidance, the Seaman's Aid Society formed a workshop that employed fifty women to make seamen's outfits and sponsored a clothing store, multiple schools, a library, and a boardinghouse.[50] Waiting for men who would never return, the women and children helped by the Seaman's Aid Society became educated and self-supporting. Both this charity and her stories show that while Hale seems to uphold the ideals of the separate spheres, wherein men should be the breadwinners, Hale accepts the frequent failure of this model. In so doing, she advances arguments for increasing women's social freedoms while avoiding sparking a culture war.

Of course, in many ways Hale's entreaty to "be actively useful, as far as our ability permits" is more a reflection of reality than a radical idea.[51] Abigail Adams's 1776 letter to John Adams (written in two parts, on March 31 and April 5) demonstrates the necessity for women to be "actively useful" while waiting. In the past forty years, the epistle has rightly received attention for Abigail's admonition to "Remember the Ladies" and John's mocking reply. Yet Abigail's full letter illuminates how she is in much the same position as Hale's female characters. Her husband is away aiding the revolutionary cause, and she is hoping for news, hoping for revolution, and hoping for his return. And yet this waiting is ripe with both intellectual work and physical labor. Abigail is thinking hard about what a new republic might look like, as she shows in the famous sentence that links her waiting and her feminist plea: "I long to hear that you have declared an independency—and by the way in the new Code of Laws that I suppose it will be necessary for you to make I desire you would Remember the Ladies." Before and after this demand for women's legal protections, Abigail reports how she has arranged someone to visit the family's home in Boston (which had been occupied by the British) and is organizing a method of cleaning and shutting up the house. She has supervised the farm, cared for the Adams children, and, most poignantly, she has been sitting in the sick chamber of her "Neighbor Trot," who has, within the past week, lost two of his young ones from the "canker fever, a terrible disorder." So too John's "brothers youngest child lies bad with convulsion fits."[52] Like so many of Hale's characters and, no doubt, like so many of Hale's readers, Abigail Adams engages in women's work—work that is about life and death—while her husband is away. She is helping, watching, thinking, cooking, sewing, farming, and doing while waiting for the men. Although her work is hidden and her waiting taken for granted, it is essential to the Revolution and the beginning of the nation.

History tends to focus on the dramatic actions—the battles and the elections—but two of the moments most formative to the United States were about committing to words that projected themselves into the future—words that wait. Penning the first draft of the Declaration of Independence in a matter of weeks, Thomas Jefferson did intellectual labor intended to create and guide a prospective nation. He then watched his colleagues in the Continental Congress spend two days demanding deletions, additions, and alterations. The final document, approved on July 4, 1776, only really became foundational because colonists won the Revolutionary War and were able to establish a country separate from Great Britain. From May to September 1787, delegates to the Constitutional Convention in Philadelphia debated words that would create a new federal government, with a separation of powers and a system of checks and balances. Two years later, after a contentious ratification process, James Madison introduced a draft version of the Bill of Rights and waited three months for his colleagues to edit and approve it. Judges, politicians, and citizens today still rely upon these ten amendments and debate their meaning. In combination with the Declaration and the Constitution, the Bill of Rights is a document that, then as now, defines a present and future nation. Unlike England, which has an unwritten constitution, the United States has been formed by writing. Words, drafted mostly by one person and then wordsmithed by many, have called the nation into being over the course of long years. In a form of productive waiting, the authors of all these documents labored in their present moment for things not yet realized, as they, like Hale's female characters, framed a country coming into existence.

In 1848, Hale would articulate her vision of productive waiting as quintessentially American and female in a thirty-three-page poem called *The Three Hours; or The Vigil of Love*, which she denominated as "an attempt to impart poetical interest to the ordinary events of woman's life, and show glimpses of domestic character connected with early American history."[53] The main character, Grace Tudor, staves off evil through ritualized prayer, tends her son's sickbed, and ventures into the pitch-black night to retrieve water, all the time fearing a Native American raid and awaiting her husband's return to their frontier cottage. The footnotes on "The Third Hour" mark Grace as a Puritan, the "last Lord Talbot's heir," a fact that Hale insists is historical.[54] That Grace's cottage stands on the edge of the Boston Common, the oldest public park in the United States, further underscores her status as a female American beginning. More importantly, resourcefulness and faithfulness like Grace's "was the true Yankee spirit."[55] Whether Jeffersonian or Emersonian, self-reliance was critical to the (white) national character: it explained subsistence farming, the expanding western border, the ability to "tame" the wilderness, and the roughness of citizens far from urban centers. While Jefferson thought of farmers and Emerson of statesmen, philosophers, and divines, Hale depicts white women as embodying this centrally American quality. Like Abigail Adams, Grace Tudor's active waiting, her self-reliance, allows her to join the culture of beginnings and the national imaginary.

The temporal gap between the two sketch parts of "The School Mistress" and "William Forbes," which I introduced before purposefully delaying fuller explanation, worked toward this same aim in two ways: it brought individual women into a shared story world and imagined social network, and it made the sketch feel real. As Paul Ricoeur notes, "Time becomes human to the extent that it is articulated through a narrative mode, and narrative attains its full meaning when it becomes a condition of temporal existence."[56] In linking story time and reference time, Hale writes Elizabeth's story and her productive stint as schoolmistress into the life of her readers.

She also likely engaged actual communities of women who read the sketch aloud together. We get evidence of this readerly engagement in the reader's letter appended to the end of "William Forbes." In an exchange "intended entirely for the ladies; *gentlemen*, therefore, will please to pass it over," the letter writer compliments "The Village Schoolmistress," which is "characterized by a more than usual degree of depth, originality and boldness—it was full of reflections that made the reader *think*."[57] That is exactly what Hale intends through the rupture of the story world. She jokes at the beginning of "William Forbes" that "we have given her [Elizabeth] six months to consider the matter, and in this steam age of the world, no woman ought to require a longer time to make up her mind." And yet, Hale is hardly eager to cut to the chase, providing yet another wordy introduction that talks about time and the "interminable, prosing articles, many of our writers are even now, inclined to perpetrate."[58] Just in case six months had not been long enough, Hale will make the readers wade through this slow beginning and then ten more pages on William's past life before finally revealing Elizabeth's reply. Women will learn to become intellectually resilient and active in the slow opening passages of "William Forbes," like Elizabeth learns through William's absence. So what answer did Elizabeth give? As Hale puts it, "She said no! unhesitatingly, as any woman of refinement and delicacy treated as she had been, would say."[59] This denial reaffirms the importance of Elizabeth's work as a schoolmistress: Elizabeth sees more good in that employment than in becoming someone's wife.

The good is both national and personal, for at her school in a small New Hampshire town, Elizabeth teaches "curly-pated boys" with the names of "all the presidents and great men of America."[60] While mocking a culture of beginnings that results in country urchins named George Washington and Marquis de Lafayette, Hale illustrates how women can have a useful position in it because their work strengthens the national fabric. Never the great men themselves, they can be the teachers (or mothers and wives) of these patriotic figures, and they can exemplify the American spirit through useful, meaningful lives. (Notably, many of Hale's contributors had themselves been teachers, and a good proportion of those taught at female academies.)[61] Thus when Elizabeth reconsiders under pressure—her friend's father refuses to send William the negative answer, and when William comes in person, Elizabeth is unable to say no—the decision is couched less as one of romantic love and more as one of teacherly duty. Elizabeth reports "that she should not have consented to wed Mr. Forbes but for the sake of his children, his little girls who, he said, so much needed her care and instructions."[62] That their love is renewed because of Elizabeth's educational skills recalls the manner in which Elizabeth and William first fell for each other while pondering books and sharing letters. The thematic consistency of this ending aligns with Hale's explicit remarks on female education and independence at the end of "William Forbes": "I would have [women] seek some employment, have some aim that will, by giving energy to their minds, and the prospect of an honorable independence, should they choose to continue single, make them less dependent on *marriage* as the means of *support*."[63] These linked sketches, then, not only elongate the beginning for six months; they also emphasize it recursively. "The Village Schoolmistress" and its prosy introduction are invoked as a necessary reference at the start of "William Forbes" and necessary ending to the two-part story.[64] Hale undercuts the happy closing of this two-part sketch to remind her readers of the inherent uncertainty of women's position. One day, even after marriage, William may not return home, and when female readers recognize that, they are better equipped for the future. "Recognition is not repetition," Rita Felski reminds us; "it denotes not just the previously known, but the becoming known."[65] Hale's readers, like Elizabeth, must see themselves as self-determining individuals—and by extension as Americans—to become paragons of American character.

These United Sketches

As *The Sketch Book* did for Irving's ambitions, the physical *Ladies' Magazine* expressed Hale's intentions. Juxtaposing sketches and poems and essays about various characters and ideas, and often mixing fiction and nonfiction, Hale presented a miscellany that posited imagined relationships between various pieces. The physical artifact shows who is included (and excluded) and how the juxtaposition, expressed through page placement, makes equal the labor of men and women. Her grieving widows, hopeful soldiers, and practical schoolmarms all live within the *Ladies' Magazine's* simulacrum of America. Bumping up against editorials about female education, these fictional constituents, with their sewing and knitting, bind together Hale's United States with loose stitches in creamy paper. Hale's readerly network served as a microcosm of this America, for the magazine had a sizable six hundred subscribers for the first issue and, by the end of the first year, was circulated at least in Massachusetts, Maine, New Hampshire, Vermont, Connecticut, Rhode Island, Pennsylvania, New York, and North Carolina.[66] Although the subscription base was concentrated in New England through-out the life of the *Ladies' Magazine,* Hale said that distribution of the maga-zine was "extensive, embracing every section and state in the Union" by the fifth volume.[67] Subsequent years saw further circulation growth, likely coming to include multiple thousands of subscribers.[68] The format of the periodical, which linked readers in space and time, enacted the project that Hale plotted in her sketches, that of women becoming part of the story of the United States—*e pluribus unum,* as Thomas Jefferson, John Adams, and Benjamin Franklin might say. To attract this notable following, Hale styled herself, as Patricia Okker has shown, as a "sister" to her readers, some-one who understood and wanted to help those who received her magazine. Even as she was the teacher, Hale was part of a community of equals all striving for a shared purpose that they were able to envision through the re-ception of a magazine that brought ideas and encouragement and, because of its existence, the indication that many other hundreds of women thought this way as well. These magazines could even feel like papers sent among friends. Hence, when Hale introduces the letter in "William Forbes," she says, "Reader, the 'Sketch' is finished," as if she is addressing one person, a unique reader who is at the other end of the pen.[69] This letter and Hale's response is a form of what would become a frequent and popular inclusion of readers' letters and Hale's replies—a nascent version of today's advice columns—in the *Ladies' Magazine.* They reinforce the sense that readers are encouraged to do intellectual work, to engage with the ideas of the maga-zine and, through the magazine, with each other, rather than merely receiv-ing information. And they provide firsthand illustrations of the ideas Hale most wants to communicate. In 1834, for example, Hale included an epistle with a dramatic story about one woman's perseverance. The letter writer from Tennessee reports:

> The dwelling of a woman was lately pointed out to me, who with a family of grand-children, left, at the age of sixty, her native State (North Carolina) and travelled here on foot, supporting herself on the way by knitting purses, *as she walked,* which she sold to travelers. . . . I have lately conversed with a[nother] woman who came to Tennessee. . . .

The length of her journey was eight hundred miles, which she accomplished on foot in nine months. . . . The most remarkable feature in her history is the fact, that though unable to read, herself, she taught her children to read. They had indeed learned the alphabet, before leaving home, and the manner in which their mother proceeded to teach them to read words was this: she had an old hymn book, the hymns in which she knew by rote. The boys would pronounce the letters to her, and by counting the words and lines she would discover what they spelt.

Capping off these stories of amazing resilience, Hale closes the extract with this pithy thought: "We are apt to prize highly what we obtain with difficulty."[70] Waiting is a form of endurance. When used productively, these interludes—like the walk from North Carolina to Tennessee—can result in marketable goods (knitted purses), the next generation's literacy, and self-knowledge. As Hale says, "Should any New England woman, feeling that her lot is hard, complainingly inquire, what can a woman do?—let her be referred to the examples her sisters in the West have given, and *do all she can*."[71] Such productivity befits the pioneer and urban dweller alike because it is quintessentially American. Even as it is highly gendered, knitting while migrating functions as a metaphor for what is good in the US character, and the letter shows that women across the United States are woven—are knitted—together because they all believe in the value of resilience. The sense that the magazine represented actual readers linked through a periodical furthered Hale's goals of empowering women to learn and to consider themselves as equal members of the American family.

The periodicity of magazines and of letters also enacts the productive waiting that Hale dramatizes in her sketches and that she hoped to inculcate in her growing readership. Each letter, magazine, or newspaper has a structured period of waiting both before and after it, a period that is culturally gendered. Whereas both John and Abigail Adams must wait for letters, Abigail feels she has less information and must wait also for John's return. ("I wish you would ever write me a Letter half as long as I write you," Abigail laments before peppering John with questions about American war preparations.)[72] Hers is—to borrow the title from Hale's poem—the vigil of love. And such a vigil is profoundly female, as the history of epistolary fiction suggests. Many early women's novels, including Aphra Behn's

Love-Letters Between a Noble-Man and his Sister (1684–87) and Hannah Webster Foster's *The Coquette* (1797), were structured through letters. This narrative strategy allowed women authors to avoid taking on an overtly public, and thus masculine, narrative stance.[73] Instead, the often female narrators spoke to other characters within the story world through ostensibly private letters that the reader eavesdropped on. Understanding such conventions, Samuel Richardson used an epistolary structure to ensure his eponymous Clarissa remained sympathetic rather than forward like Daniel Defoe's scandalous Moll Flanders. While the oblique narrative presentation of epistolary fiction was of great importance and utility for women writers, it is also suggestive that epistolary fiction, a genre so successful for women, codes waiting into the narrative arc. With her elongated serialization, Hale picks up on a long-standing and clever narrative strategy to wrap her readers into her world. Her productive waiting is a distillation of the principles of letter writing both in real life and in novels. In short, waiting was part of reading for most nineteenth-century females. When children and husbands were not interjecting when the women tried to read, these readers may well have been forced to wait for the next letter, the next issue of a periodical, or the next volume of the novel. If not actually serialized in a newspaper, mid-century novels for ladies usually appeared in multiple volumes designed to be borrowed one at a time from the subscription-based circulating libraries. They could also be, like most of Dickens's work, issued in numbers. (*Jane Eyre* and *Shirley* were both three-volume novels, a format particular to English circulating libraries. In the United States, novels like Susan Warner's *The Wide, Wide World* were two volumes, the format favored by American circulating libraries, which were central to the reading of most people in the first third of the century.[74] Because they did not target a female audience, Hawthorne's *The Scarlet Letter* and Melville's *Moby-Dick* were published as single volumes.) The waiting and narrative elongation of Hale's *Ladies' Magazine* is thus gendered not just in how it schools women to act but also in that it reflects the reality of how women waited to read letters, magazines, and novels. Pulling on the authenticity baked into the genre, Hale's sketches mirror life to give women impetus for self-improvement.

If the format of the nineteenth-century magazine helped readers imagine the United States, the genre of the sketch helped envision it. Because it pivots on incompletion and suggestion, the sketch gestures to more than what it says. In the ninth sketch of American character, "Prejudices," Hale declares she "can only give an abstract of Mrs. Ranson's story," counseling those who are dissatisfied to "invest these simple facts with all the complex circumstances, enchanting descriptions and interesting colloquies, of a long romance."[75] So too Hale refused to give Fanny, the heroine of "Walter Wilson," a "full length description of beauty" and could not even "be positive of the color of her hair."[76] Readers must fill in the lines of these sketches, exercising their minds and making their reading (and waiting for a new issue) productive. This readerly participation reinforces the idea that despite the strength of American origin myths, the American story is *not* already fixed. American beginnings are, like the sketch, incomplete. The sketch was attractive to Hale and her readers for other reasons too. Indeed, sketches "were imagined to provide writers and readers the leisure of escaping the flux of early nineteenth-century society, of stealing a moment for the contemplation and communication of a place, a person, a social ritual or transgress, and a self."[77] This versatile genre provided a way to slip away from one's cares and to get to know one's own desires through escapism. This leisure made the invitation to work—to filling in the spaces supplied by the sketch—more attractive. The readers of the *Ladies' Magazine* became part of the sketch when they, like Hale's characters, pondered the quirks of a town ("The Apparition"), the merits of an education ("The Village Schoolmistress"), or the proposal of a suitor ("William Forbes"). These sketches taught them to think and envision themselves as thinkers. Ann Ellsworth, the heroine of the second sketch of American character, "pass[ed] her bridal year busily employed with her needle, or her books" while her husband was at the office. When he returned home each evening, she "delightedly . . . told him all that she had read, and all that she had thought."[78] She awaits her spouse with an active mind because "the spirit . . . of improvement pervades our citizens."[79] This mind-set spurs Ann's intellectual work and allows her to be included, if not with full rights, in the group of citizens. She becomes an American by exemplifying American character and doing her duty—waiting—so actively and productively. The thinking encouraged by these twelve sketches conscripts Hale's readers into worlds frequented by American Founding Fathers—veterans, Pilgrims, and patriots—and thereby allows them to claim the American story as their own.

In Hale's hands, the sketch becomes a critical tool for building the perseverance inherent in American character and for expanding American national stories to include white women. The phenomenon of the series helped too. According to Frank Kelleter, popular series, of which "Sketches of American Character" was one, "have a special ability to generate affective bonds and to stimulate creative activities on the part of their recipients, who, for all practical purposes, operate as *agents of narrative continuation*."[80] In addition to their letters to the editor and amateur riffs on the serial (fanfic in modern parlance), readers influence the series. In fact, Hale credited the enthusiasm of her readers for the publication of her "Sketches of American Character" in volume form, and she restarted "Sketches of American Character" in the second volume of the magazine because of readerly demand. (She went on to publish a second volume of these sketches under the title *Traits of American Life,* 1835). This interaction with the series drew readers into the world of the *Ladies' Magazine.* To use Kelleter's words, "seriality can extend—and normally *does* extend—the sphere of story-telling onto the sphere of story consumption."[81] Each month a reader waits for the next installment, and each month the installment introduced with the header "Sketches of American Character" and under that same running title points forward and backward in time to the previous and subsequent issues of the *Ladies' Magazine.* In this way, serialization, like periodicity, suggests an ever-expanding universe: there will always be another installment and there is always further possibility. These installments might be individual episodes that reference a shared story world (and used a shared series title), or directly serial stories, as in "The Village Schoolmistress" / "William Forbes." It does not matter, since the frame of the series joins them together in a single world that the reader helps create through her subscription (commonly for a year's worth of magazines) and through her reading and thinking. Her engagement allows revolutionary heroes and Puritan divines to become figures in *her own* world, a world that might possibly be represented in a future installment. Like a child might think up a new *Twilight Zone* episode, these readers could project their version of American beginnings into their own lives. The format of a series meant that Hale's female readers developed a more vital, personal relationship with an advantageous past. "Sketches of American Character" made American history converge with the nineteenth-century present.

The affective bonds created by reading sketches in serial form helped the national project at the heart of Hale's magazine. Hale says in the periodical's introduction that through the *Ladies' Magazine,* mothers will become "competent to the task of instructing their children. . . . The sons of the republic will become polished pillars in the temple of our national glory, and the daughters bright gems to adorn it."[82] Domestic labor, including teaching Hale's version of history, goes hand in hand with the reading of Hale's magazine. Moreover, this patriotic language codes a love of reading as socially good.[83] At the beginning of the nineteenth century, some 25 percent of Americans were illiterate, but by the 1840s the rate was about 9 percent. "Women were frequently identified *as* the new readership"; they were certainly the majority of the readers of the *Ladies' Magazine* and later of *Godey's Lady's Book*.[84] And they were the backbone of the American people.

Periodicals and Volumes

Between 1825 and 1850, the average lifespan of the thousands of US magazines that were started was less than two years.[85] In contrast, Hale edited 108 monthly issues in nine years of the *Ladies' Magazine*. That Hale's magazine survived until it merged with *Godey's Lady's Book* shows the success of Hale's timely venture. Perhaps more to the point, Hale's *Ladies' Magazine* set standards of content—mostly original and American with many female contributors—that Louis Godey imported into his famed *Lady's Book* when he hired Hale as chief editor. These features helped make *Godey's* the single most successful US magazine of the nineteenth century and meant that magazines as a medium reached their professional zenith through Hale's successful formula and her editorial ability. Put another way, this realm of American letters was built on a foundation of women's periodicals. Even before *Godey's* success, Hale's *Ladies' Magazine* elevated American letters and supported women authors, including, according to a list she provided in January of 1834, Lydia Sigourney, Catharine Maria Sedgwick, Caroline Howard Gilman, Emma Catherine Manley Embury, Elizabeth Oakes Prince Smith, Lydia Maria Child, Hannah Flagg Gould, Anna Maria Foster Wells, Emma Hart Willard, Almira Hart Lincoln Phelps, and Elizabeth Fries Lummis Ellet.[86] All of these women went on to publish one or more volumes during the nineteenth century. Fifteen centimeters wide and twenty-three centimeters high, the magazine was printed on good paper with neat typography, sizable margins, and forty-eight tightly packed pages.[87] The first number included an engraving of Hannah Adams, the notable US historian, who published many well-received works in the late eighteenth and early nineteenth centuries, including *A Summary History of New England* (1799). (A sketch about her appeared in the July number.) The magazine championed female education and female authors, communicating the value of both of these projects with its physical form.[88]

Issued in twelve installments per year, the *Ladies' Magazine* worked in two temporal frames. Readers were supposed to appreciate each individual issue and then, at year end, receive the index for the volume and take the entire work to be bound. Indeed, that an entire year's worth of issues of a magazine is called a "volume" indicates the assumption that readers would make a year's worth of a magazine into a book and then keep it on a shelf. In this way, the periodical became a volume that superseded its original temporally specific life. That is to say that the meeting of reference time and story time worked only as I have described as the magazine was serialized in 1828, no doubt part of the reason no one has noticed the narrative elongation before now. Thereafter, the periodical functioned as a volume because it usually *became* a volume. Collecting pieces that had been published in periodicals and republishing them in volume form was common during Hale's life, and Hale herself did so multiple times.[89] Catharine Sedgwick, Nathaniel Hawthorne, and Edgar Allan Poe all also assembled short fiction collections from work previously printed in newspapers, magazines, and literary annuals. At midcentury, as serialized novels became popular, Harriet Beecher Stowe published her blockbuster *Uncle Tom's Cabin* piece by piece in an antislavery newspaper and then in two-volume form. Both magazines and volumes could be equally useful and prestigious. Seeing a symbiotic relationship between the formats, Hale penned both magazines and volumes simultaneously, letting them advertise each other. When Hale wrote the massive *Woman's Record, or Sketches of Distinguished Women* (1853), which included profiles of over two thousand women in its final version, her authorial byline listed her as "Sarah Josepha Hale, Editor of 'The Lady's Book;' Author of 'Traits of American Life,' 'Northwood,' 'The Vigil of Love,' 'The Judge,' etc., etc., etc." Readers learned about *Woman's Record* from the pages of *Godey's Lady's Book* and then were reminded about the magazine from the first page of the volume. More generally, volumes were hugely dependent on magazines for reviews and advertising. Without such acknowledgments and notices, volumes simply did not sell well. Hale very mindfully reviewed books she thought would be of interest or benefit to her readers, like *Notice of an Address on Female Education, delivered in*

Portsmouth, N.H. by Rev. Charles Burroughs, which was mentioned in the first issue of the *Ladies' Magazine.* In November of that same year, Hale encouraged people to buy, not borrow, Hawthorne's *Fanshawe,* and in 1830 she gave one of the few encouraging reviews of Poe's *Al Araaf, Tamerlane and Minor Poems.*[90] She also gave notice of literary annuals, those vehicles for much short fiction, including many of Sedgwick's and Hawthorne's tales and sketches. Books sold because editors like Hale praised them, and Hale used her platform and sharp critical eye to encourage young American authors—particularly women.

Although modern readers might assume there is a clear line between periodical and volume, then, in the first half of the nineteenth century the two formats were kissing cousins. And the *Ladies' Magazine,* like the Constitution and the Bill of Rights, was designed to have influence, to frame a national community, beyond its moment of serialization. In addition to what the *Ladies' Magazine* reveals about the workings of American letters in the early nineteenth century, the double temporality—monthly and then permanent—can help us understand the significant and prolonged influence this magazine had. Until 1833, Hale claimed her magazine was the most successful in New England.[91] As Hale acknowledged when she praised the *Ladies' Magazine* as a supportive forum for female writers, periodicals helped authors cultivate a readership and create a name (even if a pen-name) for themselves. Since the more direct route toward success—that of being chummy with the gatekeepers at publishing houses and prestigious literary magazines—was usually closed to women, magazines were even more crucial to the literary careers of female authors. These authors would wait while they built up a reputation or a following before attempting more ambitious literary projects. Like Fanny Fern, who wrote newspaper sketches before publishing short fiction collections and a novel, many of these women authors used their contributions to periodicals as a form of productive waiting. If their pieces were well received and if their byline gained credibility, they could earn higher wages and seek out other opportunities. As the first successful magazine for women, the *Ladies' Magazine* was a beginning for many American women authors who went on to publish volumes. It taught its readers to imagine themselves as productive Americans at the same time as it helped grow a professional space for women authors, all under the guise of passive moral instruction.

Bunker Hill by Women

A mother of five (one of whom died serving in the armed forces) and a daughter of a Revolutionary War veteran, Hale was never radical like her acquaintance and contributor Lydia Maria Child. Supporting interracial marriage and immediate abolition in *An Appeal on Behalf of the Class of Americans Called Africans* (1833), Child scandalized Boston and lost her editorship of the *Juvenile Miscellany*. (Hale took it over.)[92] Strongly prounion and, by twenty-first century standards, racist, Hale instead tried to appease on slavery, hoping the issue would vanish through colonization and wishful thinking. Still, Hale was active in the service of the social causes she championed, most particularly female education and the celebration of American beginnings. Hale is rightly known for her fifteen-year crusade—culminating in an 1863 proclamation by Abraham Lincoln—to enshrine Thanksgiving as a national holiday, but Hale's efforts to celebrate American forefathers in the public sphere began much earlier. In Boston, the fiftieth anniversary of the Battle of Bunker Hill had seen great enthusiasm for a monument on the site. By 1830, however, the four-sided, forty-foot pillar was missing over 180 feet of height, plus the pyramid on the top, and the monument committee was stymied. Through an editorial in the *Ladies' Magazine*, Hale requested donations from all her subscribers. In 1834, with the help of the Ladies' Fund and the Boston Mechanic Association, the monument grew eighty feet—and then money troubles stalled progress once more. Hale again stepped in, leading a committee of women in organizing a massive sale of domestic crafts at Quincy Hall in Boston that netted over $30,000, enough to complete the monument. On June 17, 1843, eighteen years after the cornerstone was laid, President Tyler and members of his cabinet attended the dedication, at which Daniel Webster gave a stirring oration recognizing "the mothers and the daughters of the land" who "contributed . . . most successfully to whatever of beauty is in the obelisk itself, or whatever of utility and public benefit and gratification in its completion."[93] In a twist, the long wait for the phallic monument's completion was ended by the efforts of women. Indeed, the productive wait had allowed women to enter the celebration of heroic American beginnings. Their successful fundraising meant that "Women Fought at Bunker Hill," as Lawrence Martin titled his somewhat dismissive 1935 article on Hale's efforts.[94]

Hale's personal, political, and creative work reveals a foregrounding of women's labor in ways that anticipate contemporary feminist concerns about the value of women's work to family and to society. Enmeshed in the culture of beginnings, Hale offered not just Founding Fathers who exemplified duty, honor, diligence, and patriotism but also female characters who enacted these national characteristics through waiting and working in her "Sketches of American Character." Hale thereby revolutionized the role of women in nation building, casting light on the too-often hidden acts involved in staying behind to care for the school, the farm, and the children—the constituents and the future of the country. As they bide time until their men's return, white women come to represent what is best about the United States, from defiant self-sufficiency in the homespun movement to hopeful futurity in narrative projections like the Constitution. They also secure the racial foundations of the country through their fidelity and denial of desire. Despite relying on essentialist gender tropes of female domestic waiting, Hale's sketches subvert entrenched conceptions of American beginnings as the purview of the Founding Fathers. In this way, Hale asserts women's waiting as equally constitutive of the American story and as critical to American literary professionalism. For Hale's magazine not only started the careers of many female writers; it also provided a model for other periodicals to follow. The Ladies' Magazine made it popular to focus on native literature, credit authors, and offer fair compensation, three things that, as I discuss in the next chapter, became critical elements in early literary annuals. Moreover, Hale's agented view of women's waiting aligns with the format of the Ladies' Magazine, which, through serialization and prosy introductions, provided subscribers with intellectual training. Through patience, they would learn to hold and develop ideas about their active place in the national imaginary.

3

Nonsynchronous Synchronicity in Sedgwick's Gift Book Stories

Although men contributed poems, stories, essays, and images and bought the magazines that Sarah Josepha Hale edited—some Union soldiers subscribed to *Godey's* during the Civil War—both of Hale's periodicals targeted white women readers. Understanding that this growing demographic was critical to a nascent American literature, publishers designed many a literary annual with middle-class white women in mind. Featuring a mix of poetry, prose, and images, literary annuals, also called gift books, became ubiquitous during the 1820s and 1830s.[1] In the decades that they remained popular, annuals served as mementos of the year, and the titles, which habitually included a date, communicated this purpose: *The Flowers of Loveliness, a Token of Remembrance for 1852; The Talisman for 1828; The Christian Offering for 1832;* and *The Gift, a Christmas and New Year's present for 1836* are just a few illustrative examples. In serving as records for the year, American literary annuals followed the lead of the British annuals that preceded them. Rudolf Ackermann's 1823 *Forget Me Not*, which started the phenomenon of English-language literary annuals in the United Kingdom, included "a Chronicle of Remarkable Events during the past year: a Genealogy of the Reigning Sovereigns of Europe and their Families; a List of Ambassadors resident at the different Courts; and a variety of other particulars extremely useful for reverence to persons of all classes."[2] Although this section was discontinued in later editions of *Forget Me Not*, it reveals the annual's descent from the yearly almanac, which contained calendars and weather forecasts and, particularly in Ben Franklin's *Poor Richard's Almanac*, witty prose. While American literary annuals never included news of the day or book reviews like a monthly magazine did, they presented themselves as *of the moment* and acknowledged contemporary concerns. One US annual for 1830, for example, featured an image and poem referencing the then-ongoing Greek War for Independence, and in 1834 Sedgwick tied past "party strifes" between Democrats and Federalists to the then-current tensions over slavery.[3] Even when the poems and prose did not gesture to current events, readers expected currency in the sense of originality as part of the literary annual. The outrage that greeted swindling publishers who tried to pass off an old annual as a new one with the addition of a different title page underscored how the annual was meant to be specific to its moment. It was a yearly version of the nineteenth-century magazine and a highly temporal medium attuned to the culture of beginnings.

The standard contents of a literary annual were sketches, tales, and poetry, a mixture of writing borrowed from ladies' magazines. In turn, literary annuals inspired ladies' magazines to include more of the engravings for which gift books became so celebrated. The success of literary annuals, in other words, is partly responsible for the famed fashion plates of *Godey's Lady's Book*. More generally, ladies' magazines and literary annuals shared readers and strategies to the point that they became interlinked forms. Hence, Snowden's *Ladies' Companion,* in which Poe serialized his second whodunit, declared the magazine's proximity to literary annuals in the 1843 title page, introducing the bound volume of twelve issues: the *Ladies' Companion; or Peoples' Annual: Embellished with Elegant Steel Engravings and Choice Music.* And yet, though literary annuals, like ladies' magazines, projected female readers, they hoped for male buyers, for women were supposed to be gifted the volumes on Christmas or New Year's Day, or sometimes, as the subtitle of Sarah Hale's own literary annual, the *Ladies' Wreath,* indicates, they were *a gift book for all seasons.* Catharine Sedgwick had a story in the first American literary annual and contributed regularly to annuals after that. In so doing, she placed her stories in a complicated exchange in which ideals of femininity were commodified and presented to white women by white men as a vehicle for memory. As Sedgwick's stories about women in the US past dramatize, this process allowed for a refashioned mode of creating national memory and beginnings—one that included white women in the culture of beginnings and proffered a nonsynchronous synchronicity marked as female and American.

American Gift Books

Catharine Maria Sedgwick was one of only two women selected for inclusion in the first volume of the *National Portrait Gallery of Distinguished Americans* (1834), a series of verbal sketches about cultural, military, and political leaders who had helped form the nation. (The other woman was Martha Washington.) Sedgwick was also one of just four authors featured within the volume and, after Irving, she had the longest entry: Joel Barlow and James Fenimore Cooper both earned less than half the description Sedgwick merited. Notably, such a testament to Sedgwick's cultural import was made when Sedgwick had yet to publish three quarters of her writing, including her incredibly successful domestic tracts, her collections of short fiction, and two longer romances. Despite the way in which Sedgwick was later dismissed from the nineteenth-century canon and only partially recovered through feminist efforts in the 1980s—many of Sedgwick's texts still remain out of print—she was a hugely important cultural figure from the 1830s until the Civil War. Members of Queen Victoria's court as well as other feted international guests and accomplished American authors made a point of visiting Sedgwick's Berkshire home and taking part in her lively and refined conversation.[4] Moreover, Sedgwick commanded the respect of her fellow writers. Among gestures from other notables, Hawthorne arguably referenced Sedgwick's prose through the prison-door rosebush within *The Scarlet Letter,* and Poe extoled Sedgwick as "one of our most celebrated and most meritorious writers."[5] My argument below helps in this recovery of Sedgwick's work, which has focused heavily on her novels at the expense of her successful and well-liked short fiction. And since Sedgwick gained prominence from two longer romances, *A New-England Tale* (1822) and *Redwood* (1824), before publishing any short fiction, she denies the hackneyed narrative of major authors starting with brief sketches and tales before moving to novels. Instead, Sedgwick, who wrote forty pieces for literary annuals starting in 1826, demonstrates the purposeful and strategic use of short fiction by a master writer.

Like her position in the nineteenth-century canon, Sedgwick's relationship to the culture of beginnings was complicated. She both celebrated her connection to the US story and resented its gendered exclusions. As she reminds the reader in her tale "A Reminiscence of Federalism" (*Token* 1834), Sedgwick was descended from a long line of accomplished patriots and had a front-row seat to early national history. Her grandfather Joseph Dwight was an officer during King George's War and the French and Indian War. Her father, Theodore Sedgwick, was a major in the Revolutionary War, a delegate to the Continental Congress, a US senator, the fifth Speaker of the House of Representatives, and a justice for the Massachusetts Supreme Court. He was also Sedgwick's educational guide. Later in life Sedgwick recalled that "my school life was a waste. My home life my only education."[6] In a very real way, Sedgwick entered the culture of beginnings and an authorial career through her (founding) father. And yet, Sedgwick's stories often show her frustration with the way that patriarchal authority limits women's speech and history. "A Reminiscence of Federalism," for example, features a bigoted country squire who bullies and then disowns his daughter, and whose lukewarm praise for the story's heroine consists of "I have no fault to find with the girl; never heard her speak; believe she's well enough," as if silence were a woman's biggest recommending feature.[7] In "Modern Chivalry" (*Atlantic Souvenir* 1827), a tale set before and during the American Revolution, Perdita is forced by her "incensed" English father to "solemnly [swear] never to divulge" the story of her past, which involves being forced into slavery in the United States.[8] Throughout the story, Perdita, who accepts the first name chosen by her slave plantation mistress, refuses to reveal her surname, which, she maintains, belongs to her father and has been "forfeited by [her] folly."[9] In both of these stories, American history is a setting and a theme, elaborating historic tensions between Britons and Americans or Democrats and Federalists to develop the characters and the plot. Yet the stories' representation of American history highlights serious limitations on the freedom US women have had to speak and act. In this way, these pieces hint at the kind of narratives—those that support gender stereotypes and female silence—common in literary annuals and in the culture of beginnings. Eight years after the first US literary annual, Sedgwick's "A Reminiscence of Federalism" challenged how American history was told and who could tell it, even as Sedgwick, the narrator-character of the tale, wore an eagle badge to mark herself as a proud member of the Federalist Party.[10]

The overt nationalism of the best literary annuals no doubt informed Sedgwick's story choices and careful narrative posture. The *Atlantic Souvenir* of 1830, for example, opened with a piece called "The American Eagle" and included "Seneca Lake," "A Legend of the Hurons," and "The True

Glory of America."[11] Such writing advertised its attention to the history and images that supposedly made America distinct. While midcentury reviewers sneered at the low quality of literary annuals, which is generally accepted to have dropped in the 1840s, the medium was prestigious in the 1820s and 1830s. In fact, the *Token* of 1834, in which Sedgwick's "A Reminiscence of Federalism" appeared, also included a poem by former president John Quincy Adams. Singling out both Sedgwick's and Adams's pieces for praise, the *North American Review,* that bastion of male literary privilege, lauded this *Token* as "highly creditable to the state of learning, as well as of the arts, in this country" before noting, "It is quite desirable that volumes, which circulate so widely as these do, especially among the younger part of the community, should not only gratify the eye of taste by the beauty of their embellishments, but should be made the vehicle of good principles and valuable information."[12] In their function as mementos of the year, these literary annuals reflected the ongoing concerns of its readers, the continuing and permanently renewed construction of an American people through textual means. Building the idea of the United States went hand in hand with professionalizing American letters and culturally elevating the US readership, an explicit project of the *Token* and the *Atlantic Souvenir.*

I pause here to caution that the reach of literary annuals should not be underestimated. Because of the national and relational work they did, and because they were pleasing aesthetic objects, literary annuals saturated the middle-class market for decades before the Civil War. They served as important publishing outlets for authors seeking to make a living by their pens and publishers hoping to earn a profit. Carey and Lea, who put out the first American literary annual, the *Atlantic Souvenir* of 1826, saw a huge jump in sales, from two thousand copies of the first volume to ten thousand copies per annum by 1832.[13] They made a profit of nearly 50 percent the first year, one of $4,700 for 1831, and one of $4,200 for 1832.[14] Selling at different price points depending on the expense of the binding, from $2.50 for a plain binding of the *Atlantic Souvenir* to $3.75 or $4.50 for fancier bindings, many gift books were financially successful enough for the publishers to offer more generous pay to their contributors.[15] Samuel G. Goodrich's the *Token* of 1842 promised James Russell Lowell a hefty payment of five dollars per page, and the *Legendary* (another annual where Sedgwick published) offered one dollar per page for prose to the average author. Literary annuals paid roughly the same as what established, successful magazines like *Godey's Lady's Book* (one to two dollars per page for prose) offered in the late 1830s. But higher payments were possible for established writers: Sedgwick earned over fifty dollars for each of the five stories she published in various editions of the *Atlantic Souvenir*.[16] Because she was one of the most successful and popular American gift book contributors, the inclusion of a sketch or tale by Catharine Sedgwick set a volume apart from its competitors.[17] And competitors there were. According to Ralph Thompson, who wrote the first and still best extensive treatment of American literary annuals, "A list of all the American publishers of gift books would contain over 250 firm names—probably a generous share of the literary entrepreneurs active in this country during the pre-Civil War decades." Twenty-odd firms published at least six different series of literary annuals each, including D. Appleton (New York), G. P. Putnam (New York), J. B. Lippincott (Philadelphia), and Philips and Sampson (Boston).[18] This production reflected demand: Americans bought tens of thousands of gift books between 1826, when the craze began, and 1850, when gift books began to wane in popularity.[19] During these years, which roughly coincide with the culture of beginnings, literary annuals were a ubiquitous part of white middle-class culture in the United States. Knowingly, Mark Twain places one, a *Friendship's Offering*, along with a Bible and a copy of *Pilgrim's Progress* on the corner of the Grangerfords' parlor table in *Huckleberry Finn*. On the walls are pictures of "mainly Washingtons and Lafayettes, and battles . . . and one called 'Signing the Declaration,'" which was surely a print of the painting from the US Capitol Rotunda that now appears on our two-dollar bill.[20] These details conjure the homes of whites in the Mississippi valley of the 1830s which, like the rest of the country, was steeped in celebrations of beginnings and crazy for gift books. American identity, according to Twain's description, is derived from religious touchstones (Bunyan and the Bible), American beginnings (Washington and the Declaration), and gift books.

The national work of literary annuals was framed with gift giving by men to women, that biggest growing readership in the early nineteenth century. Fathers would give literary annuals to daughters, uncles and aunts to nieces, husbands to wives, and even young men to the women they fancied. Of all of these exchanges, the popular imagination fixed most on the last one. In fact, gift books became so strongly associated with courtship that in her 1851 conduct manual, Eliza Leslie (who herself edited and submitted to annuals) designated them one of a limited number of appropriate gifts a lady could receive from a courting gentleman, along with "a bouquet," "one or two autographs of distinguished persons," and "a few relics or mementos of memorable places."[21] Literary annuals were relational, conjuring feelings of gratitude and obligation. Offering many internal narrative levels and much multivocality, Sedgwick's gift book short fiction thematizes and capitalizes on the exchange of the literary annual. In her stories, groups of women recount past events and fashion alternative truths together. Through inclusion within literary annuals, these stories are themselves circulated and authorized by networks of readers and givers. As such, men, if inadvertently, participated in a communal remembering that widened the range of American beginning stories and challenged notions of a singular, fixed origin for the nation. In ancient Mesopotamia, according to Anna Reading, when memories were formed through rituals at local temples, men and women shared equally in their creation. But when Babylonian society turned to writing, "the names retained in cultural memory were decided by male scribes."[22] Reading argues that literacy shut women out of crafting stories about the past in Western cultures. Perhaps having come to this same conclusion, Sedgwick puts women back in history by a strategic use of orality within written stories. Indeed, the feminist and multivocal narration of Sedgwick's gift book short fiction evokes a unique sense of space and time (a nonsynchronous synchronicity), refiguring storytelling practices to give white women the opportunity to claim American beginnings and "American-ness."

Female Martyrs

Sedgwick published in both the *Token* (starting with the volume for 1828) and the *Atlantic Souvenir* (starting with the volume for 1826), the two earliest American literary annuals. The annuals ended up joining in 1832 to form the *Token and Atlantic Souvenir* of 1833, but before that, the *Token* was thoroughly a Boston production, overseen by Samuel Goodrich, who made his name as the children's author Peter Parley and would be instrumental in Nathaniel Hawthorne's career. The *Atlantic Souvenir,* whose title more directly alluded to the literary annual's debt to British forms, was based in Philadelphia and edited by Carey and Lea, who would oversee Sedgwick's collection of gift book short fiction *Tales and Sketches* in 1835. Goodrich saw

the advantage of a merger in part because both of these productions advertised themselves as distinctly American, concerned with original material
by native-born authors who wrote about the United States. In 1830, one
reviewer had even counted the number of pages in both the *Token* and the
Atlantic Souvenir that featured national stories before concluding that "on
American subjects (purely,)" literary annuals "are without rivalry."[23]

One such American sketch, Sedgwick's "Mary Dyre," about a Quaker
woman hanged on Boston Common in 1630, appeared toward the end of
the *Token* of 1831 (starting on page 294 of a 320-page volume) and offered
a self-conscious opening: "The subject of the following sketch, a Quaker
Martyr, may appear to the fair holiday readers of souvenirs, a very unfit
personage to be introduced into the romantic and glorious company of
lords, and ladys loves; of doomed brides; and all-achieving heroines; chi-
valric soldiers; suffering outlaws; and Ossianic sons of the forest."[24] And
yet, although the sketch might not be stereotypical gift book fare, the literary annual was key to the workings of "Mary Dyre," for the circulation
patterns of gift books authorized the story and affirmed it as nationally
important. The third Quaker and only female to be hanged under Massachusetts's anti-Quaker law, Mary Dyre played a supporting role in William
Sewel's well-respected *History of the Rise, Increase and Progress of the Christian People Called Quakers* (1717), which Sedgwick knew. Modifying this
telling with interpolated accounts of the historical events actually written
by Mary Dyre herself, Sedgwick recasts the life of this Quaker as an American origin narrative about female resolution and authorship. Through the
Token, Sedgwick established a paradigm for leveraging male networks to
tell alternative stories about women in American history and articulated a
female poetics of historical fiction and memory.

The Quaker William Sewel first published an English version of
his *History* in London, where it received wide praise before making the
jump to American markets. In the years that followed, notables such as
Charles Lamb and Ralph Waldo Emerson came to regard the text as the
definitive work on Quaker history, and Nathaniel Hawthorne used it as
a source for his portrayal of Quakers in "The Gentle Boy," a tale I discuss in the next chapter.[25] Although Sewel's eight-hundred-page history
was accepted and revered as *the* account of a particular American religious
beginning—the Quaker equivalent of Cotton Mather's *Magnalia Christi
Americana*—Sedgwick revised Sewel's account of Dyre in two important

ways. First, Sedgwick separates Dyre from two other Quaker martyrs, William Robinson and Marmeduke Stevenson, with whom Dyre was first sentenced to death and with whom Sewel lumps her. (When the other two are hanged, Dyre was given a reprieve on the condition that she never return to Boston. She did return and did finally meet her death.) Second, Sedgwick foregrounds Dyre's own voice. While Sewel depicts Robinson and Stevenson as literal authors of their own destiny, he suggests that Dyre passively accepts the courtroom drama. Robinson and Stevenson hurriedly prepare papers in their jail cell in the hope that John Endicott, their judge, will allow the papers to be read in court, but Dyre calmly awaits Endicott's pronouncement of death. Sewel's account then has Robinson and Stevenson reply to Endicott—desiring their papers to be read and threatening Endicott with God's disfavor—while Dyre says only, "Yea, joyfully I go" when Endicott orders the marshal to lead her away.[26] The historical Dyre was not actually as passive as this moment makes it seem. In jail after receiving her death sentence, Dyre authored a missive with which Sewel does not engage. Sewel includes Dyre's letter—though he excludes an important later letter—but he forgoes any comment, as if the letter does not actually impact the historical record. Sedgwick corrects this neglect by quoting directly from Dyre's "Appeal to the Rulers of Boston" within her story and by highlighting its significance. A request not for life but for a revocation of the Massachusetts laws discriminating against Quakers, Dyre's letter displays nobility and bravery of spirit. In Sedgwick's sketch, Dyre herself pleads, in quotation marks, the case of non-Puritan Christianity: "Let my counsel and request be accepted with you to repeal all such laws, that the truth and servants of the Lord may have free passage among you, and you keep from shedding innocent blood, which I know there be many among you would not do, if they knew it so to be."[27] Using Dyre's own words allows Sedgwick to invite this historical actor to speak back to her son and her husband, who want to defuse Dyre's words, and her judge, who wants to eliminate them. Dyre's voice is so important to this sketch that Sedgwick includes a second letter, one that Dyre writes during her second imprisonment (after Robinson's and Stevenson's deaths), which Sewel omits from his history. Knowing that she will be hanged, Dyre declares that she is "freely offering up [her] life to Him that gave it [her], and sent [her] hither so to do."[28] While the Puritans imprison, condemn, and hang her, Dyre remains the author of her own destiny. Her voice, marked off with quotations and working with Sedgwick's, enriches and alters the depiction that Sewel gives. Dyre is not merely one of three Quakers sentenced to death on the Boston Common. Rather, Dyre offers an early and impassioned declaration of religious freedom. Her high principles are beyond the narrow-minded understanding of male Puritan elders and perhaps of her chronicler William Sewel. In the end, Dyre gives up her life for "the best cause, the fountain of all liberty—liberty of conscience."[29] Dyre thereby supersedes the category of woman to become *American,* and the various narrative modes, from direct narration to interpolated letter, all of which converge in the story time of "Mary Dyre," provide a multivocal affirmation of that estimation.

The cultural expectations around literary annuals helped circulate Dyre's story and achieve Sedgwick's hope of redeeming this early American heroine. Although mass-produced, literary annuals were an embodied representation of a relationship, a *Token,* as Goodrich's title pointed out. Perhaps most clearly articulating this fact, literary annuals came with a presentation plate, an engraving included at the beginning of the volume that had, within the design, space for the giver to fill in the receiver's name. Notably, these presentation plates often did not leave space for the giver to include his name. Instead recollection of the giver was supposed to have suffused the entire volume, obviating the need to record it, but lending the giver's indirect approval to the contents. This personalization of the literary annual helped the mass-produced item feel intimate. The *Offering* of 1834 began with a poem "addressed to the ladies," to remind them of this transmogrification of book to sentiment: "When from the husband, the lover, or friend, / You receive, as a proof of affection, / The Offering, oh, say what emotions must blend / With the gift, and cement the connection!"[30] Small and easily held, gift books were much different from the grand glossy coffee-table books of today. In fact, the *Token* before 1838 and the *Atlantic Souvenir* for its full run were cozy quartos, roughly 14.5 centimeters by 9 centimeters (5.75 inches by 3.5 inches), slightly smaller than the average woman's extended hand.[31] Even as they were often displayed in the parlor, then, these literary annuals could be and were cradled, clutched, and read. The size both addressed economic requirements of publishers and helped literary annuals become the marks of emotion that they billed themselves as being. Sparked by the initial gifting, the volumes invited somatic responses and active identification. In this way, although it precedes the heyday of sentimentalism, the literary annual is a sentimental genre that seeks to conscript the reader's body into the project of feeling and identifying with a text. With its inclusion in the *Token*, "Mary Dyre" entered this exchange, becoming, if indirectly, endorsed by the male gift givers and primed for the sympathy of female recipients. The literary annual thus furthered Sedgwick's project by assuring that Dyre was not just redeemed from Sewel's lopsided account but was also widely circulated and accepted by nineteenth-century Americans. As one reviewer with an eye on the popularity of the *Token* and the success of beginning stories declared happily, "'Mary Dyre' will be read by countless thousands."[32]

Following Ernst Block, Rita Felski has theorized the concept of synchronous nonsynchronicity in which "individuals coexist at the same historical moment, yet often make sense of this moment in strikingly different ways."[33] Flipping this concept to make *nonsynchronous synchronicity* allows us to understand the working of Sedgwick's sketch wherein characters and readers are brought from different moments—1630 of Dyre's letter and 1831 of Sedgwick's narration, most obviously—into the same story. As these narrative layers contribute to the story, as Dyre's words, Sedgwick's storytelling, the gift book recipient's reading crystalize into meaning, they come together in an intimate chronotopic palimpsest, a multilayered story that is joined temporally, by sharing a narrative, and spatially, by sharing a page, even as the layers remain separate and stacked. Dyre shows that women have exemplified US character and principle, and through their reading and holding of the *Token*, the sketch invites nineteenth-century readers to see themselves as quintessentially American like Mary Dyre. In a sly aside about "one of our most celebrated surgeons" who admiringly says to a patient, "Sir you have borne it like a man, you have done better than that, you have born it like a *woman*," Sedgwick directly connects past and present within the story of this Quaker heroine.[34] Joining temporal moments together in a stacked coherence, "Mary Dyre" claims American beginnings for female readers in 1831.

Upon the release of the *Token* of 1831, "Mary Dyre" became the first published text with Sedgwick's name rather than a pseudonymous byline. This sketch, then, was important in Sedgwick's oeuvre, publicly marking her as "Miss Sedgwick," the author. This first named attribution followed a trend of connecting Sedgwick and short fiction: the 1826 *Atlantic Souvenir*, the first American gift book, listed Sedgwick as a contributor in the preface, even while it did not identify which piece was her work. Short fiction in literary annuals thus had a particular status as named productions for Sedgwick, for while Sedgwick's authorship of her novels became an open secret, her "Miss Sedgwick" byline publicly claimed only sketches and tales—not longer romances—during her lifetime. In fact, her 1835 collection of gift book stories was the only volume published under Sedgwick's name before her death.[35] This fact reflects the relative ease with which short fiction could be reprinted, the cultural work it did, and the interest a writer and publisher would have in marking it as authored.[36] The byline might also be taken as a radical statement declaring female freedom in a literary market where women rarely signed their works "Miss," acknowledging themselves as unprotected and unchosen by a husband.[37] Most of all, though, Sedgwick's byline exposes the power dynamics at work in literary annuals like the *Token*. Melissa Homestead conjectures that "Miss Sedgwick," rather than "Catharine Sedgwick," "C. M. Sedgwick," or even "Miss Catharine Sedgwick," was a name chosen by *Token* editor Samuel Goodrich rather than Sedgwick herself since none of Sedgwick's (admittedly highly incomplete) correspondence mentions her byline.[38] If so, Goodrich probably selected the byline to advertise to the many readers who knew Sedgwick's name, that, as promised, the *Token* would be both visually and literarily from "the resources of our country."[39] Goodrich, a man, was authorizing both Sedgwick's stories and her authorship while also indicating through the title "Miss" that she lacked the cultural authority of wife or mother. In some sense, Sedgwick becomes most visible as she loses control over her self-presentation, much like how Dyre becomes notable through her disappearance and death. Put another way, Sedgwick's authorship is most apparent when her agency is undermined. Indeed, previous to this *Token*, Sedgwick had been unwilling to name herself on title pages because it was seen as indecorous and unladylike. Goodrich, in contrast, could and did proclaim her identity on "Mary Dyre," and on all Sedgwick's subsequent stories in the *Token* and the *Token and Atlantic Souvenir*. My point here is that this act mirrors the exchange of literary annual—in which women's stories become heard, become American, through the men who select them—and that literary annuals and Sedgwick's use of them reveal a complicated set of restrictive and promising narrative realities for female authors. Told with a combination of Dyre's and Sedgwick's voices, "Mary Dyre" enacts community narration through its instantiation in the literary annual, for its authorship is named—and thus in some sense it is *told*—by both Goodrich and Sedgwick. Sedgwick's sketches and tales posit this type of communal narration and spatiotemporal coexistence as the beginning condition for beginning stories about women.

In two other stories about female martyrs of the past, one before and one after "Mary Dyre," Sedgwick similarly probes the limits on what women can safely say. "The Catholic Iroquois" appeared in the *Atlantic Souvenir* of 1826 (the first US literary annual), and "St. Catharine's Eve" was printed in the *Token* of 1835. Like "Mary Dyre," these pieces feature early martyrs, a Canadian Catholic Iroquois woman killed at the hands of her tribe around 1700 and a thirteenth-century lady-in-waiting at a French court. All three of these pieces rely on the sketch's association with authenticity and documentary authority. They are history. At the same time, however, the incompletion of the sketch allows these three stories to exceed their telling, suggesting that readers should see how every narrative has an arbitrary boundary around it. Even as Sedgwick writes her female martyrs into the story center, the sketches show the essence—not the totality—of these women. As such, the characters, filled with life, exceed their many tellings. In "The Catholic Iroquois," a young Iroquois martyr, Françoise, exists above and beyond a host of narrative frames supplied by men—a traveler, the traveler's host, a manuscript copier, a manuscript writer, and an on-site witness. As the narrator tells us, the traveler meets a Canadian farmer who shares an aged copy of a manuscript written by Pere Mesnard, a French Catholic priest. This illiterate farmer reports that, many years before, around 1700, a Frenchman named Bouchard had witnessed some indigenous peoples leaving an offering in a hidden cave, which he then stole "as a holy relic" and copied for the farmer's grandfather.[40] Robbed from a shrine, the manuscript, which climaxes in the immolation of a young woman, becomes idle entertainment for a gentleman traveler much like Geoffrey Crayon. Sedgwick's portrait rehearses the imperialistic process of acquiring American beginning stories and the exploitation of women (of color) inherent in such stories.

And yet even as the gentleman traveler is a quintessential sketch writer, "The Catholic Iroquois" is not like any of Crayon's sketches. Its geographical ranging—the farmhouse is near Niagara Falls, but the manuscript was found near Lake Huron, and the action of that story takes place closer to Montreal—shows that the piece is not an illustration of a location or its customs. Instead it is a portrait of a female martyr. Thus the various figures who introduce the story (the gentleman traveler, the farmer, the farmer's grandfather Bouchard, and even Pere Mesnard) recede one by one to leave Françoise, defiant, proud, and pious, choosing her own death. The disrupted beginnings of her life dictate Françoise's final difficult choice. Seized by a rival tribe (the Utawa), the Iroquois Françoise and her sister Rosalie are handed over to Pere Mesnard, who trains them for the convent. Rosalie takes to the teachings and becomes a nun, but Françoise falls in love with Pere Mesnard's nephew Eugene when he rescues her from an Iroquois ambush. After Françoise and Eugene marry, the Iroquois raid the Utawa encampment, kill Eugene and many of the converted Utawa, and take Françoise. She is asked to abjure her crucifix and marry a young warrior. When she refuses, her father, the Iroquois chief, slices a cross in her breast and orders a pyre. Despite her father's demand for submission, Françoise, after assuring that her story will be told to her sister by a freed Utawa girl, dies with "victorious constancy." She is a "voluntary sacrifice, not a victim" to her father's unyielding rage and his masculine authority. Françoise can fulfill neither the narrative trajectory laid out for her by her Iroquois family nor that created by her Christian mentor. She cannot return to a state before her conversion, nor can she become a nun. Instead she chooses death in an attempt to craft her own narrative and reconcile her multiple origins: "Happy am I," Françoise declares while on her funeral pyre, "thus permitted to die in my own country and by the hand of my kindred, after the example of my Saviour, who was nailed to the cross by his own people."[41] In her conflagration, she remains both Iroquois and Christian. She recognizes God, but she also claims Native American land as her country and her birth family as her kindred. And yet, while Françoise seems to die precisely because she is neither fully Christian nor fully Iroquois, her capture and killing—after refusing marriage—recall the sexual-racial threats of the captivity narrative, that best-selling early American genre, which opposed Native American savagery to white Christian femininity. With this master narrative of Native American–white contact hovering over the story, Françoise reads as most white at the moment when she chooses death over marriage to an Iroquois warrior. She enacts familiar racial scripts that reinforce the projection of a white American people.

Françoise's self-sacrifice shares much with the Quaker Mary Dyre of "Mary Dyre" and the Paterin (a religious sect) Clotide of "St. Catharine's Eve." All three women bravely die for their version of Christianity, and all three are condemned to death by men, respectively, an aggressive Iroquois father, a bigoted Puritan divine, and a duplicitous Catholic archbishop. Placed at the court of the French king Philip's mistress, "St. Catharine's Eve" is the most radical stretch of American beginnings. Yet, like "The Catholic Iroquois" and "Mary Dyre," it considers the fundamental disadvantages that women start with as well as the relationship of woman to nation. Indeed, Clotide meets her death because she does not approve of how Philip II (1165–1223) has abandoned his lawful wife and "married" his mistress Lady Agnes, whom Clotide serves. (Historically, the pope also disapproved and placed France under an interdict.) While she seems concerned about the theological implications of bigamy, Clotide tells her daughter that she is most outraged at how the rightful queen's "wrongs are unknown, or never mentioned" in Philip's court when "every true heart in Christendom is for" Queen Isemburg.[42] Although the sketch takes place many years before the founding of the United States, "St. Catharine's Eve," like "The Catholic Iroquois," expands Sedgwick's consideration of patriarchal authority and its tie to national stories. Just as Françoise's father and Pere Mesnard decide how to read Françoise's soul and body—as Christian or Iroquois, as civilized or savage—Philip II and his crony churchmen have decided, despite Queen Isemburg's protestations, to read her as an invalid wife.[43] The truth that King Philip is denying his lawful wife only comes out when Clotide speaks to her daughter in a scene of dialogue. Yet again, Sedgwick uses her characters' voices to construct an alternative and more valid account that disrupts patriarchal authority through exchange and community and pulls women separated by time and space into a shared moment of narration. But, of course, for this revelation of truth, Clotide is sentenced to death. Communal truth can challenge phallocentric origin stories, but the risk is great since vested interests will silence disruptive voices.

"St. Catharine's Eve" and "The Catholic Iroquois" are centrally stories about women for women. As I said above, Françoise's story comes from a manuscript written by one man (with material from another), copied by a third, framed by a fourth, and translated by a fifth. But, caught in this web of men, Françoise's story is intended for her sister Rosalie. Similarly, a man, the archbishop, overhears Clotide's daughter Rosalie talking to her lover and the archbishop's one-time (male) protégé Gervais and weaponizes that information for vengeance. Meant only for her daughter, Clotide's story is carried into the circuits of male power. The men thus enable the telling of these tales, either because the traveler reads the ancient parchment with Françoise's story or because Gervais rescues Rosalie, who carries her mother's story away from a death sentence. But the price is heavy: like Dyre, both Clotide and Françoise die. Still these women's stories retain their power and their identity as stories by women for women. Françoise's sister Rosalie and Clotide's daughter Rosalie can remember and retell. The gift exchange of the literary annuals aligns Sedgwick's female readers with both Rosalies: they are the women who receive these inspiring stories of female martyrs after they pass through the hands of men. And they, following the celebrated surgeon in "Mary Dyre," will understand that these pieces illuminate the perennial strength of women. While all three of these martyrs underline how difficult it is for women to control their stories—a fact that Sedgwick's almost certainly not chosen byline on "Mary Dyre" similarly illustrates—they also hold the promise of leveraging the circulation patterns of literary annuals. In using men to disseminate their history, these female storytellers can speak alternative truths about the past and the present United States to their sisters and daughters. The literary annual, that record of the year, provides the sense that these many voices can meet in the space-time of the story to form what Lauren Berlant has called an "intimate public," that "porous, affective scene of identification among strangers that promises a certain experience of belonging and provides a complex of consolation, confirmation, discipline, and discussion about how to live."[44] Through the formation of this social space, the tale tellers expand the culture of beginnings and invite white women into the collection of US stories as authors, speakers, characters, auditors, and readers.

Female Communities Producing True Female Origins

While she foregrounds the heroine's words in the three historical sketches, Sedgwick more fully places conversations at the centerpiece of a number of other tales. In these, groups of female storytellers and listeners together make manifest a new truth. Like the Old Dutch farmers in Irving's Knickerbocker tales, these communities affirm their own vantage on life and reality, one tinged with local experience and knowledge. But because the intradiegetic (that is, *in the story*) tale tellers choose their stories to influence their fellows, these narratives have didactic purposes enacted within the story world and, Sedgwick hopes, in the real world. In "The Country Cousin"

(*Token* 1830), for example, Sedgwick presents an English grandmother who describes the actions of two American sisters during the American Revolution to her English granddaughter and her granddaughter's American cousin in an attempt to improve relations between the girls. According to the grandmother, after the British soldiers take over an American town, Emma and Anna must care for a gravely wounded British officer, McArthur, who falls in love with, serially, Emma and then Anna. When their father denies permission for Emma to marry McArthur, the British officer convinces Anna to elope while Emma is traveling through the war-torn country to seek her father's approval for her sister's match. When Emma returns home with her father's certain and final "no," she finds her sister newly married and McArthur transferred to the South. The pregnant Anna is thrown out of the house and survives only through her sister's help until she is finally reunited with her British husband at war's end.

Clearly the grandmother's story showcases proper female behavior, that frequent topic of female sketch writers. Emma, who is exemplary and Christian, lives a contented and happy life that the capricious Anna, who suffers for many years, cannot. But the more important truth the story offers is a revelation of family history for two young female cousins. "Grandmamma!" Isabel exclaims at the end of the story, "You have been telling us of our mothers!"[45] Isabel's mother, Anna; Lucy's mother, Emma; and the grandmother's son (and Isabel's father) McArthur are the protagonists. Though both the grandmother and the narrator initially claim the tale is a "ghost story," the most ghostly aspect of the tale seems to be the facts of Lucy's and Isabel's unknown past.[46] The reader, in discovering what the true ghost is—not the somnambulate and bedsheet-wrapped Anna making a nocturnal visit to her son's grave but rather the secret past of the girls' mothers—helps reconstitute personal history as national history. To borrow Susan K. Harris's words about Sedgwick's novels, in these tales "family and social relationship" work "as models for political relationships."[47] In making major historical events like the American Revolution an explanatory part of lineage, Sedgwick retools American beginnings, shifting them from the public to the domestic realm. As part of their family story, the American Revolution and the suffering endured belongs to Lucy and Isabel as much as it ever did to the men who fought in the war. Through these two characters, this momentous American war becomes part of the reader's world as well, for Sedgwick authorizes her female narrative voice by directly speaking to her "gentle reader."[48] The direct address includes both unnamed narrator (unlike the named grandmother) and tale reader into the community of (female) story producers who reconstruct the American past and reveal that an authentic American beginning has blood ties to the nineteenth-century present. It stacks three distinct temporalities (the American Revolution, the grandmother's telling, and the reader's reading) so they can touch, evoking a sense that events and narration are shared property.

Like "A Country Cousin," "Old Maids" (*Offering* 1834) has a story that unfolds through dialogue that emphasizes the productivity and possibility of female fellowship. In "Old Maids," after a younger woman named Anne displays disgust about the possibility of being an old maid, Mrs. Seton sets out to enlighten her friend through the sketching of four unmarried ladies who selflessly serve others. It is the last of these, Agnes Gray, whose "true story" forms the bulk of the sketch.[49] Agnes's narrative, like "The Country Cousin," features a pair of sisters who fall for the same capricious man. Agnes, the Emma of the sketch, is a paragon of Christian self-effacement, and when she discovers that her sister Lizzy is in love with her beau Henry, she encourages her sister to follow her heart, breaks off her engagement, and accepts her own "self-immolation."[50] Although she gets the man, poor Lizzy goes on to suffer from an inconstant husband and has a life "chequered with many sorrows," for "you can not expect much from a man, who, at eight and twenty, acted the part of Henry Orne." Agnes, in contrast, maintains her profitable school and devotes herself, "with a courageous heart, and serene countenance," to assisting Lizzy with her troubles and her many children.[51] Though her heart has been broken, Agnes has the better ending because, as if she has read the *Ladies' Magazine*, she is the more actively useful. Sedgwick redeems old maids both through plot and through the exchange and interaction of multiple voices. For this reason, Harriet Martineau, the never-married English writer to whom Sedgwick's *Tales and Sketches* was dedicated, called "Old Maids" "a dialogue," and added that it was "perhaps the most beautiful of the author's single pieces."[52] When Mrs. Seton narrates the story from Agnes's point of view, she is bringing an "old maid" into a community of women wherein, after Agnes's story is aired, Agnes will be respected and admired. Indeed, through her participation in the narration by means of interruptions and questions, Anne comes to join Mrs. Seton in an embrace of old maids, validating Agnes as useful, attractive, and moral. Anne, in fact, ends the tale by crying over Agnes's nobility and generosity because Agnes has so effectively entered Anne's temporal moment. Agnes's story is formed of more than just the work of two speakers, however, for internal to Mrs. Seton's story are many layers of marked narration. Lizzy's lament about her questionable love, for example, exists within quotation marks that are within quotation marks, reminding the reader that there are at least three levels of discourse: Lizzy's speech inside Mrs. Seton's story inside Sedgwick's reporting. The piece thus uses formal means—quotation marks—to emphasize the multiplicity of voices creating the anecdote and, once again, the joint formation of an alternate truth that redeems women. When women band together, their voices reinforce each other's, and they learn meaningful knowledge through female-to-female exchange.

Sedgwick's conversational frame provides a model for how beginning stories become culturally accepted: people tell and retell them, bringing them into their own temporalities. Because of the yearly cycle of literary annuals, volumes like the *Token* and the *Atlantic Souvenir* became part of such iterative conversations as soon as they were released in the late fall.[53] "Just at that season when Nature commences her preparations of a winter's nap, changing her green summer dress for the russet and brown of Autumn; . . . when little boys and girls burst out in the exuberance of childish joy, quickened by the inspiration of the free fall air, and great boys and women forsake watering-places and country residences for the comfortable parlors of the city," the *Iris, or Literary Messenger* mused, "just then, i.e. early in October of each year, come the Annuals."[54] This yearly cycle made literary annuals part of a temporally specific and concentrated conversation. For the three months before the new year, reviewers' eyes were turned toward the annuals. Then, by January, reviewers of gentlemen's and ladies' magazines assumed their readers had either given or received the volumes, and it was time to move on from printed evaluations of the gift books. In December, one late-to-the-game review in Hale's *Ladies' Magazine* acknowledged that "Christmas and New Year are approaching, when the books will doubtless be in the possession of *all* our fair young readers, and they can select the beautiful passages for their own amusement."[55] When they became owners of their own copies, these readers extended the discussion started by the reviewers by reading and considering the parts of the miscellanies in front of them. Because they were an annual phenomenon and because they

targeted both men, as gift givers, and women, as readers, literary annuals were gendered literary material that was nonetheless embraced across
the cultural spectrum. Reviewers, editors, givers, and receivers created a
community that exchanged and considered gift book stories. And the reprinting of sections of literary annuals and complete stories, as when the
Lady's Book reprinted Sedgwick's "A Story of Shay's War" (*Atlantic Souvenir*
1831) in its January 1831 issue, helped these annuals and their contents become shared public discourse, adding another level to the nonsynchronous
synchronicity of Sedgwick's gift book fiction.

Carolyn Karcher, Charlene Avallone, Victoria Clement, Lucinda Damon-
Bach, and Susan K. Harris have all acknowledged the polyvocality of Sedgwick's novels.[56] But this strategy was certainly not limited to longer prose
works. Sedgwick also includes her characters' thoughts and speech in short
fiction through means of dialogue, letters, and other interpolated texts.
Arguably this technique is even more overt and powerful because the concision of these stories allows for the entire tale to be a single exchange of
dialogue, as in "Old Maids" and "The Country Cousin." The concentrated
impact of this narrative technique makes the piece into the chronotopic
palimpsest that I have described. Sedgwick so frequently composed stories
that foreground their communal narration because this strategy offered an
alternative means by which to arrive at the truth, a truth that reflected the
lives of nineteenth-century white women by shifting standard patriarchal
narratives. A reviewer, who was most likely Edgar Allan Poe, showed the
power of this strategy when he called Agnes "the beau-ideal of feminine
disinterestedness—the *ne plus ultra* of sisterly devotion," applying traditional
praise for women to a social category, old maids, that would not normally
receive it.[57] Relying on the authenticity of the sketch and the orality of the
tale, Sedgwick's pieces—which often resist clear genre classification—call
themselves "true" and feature recognizable and ideal female types who
use words as challenges. The in-story tale tellers of Mrs. Seton and the
grandmother effect change through exchange with their auditors. They *act*
through their stories and their exposure of deep truth. Published in literary
annuals that would have been placed on the parlor table and read and discussed in groups as well as individually, Sedgwick's tales invite their female
readers to create the communities that reform American stories.

Embellishing Femininity

Even as Sedgwick challenged patriarchal narratives, her tales and sketches were not in direct conflict with the idealized feminine types captured in gift book engravings. Within these images, literary annuals generally featured generic and stereotyped women along with grandiose American scenes and the occasional exotic image. The *Token* of 1830, in which "A Country Cousin" appeared, had a view of Mount Chocorua in New Hampshire, the Juniata River in Pennsylvania, and multiple ideal women in "Genevieve," "The Doomed Bride," and "The Sibyl." All three of these women display the ivory neck and bosom that underline how a certain type of whiteness was the height of beauty in the nineteenth-century United States. Genevieve, with her low-cut dress, looks directly at the viewer, a cross between flirtation and challenge, but the other two women look away, their demure gazes and shapely bodies expressing inner goodness for a culture in which external appearance was widely accepted to reveal interior morality. These engravings, commonly called embellishments, communicated the volume's aesthetic value and were critical to the marketing of literary annuals. As such, they were usually billed on a separate table of contents that appeared before the table of contents for the literary matter. The allure of these embellishments was twofold. First, they offered visual pleasures to a middle-class readership relatively bereft of high-quality images. Second, they played to nationalist sentiments, both by depicting those things—women, mountains, Native Americans—deemed quintessentially "American" and by supporting the nascent American visual arts.[58] The *North American Review* noted in 1833, "The art of the engraver . . . required in this country some such encouragement," which it found in the gift books. As a result, "Deserving artists have been incited to excel by the liberal compensation which the publisher of works like these is able to offer. If no other benefit be derived from them, this, at least, may be justly mentioned to their praise."[59] Gift books did indeed provide the first general circulation of what Ralph Thompson calls "consciously artistic illustration" largely because of technological developments.[60] In the 1820s, just as the gift book craze began, steel plate engraving became more widespread, offering a medium that was cheaper, longer lasting, and better able to craft the soft idealized images then in fashion.[61] When described in reviews and notices, and when flipped through in a book shop, steel engravings communicated the safety and value of the volume's contents for gifting.[62] The power of this exchange and its potential implications are suggested by an engraving that appeared just a few pages before Sedgwick's "The Country Cousin." Called "Meditation," it features a classically beautiful woman lounging in a chair with her foot peeking out from her dress. The woman holds, in her right hand, a book partially tucked behind her skirt. Her finger is caught in the pages, as if she has just closed it to consider what she has read. This engraving articulates the promise and possibility of the literary annual: even while broadcasting narrow ideals of femininity, the annual invited *meditations* about the relationship between its disparate pieces and about the content of those individual items. It is seemingly contradictory that a gift book that encouraged limited views of women might also foster critical thought. Yet this contradiction was elided by the temporal relationship between images and texts in a literary annual. One young woman, within the pages of a gift book story, opens her literary annual carefully, "that it might not be soiled in the slightest degree," and then "eagerly looked all through it" and "commenced again, and examined the plates with the most minute attention." After this second examination of the embellishments, "She then showed them to her little brother and sister."[63] As they do for most readers of the modern-day *New Yorker* who look at the cartoons before reading the articles, the gift book images came first. The reading comes later, after the gift giver has gone and when a woman—or a group of women—have a space of time. That the images are followed by the stories allows the female reader to reinterpret both stories and images in light of her increasing knowledge about the contents of the volume and, perhaps, with changing or growing feelings about the male who had given it. The suspended serialization of the annual—lasting for a whole year on the parlor table—increased the likelihood of this (re)meditation and participated in one of the explicit aims of the culture of beginnings, continually (re)fashioning the past for nineteenth-century needs.

On the table next to the lounging woman in "Meditation" is a vase of flowers, an accessory that references the organizing structure of the miscellany and brings us back to John Adams, Thomas Jefferson, and Benjamin Franklin's selection of *E Pluribus Unum,* a phrase appearing next to a handful of blooms, as a motto for the Great Seal. Many literary annuals had names inspired by flora—the *Amaranth,* the *Chaplet of Roses,* the *Dahlia,* the *Forget-Me-Not,* the *Floral Offering, Flowers of Loveliness,* the *Garland,* the

"Meditation," an embellishment from the *Token* of 1830 showing a
woman, with book in her right hand, considering what she has just
read. (Courtesy American Antiquarian Society)

Hyacinth, the *Iris,* and the *Lily,* to name a few. Not only were flowers appropriate for the young women who were to receive these gift books, but
these titles conjured the idea of, to employ the title of yet another annual, a
Bouquet. Hence, the *Token* of 1832 offered a presentation plate with a stone
vessel spilling over with flowers on top of a wall with a space for the receiver's name. The *Atlantic Souvenir* of 1829 had a title page of two angels
with garlands of flowers, surrounded by border of woven blooms. Such
floral bounty, unified by vase or hand, was a metaphor for the contents
that followed, which reviewers would recognize, sometimes by reviewing
every single piece—poetry, prose, and image—of an annual.[64] In 1828 one

reviewer noted that the *Atlantic Souvenir* must be read "not as the work of one, but of many authors," who are "all reaching after the same reward, all striving together for the same notoriety."[65] These various pieces made a single coherent volume. But the many floral names of literary annuals and the pervasive metaphor of a bouquet also reveal how variety, as an aesthetic, was marked as female, and sketches and tales, the major prose forms of such gift books were gendered by association.[66] Lest the femininity of the literary annual and its variety not be clear enough, the presentation plate in the *Offering* 1834 is a semicircle of seven women enthusiastically greeting a

Title page from the *Offering* of 1834 showing a community of women sharing the news brought by a male traveler. (Courtesy American Antiquarian Society)

man dressed in a traveling clothes. With a blank space for the presenter to write his beloved's name underneath the curly letters of the gift book title, the plate suggests that the offering of the *Offering* is ability to receive and process new information in a group of women. The literary annual is the formal instantiation of Sedgwick's narrative strategy in which many voices and many stories come together in time-space: it enacts and illustrates the male-sponsored creation of communal female histories.

Reconstructing Memory

While the gendered nature of variety is coded into all of Sedgwick's gift book short fiction, "Romance in Real Life" (*Legendary* 1828) might best explain how this aesthetic provides a radical challenge to a phallocentric culture of beginnings. When the heroine embraces two identities and two stories, she models how feminine variety does not just supply different origin stories. It offers a different mode of constructing origins. The tale consists of two letters and some four conversations, portions of which are originally in French and "put into plain English," a miscellaneous structure that recalls both the dialogue of pieces like "Old Maids" and the restructured historical accounts like "Mary Dyre."[67] These different types of texts work within Sedgwick's narration to recount the heroine's complicated history. In 1777, Mary, a young girl, is abandoned by her French father in western Massachusetts and adopted by Mr. and Mrs. Reynolds, a childless innkeeper and his wife. Some years after the Revolution, a pair of travelers—one French, one English—arrive at the inn in search of a Marie Angley de Creve-Coeur, the long-lost daughter of their friend. Near the beginning of the Revolutionary War, Marie's father had been seized by the British while traveling and forcibly transported back to Europe. He did not, then, purposely abandon his children. Rather, he was unable to get word to or retrieve them during the continuing hostilities. While the innkeeper's wife considers dissembling so as not to lose her adopted daughter (who has been separated from her brothers), she eventually confesses to the gentlemen that her charge is the little French girl. Mary, in turn, is taken to Boston and placed under the care of a French woman, but she leaves with the promise that she will never forget Mrs. Reynolds. This story, then, has obvious double origins: Mary's existence as Marie, and Mary's time with the Reynoldses. The adult Franco-American Mary also lives a doubleness of being in love and denying it. Unwittingly, she falls for M. Constant, the French ambassador to the United States, and the fiancé of one of Mary's friends. Living up to his name, Constant marries his fiancée despite his feelings for Mary. But when his first wife conveniently dies a year later, he courts and wins Marie Angley's hand in marriage, a second beginning of his domestic life.

In this story Sedgwick encourages a recognition of duality: Mary is also Marie (a curious foreshadowing of Poe's 1842 "The Mystery of Marie Rogêt," which also features a Mary/Marie and which I discuss in chapter 5). She is simultaneously French and American (again like Poe's Mary/Marie), and she has both a French and an American family. As Sedgwick tells it, Marie's tale starts as an American one. After her French father is lost during the Revolution, she becomes part of her Massachusetts community as Mary. When her father's friends discover her, however, she goes to Boston to be tutored in French, acquires a French beginning, and becomes Marie again. Yet, by being two things at once, like the Catholic Iroquois Françoise, Mary/Marie is fully neither. So too the story cannot be unequivocally happy. Her father has lost his daughter, and when his European friends discover her, Mrs. Reynolds loses her daughter. Like Mary/Marie's doubleness, the European and American connections these characters possess serve to question the exclusivity of American origins in both gendered and national terms. It is through Mary/Marie's doings, not her father's, that she maintains contact with Mrs. Reynolds and stitches together the two stories of her life, achieving a version of personal nonsynchronous synchronicity, a both/and of identity, even as she lives under one of her two names. As Irving's *Sketch Book* does, "Romance in Real Life" asks whether an American beginning like the Pilgrims and the Revolutionary War can ever fully be separated from Europe. Read through the lens of Sedgwick's tale and Mary/Marie's life, the answer is no, and it is women's work to embrace such multiplicity. Edward Said argues that the origin is a myth that tries to shut down multiplicity, providing a single explanation for all that comes after, but in theorizing a narrative multiplicity, Sedgwick offers a method for holding open this foundational story to include variety and women.[68]

When we accept the multiplicity of Mary/Marie's story, it offers two resonate connections to early American founders. Mary/Marie, we learn in the penultimate paragraph, "delighted in relating the vicissitudes of her life, and dwelt particularly on that period, when, as Mrs. Reynolds's handmaid, she considered herself honoured in standing behind the chair of the wife of the great General Knox."[69] Mary/Marie's early life links, in some essential way, to the great revolutionary hero('s wife) and canonical understandings of American genesis. Yet, at the same time, it hardly seems a coincidence that Mary/Marie's surname is Creve-Coeur, the same surname of the French author who first answered "What is an American?" in his *Letters from an American Farmer* (1782). Like Marie's father, J. Hector St. John Crèvecoeur left his New York farm and family to visit his ailing father in France during the American Revolution. After being detained in British-occupied New York City and then staying in France for some time, he returned to New York to find his wife dead and his children farmed out to neighbors. Marie is the fictional daughter of the actual man who declared that the American was not defined by consanguinity, shared language, or joint history but rather was a type of modern figure who valued equality, hard work, honesty, and self-sufficiency. While the Anglo-American Founding Father General Knox is explicitly named, the Franco-American Founding Father is a shadow story, an oblique acknowledgment of the transnationalism inherent in the formation of a national literary tradition. The multiple speakers who voice parts of Mary's truth indicate the need to interrogate origins by retelling beginning narratives and considering their erasures, for the gentlemen who go looking for Mary only find her after they consider the possibility that she lives under a new identity. Mary finds happiness, with her adopted mother and later with her husband, exactly because she is willing to hear the missing story of her past and layer it with her present in a chronotopic palimpsest. Taking a cue from Mary/Marie, the readers of the tale should similarly display concern for how history is (re)constructed.

Literary annuals were an overt means by which memories were formed as a *Souvenir*, a *Memento*, or a *Token* of remembrance. Beyond their function of memorializing a certain year, many of these literary annuals and particularly the *Token* and the *Atlantic Souvenir* were involved in the overtly nationalist project of bolstering US letters through support for native-born writers and engravers. These two projects, remembering the year and fostering American literature, dovetailed most closely in stories about the American past that considered the condition of remembering. Perhaps most obviously Sedgwick recognizes this fact in "A Story of Shay's War" when a participant in Shays' Rebellion rejects the label of "rebel" offered by his mother. He rejoins: "My father," a Revolutionary solider, was also called a rebel, "and he changed the name to patriot."[70] The point is that narrative terms fashion the reception and meaning of history. Helping to craft shared ideas and values for gift book readers, many of these sketches and tales provided authentic, if not strictly true, accounts of American beginnings for two reasons: to leverage women as storytellers and story characters into the culture of beginnings and to question how women were remembered and beginnings were constructed. The accepted transmission of literary annuals, from man to woman, increased the authority of Sedgwick's stories; men implicitly approved the contents as they gave them to their lovers, wives, and daughters. In turn, women, who were supposed to imbue the books—and their contents—with affection, cradled and displayed the annuals, experiencing the contents in private moments and in public groupings. The mass-produced item became personal and intimate even as it remained linked to the larger cultural discussion of magazine and newspaper reviews and the larger cultural ritual of Christmas and New Year's gift exchange. This simultaneous personal and public dialogue, one replicated in the conversational frames and multivocal tellings of Sedgwick's narratives, pulled female martyrs, old maids, and storytelling women into the patriotic mission of constituting the American people. Recognizing the power of the patriarchal authorities, from Perdita's silencing father to William Sewel's lopsided historical account, Sedgwick's sketches and tales slyly pervert male authority to know themselves and each other by meeting in the time-space of a layered truth, a chronotopic palimpsest. To better reach and more significantly impact Sedgwick's targeted female readers, these stories capitalized on the bonds of affection and gratitude built into the giving of these literary annuals. Like involved reading, memory itself, as the phenomenon of literary annuals remind us, is an emotional act. Through the shared conversation and the nonsynchronous synchronicity of the literary annual, Sedgwick's short fiction conjured alternative communal memories that celebrated the feminine variety of American origins.

❖ 4 ❖

The Chronicle, the Reckoning,
and Hawthorne's Puritan Tales

Through her brother Theodore Sedgwick, Catharine Sedgwick sent the Philadelphia publisher Carey, Lea and Blanchard a packet of stories, almost certainly the actual pages of the literary annuals where each sketch or tale had first appeared, and requested they produce a collection.[1] Published in 1835, *Tales and Sketches* proffered a jumble of short fiction with neither a unifying narrator like Geoffrey Crayon nor overarching theme like *Sketches of American Character* (Hale's 1829 volume). According to John Austin, Sedgwick's successful text thereby "marks the emergence of a new and distinctly American genre: the miscellaneous collection."[2] Transferring the variety of the US magazine to a single-authored volume, *Tales and Sketches* once again illustrates that *e pluribus unum*. Following in Sedgwick's footsteps, Hawthorne put out *Twice-Told Tales* (1837), his own miscellaneous and distinctly American collection of fiction from literary annuals and magazines.[3] But Hawthorne's collection is different from Sedgwick's. While *Twice-Told Tales* has no overriding structure, Hawthorne's Puritan tales, including "The Minister's Black Veil," "The Maypole of Merry Mount," and "The Gentle Boy," which had all appeared in the *Token*, provide a through line. This fact reflects the different agendas that Hawthorne and Sedgwick had. That is, instead of challenging who belonged in the culture of beginnings, Hawthorne asked how much free will an author who engaged deeply with the historical record had when the culture of beginnings was the easiest path to writerly security. How could one reconcile the tension between the Puritans' abhorrent acts and their apotheosis in the culture of beginnings? Mirroring the existential dilemma of Puritanism itself, Hawthorne's tales question the presence of volition in literary nationalism. The collection's success—Frank Luther Mott identifies it as a best seller—suggests that Hawthorne's probing had wide appeal to those who celebrated forefathers. That it sold in editions into the 1840s and 1850s implies it also resonated with the growing disenchantment with the culture of beginnings.[4]

Tales Told Twice

Nathaniel Hawthorne's *Twice-Told Tales* (1837) are twice told because they are twice printed—each sketch and tale appeared in a periodical or literary annual before being collected in a volume. But these tales and sketches are twice told in yet another, more interesting way as well. Each story—and particularly each Puritan story—functions on a dual temporality, both a chronological and a retroactive way of understanding the plot. Baked within each tale, then, is a double telling. First, the reader comprehends the story in a chronological fashion; she adds to her understanding as unfolding events give more information about a character's personality and his choices. Second, the reader understands the entirety of the text as well as its constituent parts in light of the story's ending. For example, if a protagonist goes on to become president of the United States, her election as kindergarten line leader takes on new, even typological, significance. We can understand her as predestined to be president. While viewing prior events through a story's ending often happens after a reader has read through the text in a chronological fashion, the second mode of understanding does not always follow the first. With *Hamlet*, for example, most have an idea of the ending, of Hamlet's tragic flaw, and of the play's cultural significance before hearing the first line. They thus have some sort of reckoning of the character and the play before they read or see it. Moreover, the chronological end that forces, encourages, or allows a reader to (re)conceptualize a chronologically prior happening does not have to be in the final paragraphs.[5] A story can be told out of order. In reading, as in life, our opinions and understandings of previous occurrences are constantly revised in the light of new information and happenings, no matter where such data appear. A pull between the chronological understanding and final judgment characterized the world of seventeenth-century New England Calvinists, a fact that Matthew P. Brown has recently shown was coded into their textual practices of reading and writing. Their lives were twice-told tales. But these competing modes of reading also describe a tension implicit in most if not all fictional narrative, and they reveal a paradox at the heart of crafting American beginning stories to reflect nineteenth-century values. On the one hand, nineteenth-century authors were trying to write authentic tales of the past; on the other hand, they were doing so with preconceived ideas about what the past was and what it meant.[6]

I call the more straightforward of the temporalities described above, that of considering a narrative (and life) chronologically, the *chronicle*, by which I mean the forward movement of time that governs our understanding of human actions. The term is supposed to conjure up daily records like John Winthrop's diary as well as the biblical books of Chronicles, that linear account of Jewish happenings from Adam to the Babylonian captivity. In particular, with its record of who begat whom, the first nine chapters of 1 Chronicles serve as a potent illustration of human chronology plodding onward. Events lead to other events just as Noah's sons father other sons. In contrast to this forward-moving temporality is the *reckoning*, the manner by which we (re)conceive that which has come chronologically (though not necessarily narratively) before. The term gestures to the act of giving an evaluation of what has previously come ("to give a reckoning of"), the act of accounting for and settling differences and inconsistencies ("he reckoned with her"), and, of course, the idea of final judgment ("the day of reckoning"). All these senses have embedded within them a way of viewing time backward, of reconstructing events from the ending to the origin. While humans naturally think and live by the chronicle, we inevitably also employ the retrospective logic of the reckoning. These two forms of temporality are as irreconcilable as they are simultaneous and inevitable. They create a potent narrative paradox that captured, for Hawthorne, the difficulty of writing American beginning stories and that raises questions about the aesthetic compromises inherent in using American history to advance US letters.

For seventeenth-century Puritan New England, the subject of Hawthorne's most famous tales, this temporal dilemma was more than just a quirk of narrative—it was a life-and-death issue. A form of Calvinism, Puritanism relies on double predestination, which holds that, due to God's prior decree, some are elected to heaven and others are damned to hell before birth.[7] A Puritan's final "reckoning" thus retells the narrative of a

Puritan's life, for after death, the life's "theme" (Paul Ricoeur's term) or moral becomes salvation or damnation and effectively recasts all the happenings of that person's life as sainted or damned.[8] While such inverted temporality is, perhaps, the closest human approximation for the atemporality or other-temporality of God and God's predestination, it is clearly not the normal conception of time. In human terms, the reckoning serves as the inverse and negation of the chronicle, a powerful force within Puritan life despite Puritan belief in double predestination. Spiritual diaries, which many Puritans kept, and the staunch belief in successive stages of the spiritual purification that readied one to receive God's grace displayed how Puritans put stock in forward-moving time.[9] Puritans were thus both constrained by God's prior determination of their salvation or damnation *and* able to act freely as time marched on. They believed that, as Dewey D. Wallace Jr. writes, double predestination "harmonized with the freedom of the will understood in the Augustinian sense as a voluntary necessity whereby no sinners were compelled to sin but did so freely."[10] The chronicle, which constructed life one moment at a time, and the reckoning, which constructed a person's life only after it had ended, competed as *and* together formed the explanatory mode of Puritan life.

Hawthorne's original *Twice-Told Tales* showcases this temporal paradox within New England Puritanism, within nineteenth-century historical fiction, and within narrative more broadly.[11] As the narrator in Hawthorne's "Wakefield," a twice-told tale of a man who abandons his wife, observes, "An influence, beyond our control, lays its strong hand on every deed which we do, and weaves its consequences into an iron tissue of necessity."[12] A higher force impacts action and confuses—if not confounds—forward-moving causality with a predetermined, reckoning script. This tension produces at least some of the irony and ambiguity that have fascinated generations of Hawthorne scholars. More importantly, it reveals the difficulty of identifying beginnings that are anything but hollow retrospective constructions. The end informs our appointment of the beginning. It was thus through a contemporary lens that early nineteenth-century politicians, orators, historians, and writers sought to shape the American origin. When Rufus Choate spoke in Hawthorne's hometown of Salem in 1833, he asserted that American history and prehistory needed to display the democratic virtues of the republic. He told authors to "begin with the landing of the Pilgrims, and pass down to the war of Independence, from one epoch and one generation to another" and to select "whatever of illustrious achievement, of heroic suffering, of unwavering faith" was useful.[13] According to Choate, authors writing in the service of the nation should tell a story that moves forward chronologically and skips over any events deemed unsavory by their descendants. Choate wanted a selective (even false) chronicle that served and was created by a very specific reckoning.

Of all US writers, Hawthorne is perhaps most closely associated with historical fiction. Yet the temporal paradox baked into his tales reveals his ambivalence, even repugnance, not just with the actions of the Puritans but also with writing about these figures. While Hawthorne does use the terms "chronicle" and "reckoning" in one of his sketches, he does not directly cite Puritan theology in any tale.[14] Yet, as I show, *Twice-Told Tales* displays investment in this temporal dilemma. My theorization of these two temporalities elucidates how Hawthorne's Puritan stories offer a commentary on the location and dislocation of American beginnings, both through their subject matter and through their treatment of narrative time. Indeed his articulation of the chronicle and the reckoning speaks to the limits of writing during the culture of beginnings. Even as historical fiction and nationalism supported the development of a self-consciously American tradition, it limited authors' ability to tell unsavory tales. With his own biographical and literary origins in the Puritans, Hawthorne challenges the judgment that appoints these Calvinists as forefathers even as he employs the common nineteenth-century evaluation of them. Put another way, while Hawthorne did research with the primary source chronicles of seventeenth-century Massachusetts, he put stock in the reckoning as a meaning-making device.[15] As Millicent Bell notes, the past for Americans in the first part of the nineteenth century "was not dead because it was refigured in the present."[16] Hawthorne helped make it so.

Preparationism and Predestination

Before looking at *Twice-Told Tales*, I want to take a short detour to explain the intellectual and religious culture of seventeenth-century Boston. I also want to show how historical actors wrestled with the temporal paradox of the chronicle and the reckoning. Increase Mather (1639–1723), the major preacher of the second generation of Massachusetts Puritans, underlines the importance of both the chronicle and the reckoning to the quotidian life of those within the Massachusetts Bay Colony. On the one hand, Mather believed that sinners were damned on the whim of God. As he wrote in 1710, "I say, God is not bound to give Sinners Grace: He is an absolute Sovereign, and may give Grace or deny Grace to whom he pleaseth. Shall the thing formed, say to him that formed it, why have thou made me thus? . . . If He giveth Grace to any man in the world it is from His Sovereign good pleasure."[17] God's creations were but actors in a fixed world where they were granted or denied Grace based on God's absolute and inscrutable will. On the other hand, however, Mather thought that humans controlled their actions: "Altho' it is true, (as has been shewed) that Sinners cannot Convert themselves, their Cannot is a wilful Cannot."[18] According to Mather, even though they were predestined to be reprobates, sinners retained free will in their choice of rejecting Christ. Sinners were thus responsible for the condition of being sinners even as God determined them to be such ahead of time. Such a paradoxical stance was integral to Puritanism, which tried to walk a thin line between antinomianism, the idea that one could be involuntarily ravished by God (thus making the sanctified life irrelevant), and Arminianism, the idea that one could by means of actions *force* God to elect him to heaven. In essence, holding sinners responsible for sinning meant that, despite the fact that they lived in a world of reckoning where one's election or damnation was prejudged, Puritans believed in free will and forward-moving time and found it relevant to (though not determinative of) their ultimate destiny.

Exactly how much stock a Puritan could put into the chronicle was a pressing seventeenth-century question. Consequently, while Puritanism, which placed a good deal of control at the level of individual churches, was never monolithic, the most disruptive conflicts in Puritan theological history relate to the issue of free will and predestination.[19] The stakes, after all, were high. In the tension between the chronicle and the reckoning lay the choice of claiming or refuting influence over one's eternal soul and of seizing or ceding control over the explanatory moment of one's life—a final judgment that occurred before one was born but was revealed, and thus in a sense happened, only after one died. The paradox between these two modes of understanding life became extremely well articulated with the advent of what is known as preparationism, a doctrine that caught hold in New England and then traveled to Old England. Preparationism held that though the elect and damned were predetermined, Puritans could *prepare* themselves for grace through proper moral behavior. (In essence, the most prepared were those who best followed the dictates of the church elders about what constituted a sanctified life.) A number of political reasons, most significantly the clergy's need for better control over their New England congregations, gave rise to this doctrine in the late 1630s.

Thomas Hooker (1587–1647), the founder and leader of the Puritan colony of Connecticut, was the single most influential articulator and proponent of preparationism. Indeed, preparation and its role in redemption is, according to Hooker biographer Sargent Bush Jr., "the chief topic of more than six thousand pages of his writings."[20] In these many pages, Hooker describes preparationism as a stage in which the Puritan can better receive inclinations to holy action and thought and thereby become ready for grace. The implication is clearly that Puritans could impact their final judgment and encourage, if not force, God to save them. While Hooker vehemently denied that preparationism constituted Arminianism, he understood that the doctrine encouraged action as if it were causal. Indeed Hooker was "constitutionally adverse" to the idea that Puritans must be fully passive in their reception of salvation, for he was aware of the "psychological danger" in advocating such a stance.[21]

Hooker justified his doctrine in two ways. First, most Puritan theologians accepted that there were four spiritual stages one went through on the way toward union with God: calling or vocation, justification, sanctification, and glorification. Still, the exact significance of each stage was a matter of debate. In particular, there was disagreement over whether Puritans received grace at the beginning or the end of the first stage. This uncertainty allowed preparationists to insert two preliminary steps before justification and after vocation, steps that required the elect to exert himself to receive God's grace. Hooker knew that these two steps—contrition and humiliation—did not have mainstream Puritan support. For example, Hooker's notable English friend Thomas Goodwin, president of Magdalen College, Oxford, and chaplain to Oliver Cromwell, disagreed with Hooker's emphasis on preparation. Nonetheless Hooker's ideas had "ample precedent" from English predecessors, including William Ames (1573–1633), a noted Puritan divine who never made it to New England but had considerable influence on the colonists.[22] (Puritans, like early nineteenth-century US writers, were necessarily thinking transatlantically. After all, the original aim was for the Puritans to serve as a light on the hill for other Englishmen—to influence English religious life—not to found a new country.) Second, Hooker justified preparationism through Puritan Christology: since Christ could not have died for unredeemed sinners and since it does not make sense that he would die for those already elect, Christ must have died for sinners who *would become* elect. As Hooker wrote, "*This precious blood of Christ was shed for Sinners,* BUT NOT AS SINNERS."[23] The logical conclusion was that sinners could and should impact their salvation. Hooker warned, "You must not thinke that Christ will pardon all, and you doe nothing."[24] To avoid charges of Arminianism, Hooker stated the case in an inverted fashion. Sinners, he maintained, could prepare for grace or, at the very least, ward off the devil through effort and action. While keeping evil at bay is not equivalent to attaining salvation, one can see how one idea leads to, even bleeds into, the other. Hooker's preaching about preparationism thus paved the way for two famous causal chronicles of reformed salvation—John Bunyan's *Pilgrim's Progress* (1676) and Daniel Defoe's *Robinson Crusoe* (1719).[25]

Though Hooker and others maintained that preparationism did not undermine Calvinism's central tenet of predestination, those who disagreed with preparationism on theological grounds, including Hooker's contemporary and friend John Cotton, contended that the doctrine constituted a challenge to God's arbitrary preordination of grace and damnation. For Cotton and for strict Calvinists, human action had no effect on salvation. As Cotton wrote, "There is no promise of [eternal] life made to those that wait & seek in their own strength, who being driven to it, have taken it up by their own resolutions."[26] In the Bay Colony's crisis of Antinomianism (1636–38), Anne Hutchinson, the most famous religious defector of the first generation of New England Puritans, also disagreed with preparationism and cited Cotton's stance in her trial. Both she and her followers (including Mary Dyre and her husband) held that the Puritan leaders had begun preaching a "covenant of works" and were hoodwinking congregants about the true nature of grace through the suggestion that their actions, their works, could earn salvation. Ultimately, Hutchinson was expelled from the community (to the delight of Thomas Hooker, one of the principal prosecutors in her trial), Cotton became less outspoken in his opposition to the doctrine, and preparationism was officially sanctioned throughout New England.[27] When English Puritans were faced with their own crisis of Antinomianism starting in the 1640s, they too adopted the doctrine.[28] This fact had huge consequences for the Puritan world. According to Perry Miller, "Here at last was a fulcrum for the lever of human responsibility, even in a determined world. Here was something a man could do, here was an obligation that could be urged upon him, no matter how impotent his will."[29] While Hooker could not and did not frame preparationism in the same terms as Miller, it is indisputable that the doctrine placed emphasis on human effort and causality. Despite God's predetermination of salvation, despite God's temporally prior position, despite the denials of some Puritan clergy, human actions could (at least in some way) affect the outcome of one's life. Preparationism magnified the chronology and causality of Puritan life. It offered the godly free will even while they remained chained within a predetermined and retrospective world. Caught between the chronicle and the reckoning, Puritans lived the temporal paradox that Hawthorne encodes in his tales.

"The Gray Champion" as American Beginning

As published in the United States in 1837, before the 1842 addition of "The Toll-Gatherer's Day," *Twice-Told Tales* contained eighteen pieces that can be split roughly into three groups: sketches, fantasy tales, and historical tales.[30] As frequently emphasized through the bibliographic footnotes or citations Hawthorne offers, the history tales purport to represent real events and often feature actual personages, like Simon Bradstreet and John Endicott. Such authenticating features point to the cold facts that Hawthorne weaves into an imaginative and artistic story. As Hawthorne once said, "The knowledge communicated by the historian and biographer is analogous to that which we acquire of a country by the map,—minute, perhaps, and accurate, and available for all necessary purposes, but cold and naked, and wholly destitute of the mimic charm produced by landscape painting."[31] In contrast, fiction (with a dose of reckoning) made history breathe. Located mostly in the first half of the collection, "The Gray Champion," "The Minister's Black Veil," "The May-Pole of Merry Mount," "The Gentle Boy," and "The Prophetic Pictures" all take place within the greater Boston of the seventeenth and eighteenth centuries, and all show a preoccupation with temporality, causality, and providence. These histories allow *Twice-Told Tales* to comment upon the Puritan paradox of the Massachusetts Bay Colony, reflecting, in turn, the larger difficulties of narrative and of narrating the beginnings of the United States.

The first tale in *Twice-Told Tales* strikes a patriotic note in its record of a moment of English-American conflict. As G. Harrison Orians has shown, the kernel of "The Gray Champion" is the Angel of Hadley legend, first recorded in a 1794 history and then picked up by others as various as Sir Walter Scott (*Peveril of the Peak,* 1822) and James Fenimore Cooper (*The Wept of Wish-ton-wish,* 1829).[32] According to the legend, two of those who had condemned Charles I to death had taken refuge in Hadley, Massachusetts, when, as the townsfolk were at church, a Native American raid began. One of the regicides (General Goffe) suddenly appeared to calm, organize, and lead the colonists in a successful defense of Hadley. Once the town was safe, the defender vanished. Hawthorne notably alters the historic situation of the legend, for, unlike Scott's and Cooper's, Hawthorne's Gray Champion challenges Britons, not Native Americans, in a moment typologically predictive of the conflict between colonists and Redcoats. Fittingly, "The Gray Champion" opens with confidence: "There was once a time when New England groaned under the actual pressure of heavier wrongs, than those threatened ones which brought on the Revolution" (*TTT* 11). By moving backward from the American Revolution in favor of earlier skirmishes against the British, Hawthorne's tale asks the question, can an author elect British subjects as Americans, a category that cannot exist during the seventeenth century, and still be true to the chronicle? Put in the terms of Puritan theology, can God elect the saved before their birth? "The Gray Champion" answers in the affirmative, for these proto-Americans are opposed to monarchal power. The story is set in 1684 when the Catholic and "bigoted" James II had annulled the charter of the Massachusetts Bay Colony, and the royal governor's administration "lacked scarce a characteristic of tyranny," a word Jefferson used to describe the actions of George III in the Declaration of Independence (*TTT* 11). The lengthy first two paragraphs of the history-tale provide a list of British misdeeds before focusing in on an April afternoon in 1689. Drunk with wine, Sir Edmund Andros, appointed royal governor of all New England by James II in 1686, sends the Governor's Guard into the streets of Boston. Notified by the martial drum that the Redcoats are out en masse, the demurely dressed and devout Puritans collect in the street looking for guidance from such patriarchs as the almost ninety-year-old former governor Bradstreet. "Oh! Lord of Hosts," someone cries from the crowd, "provide a Champion for thy people!" (*TTT* 17).

Immediately, the aged Gray Champion does appear, in his out-of-date Puritan dress, to drive back the Redcoats. When challenged by Sir Edmund Andros, the champion declares: "I am here, Sir Governor, because the cry of an oppressed people hath disturbed me in my secret place; and beseeching this favor earnestly of the Lord, it was vouchsafed me to appear once again on earth, in the good old cause of his Saints. . . . With this night, thy power is ended—tomorrow, the prison!—back, lest I foretell the scaffold!" (*TTT* 20). According to the Gray Champion, someone's cry— a story event—gave rise to his (the Gray Champion's) appearance—another story event—that in turn caused the crowd to attack the Redcoats and force Andros to withdraw. Even before the champion's speech, the forward-moving chain of causality is clear. A plea to God made the almighty send the Gray Champion as defender of the Puritans. Later, seemingly as a result of their victory, the Puritans confirm what the Gray Champion has foretold: the Catholic James II has been deposed and the Protestant William is on the throne. Despite the Puritans' heinous actions against the Indians, actions that the narrator notes in an aside and that Choate wanted erased from the historical record, the tale celebrates a proto-American challenge of British hubris, pushing the American beginning back nearly a century before the American Revolution.[33] The tale answers Choate's call to celebrate Puritans as *the* origin. Such is the once-told version of this twice-told tale.

The second telling of the tale—both equally valid and fully in conflict with the first—aligns with the Calvinist dogma that extirpates free will and views narrative retrospectively. Taken to its extreme, this doctrine disallows the caller's plea from having any causal effect. The Gray Champion has always already been ordained to come, and the result of his visit is likewise already foretold—a word the Champion himself uses to highlight the power of the story's end. In line with Calvinist theology, the narrator's final dictum reverberates back through the story and eliminates human causality: "But should domestic tyranny oppress us, or invader's step pollute our soil, still may the Gray Champion come; for he is the type of New England's hereditary spirit: and his shadowy march, on the eve of danger, must ever be the pledge, that New England's sons will vindicate their ancestry" (*TTT* 22). In other words, the Gray Champion came because the

New England (Puritan) narrative so dictates. Despite the slightly equivocal "may . . . come," Hawthorne's sentence indicates necessity: the champion's march "must ever be the pledge" of a Puritan social order. Moreover, though the idea of sons evokes the most pointed example of human chronology—that of succeeding generations so well demonstrated by the lengthy genealogy of 1 Chronicles—the text inverts the timeline by highlighting the power of the ancestors, forefathers who will be vindicated in the future and who are American in their opposition to British control. The authority of the fathers and of God the Father over Puritan progeny means that sons and their actions are constrained and, of course, predestined. The end determines the beginning, a fact heightened by the tale's brevity, which places closing in proximity to opening. The causality and temporality inherent in chronology are superseded by the temporality of predestination and reckoning, which in its backward movement recalls the Puritan jeremiads that posit not progress but decline and thus privilege the past as destination rather than origin. Like a Calvinist's grace or damnation, this narrative logic is exposed at the tale's end, and it effectively retells the story, making it twice told. Indeed, in the penultimate paragraph, as the narrator recalls other appearances by the great defender, he sometimes positions the champion's coming as prior to the terrible situation he arrives to defuse: "Five years later, in the twilight of an April morning, he stood on the green, beside the meeting house, at Lexington, where now the obelisk of granite, with a slab of slate inlaid, commemorates the first fallen of the Revolution" (*TTT* 22). Even as the Battles of Concord and Lexington temporally start before the champion's arrival, narratively and syntactically—that is, according to the structure of Hawthorne's sentence—the battles occur after the champion's appearance. Through synecdoche, this moment showcases how the story's two logics remain in tension. Challenging the progression inherent in human chronology, the tale reveals the champion's already determined arrival and apologia, but the story is also told so that each event begets a subsequent happening. Though the tale, then, is superficially about the political hierarchy of the New England Puritans and the political loyalties of the tale teller as twentieth-century critics like G. R. Thompson and Frederick Crews suggested, "The Gray Champion" explores the central contradiction within Puritanism—the issue of predestination and free will—and how that paradox articulates the difficulties in crafting Puritan tales from a nineteenth-century position.[34] "The Gray Champion" portrays prerevolutionary America in its chronicle, but the tale relies on postrevolutionary patriotic sentiment for its reckoning. Hawthorne represents the Gray Champion as American because he knows that the champion's descendants, including Hawthorne himself, will be so. As Peter Brooks has pointed out, the "anticipation of retrospection" becomes "our chief tool in making sense of narrative." We read both "in a spirit of confidence, and also a state of dependence" because of the knowledge that there are "forgone eternal narrative ends" that will shift the story's meaning when we arrive at them.[35]

The historical truth behind "The Gray Champion" also displays tension between the chronicle and the reckoning. Enraged by Sir Edmund Andros's policies (especially his steep taxes and his enforcement of the Navigation Act), Bostonians, likely led by Cotton Mather, staged the Rebellion of 1689. News had come to the colonists that the Protestant William of Orange had been warmly received by the nobility in England, and many suspected and hoped there would be a coup d'état against the Catholic James II. (The Gray Champion foretells this in Hawthorne's tale.) As such, the colonists wanted to declare their loyalty to William (and against James's governor, Andros) and get their commonwealth charter reinstated. To avoid possible legal recourse, however, the uprising, which leaders planned on an almost hourly timetable, was constructed to look spontaneous and draw spontaneous support.[36] In other words, for the rebellion leaders, the constructed (and retroactive) perception of the uprising came before the seemingly instantaneously sparked protest, even as many did truly participate because they were inspired in the moment. Hence, the rebellion was both a product of chronicling—the oppression of a people giving way to a cathartic and extemporaneous demanding of their rights—and a product of reckoning. Like preparationism, the historical truth behind "The Gray Champion" explores how Puritans could and could not impact their world: Did the street mob have the free will to begin an insurrection, or did the Puritan leaders preordain the happenings of the rebellion? The answer is significant, for it indicates the extent to which these Puritans and the Gray Champion can be proto-American. In the end, if these colonists were chained in a predetermined world, they cannot serve as the type of American independence so desirable in the culture of beginnings.

In opening his collection with "The Gray Champion," Hawthorne offers a generally patriotic account of American resistance to English rule, a message that was resonant enough that Hawthorne's publisher proposed "The Gray Champion, and Other Tales" as the collection's title.[37] Moreover, likely due to its celebration of American beginnings, the story remained first throughout all American editions of *Twice-Told Tales* in a sequence seemingly chosen by Hawthorne. (More on the British editions later.) Because Hawthorne had previously published either anonymously or under such authorial phrases as "the author of 'The Gentle Boy,'" Hawthorne's name had not been connected to any of his fiction before *Twice-Told Tales* (save an 1836 puff by Park Benjamin).[38] "The Gray Champion" can therefore be considered a purposeful and staged literary beginning, one approved by Hawthorne as the piece to herald his authorship to nineteenth-century readers. Hawthorne resented the legacy of Puritanism, but *Twice-Told Tales*, with his name centered in bold capital letters on the title page, advanced his reputation, career, and, critics like Poe and Melville would later argue, American literature itself.

Discomfort with the Historical Reckoning

Belief in Puritans as representative of American origins started in the 1760s, strengthened after the American Revolution, and was solidified by nineteenth-century histories—a cultural trend that deeply influenced what printers would print and what they could sell.[39] And yet Hawthorne's contemporaries knew of the atrocities committed by the Puritans. Ashamed of his ancestor's actions during the Salem witch trials, Hawthorne himself had added a *w* to his surname to create distance from his family's past, and in transcendental and liberal Boston, the Puritans were widely seen as intolerant ideologues whose excesses resulted in the deaths of "witches," Quakers, Pequots, and others. The idea that Puritans were *puritanical* had currency even before the religious liberalism of the nineteenth century. According to the *Oxford English Dictionary,* the word is in use as early as 1598 and with an unmistakably negative implication by at least 1793. To deal with what Michael Davitt Bell has called this "double view" of Puritans—that they were both laudable and abhorrent—authors often wrote historical fiction that pivoted on a contest between a kind proto-nineteenth-century Puritan and a single bigoted reprehensible Puritan.[40] The presence of the Puritan villain allowed authors to condemn the extremes of Calvinist dogma while maintaining the Puritans as the genesis of the democratic United States. Within

"The Gentle Boy," Hawthorne both employs and destroys this double view. On the one hand, even while he declares that "an indelible stain of blood is upon the hands of all who consented" to the fining, banishing, and hanging of Quakers, the narrator presents one sympathetic and generous Puritan (*TTT* 99). On the other hand, this same character is Quaker by story's end, suggesting that tolerance and Puritanism are antithetical. If the American nation-state requires liberty, Hawthorne's tale says, the Puritans certainly did not found the United States. In other words, even as "The Gray Champion" strikes a patriotic note to open *Twice-Told Tales*, Hawthorne's writing—as any reader of nineteenth-century literature knows—offers conflicted stories about America's Founding Fathers.

"The Gentle Boy" begins with a damning list of Puritan crimes against the Quakers before turning to a sentimental story that vilifies Puritan society. The young Quaker Ilbrahim, whose father has been hanged and mother banished, is adopted by the childless Puritan couple Tobias and Dorothy Pearson. Before the tale jumps years forward in time, Ilbrahim meets with terrible prejudice and even violence from the Puritan townsfolk. In particular, after Ilbrahim befriends a Puritan child in need, that boy orchestrates a group beating of his friend. As a result, Ilbrahim's adopted father, Tobias Pearson, the extremely tolerant Puritan, converts to Quakerism. The end of the tale features a Quaker gathering of the Pearsons and Catharine, Ilbrahim's biological mother, at Ilbrahim's deathbed. The causality inherent in the story is fairly straightforward. Had Ilbrahim's father not been Quaker, the Puritans would not have hanged him. If the Puritans had not so condemned Ilbrahim's father, the boy would not have been weeping in the cold at his father's grave, thus moving Tobias to pity. And most importantly, had Tobias not taken in Ilbrahim, Ilbrahim's spirit—once again willing to trust Puritans because of his adoption—would not have been broken when his peers beat him, Ilbrahim would not have died, and Tobias would not have converted to Quakerism.

The retrospective reading of the text, however, challenges this paradigm of event giving way to event by showing that Tobias is always already Quaker. With the legalized persecution of Quakers and the distaste for such "fanatics" within the Massachusetts Bay Colony, the story implies that only a Puritan who had deep empathy with the sect would ever adopt a Quaker boy (*TTT* 129). More importantly, the tale goes out of its way to mark Tobias as Quaker-like from the start. As Tobias himself declares, "From

my youth upward I have been a man marked out for wrath" (*TTT* 135).
The retributory punishment he has received, the wrath, is something reserved for Quakers within the story's logic. Quaker Catharine loses her
Quaker husband because of his hanging and her Quaker son because of
her banishment. After Ilbrahim helps nurse a Puritan boy back to health,
it is that boy who eggs the other children into beating the young Quaker
and, in the largest betrayal, strikes Ilbrahim on the mouth with his staff.
Finally, Catharine and the openly Quaker Tobias both suffer imprisonment,
beatings, and fines at the hands of the intolerant Puritans. Associating such
pain with Quakers, not Puritans, the tale shows how Tobias's early experience is also marked by Quaker-like punishment: Tobias and Dorothy lose
multiple children before the start of the story. Accusing them of ungodly
worldly preoccupation and corresponding godly retribution, their neighbors, "more bigoted Puritans," shun and harass them because of the deaths
of their children and their subsequent adoption of Ilbrahim (*TTT* 108).
These occurrences—and the death of the gentle boy—are the reckoning for
which Tobias declares he has always been ordained. In this way, Tobias is
Quaker before his conversion, even before his adoption of Ilbrahim. His
conversion is not causal, for his Quakerism is an ending revelation of a
prior condition, a reality that undercuts the Puritan position as the font and
creators of a tradition of American liberty. There is no freedom to choose a
new religion or government if all runs according to a godly script.

"The Gentle Boy" was the only story that Hawthorne substantively
revised between its first appearance in a periodical and its inclusion in
Twice-Told Tales.[41] Most of these alterations were actually deletions which,
in Seymour Gross's words, "clarified the terms of his tragedy," and kept the
Puritan and Quaker forces better in balance.[42] To that end, Hawthorne ex-
cised a lengthy initial explanation of Puritan actions. After declaring that
these Puritans "responsible for innocent blood" in the literary-annual version, he expressed that religious conformity was necessary to the survival
of their government and colony "especially at a period when the state of
affairs in England has stopped the tide of emigration, and drawn back many
of the pilgrims to their native homes."[43] While not a defense, the paragraph
was a sympathetic explanation of Puritan actions built out of Hawthorne's
understanding of the seventeenth century. So too Hawthorne deleted the
final words of the tale as it had appeared in the *Token*: he did not close with
a "kindlier feeling for the fathers of my native land."[44] Rather, in *Twice-Told*

Tales, he ended with "Ilbrahim's green and sunken grave" (*TTT* 145). These changes lessen the reckoning of Puritans as protodemocrats, forcing the *Twice-Told Tales* reader to ponder the truthfulness of how Puritans are figured in the culture of beginnings.

Hawthorne, who enjoyed reading primary sources and histories alike, was considering just that.[45] He felt conflicted by the cherry-picking that ennobled forefathers when historical sources illustrated Puritans as short-sighted killjoys. But Hawthorne also needed income from his writing and had to make his tales attractive to, first, the editors and readers of the magazines and periodicals where he published his tales and then, second, to buyers of *Twice-Told Tales.* Like his Puritan ancestors, Hawthorne was caught between the chronicle and the reckoning, but unlike his forefathers, Hawthorne's conundrum was born from knowing both what the public wanted and what the historical sources said. His were the problems of an author in a moment with a particularly opportunistic relationship to history. Hawthorne coded his preoccupation into his tales in part by means of historical footnotes. In "The Minister's Black Veil," the narrator uses such a footnote to tell the reader that Reverend Hooper was inspired by "Mr. Joseph Moody, of York, Maine" who wore a veil because "he had accidentally killed a beloved friend" (*TTT* 53). This historical antecedent offers an easy and attractive causal explanation for Hooper's own inexplicable black crepe veil. Hooper is based on Moody, and Hooper wears a veil. Moody killed a friend, and Moody donned the veil. That Hooper committed murder is thus a tempting assumption even though Hawthorne insists that Moody's veil has "a different import" from Hooper's (*TTT* 53). Indeed, certain identification of that different import remains tantalizingly impossible throughout the tale, unnerving both congregants and readers. Though the facial shroud makes Moody a more effective preacher—we assume because he illustrates that secret sins have (terrible) results—his congregation and even his fiancée shun him when he refuses both to remove the veil and to give adequate explanation. Working to maintain the veil's inscrutability as "a type and a symbol," Reverend Hooper emphasizes the importance of not knowing the veil's significance (*TTT* 65). As he makes clear on his deathbed, the "mortal veil" symbolizes the epistemological limits of a Calvinist reckoning in which all live with an unreadable symbol of their election or damnation (*TTT* 66). But the townsfolk are not mollified. They speculate about an awful crime—a sexual one thought Edgar Allan Poe—and refuse to accept that causality is impotent or that meaning is revealed only after death.[46] So, too, we readers look for connections between actions and a final explanation of the story events as we move from paragraph to paragraph and page to page. Much as we are tempted to do, congregants think that Reverend Hooper must have done something to cause the veil's appearance—his actions must have chronological explanation. While the confounding of a reason for the veil makes the tale unsettling, our insistence on looking for one makes our search compelling in human and narrative terms. Stymied in the end, we reckon, we re-collect the tale, making it function as a metaphor for the problems of interpretation. The desire to understand Hooper's veil is emblematic of the impetus behind the culture of beginnings wherein readers and authors alike searched the past for comfortable explanations of the present.

Narratives Wrought Themselves Almost Simultaneously into Tales

While Hawthorne clearly saw more nuance in the historical record than simplified praise of proto-American Puritans allowed, his tales, including "The May-Pole of Merry Mount," demonstrate an appreciation and even awe for the master narratives under which authors struggle. Hawthorne's retelling of the Fall takes place in present-day Quincy, Massachusetts, where, much to the dismay of the Puritans, especially those in nearby Plymouth, Thomas Morton, the so-called Lord of Misrule, leads a band of merry followers in the settlement of Mount Wollaston. The historical William Bradford, governor of the Plymouth colony, complained of the "drunkenness, riot and other evils" of Merry Mount, the sobriquet given to Mount Wollaston by the revelers.[47] Tensions escalated until the Puritans arrested and banished Morton to England—twice. Persistent to the end, Morton died in a Maine prison after returning and incurring the Puritans' wrath. The most notable story about Merry Mount concerns a May Day maypole under which, in Hawthorne's tale, Edgar and Edith, the Lord and Lady of the May, are to be married. In contrast to the happy couple, the Puritans lurk gloomily in the forest, exuding disapproval until they finally intervene and disperse the dancers. John Endicott, leader of the Massachusetts Bay Colony, singles out the cleric for upbraiding, chops down the maypole, and orders a whipping of the revelers. As the narrator says, "The Puritans had played a characteristic part in the May-Pole mummeries"—they disrupt and end them (*TTT* 88).[48] Edith and Edgar, however, are so pure and lovely that John Endicott spares them from the birch switch, pronounces the end of their Merry Mount life, and marches the young couple away to the Puritan settlement and thus to "America." This causal and chronological plot, based on human agency, is the once-told version of the tale.[49]

The tale's teleology toward the determined end of Eden forms its second telling. Before they are married, Edgar catches a pensive look on Edith's face and chides that "nothing of futurity will be brighter than the mere remembrance of what is now passing" (*TTT* 82). Sensing a Calvinist truth, Edith replies that such ephemerality is precisely her worry. As John Calvin preached, Adam and Eve were predetermined to fall—paradise was never real insofar as it was a temporary state that humans were always already ordained to lose. Though responsible for their actions, Adam and Eve were destined to choose sin. In some sense, then, the Fall precedes any bite of the apple, and the Puritan world is necessarily postlapsarian.[50] As such, Edith and Edgar's sense about their fate is allegorically Edenic and theologically Puritan. Their story is a twice-told Calvinist Genesis. And truly, Edgar and Edith end up in a fallen world, for they are taken to Salem, the locale of the infamous witch trials presided over by Hawthorne's ancestor. The tale tells us that, for Puritans and for nineteenth-century Americans, the paradisal origin is as irrecoverable and false as it is attractive and necessary. As Hawthorne made even more explicit in *The House of the Seven Gables* (1851), the sins of the fathers shadow the lives of their descendants. In that vein, we might even say that established narratives force themselves onto stories. Puritans are either noble proto-American democrats (as in "The Gray Champion") or intolerant ideologues (as in "The Gentle Boy"). They are the first modern men who worshiped God directly, not through intermediaries from a corrupt priesthood, and they are the educated resisters of the British Crown. Or, misguided by their religious zeal, they are superstitious perpetrators of murder and witch hunting. In some sense, these conceptions of Calvinists have already written all Puritan tales. As the narrator says in a prefatory note to "The May-Pole of Merry Mount," one that critics have largely ignored, "In the slight sketch here attempted, the facts, recorded on the grave pages of our New England annalists, have wrought themselves, almost spontaneously, into a sort of allegory" (*TTT* 77). The nineteenth-century narrator loses full control of beginning stories because the story's moral is predetermined. And yet, of course, the author has selected which story to tell and how to tell it. Indeed, as Neil Frank Doubleday notes, Hawthorne takes some liberties with historical sources.[51] For example, Hawthorne places Reverend William Blackstone in Merry Mount though the actual historical figure had nothing to do with the location. Still, Hawthorne feels the need to add an apologetic footnote to Blackstone's appearance because history compromises his narrative control: "The Rev. Mr. Blackstone, though an eccentric, is not known to have been an immoral man. We rather doubt his identity with the priest of Merry Mount" (*TTT* 89). Working with an already extant chronicle and a predetermined reckoning is the tension of historical fiction—especially at a time when politicians and writers were actively trying to form the past into a typological narrative of American republicanism. Authors who wanted artistic control and strong sales had to make careful calculations about using historical chronicles while meeting readerly expectations. However one looks at this temporal paradox, the issue is really one of free will. How much could an author alter the historical record and still have his story received as an authentic account of American beginnings? How much could he challenge common wisdom about events and people and have his tale sell? How much could he resist the master narratives that form the facts "almost spontaneously, into a sort of allegory"?

Hawthorne caustically recognizes the limits on what he could write in *Grandfather's Chair: A History for Youth* (1841), which, though it appeared later, he drafted for money while waiting for *Twice-Told Tales* to be published. By and large, the text reifies the Puritans as the founders, going so far as to compare them to "the granite rocks on which New England is founded."[52] And yet here too Hawthorne knowingly exposes the boundaries of acceptable history. After Grandfather, who is a clear stand-in for Hawthorne, has mentioned the colonization of Canada and all the New England states, and when he "might have gone on to speak of Maryland and Virginia," he realizes that one of his little listeners is "growing impatient" and "suspend[s] the history of his chair."[53] Neither Maryland nor Virginia ever returns because Hawthorne's Boston-based publishers and readers desired a story of American beginnings that starts with the Pilgrims, "the best men and women of their day," and ends with the Revolutionary Age.[54] Nineteenth-century Americans wanted to hear about the heroic locally inflected actions of their American forefathers so they could imagine themselves as part of an American people. As a result, history served to affirm self and nation and to stifle literary creativity and inventiveness. Hawthorne, like Grandfather, whose listeners would only sit for certain stories about American beginnings, felt this acutely.

Prophetic Pictures

The last of Hawthorne's twice-told history tales has nothing to do with the Puritans. Nonetheless, perhaps more than any other tale, "The Prophetic Pictures" explicitly considers the struggles of narrative and actor to escape the temporal paradox of chronicle and reckoning that energized both the culture of beginning and *Twice-Told Tales*. Based on "an anecdote of Stuart, related in Dunlap's History of the Arts of Design," "The Prophetic Pictures" concerns a young Boston couple, Walter and Elinor, who shortly before wedlock commission a talented European portrait painter to capture their likenesses (*TTT* 237). The single portraits produced by the painter are technically magnificent but somewhat disturbing since Elinor's expression appears rather horrified and Walter's expression appears rather insane. The painter claims to have painted what he saw, and no one can deny the verisimilitude. Still, the paintings become more and more frightening to the couple, who eventually hide the works behind a curtain. Years later, when the painter returns to the colonies, he asks permission to view these, his most skilled works. Startled by the visit, Elinor and Walter draw back the portraits' curtain. At that moment Walter shouts, "Our fate is upon us!" and seizes a knife to kill Elinor (*TTT* 257). Though the painter prevents the murder, Elinor's and Walter's expressions finally perfectly match their painted depictions. These portraits, then, are the prophetic pictures. The title also refers, however, to the sketch that the painter has shown Elinor while he is painting the original portraits, a sketch of Walter's trying to kill her.

The two common interpretations of the tale underline the two temporalities that I have been tracing.[55] In the first reading, the chronicling one, the artist's actions have caused Walter to attempt murder just as the artist's interposition saves Elinor's life when Walter does lunge. When the artist shows Elinor a picture of a murdering Walter, she, startled, turns to realize that "Walter had advanced near enough to have seen the sketch." Elinor cannot "determine whether it had caught his eye," but Walter may well have seen the sketch and been inspired to commit murder (*TTT* 250). The tale is marked by forward-moving time and seemingly free choices: Elinor still marries Walter after the warning, and Walter chooses (perhaps because of the painting's inspiration) to kill. The other customary reading of the tale suggests that the tale's teleology toward attempted murder fashions the course of Elinor's and Walter's lives. As the painter asks Elinor in reference to the portraits, "I might change the action of these figures too. But would it influence the event?" (*TTT* 249–50). The question implies that the event has already been fixed—its future occurrence reverberates backward onto the scene. Correspondingly, at the tale's finale, "A strange thought darted into his [the painter's] mind. Was not his own the form in which that Destiny had embodied itself, and he a chief agent of the coming evil which he had foreshadowed?" (*TTT* 257). If so, the painter is enacting a preordained narrative.[56] The narrator sums up the tale's double logic in the final sentence: "Could the result of one, or all our deeds, be shadowed forth and set before us—some would call it Fate, and hurry onward—others be swept along by their passionate desires—and none be turned aside by the Prophetic Pictures" (*TTT* 258). Here the narrator endorses fate, that which determines the end before the beginning, as a possibility, even a reality. Yet his question about passionate desires indicates some presence of free will, some forward-moving sequence of events. It is an articulation of the same paradox at the heart of Puritanism: free will both is and is not connected to and determined by predestination. At the end of the tale, then, the narrator leaves both temporal logics in play. Either despite the (possible) existence of fate, people act with full agency or fate has decreed that all will ignore the prophetic pictures and humans cannot gainsay the predestined. Within a story world, the chronicling mode allows characters control over narrating their own lives—writing diaries, making choices, and ignoring prophecies. Yet the reckoning, which snatches away control from these characters as it did from Puritans necessarily converts the chronicle into a meaningful account by retroactively making connections, finding themes, and giving judgment. Notwithstanding the seeming paradox, the universe is both providential and nonprovidential, and this tale pivots on keeping in tension both human causality and godly destiny and disallowing either from being a full explanation for the story's events.

Even with a final sentence that can be read to endorse both temporalities, however, the painter's position within the dilemma that I have been outlining is a bit uncomfortable. The painter has, at the very end, "the same sense of power to regulate their [Elinor and Walter's] destiny, as to alter a scene upon the canvas. He stood like a magician controlling the phantoms which he had evoked." Moreover, as the painter stops the murder, Walter asks: "Does Fate impede its own decree?" (*TTT* 257). In these instances, the painter becomes more than a human figure within the narrative. His godlike capabilities align him with the author and illustrate anxiety over narrative control. Does he, like the Puritan creator, constrain human actions? Or do Walter and Elinor, like Puritans after preparationism, have the ability to effect their own ending? That both these possibilities are equally plausible within "The Prophetic Pictures" not only attests to Hawthorne's famed ambiguity but also, I would argue, expresses the conundrum at the heart of an ascendant culture of beginnings, a culture that subsists on the production of new stories that retell familiar themes. As the critical tendency to read this painter as a figure of Hawthorne specifically and of an artist generally displays, the tale functions allegorically. It underlines the apprehension and the responsibility of fashioning narrative, especially in the culture of beginnings, wherein authors must determine a dénouement or a moral as well as make their characters volitional. To some extent, the narrator/author positions himself as a Calvinist. The end (theme, historical outcome, salvation, damnation, and so forth) comes before the tales even begin, and the narrator/author is subject to that prior decree. As Poe writes in his review of Hawthorne's *Twice-Told Tales,* a wise literary artist "has not fashioned his thoughts to accommodate his incidents; but having conceived, with deliberate care, a certain unique or single effect to be wrought out, he then invents such incidents—he then combines such events as may best aid him in establishing this preconceived effect."[57] This "effect" dictates the story. It is telling that Poe sets forth his theory of tale writing—working backward as well as forward—in a review of Hawthorne's collection, for Hawthorne's stories foreground the related temporal paradox of the chronicle and reckoning.

Though Hawthorne's Puritan tales illustrate an extreme case, the dualities (the chronicle / the reckoning and free will / predestination) that I have been tracing exist in some way within many narratives. Whereas authors, like gods, determine the ends of their stories and the actions of their characters, story actors must seem to have free will and volition—they must appear to cause results within the story world—for the narrative to have power. The reader needs to accept the happenings of the story world even as she knows that the god/author has put his or her characters within a universe whose predetermination is revealed at narrative end. These dualities, then, also illustrate the illusion of mimesis inherent in realist narrative: characters seem to act autonomously when they are actually a part of authorial design. Even the selection of characters is both volitional (the character acts interestingly and thus offers herself as a subject) and predestined (the author makes the character worth following). Just so, George Eliot's famous query, "But why always Dorothea?" both challenges Dorothea's status as an object of interest and seems to recognize an inevitability (or predetermination) of that status.[58] These difficulties with mimesis are perhaps most acute in historical fiction, where the author has to worry about readerly preconceptions of characters and events. The challenge lies in being true to the historical account while still assuring that the figures and events within the tale serve the author's purpose. When, as was the case for Hawthorne, the historical record partially conflicts with contemporary acceptance of that chronicle, claiming the past becomes even more fraught. Hawthorne's depiction of John Hancock within the last piece of "The Legends of the Province-House," a series of revolutionary tales that begins the second volume of *Twice-Told Tales* (1842), ironically dramatizes the imposition of contemporary ideas into historic situations. Hancock exclaims to his fellow Bostonians: "We are no longer children of the Past!"[59] The narrator wants to underline the way in which Americans "represent a new race of men, living no longer in the past, scarcely in the present—but projecting [their] lives forward into the future."[60] Nonetheless, Hawthorne is deeply invested in Hancock because he is a historical figure and because, reading backward from the nineteenth century, authors can say that Hancock's actions foretell everything that is to come. Hancock may declare that he is a man of the future, but it is our retrospection, our reckoning of our fledgling democracy and its founders, that makes him historically significant. Without Hawthorne and others willing to narrate Hancock's life, Hancock *is* a child of the past.

While all narrative displays the tension between the chronicle and the reckoning, tales do so particularly well. With their capacious nature, novels can better emphasize seemingly indefinite chronicles. Some like *Robinson Crusoe* even painfully track the passage of days and years. Traditionally written novels pivot on temporal linearity, providing a marked narrative procession through a beginning, middle, and end. (That *David Copperfield* begins with David's birth takes the idea of beginning at the beginning to its logical extreme; the text finishes with David's hope that his wife Agnes will be by his side at his death—death being the most logical ending point of any life narrative.) With its truncated nature, however, short fiction undermines any prolonged process of beginning, middle, and end. As a result, the reckoning is not long deferred. And its immediacy makes it feel even more in contest with the chronicle. The tale's commitment to brevity and the reader's experience of that shortness (according to Poe, one reads a tale in a single sitting) forces a distillation of chronology and retrospection unique to short fiction.

Particularly American: The Reception and Reprinting of *Twice-Told Tales*

When collected into a volume like *Twice-Told Tales*, individual stories have both their own internal chronicle and reckoning—the sequential events and ultimate judgment of that tale—and a larger interstory layer of relationships wherein, for example, "The Gray Champion" establishes concerns and issues that resonate through the volume. Above these two layers, though still very much related to these individual tales, *Twice-Told Tales* has experienced a series of judgements, of reckonings, as a volume, both in the form of reviews and in the form of reprintings. In some sense, like a Puritan's discovery of salvation after death, a nineteenth-century author only found out if his writing was elect after its publication, wherein English reprintings become a volume's transatlantic afterlife. (The long-standing metaphor of book to body—both have heads, feet, and spines—makes the comparison even more plausible.) And praising reviews were the preacher's encouraging words that one was on the righteous path. For Hawthorne, both those reviews and the reprintings suggested that his history tales felt quintessentially—even, for the British, worryingly—American. Certainly, nineteenth-century critics and readers on both sides of the Atlantic praised the sketches in *Twice-Told Tales*—pieces that I have not here discussed—for their repose and style, and Hawthorne included them purposefully in his collection. In the same review in which he laid out his theory of the tale, Poe wrote of the sketches, "They are each and all beautiful, without being characterized by the polish and adaptation so visible in the tales proper."[61] The beauty of the sketches lies in their style and their

stasis; as one reviewer admiringly said in 1838, they "give us merely a transcript of the author's own musings, with barely a thread of incident to bind
them together."[62] In the sense that the reader looks back on the beginning
of the sketch after she has gotten to the end and in the sense that the author has an intention for the sketch's ending before he has reached it, these
pieces do mobilize the chronicle and the reckoning. They do so, however,
in a perfunctory manner. Hawthorne's meditations on temporality, made
amid the nineteenth-century calls for a national literature and codifications
of national history, are left to his tales and are particularly pointed in his
history tales. Hence, while impressed by the "soft and musical flow of language" in the sketches, Longfellow commended the tales for being "national
in their character." He continued, "The author has wisely chosen his themes
among the traditions of New England; the dusty legends of 'the good Old
Colony times, when we lived under a king.' This is the right material for
story. It seems as natural to make tales out of old tumbledown traditions, as
canes and stuff-boxes out of old steeples, or trees planted by great men."[63]
According to Longfellow, making American (pre)history part of the present is both narratively and politically praiseworthy; it is also materially
functional, like a cane or snuffbox. Elizabeth Peabody, before becoming
Hawthorne's sister-in-law, similarly singled out the patriotic work of the
history tales, writing of the Puritan stories: "When we first read them, we
wanted to say to the author, 'This is your work:—with the spirit of the past,
chrystallized thus, to gem the hills and plains of your native land; especially
let every scene of that great adventure which settled and finally made free
our country, become a symbol of the spirit which is too fast fading." For
Peabody, Hawthorne's Puritans are clearly typological: their actions foretell the struggles of the American Revolution and serve as an example to
nineteenth-century citizens. Thus, even as she feels "that we cannot spare
him from" sketch writing, Peabody recommends Hawthorne "frequently
to walk" in the "patriotic" path of historical tale writing.[64] In short, while
sketches greatly appealed to American readers, Hawthorne's reviewers saw
the history tales doing temporal and cultural work that the sketches could
not achieve.

Two pirated British versions of *Twice-Told Tales,* which exclude most or
all of the history tales, further suggest something felt particularly American
about the Puritan subject matter and Hawthorne's temporal considerations.
In 1850, William Tegg, a second-generation London bookseller, published

his version of Hawthorne's *Twice Told Tales*. Although the volume retains Hawthorne's title, the contents make clear that the collection is hugely different.[65] In fact, of four Puritan tales in Hawthorne's original volume ("The Gray Champion," "The Gentle Boy," "The May-Pole of Merry Mount," and "The Minister's Black Veil"), not a single one appears in this British reprinting. Nor does Tegg's publication include "Endicott and the Red Cross," a Puritan tale from the second volume of *Twice-Told Tales*. Instead, like *Little Annie's Ramble: And Other Tales*, a version of *Twice-Told Tales* put out in 1853 by Milner and Sowerby, a regional publisher based in Halifax, England, these two collections submerge the stories of American beginnings in favor of picturesque sketches. Rather than the patriotic march of the Gray Champion, these two volumes start with calm walks, along the beach in Tegg's *Twice Told Tales* and through town with a neighborhood girl in Milner and Sowerby's *Little Annie's Ramble*. The collections then proceed apace with various pieces on different topics in a rhythm more like Irving's *Sketch Book* than Hawthorne's *Twice-Told Tales*. Eschewing the disruptive chronology of predestination, *Little Annie's Ramble* offers a broadly chronological arc, from the spritely village girl to a sketch about a gravestone carver.[66] (It is within this vector from childhood to death that Milner and Sowerby place the only two Puritan narratives of their collection: "The Gentle Boy," a tale of young Ilbrahim's early death, fits nicely within the first half of the volume, and "Endicott and the Red Cross," a marker of times long gone and dead, is penultimate.) More than their refutation of the reckoning and its backward temporality, both these British reprintings shift the focus from Hawthorne's American tales to his less historically and geographically specific sketches. Indeed, while the 1842 two-volume version of *Twice-Told Tales* published in Boston contained thirty-nine pieces of which twelve were sketches, Tegg includes eleven sketches of a total twenty-five pieces, and Milner and Sowerby offer six sketches in a volume of fourteen pieces—barely more than half of the two collections that purport to be "tales" in their titles are actually tales. Such shift toward the sketch radically rewrites the original *Twice-Told Tales*'s keen interest in tales about American beginnings and thereby suggest that such tales were too "national" in form and content to appeal to British readers.

Hawthorne did not, like Irving, mark the sketch as British and the tale as American in *Twice-Told Tales*. Yet I am arguing that his tales (especially his Puritan ones) suggest a link between that genre and the United States in theme, in temporal complexity, and in reception. Dramatizing the chronological knot of US prehistory, tales were particularly nationally useful. In seeking to define what was "American," they formed part and parcel of the ongoing project to (re)construct a social community around stories of the US past. Hawthorne's later writing underlines this connection. When Hawthorne became consul in Liverpool, England, in 1853, he wrote multiple drafts of three different English romances, but, incapable of bringing conclusion and coherence to his projects, he abandoned each one. Instead, in September of 1863, Hawthorne published *Our Old Home: A Series of English Sketches* simultaneously in England and the United States. In the preface to the volume, he attributed his inability to write fiction, to write tales, to "The Present, the Immediate, the Actual" that had "proved too potent." Hawthorne continued, reality "takes away not only my scanty faculty, but even my desire to imaginative composition, and leaves me sadly content to scatter a thousand peaceful fantasies upon the hurricane that is sweeping us all along with it, possibly, into a Limbo where our nation and its polity may be as literally the fragments of a shattered dream as my unwritten Romance."[67] The fracturing of the United States in the run-up to the Civil War dissolved Hawthorne's fictional abilities—his English romances, the literary attempts of his later years, remained unfinishable and unfinished—and left him only able to publish political essays and biographical sketches. In this way, at the end of his life, Hawthorne indicated that tales, and fictional stories more broadly, were tied to the projection of a coherent white American people. (Whiteness was critical to Hawthorne's own projection of the United States. He supported the Democrat Franklin Pierce, had little sympathy for enslaved African Americans, and thought that the southern states should be allowed to form a separate slave-owning country.) Once "the Present, the Immediate, the Actual" of the Civil War came, with its corresponding questions about the place of African Americans in the national body, the culture of beginnings was dead. But even a decade and a half earlier, the "thousand peaceful fantasies" of American beginnings, with their wishful projections of an all-white republic, became less and less plausible to both apologists and opponents of slavery.

This chapter has shown that Hawthorne, the author most closely associated with fiction about Puritans, offered not just ambiguous portraits of proto-Americans but also an articulation of the difficulties in writing to an early nineteenth-century readership deeply invested in beginning stories.

Ironically, although he theorized a resistance to advantageous historical reckonings, Hawthorne's work was incorporated into the culture of beginnings as exemplary, and Hawthorne himself has often been reduced to a writer of Puritan stories. In truth, after *The Scarlet Letter* (1850), Hawthorne centers no work of fiction on the Puritans, and the Puritan tales that ended up in collections following the original *Twice-Told Tales* were actually composed early: "Endicott and the Red Cross," the only Puritan tale in the second volume of *Twice-Told Tales* (1842), was first printed in 1838; "Young Goodman Brown," the only Puritan tale included in *Mosses from the Old Manse* (1846), was first printed in 1835.[68] Thinking about Hawthorne as solely a writer of Puritan tales, then, is reducing him to the beginning of his literary career.[69] The Puritan as origin offers as powerful and attractive a reckoning today as it did during the culture of beginnings.

5

Beginning Detection with Poe's Mary/Marie

Famous for his gothic tales and his penury, Edgar Allan Poe might seem a strange inclusion in a book about the culture of beginnings, the rise of American literary professionalism, and the construction of a white fictive ethnicity. But in his own way, Poe was very interested in American beginnings, US whiteness, and literary nationalism. And he actively engaged with the prominent literary figures in the culture of beginnings through reviews, submissions, letters, and friendships. Poe had been at West Point with one of Sarah Hale's sons and exchanged letters with her about *Godey's Lady's Book* and the *Opal*, a literary annual she edited. He publicly praised her in the *Southern Literary Messenger*, declaring in a review of *Traits of American Life*, the second collection of "Sketches of American Character," that "Mrs. Hale has already attained a high rank among the female writers of America, and bids fair to attain a far higher."[1] Poe may really have liked the volume, but he was also returning the favor, for in 1830, Hale had written that Poe "is evidently a fine genius."[2] So too Nathaniel Hawthorne and Poe held each other in mutual admiration. In a letter, Nathaniel Hawthorne recognized Poe's ability with tales and, less enthusiastically, his sharp critical pen: "I admire you rather as a writer of tales than as a critic upon them, I might often—and often do—dissent from your opinions in the latter capacity, but could never fail to recognize your force and originality in the former."[3] Even the doyen of short fiction, Washington Irving regarded Poe's stories highly. In a note that Poe later used as an advertisement, Irving reported, "I am much pleased with a tale called 'The House of Usher,' and should think that a collection of tales, equally well written, could not fail of being favorably received."[4] While Poe was not close to Catharine Sedgwick, he wrote reviews of her writing and managed to nab Sedgwick's signature—along with Irving's and Hale's—for his "Autography" series in the *Southern Literary Messenger*. Poe's personal and professional connections with these authors assured that he was aware of the beginning stories they penned and aware too that by the 1840s these stories were losing their luster. Immigration was remaking the urban core, land acquisition was shifting national borders, and race riots were threatening people and property. All these phenomena sparked debates about the composition of the country and fanned tensions over slavery. Grounded in the industrializing city centers of the 1840s, Poe's detective fiction shows how changing forces eroded the culture of beginnings as the explanatory narrative mode of American character and as a major vehicle for projecting a white American people.

Confused Beginnings

In Poe's well-known tale "The Murders in the Rue Morgue" (1841), the detective C. Auguste Dupin solves the case of a double murder that has been committed by an orangutan.[5] This story, the first of three detective tales featuring Dupin, is accepted as the origin of modern detective fiction, which plays curiously with narrative time. By repositioning the start of the story (the murderer killing a victim) to the end of the tale (the moment in which the detective reveals the criminal), the story moves forward only, paradoxically, to get closer to history. Each new clue brings the detective nearer to an exposé of the crime that took place before the detective assumed the case. The genre denies linear chronology and the primary position of beginnings because, for Poe, the origin is something we, like the detective, create to bring sense to our story. Poe's second whodunit does not quite follow this pattern, however. "The Mystery of Marie Rogêt" (1842–43) translates the true unsolved murder of New Yorker Mary Cecilia Rogers into the fictive and solvable murder of Parisian Marie Rogêt. For the full month of August as well as parts of September and October 1841, the New York press published almost daily updates, speculations, and remarks upon Mary Rogers, the "beautiful cigar girl" who was found floating in the Hudson River with marks of sexual violation upon her body. Had she been kidnapped and mistreated by a gang? Was one man responsible for the murder? Was the culprit someone she knew? Without leaving his home, Dupin answers these questions through the examination of affidavits and newspaper clippings, all of them excerpts from actual American journalistic coverage of Mary Rogers's death.[6] And yet, Poe, realizing he had identified the wrong culprit—a swarthy sailor—as Mary Roger's murderer before the final story installment was serialized, offers an ambiguous and problematic resolution to his story. In the *Omnibus of Crime,* Dorothy Sayers asserts that of the three Dupin stories, "The Mystery of Marie Rogêt" is "the most interesting of all to the connoisseur."[7] Sayers's own stature as a giant of detective fiction may be undisputed, but Poe's "Marie Rogêt" has had more than its fair share of detractors. Perhaps what Sayers noticed and what others dislike is exactly how the tale refuses any comfortable and singular beginning, both in its confusion of fact and fiction and in its abortive exposure of the criminal. In some sense, "Marie Rogêt" has no true beginning because it has no full revelation of the crime.

Although Poe's second whodunit does not have a satisfying conclusion, it too lends itself to the racial readings that recent critics have given "The Murders in the Rue Morgue." It makes sense that Poe, a displaced southerner who grew up near slaves and slaveholders, would be aware of growing white fears at the changing demographics of the United States. Millions would immigrate to the United States in the later nineteenth century, but some 743,000 foreigners came between 1819 and 1840 in the first massive wave of immigration. New York City welcomed more than 70 percent of those who entered the United States after 1816.[8] While some boarded trains and boats for the West, many, especially those too poor to pay for further travel, remained in the city. As a result, the population of New York City jumped from 156,056 in 1820 to 391,114 in 1840, and by 1860 was over 1 million.[9] Such a growing, complicated, and diverse urban space informed new theories of criminality that fed on ideas of racial difference, complicated the coherence of whiteness, and justified much antiblack violence. In 1838 and 1842, years when Poe was conceiving and writing Dupin stories in Philadelphia, massive race riots broke out in that city—the first in response to rumors that the Anti-Slavery Convention of American Women supported interracial sex ("amalgamation"), and the second when white onlookers decided an African American temperance parade was making unacceptable allusions to slave insurrections.[10] Also in 1838, Pennsylvania voters ratified a new constitution that withdrew the franchise from African

American men, giving it only to "white freedmen." The culpable parties in Poe's two whodunits betray the same racial anxiety that caused such events. They are travelers who bring foreign creatures (in "Murders in the Rue Morgue" there is a sailor with a pet from Borneo) and foreign skin tones (in "Marie Rogêt" there is a sailor who is described as "swarthy" and with a "dark complexion") to the city. Reflecting common racist notions that non-whites were other, dangerous, and immoral, Poe's detective fiction shows the difficulty of celebrating a single, uncomplicated American origin at the time when many whites, especially those of northern European Protestant descent, felt the demographic and geographic contours of the United States to be under threat.

Building on the criticism that sees Poe's "Murders" as racialized, I offer a reading of Poe's second detective tale and the second-ever whodunit, "The Mystery of Marie Rogêt." With their racial concerns and innovative narrative time, both Poe's whodunits respond to the culture of beginnings. Poe once ridiculed the critics who could not "discuss with discrimination the real claims of the few who were *first* in convincing the mother country that her sons were not all brainless, as at one period she half affected and wholly wished to believe." It annoyed Poe that "Mr. Cooper, for example, owes much, and Mr. Paulding nearly all, of his reputation as a novelist to his early occupation of the field."[11] In other words, Poe believed the American fixation on primacy and beginnings swayed critics into endorsing poor quality literature, and he thus thought that beginnings themselves, as they were identified in the literary world, were arbitrary and suspect. Poe's whodunits correspondingly display a perversity in displacing the murder to the end of the story where it is both of primary importance (it is the story's payoff) and of little consequence (since the story is set into action and takes place while the beginning remains a cipher). Yet, because these stories rely on a ratiocination borne of racial difference, Poe's cheeky genre falls apart with the second instantiation. I argue that "Marie Rogêt" fails the genre rules that Poe himself sets forward exactly because beginnings were becoming increasingly unstable, and Poe, despite his disdain for primacy, was invested in the racial logic that undergirded the culture of beginnings.

The Race of Guilt and Logic

Because I am tracing the development from "Murders in the Rue Morgue" to "Marie Rogêt," it only makes sense to start with Poe's first whodunit. When the French police are stumped by two grisly murders in a locked room, C. Auguste Dupin steps in and, after reading all the relevant police and newspaper reports, methodically investigates the premises. As it turns out, various passersby, having been attracted by screaming, have heard two figures speaking. Whereas all agree that one speaker is French, the other speaker's language is hard to pinpoint. The listeners, four of the five of whom are immigrants, believe the shrill voice to be Spanish, Italian, French, German, Russian, and English—each identifies the words as a language that he does not speak or understand. This confusion of tongues gives Dupin the first clue to the identity of the nonhuman murderer. It also points to the discomfort with nonnatives in Poe's story world and in 1840s America. Perceived as foreign, nonwhites in the United States routinely suffered hostility and disdain. In 1834, an anti-Catholic mob in Massachusetts burned down the Ursuline Convent close to where Poe was born. (Italian and Irish Catholics are not subsumed into the category of whiteness until the mid-twentieth century.) Similarly, a nativist riot occurred in Philadelphia just months before the appearance of Poe's "The Purloined Letter" (1844). And the 1830s generally saw a number of riots against abolitionists, both black and white, including New York's Farren Riots in July of 1834. These eruptions sought to control the definition of the American people by attacking those seen as non-American, those not featured in beginning stories. Through violence, the mobs communicated that nonwhite and non-Protestant people and customs were—like the language that the passersby hear in the Rue Morgue—unintelligible to Anglo-Saxons. Dupin thus speaks very much like an American when he fingers the murderer in "Murders" as necessarily nonwhite. Incomprehensible to "denizens of the five great divisions of Europe" and characterized by "harsh" and "unequal" sounds, the language heard by the witnesses in the Rue Morgue should, Dupin notes, logically be that "of an Asiatic—of an African."[12] Dupin is more than willing to agree that a nonwhite would commit such atrocities.[13] Only that the murderer enters the house by climbing a lightning rod and swinging on a shutter clears the phantom African and Asian suspects. The culprit's preternatural acrobatics, along with some corroborating hair, force Dupin to conclude that the criminal is an orangutan.

Yes, the murderer is neither African nor Asian, but he is racialized as nonwhite in myriad ways. The ape is regularly whipped by his master, and when his master departs, the orangutan is locked in the closet but escapes. Later, in trying to shave her with the razor that his master has used, the orangutan accidentally slits the throat of his victim. Enraged by the sight of blood and impetuous and irrational, the ape strangles the woman, who has swooned. He then shoves her body up the chimney and throws her mother's corpse out of the window. Later his master punishes "the brute" by selling him. But first Dupin plays the slave catcher, pretending to have located the "fugitive" orangutan for his owner and placing an ad in the local paper.[14] The sailor, coming to retrieve his valuable "property," happily offers Dupin a reward.[15] If this straightforward resemblance to keeping and pursuing enslaved African Americans is not enough, there are other excellent reasons to read the tale racially. When Dupin reveals to the narrator the nature of the murderer, he cites Frederic Cuvier as the authority on orangutan abilities, even including some of Cuvier's writing. In so doing, he imports into his tale a naturalist whose "scientific" racism was well known. Cuvier, whom Poe had translated, was associated with the cruel exhibition of Saarjte Bartmann (the "Hottentot Venus"), and his writings propagated the theory that blacks were a less evolutionarily developed race, one genetically close to apes.[16] Moreover, Borneo, the orangutan's home country, was a British colony long associated with primitivity. Indeed the Norwegian explorer Carl Alfred Bock traveled there in the 1870s to find the "missing link" between human and animal.[17] Given that Africans represented a genetic past for many Euro-Americans, we might even read the whodunit as a narrative attempt to combine "white" and "black" chronologies in which linear progress and teleological narrative is disrupted by an atavistic force. Euro-American forward movement, represented by the white women who retrieve their savings from the bank, is impeded when a racialized other murders them.

Other critics have pointed out how Dupin is personally invested in antebellum racial logics. Juxtaposing the ape's murderous impulsivity with Dupin's cold logic, the story, Lindon Barrett argues, posits ratiocination and reason as white and as diametrically opposed to the instinct and brutality of blackness.[18] The direct inspiration for the story may even have been an account of a black man murdering a white woman with a razor.[19] The invention of detective fiction, in other words, hinges on a racial difference reflective of common racist beliefs in antebellum America. Agreeing that a racial reading of "Murders" is entirely appropriate, Elise Lemire points out that local knowledge would have added resonance to certain story details for Philadelphians, who lived where Poe composed and published the tale. The moment the orangutan tries to shave echoes a well-known display of stuffed monkeys, one shaving another one, in Peale's Museum in Philadelphia, which one white museumgoer remembered as "exquisite humor."[20] The supposed humor here is that the viewer, believing that barbering was a profession particularly suited to African Americans, would see the literalization of the odious cultural association between African Americans and simians. The racist comparison of black people to apes was used to stoke fears of sexual contamination at least as far back as Thomas Jefferson's *Notes on the State of Virginia* (1785), which contends that orangutans sexually desire black women as obviously as blacks sexually desire whites, each group's romantic inclinations an attempt to move up a presumed genetic hierarchy. Taught by Jefferson and others to think of orangutans as lustful, most Americans would have understood the sexual threat inherent in the ape's visit to the private rooms of two unwed white women. Still, after the race riots of 1838, Lemire underlines, Philadelphians would have been even more sensitive to the idea of amalgamation, the rallying cry for the mob that burned down the meeting location used by the Anti-Slavery Society Convention.[21] If, as Samuel Otter encourages, we see Philadelphia as "a peculiarly American experiment" where free people of color lived alongside whites before the Civil War, then we can understand how, even while the conditions in Philadelphia were distinct, the violent racial clashes of the late 1830s and the 1840s articulate social tensions that extend across the country.[22]

Born of a divide between white logic and black atavism, Dupin's ratiocination relies on racist assumptions in "Marie Rogêt" as much as in "Murders," for the solution to "Marie Rogêt," like that of "Murders," identifies the criminal threat as nonwhite peoples. The story thereby suggests that the European setting of the story is really a veiled argument for expressing how nonwhites challenge the definition of Americanness. And yet the story's extra muddled temporality indicates that Poe has trouble maintaining his relocation of the story's beginning—that final revelation—and the simple racial logic that underpins his indictment of racial others. As the solution of his story, a solution that was intended to solve the real-life crime of Mary Rogers, falls apart, Poe both rejects and clutches ever more tightly to his guilty swarthy sailor. Even Poe, who disdained the cultural reverence for literary beginnings and who designed a genre that poked fun at the writerly inclination to give outsized importance to beginning stories, found himself unmoored without the secure white fictive ethnicity they conjured. "The Mystery of Marie Rogêt" has invited relatively little critical scrutiny and none that offers a racial reading. But in line with Teresa Goddu's advice to see the American gothic as "intensely engaged with historical concerns" rather than "escapist," my reading of the tale allows us to understand the shifting uses of short fiction, the dying culture of beginnings, and the nature of detective fiction as a genre.[23]

Muddled Time and Space in Marie's World

In "Marie Rogêt," Dupin, like any good detective, follows a trail of logic that leads him to a culprit. First he deduces that the discovered body does belong to Marie, not, as some suppose, to an unidentified other; then he concludes that she was harmed by a single criminal, not, as some suppose, by a gang. As he narrows in on a dark-complexioned sailor, he clears Marie's fiancé from suspicion. (In real life the fiancé was suspected until his death, either from suicide or heavy drink.) A sailor, Dupin reveals, not only knew how to tie the particular kind of knot found around Marie's neck, but he also would have had knowledge about the workings of various boat yards along the river, an important fact because the sailor attempts to cover his tracks by retrieving the boat that he has abandoned after dumping Marie's body in the Seine. This small clue leads Dupin to the seizure and, upon the sailor's own confession, conviction of the culprit. And yet, Poe's tale is hardly as straightforward as this sequential plot would indicate. Poe, through his fiction, attempted to solve an ongoing and sensational criminal investigation, making it, Mark Seltzer contends, an early version of "true crime."[24] The print history of "Marie Rogêt" reflected this aim. Appearing in three separate installments in Snowden's *Ladies' Companion* between November 1841 (the first issue of the magazine's volume) and February 1842, the tale, which was Poe's only serialized detective tale, existed in *real time*, not just story time. (Both the second and the third installments of the story indicated it was "continued from" a previous page, and since the entire volume of the *Ladies' Companion* was numbered sequentially, it would have been relatively easy, especially when the issues were bound in volume form, to flip back to page 20, the final page of part 1, and page 99, the final page of part 2.) While Poe's audience read Dupin's investigation of Marie's death, they watched the police and the newspaper men try to figure out what had happened to Mary Rogers. James Gordon Bennett, the editor and founder of the *New York Herald*, one of the first successful penny papers, was chief among these detectives.[25] In daily updates on the mystery, he flamed anger at the lack of progress on the case, helped to form a "Committee of Safety," and offered a reward for information leading to the conviction of a culprit.[26] These actions were less about justice for Mary Rogers and more about getting readers to buy papers. As Poe, through Dupin, cautions us: "We should bear in mind that, in general, it is the object of our newspapers rather to create a sensation—to make a point—than to further the cause of truth."[27] Penny papers, which eschewed the traditional subscription model, made their one-penny price work by sending (poorly paid) boys and girls onto the street to hawk a paper packed with advertisements. Continuing stories were especially useful to this model because they drew people into buying subsequent issues. And Mary's death was great at that for two reasons.[28] First, the coroner said that Mary had been raped and murdered—a brutal and shocking death for a young woman. Second, as Amy Srebnick has argued, Mary Rogers represented the new, sexual dangers of an industrialized, multiethnic city that antebellum tracts were busy decrying.[29] The likable and attractive young woman had exited the private domestic space ideologically reserved for the antebellum female to become a clerk in a cigar shop frequented by journalists and politicians. Mary Rogers's story thus encapsulated a timely tension: the possibilities of the city that allowed someone like Mary to sell cigars and the dangers of the city that allowed her to disappear—only to turn up battered, bruised, violated, and dead. Readers bought updates on the murder to understand the nature of New York City and the changing face of American character.

If, as David Henkin has pointed out, the words on buildings, streets, sandwich boards, money, sidewalks, and other places made the antebellum city like a newspaper, both gridded into blocks and waiting to be read, then the scandal of Mary Roger's death illustrated the pressing need for a new ability: the reading of the inscrutable, threatening urban space.[30] Dupin's central talent is just that. In "Murders" we learn that Dupin likes to saunter about at night, "seeking, amid the wild lights and shadows of the populous city, that infinity of mental excitement which quiet observation would afford."[31] His joy is the intellectual labor afforded by a teeming city of "wild lights and shadows," or perhaps we might say, of whites and nonwhites. On one midnight stroll, Dupin exactly guesses the narrator's thought process through close examination of his friend's gestures and mumblings. Although echoing the objectivity to which the sketcher aspired, this ability to unearth hidden meaning actually distinguishes Dupin from someone like the observant Geoffrey Crayon: Crayon makes the unfamiliar enjoyable, while Dupin makes the illegible legible.[32] As Dana Brand points out, in "Murders in the Rue Morgue" and "The Mystery of Marie Rogêt," Dupin reads the interpretation of languages more than the language itself.[33] That is, Dupin realizes the importance of witnesses with different nationalities all assuming that the murderer speaks a language that they do not understand—the murderer is not actually speaking a human language. So too in "Marie Rogêt," Dupin interrogates the conclusions various journalists have reached, more than he investigates the case, by collecting details from their stories and understanding the city's geography. As Dupin emphasizes to his friend, there is a difference between "the evidence itself" and the "peculiarity of the evidence"—between the facts and that which makes the facts relevant to understanding the crime.[34] Dupin's talent is thus not that he reads the crime. It is that he reads the city and (the words of) its many different inhabitants. This skill matters because murder is a byproduct of urban chaos: the narrator reminds us of "the great frequency in large cities, of such atrocities" like Mary's death, and Dupin emphasizes that Mary's death "is an *ordinary,* although an atrocious instance of crime" (*MR1* 16, 19). Detective fiction teaches us that cities are steeped in crime and filled with criminals and victims.

The urban setting of a Paris like New York, then, is worth attention. On the one hand, Poe simply followed trends in positing the equal worth of these two cities. Nathaniel P. Willis boasted in the *Home Journal*: "New-York hereafter may as well be spelt New-Yolk, for Paris, or what makes Paris the world's golden centre, is positively coming here!" He continued, "Paris has been what Bagdad was," and "New-York is to be what Paris is."[35] Copious sketch writers were putting together sketch collections about New York, which felt as interesting and as foreign as any European city.[36]

New York was various, immense, and up and coming. On the other hand, New York City was dangerous and less and less a comfortable projection of a white United States. All these sensations are coded in the Paris–New York of "Murders," where the Seine is both the Seine *and* the Hudson; the Barrière de Roule is both the Barrière de Roule *and* Hoboken, and so on.[37] While "Murders" posits a Paris that could be read as New York, in "Marie Rogêt," the spatial relationship of these locations follows New York, not Parisian, logic. The Barrière de Roule is not on the banks of the Seine, for example, although Hoboken is on the Hudson.[38] In his second story, Poe's setting also becomes American in its detail. The nineteenth-century Seine had neither the sassafras nor the ferryboats described in "Marie Rogêt," though the nineteenth-century Hudson had both. So too Paris in the 1840s was not yet the polyglot immigrant city depicted in "Rue Morgue." Nineteenth-century New York most certainly was just that. In short, although Poe tells us we are in Paris, especially in "Marie Rogêt," he is writing about a city he knew and lived in—a New York teeming with nonwhites waiting (in the racist imagination) to threaten, rape, and murder white women. In a way, Poe's story perfectly illustrates a New York that is no longer fully New York. When German immigrants in the first great wave of European immigration created lively ethnic enclaves precisely because they did not want to assimilate, they fanned such fears. In *Kleindeutchland,* New York City's Little Germany, residents could actually conduct their entire life in German since all the shopkeepers, tradesmen, pastors, and physicians were German. One midcentury observer noted, "Life in *Kleindeutchland* is almost the same as in the Old Country."[39] Such behavior, thought many upper- and middle-class whites, threatened the racial and cultural composition of the United States. Although that attitude was ossified by nineteenth-century immigration, it had precedents in the eighteenth century. In fact, in an essay published in the *Gentleman's Magazine,* the periodical that is the origin for the Great Seal's motto, *E Pluribus Unum,* Benjamin Franklin lamented: "The Spaniards, Italians, French, Russians and Swedes, are generally of what we call a swarthy Complexion; as are the Germans also, the Saxons only excepted, who with the English, make the principal Body of White People on the Face of the Earth. I could wish their Numbers were increased." For Franklin and others, yes, *e pluribus unum,* by all means—as long as everyone is white rather than, in Franklin's terms, "swarthy," "black," or "tawny."[40] A hundred years later, Poe's New York–Paris distills antebellum fears of nonwhites who could never be fully folded into the American people. It suggests that the United States is losing control of its cities and its demos and can only be saved by a white super reader.[41]

This shifty geography fits with the complicated temporality of "Marie Rogêt." As Tzvetan Todorov has shown, in the whodunit, the first temporal line includes the murder that motivates the detective's involvement and that takes place off the page, before the story begins.[42] The second temporal line is the narrative progression of the whodunit itself—the detective's investigating and solving the crime. In most instances these two temporal lines never meet. The detective appears only after the crime to bring about the story's resolution. And yet the temporal line of the crime and that of the investigation interact in complex ways. The beginning (the crime) becomes the end (the revelation of the crime) as the present (the investigation) leads to exposure of the past (the murder). The narrative doubles back on itself to finish with a final revelation of the act that started the story. Sherlock Holmes once teases Dr. John Watson, "I am getting into your involved habit, Watson, of telling a story backward."[43] But of course as Arthur Conan Doyle knew, Watson must tell stories backward to be a narrator of detective fiction. Formally, the whodunit creates a paradox wherein the past is secondary to the present even as that present relies on the past. We do not know that the butler did it until the end of the story. In a way, then, the butler has *not* done it until the final scene—and yet the butler (or in terms of "Marie Rogêt," the sailor) had to do it before the story began in order for there to be a detective narrative. Because of this temporal Möbius strip, the form denies any singular origin and works as a refutation of the two decades worth of beginning celebrations in short fiction. The butler or sailor commits and thus *authors* the crime, but the detective forms the narrative of it and thus, in some sense, *creates* the crime that the reader has previously not seen. Through the interaction of its two timelines, detective fiction dramatizes the process of narrating a beginning while simultaneously underlining the instability of beginnings and of defining a national people in the 1840s.

As a whodunit, "Marie Rogêt" expresses this double temporality and its confusion of beginnings even more than does "Murders." Indeed "The Mystery of Marie Rogêt" has not just two but three temporal lines—the murder, the investigation, *and* the actual events of Mary Rogers's death—resulting in a complexity that makes it impossible to feel placed in the story and unexpectedly highlights a desire and need for identifiable origins. To better explain the temporal complications of "Marie Rogêt," I must first briefly retell the actual known events of Mary Rogers's death. At 7:00 p.m. on Sunday, July 25, 1841, after Mary had supposedly gone to visit her aunt, Mary's fiancé, Daniel Payne, decided that Mary was not, as she had promised, arriving home on the coach. The thunderstorm that had been threatening all day had finally broken. On Monday, Payne learned that Mary had been neither seen nor heard from since the previous morning. In between calling on friends to ask for information, the anxious Payne placed a newspaper ad that, running the next day in the New York *Sun*, caught the attention of two former lodgers at the boardinghouse run by Mary and her mother. Such was the beginning of the incident's presence in the penny papers. On July 28, three days after Mary's disappearance, these two lodgers, suspicious that Mary, the "beautiful cigar-girl," could have been abducted for immoral purposes, took the ferry to Hoboken, New Jersey. Shortly after their arrival, they saw a crowd along the shore—a crowd surrounding the twenty-one-year-old Mary's drenched and battered body. A coroner's inquest that evening declared that the death had resulted from "violence committed by some person or persons unknown."[44] As the newspaper trail shows, Mary was widely thought to have been raped and murdered, either by a single man or by a gang of ruffians, until a much delayed and possibly unreliable deathbed confession from Frederica Loss in November 1842. Loss declared that Mary had actually died in a botched abortion that took place at her inn. (Loss, the inn manager, also said that her sons had staged, not found, Mary's clothing in a thicket in August 1841.) Though Loss's confession was not admitted in court and though the mystery of Mary Rogers was never judicially solved, the abortion explanation was then, and is now, widely accepted. As the press and the populace came to understand it, Mary had died during the operation.

While reliant on the above history, Poe jiggers the timeline, making it unclear who came first and if we are to understand Mary as Marie or Marie as Mary. Poe sets the events of his Parisian tale at least a full month before the actual events of Mary Rogers's death. The most specific temporal references, and thus the temporal anchors of the tale, are two. First, Marie leaves her house "about nine o'clock in the morning of Sunday, June 22" (*MR1* 17). Second, Dupin receives intelligence of the murder "early in the afternoon on the thirteenth of July" (*MR1* 16). Despite Poe's care in fictionalizing a real crime, the time when Marie leaves her house does not coincide with the facts known about Mary Rogers. In actuality, Mary had left her house on Sunday, July 25, at 10:00 a.m.—a month and an hour after Marie. Poe's redating of the events of the murder is suggestive because it means that Marie Rogêt dies and is found floating in the Seine *before* Mary Rogers disappears in New York. Mary Roger's death could thus not have inspired the tale. Yet, because Poe neglects to offer a year for Marie's disappearance, the story's temporal map doubles back and points to the United States. It turns out that June 22, the Sunday Poe identifies as the day that Marie leaves home and disappears, was not actually a Sunday in 1841, the year that American Mary disappeared. June 22 fell on a Sunday only in 1834 and 1845. Hence, either Marie's disappearance happened seven years before Mary's, or Marie's death is divorced from reality and calendric time. All this is relevant because the narrator emphasizes the similarity between Mary and Marie *particularly* as regards to temporality, even while frustrating our ability to understand whose story inspires whose.[45] In the epigraph that ran at the beginning of each of the story's three installments, Poe tantalizingly tells his reader: "There are ideal series of events which run parallel with real ones" (*MR1* 155). The sentence foregrounds the correspondence of Mary and Marie, while the tale does everything to frustrate that alignment. Because the conditions by which we are to understand the tale are so uncertain, we end up feeling unmoored in an unrecognizable city filled with murderous swarthy men. This result is both a reflection of and a contribution to the sense of increasingly unstable and threatened beginnings and ideals: white readers did not know where and when they were in Poe's story because they increasingly felt they did not know *who* they were as Americans. I do not think this sensation was the result of Poe's imp of the perverse. For Poe believed without a "shadow of a doubt" in "the need of *that* nationality which defends our own [American] literature, sustains our own men of letters, upholds our own dignity, and depends upon our own resources."[46] He wanted to bolster American literature, and he sought to express American character through his European tales. When he fails, as he does rather spectacularly in "Marie Rogêt," it is because the beginning, the powerful projection of a white American people, has slipped away.

The stakes for Poe of correctly identifying the origin—of identifying how Marie died and assuring that explanation also applied to Mary—are thus both deeply personal and more broadly about the ability of literature to intervene in the social world. The proper solution would prove his own intellectual ability and reinforce an US social order predicated on whiteness. Given this, that Poe denies his own explanation of Marie's death is deeply confusing and uncomfortable—and suggests something important about the antebellum United States. In the serialized version, after Dupin announces that a sailor must be guilty, the reader is given an odd bracketed note in which the editors state they "shall not specify" why they have omitted "such portion as details the *following up* of the apparently slight clew obtained by Dupin," but assert that the reason "to many readers will appear obvious" (MR3 166–67). Presumably this obvious explanation is Frederica Loss's confession. If so, multiple questions arise: Did Poe pretend to be these unnamed editors? Did someone at Snowden's alter the tale, and if so, was it at Poe's behest?[47] Assuming that there were changes to the manuscript, what was in the final revelation that Poe had originally written? (We will never know unless the original manuscript unexpectedly appears.) And why would the editors omit the climax of the story if they also tell us "that an individual assassin was convicted, upon his own confession, of the murder of Marie Rogêt" (MR3 167)? One hint is that in the tale's final installment (published in February of 1842), Poe suggests that the parallel between Mary and Marie exists only up to the murder: "But let it not for a moment be supposed that, in proceeding with the sad narrative of Marie from the epoch just mentioned, and in tracing to its *dénouement* the mystery which enshrouded her, it is my covert design to hint at *an extension of the parallel,* or even to suggest that the measures adopted in Paris for the discovery of the assassin of a grisette, or measures founded in any similar ratiocination, would prove any similar result" (MR3 167; emphasis in original). This repudiation of the connection between Marie and Mary at the moment of their death is quite extraordinary. What, then, is the point of Poe's tale if not to reveal Mary/Marie's murderer, as he had repeatedly boasted he would do? When Poe tries to back out of the assertion that Mary and Marie are analogous, he is rewriting the premise of his own tale, further compounding the instability and mutability of origins. Poe also tries to prove the truth of the dark-complexioned sailor's misdeeds. In denying the similarity between Mary and Marie, that is, Poe is reinforcing the notion that nonwhite men threaten white women and the nation. It is an idea that Poe cannot give up, even when he slightly alters the story for the 1845 publication of *Tales* and makes more possible—but still not clear—the death-by-abortion theory.[48] Although Poe deletes the line where the sailor is caught and convicted, Dupin still deduces that a sailor tied a knot around Marie's neck and disposed of her body. The result of this version is even more disturbing: the reader ends the tale feeling all the same anxiety about a violent sailor without any of the catharsis of the man's arrest. By 1845, then, the danger represented by the sailor, who is definitionally a traveler and an outsider, is not contained. And it only gets worse. In 1848, Poe affirmed that "The 'naval officer,' who committed the murder (rather, the accidental death arising from an attempt at abortion) *confessed* it; and the whole matter is now well understood."[49] The confusing sentence hardly helps the matter be "well understood." I am arguing, then, that as much as Poe's disinclination to revise demonstrates his well-known inability to admit himself wrong, it also reflects what Poe believed and what he thought his readers believed. Poe was attached to his identification of the criminal because it aligned with his ideas about race and confirmed, through racial difference, his sense of his own intelligence.

Poe suggests as much when he compares himself to Dupin and, even before that, when he boasts of his intellectual abilities in a series of un-signed articles in *Alexander's Weekly Messenger* (starting in December 1839) and then in a signed article in *Graham's* (July 1841). Poe challenges maga-zine readers to find difficult ciphers for him to solve and then reports tri-umphantly that "out of, perhaps, one hundred ciphers altogether received, there was only one which we did not immediately succeed in resolving. This one we *demonstrated* to be an imposition—that is to say, we fully proved it a jargon of random characters, having no meaning whatever."[50] Although the truth of Poe's claim is questionable, the braggadocio dis-plays that Poe wanted others to believe that he could interpret anything, from a cryptograph to an immigrant city. As Poe puffed in an 1841 letter, "Nothing intelligible can be written which, with time I cannot decipher."[51] In line with this boast, Poe's June 1842 letter offering the tale to J. E. Snod-grass of the Baltimore *Visiter* promises that while Dupin seems to unravel "the mystery" of Marie Rogêt, Poe actually "enter[s] into a very rigorous analysis of the *real* tragedy" of Mary Rogers. In truth, Poe continues, it is "under the pretense of showing how Dupin" solves a murder that Poe puts forth the "real" explanation for Mary's disappearance.[52] Poe's self-figuration as a detective meant that he was qualified to arbitrate the rules of detective fiction. He did so in a February 1842 review of Dickens's *Barnaby Rudge*, where Poe claimed to have solved the novel's mystery before the book was fully published and criticized Dickens's handling of the crime narrative. Dickens, Poe said, had not clearly known the ending of the novel and had thus dropped misleading clues and even allowed the narrator to lie. For example, Mrs. Rudge was never "the widow" she was denominated as being.[53] Hence, Poe said, Dickens had violated the rules of the genre Poe created—a hypocritical charge given that Poe selected a criminal no reader could ever suspect in "Murders" and declined a full final exposition of the crime in "Marie Rogêt." And yet if we understand the revelation of the criminal as being more about the exposure of comforting racial logic than about the identification of a culprit, Poe's own stories meet the genre rules he accuses Dickens of traducing. They uphold a specific sense of American reality. Poe's swarthy sailor reflects what Terence Whalen has called Poe's "average racism," by which he means that reflection of broadly held and thus generally popular racial ideas that appealed to as many readers as possible, both North and South, abolitionist and proslavery, at a time when political divisions were carving up readerships.[54] Such average racism seems to have been an on-point calculation for past and less-past readers: Poe's criminal was convincing enough that multiple twentieth-century scholars went looking for historical traces of a sailor involved in Mary Rogers's death.[55]

Pivoting on a narrative dislocation of the beginning, the whodunit reflects a disillusionment with American beginnings. It offers instead a multicultural city in which a white master reader discovers and controls foreigners by revealing them as murderers. For Poe, this racial logic felt so true that even when he admitted Mary Rogers had died from an abortion, he maintained the guilt of his dark-skinned sailor. While Poe seemed comforted by his fictional culprit, we readers do not have a restoration of social order when no murderer is caught. Instead the tale creates a whirl of temporalities, locations, and possibilities that reflect a dangerous and unknown world, one becoming more threatening with each story revision. That truth reflects what Poe and his readers likely felt as well—a dislocation of origins that made it harder to conflate whiteness and Americanness—and it can explain why Poe never wrote another whodunit. After "Marie Rogêt," Poe cannot answer the question *whodunit* because the projection of a stable, white American people no longer felt possible. With no comfortable answer to *who?*, he turns to the question *where?* in his famous final detective tale, "The Purloined Letter." The moment in which Irving's "Rip Van Winkle,"

Hale's "The Soldier of the Revolution," Sedgwick's "A Reminiscence of Federalism," Hawthorne's "The Gray Champion," and even Poe's "The Murders in the Rue Morgue" could be written was past.

Is the Detective Democratic or Imperial?

I have based my argument on the content and printing of Poe's whodunits, but now I would like to zoom out a bit and talk about how critics have argued over the political meaning of detective fiction. Is the genre, with the Dupin trilogy as its important beginning, imperial or democratic? This long-standing question about the form reflects debates about the nature of the United States and various American policies in the run-up to the Civil War and maps the decline of the culture of beginnings. On one hand, abolitionists decried the Mexican-American War and the various filibustering expeditions of the 1850s as imperial actions. Thoreau, for one, denounced how Mexico was "unjustly overrun and conquered by a foreign army"—the US Army.[56] On the other hand, apologists for slavery maintained that slave owners had a right to their property in a democracy, and any attempt to deny them that property was governmental tyranny. William Walker, the notorious American filibusterer and short-lived dictator of Nicaragua, argued that slavery was actually essential to democracy because the "African was reserved" as a "counterpoise which shall prevent" Anglo-Saxon "liberty from degenerating into license, and . . . equality into anarchy or despotism."[57] Whites received order and liberty (and free labor), and blacks received religion and civilization in Walker's depiction of slavery as mutualistic. That contention displays the tortured logic behind many of the expansion projects of the 1850s, for Walker's ideas, repugnant now, were then not far from the mainstream. When Walker was tried in 1853 for seizing Mexican land and establishing a republic with a slave-based economy, a sympathetic California jury took less than eight minutes to acquit him of all charges.

Theoretically, because detective fiction shows us the necessary clues, anyone, not just the detective, can solve the crime. Hence the genre of detective fiction, as Poe created it, trains readers to become adept critics. With each successive clue, the reader has a new opportunity to deduce the truth that the narrative reveals at the very end of the story. As Richard Kopley says, "We may learn from Dupin to become our own Dupin. His detection may be taken as an allegory of our own potential reading."[58] In this way of understanding detective fiction, the form has a democratic aim at its core. Moreover, the move from order to chaos within a detective story relies on democratic institutions. As Howard Haycraft argues, the genre, "produced in any large scale only in democracy," works by "dramatizing, under the bright cloak of entertainment, many of the precious rights and privileges that have set the dwellers in constitutional lands apart from those less fortunate."[59] Detective fiction pivots on some belief in juridically established guilt and innocence; in a regime where people are imprisoned without regard for a legal truth-discovering process, a detective would hardly be a plausible or satisfying figure.[60] Because of the association between detection and due process, Nazi Germany and Fascist Italy banned detective fiction. Arguments linking detective fiction and democracy also underline the historical coincidence of the rise of detective fiction with the increasing police professionalism that established procedures for protecting constitutional rights. The alignment is particularly obvious in the case of Mary Rogers. When, before Frederica Loss's confession, various prominent citizens were dismayed at how the police had neglected to find a culprit for Mary's presumed murder, they met in a group to decry the current practices of the New York police and to demand reform. The attention resulted in the Police Reform Act passed by the New York State Legislature in 1845. The law professionalized the police force by replacing the former rewards system with salaries. Police thus became obligated to research and solve *all* crimes, not just those for which there was a promised sum of money. Ironically, the police were required to provide their services more democratically even as the law's passage had been assisted by racialized fears of foreign others.

Despite such suggestive history, multiple critics have found the form to be illustrative not of democracy but of imperialism. Citing the control of knowledge exhibited in the detective figure, Caroline Reitz argues that detective fiction allowed British citizens to understand and accept the British Empire. Similarly, Jon Thompson contends that in Dupin, "Poe creates a figure whose omniscience is comparable to that of a panopticon."[61] As a result Thompson believes Poe's detective fiction enacts imperial means of control and knowledge: "Through Dupin's rationalism, Poe indirectly criticizes the values of democracy and the narrow empirical methods that were doing so much to industrialize American society, always implicitly contrasting these values and mechanical methods to the ennobled lifestyle and aims of the aristocracy."[62] Dupin's ratiocination is really a top-down display of power, not a democratic lesson in hermeneutics. As Poe, who was surprised, if pleased, at the praise of his detective stories, wrote to a friend, "Where is the ingenuity of unraveling a web which you yourself (the author) have woven for the express purpose of unraveling? The reader is made to confound the ingenuity of the suppositious Dupin with that of the writing of the story."[63] Poe, through Dupin, has mandated the solution. The exercise of analytical might is, in this sense, fraudulent because the crime is never actually a mystery to the author. So too because of the skewed power dynamic between the detective and his audience, few if any readers solve the crime correctly before the detective reveals the mystery. Indeed, Leland Person notes that Poe never really "cede[s] control of the reader's mind or soul. He only seems to do so." Poe, Person continues, is "the master illusionist" in making readers feel that they can think and feel independent of his narrative control.[64] In short, Dupin and his author retain an ideal position of knowledge, one that we readers can never hope to approach. Despite its democratic inclinations, this line of thought runs, detective fiction finally presents an imperial regime in which the reader and the characters are ruled by the best—a (white male) master detective.

Although the critical positions of Kopley and Haycraft, on the one hand, and Reitz and Thompson, on the other, seem opposed, they are not actually irreconcilable. As in the use of Paris for New York and the use of Marie Rogêt for Mary Rogers, the form of detective fiction encodes a doubleness. The imperial methods of the detective, even with their troubling racial coding, work to maintain a democratic social order, complete with processes for trying and convicting criminals that in practice distinctly favor white victims and criminals. So too the genre provides readerly pleasure by encouraging the fiction that a reader can discover the murderer while simultaneously assuring the final revelation is a surprise. In that last moment, when the scales fall from the reader's eyes, the feeling a good whodunit generates is an *Oh! I should have known!* What unifies these democratic and imperial tendencies is a coherent, recognizable social world in which justice is satisfyingly, but not necessarily evenly, meted out. For Poe, evoking that antebellum social world meant delineating reason and instinct and good and bad along racial lines—and thus rehearsing the same logic that underpinned the creation of the democratic United States and spurred later imperial endeavors.

Coda: Composing Backward

No formal treatment of Poe's tales would be complete without recognition of Poe's customary place as the genesis of short story theory. I thus end this chapter with a nod to how Poe's "unity of effect" means all tales are like whodunits. As noted in chapter 4, in his frequently reprinted 1842 review of Hawthorne's *Twice-Told Tales,* Poe, working from Aristotle, argues that every word, image, and idea within a tale must combine to produce a specific sensation, a "unity of effect." According to Poe, that emotion is the highest achievement of the tale, a prose form that Poe believes to be "unquestionably the fairest field for the exercise of the loftiest talent." Because of the importance of the "unity of impression," Poe advocates composing *backward* from the desired effect to the actions, images, and words of the story.[65] As Poe puts it, a "wise" author "has not fashioned his thoughts to accommodate his incidents: but having conceived, with deliberate care, a certain unique or single *effect* to be wrought out, he then invents such incidents—he then combines such effects as may best aid him in establishing this preconceived effect."[66] The murder or effect comes *before* the construction of the narrative that inevitably drives toward that murder's or effect's revelation. The end, the story's result, is actually the beginning, the place from which an author starts composing.

For scholars like Fred Lewis Pattee, the primary takeaway from Poe's review of Hawthorne has been that Poe theorizes the modern short story. Notwithstanding that "short story" is not in use as a literary term when Poe is writing, critics take Poe to be speaking directly about the genre and, in fact, originating all later theory on the form. If we accept Poe as the origin of the modern short story, then we must acknowledge how short stories begin with and rely on the refutation of beginnings similarly encoded in Poe's detective fiction. Perhaps the kinship between Poe's theory of the tale and the structure of the whodunit has gone unnoticed because Poe published his review of *Twice-Told Tales* in May of 1842, six months before "The Mystery of Marie Rogêt" and eleven months after "The Murders in the Rue Morgue." He laid out the theory midstream in his praxis. Also many readers do not consider Poe's detective fiction to have strong effects like his gothic tales do. Critics like Edward J. O'Brien have even dismissed detective fiction as "not literature" because of its amazing commercial success.[67] Nonetheless, as Poe said, "Some of the finest tales are tales of ratiocination."[68] For most readers, "Marie Rogêt" is not one of these. Still, it provides a window onto the racialized fears and dysfunctional origins that lead to the construction of novels from tales and sketches.

6

The Short Fiction Skeleton of
the Great American Novel

B y 1845, the antebellum culture of beginnings had eroded. Though the Civil War was still a decade and a half away, the acceptance of Texas, a slave state, into the Union and the subsequent war with Mexico kept sectional tensions—and the issue of slavery—prominent in national politics. The political crisis that gripped the United States made it less and less appropriate to produce stories celebrating the Pilgrims' gift of liberty and freedom. Thus, when compiling a list of historic romances about Puritans between 1820 and 1850, Michael Davitt Bell found three-quarters of the relevant titles were written before 1845; that number increases to 85 percent when Hawthorne's tales and sketches, which are published in volume form after 1845 but written before that date, are included in the tally.[1] Beginning stories did not disappear, however. Whereas in the 1820s and 1830s belletrists had celebrated Pilgrims as founders of the United States, in the 1840s and 1850s the fight over abolition—and to a lesser extent, over women's rights—challenged the relevance and plausibility of such celebratory beginnings. Instead of featuring in the kinds of short fiction Irving, Hale, Sedgwick, and Hawthorne were writing, Founding Fathers like George Washington and John Winthrop were roped into polemics about slavery as in Elizabeth Barrett Browning's "The Runaway Slave at Pilgrim Point" (1848), which decries the hypocrisy of lauding the Pilgrims as founders of a *free* country. The poem accuses the reader, "born of the Washington-race," of being shamefully reliant on myths of past greatness and, like the "pilgrim-ghosts," avoiding the scornful faces of African American slaves.[2] A Briton, Browning believed that whites, as descendants of

Pilgrims and Founding Fathers, should be horrified by what the runaway has endured in "the free America," including the murder of her black lover, her rape by her white master, her killing of her white child, her savage flogging, and her escape to Massachusetts.[3] The young woman survives all this only to die at Plymouth Rock at the poem's end—a dramatic illustration of the unequal promises of liberty for white and black in the midcentury United States. Perhaps because he saw his compatriots' reverence for the founders, abolitionist Wendell Philips took a different tack. In a fiery 1859 speech commemorating the raid on Harper's Ferry, Phillips argued that the Calvinists inaugurated both republicanism and action, principles personified in John Brown's courageous insurrection. Phillips declared, "The lesson of Puritanism, as it is read to us to-day" is that "'Law and order' are only names for the halting ignorance of the last generation."[4] Antebellum Americans must bear out the promise of liberty embodied in the self-made Pilgrims and assure the complete eradication of racial slavery. Following the principles of the Pilgrims meant emancipation—and war. That the slave trade was active in New England and present in the City upon the Hill by 1644 was not germane to this argument. Abolitionists, be they critical or reverential of the Pilgrims, were mobilizing the potent cultural associations that had been formed by decades of origin celebrations.

As Browning's poem, with its reference to Washington, suggests, both abolitionists and slavery apologists also found early American presidents to be forceful political symbols. Collected in the 1848 *Anti-Slavery Harp*, a Scottish poem called "Jefferson's Daughter" pointed out the hypocrisy of the man who had authored the Declaration of Independence and whose daughter "was sold at New Orleans for $1,000."[5] Similarly in *The Liberty Cap* (1846) Eliza Lee Follen highlighted the legerdemain of celebrating presidents as paragons of liberty when they held slaves. Writing a letter to his mother, a little boy reports seeing a "banner [that] had these words on it, 'The Almighty has no attribute that can take sides with the slaveholder,' and Thomas Jefferson's name under them: and yet," muses the boy, "Jefferson held slaves, and so did Washington, but Washington freed his in his last will."[6] On the other side of the political divide, the best-selling Anti-Tom novel, Mary Henderson Eastman's *Aunt Phillis's Cabin; or, Southern Life as It Is* (1852) contended that "God's blessing is, and always has been on . . . Washington, Jefferson, Madison, Marshall, Calhoun, Henry Clay, and not a few others" who held slaves, thus proving that slaveholding was approved by God.[7] And Charles Jacobs Peterson, under the pseudonym of J. Thorton Randolph, offered a stern defense of slavery through reference to Washington and Jefferson in his novel *The Cabin and the Parlor; or, Slaves and Masters* (1852). Peterson believed that slavery was morally just because the Constitution allowed it and "Washington and the other most influential framers of that instrument are known to have been God-fearing men, who must have had full assurance of right for all its provisions, or they would never have put their hands to it."[8] According to this logic, if the American Cincinnatus approved of slavery, no patriotic citizen could think it wrong. Despite their opposing stance on slavery, all these authors were mobilizing the resonant myths of the Founding Fathers to further their cause. To be sure, some authors were still writing beginning stories after 1845. In the 1850s, Sarah Hale penned a *Godey's Lady's Book* series called the "The Heroic Women of the Revolution" and worked to save Mount Vernon; Washington Irving published his *Life of George Washington* between 1856 and 1859 and avoided mention of Washington's slaveholding until two-thirds of the way through the fifth volume—after Washington himself has died. Yet the tide had turned, and the commitment to writing beginnings became an ineffectual attempt to conjure an obsolete idea of a unified white American people, to forestall the impending civil war, and to hold the Union together. Though they were respected both north and south of the Mason-Dixon Line, even literary giants like Hale and Irving could not prevent the secession of the Confederacy.

I want to end, then, with a new beginning and with the retooling of the sketch and the tale as midcentury authors, coached by the realities of the moment, relied on the sketch and, though I focus on it less, the tale to craft longer American fiction. More specifically, I demonstrate that the aesthetic of the sketch enabled the participation of readers, the feeling of authenticity, and the acceptance of the incomplete in four American masterpieces published within three years: Nathaniel Hawthorne's *The Scarlet Letter* (1850), Herman Melville's *Moby-Dick* (1851), Harriet Beecher Stowe's *Uncle Tom's Cabin* (1851–52), and William Wells Brown's *Clotel; or, The President's Daughter* (1853). Hawthorne, Melville, and Brown paired sketches with tales, thereby lending the sketch's formal features to the tale, a genre associated with the coherent, singular presentation of a short plot. Stowe similarly relied on the authenticity of the sketch to pull her narrative together. According to Lawrence Buell, Hawthorne's, Melville's, and Stowe's novels provide the foundation for three of the four great American novel scripts.[9] Although it has not been canonized in the same way, Brown's novel also enacts one of Buell's four classically American scripts, and each of these stories has been told and retold, read and reread, and commended and revered.[10] Yet since the dream of the great American novel is a post–Civil War phenomenon, *The Scarlet Letter, Moby-Dick, Uncle Tom's Cabin,* and *Clotel* sought and achieved different types of greatness in the 1850s. Indeed antebellum readers would have identified only *Uncle Tom's Cabin*—not *The Scarlet Letter, Moby-Dick,* or *Clotel*—as a "national" novel.[11] Still Hawthorne's and Melville's intention to produce a work of literary genius, and Stowe's and Brown's desire to effect political change have something very important in common: the authors of all four books sought to reveal a truth specific to a time and place—to the midcentury United States. To do so, they moved away from the disjunction of the miscellany to a more unified story world even as the country itself headed toward bifurcation. By the 1850s the aesthetics of *e pluribus unum* had become more threatening than aspirational. So Hawthorne, Melville, Stowe, and Brown leveraged the sketch to craft novels that responded to the politics of the moment, and they tolled the death knell for the culture of beginnings.

The Scarlet Letter: A Paired Sketch and Tale

Nina Baym has shown that by the 1850s "truth to nature became a criterion by which superior novels were known."[12] Relying on the aesthetic of fragmentation, the feeling of essence over polish, and the two dominant relationships between sketcher and sketched object, Hawthorne, Melville, Stowe, and Brown employed the formal markers of the sketch to achieve that expected sense of authenticity. In the first of the two dominant sketcher poses, the narrator is a disinterested observer, like Irving's Geoffrey Crayon, who communicates his credentials through careful description; in the second, the narrator is a participating member of the community who shares her insider information and keen observations.[13] Both relationships produce a sense of genuineness and truth: the sketcher's urbane and observant manner or personable and confiding nature validate the content of that piece and, in these novels, the linked tales that follow. As Kristie Hamilton notes, "The identification of 'tales' *as* 'sketches' imbued fiction with the specialized authority of the documentary" even earlier than midcentury.[14]

When transported into novels, this particular quality of the sketch allowed an entire longer work to feel true to the story, true to the moment, and "a source of cultural legitimation for American letters."[15]

Taking the four novels in chronological order, I turn first to the tale-sketch structure of *The Scarlet Letter*. Selling six thousand copies in the first six months of publication and almost twelve thousand copies between 1850 and 1859, *The Scarlet Letter* was an antebellum best seller.[16] Moreover, as a critical favorite throughout the twentieth century, it remains a leading contender for the title of the great American novel. Yet Hawthorne actually intended "The Scarlet Letter," the major part of his first longer work, to be the initial and most substantial tale in *Old-Time Legends Together with Sketches Experimental and Ideal*.[17] It was Hawthorne's publisher James T. Fields who, thinking it would sell better, suggested that Hawthorne lengthen "The Scarlet Letter" into a stand-alone piece.[18] In response, Hawthorne added to Hester's story and paired it with what he called the "Custom-House sketch."[19] Fields's interest in publishing "The Scarlet Letter" as a novel reflected the changing conditions of the American literary market, one part of which was improved infrastructure. Railroads, steamboats, and better roads newly facilitated book shipments from the Northeast and Mid-Atlantic to the West and South; publishers were thus better able to find national audiences for their writers. Money was also a major factor. Samuel Goodrich, a successful nineteenth-century author and editor, believed that the monetary outlay of US publishers in 1850 was five times that of 1820. This increase in capital allowed publishers to put out a larger percentage of American works: according to Goodrich, 70 percent in 1850, up from just 30 percent in 1820.[20] The firms that survived the Panic of 1837 were, by and large, on more solid financial footing in the early 1850s.[21] Printing technologies were also changing at midcentury. Although movable type was still widely used in the antebellum period, by the mid-1820s there were US firms that specialized in stereotyping and electrotyping, wherein a steel cast was made of each page of set type.[22] The method saved wear on the type, the most valuable of a printer's assets, and eliminated repeated composition costs (in which a firm paid to reset pages for subsequent editions). Stereotyping, however, was cumbersome and expensive and thus slow to catch on. Throughout the 1840s, the process became less pricey and more common. Thus, Ticknor and Fields, Hawthorne's publishers, did not stereotype any texts in 1840 but by 1846 were investing in the technology.[23] Still, the fact remained that stereotyping was rarely economical for print runs of less than a few thousand.[24] Hence, the existence of plates for a midcentury book indicated the expectation of substantial sales. That *The Scarlet Letter, Uncle Tom's Cabin,* and *Moby-Dick* were all stereotyped says something about their realized (for *The Scarlet Letter* and *Uncle Tom's Cabin*) or projected (for *Moby-Dick*) success.[25] (*Clotel* was possibly but not certainly stereotyped, as I explain later.) In sum, the technology for making type plates both enabled and reflected larger print runs, faster creation of subsequent editions, and wider circulation of texts. And as discussion of Brown's novel will help us see, it had a close relationship to racial stereotypes.

While midcentury conditions no longer necessitated that Hawthorne write short fiction, *The Scarlet Letter* remains a paired tale and sketch—a combination that refutes the canard that Hawthorne moved on from short fiction because it no longer challenged his genius. Written after Hawthorne was removed from his customhouse post for political reasons and thus filled with unflattering descriptions of his former colleagues, "The Custom-House" is a consummate sketch. It invites readerly intimacy, foregrounds its fragmentary nature, and emphasizes its truth. When Hawthorne's affable first-person narrator takes the liberty "to imagine that a friend, a kind and apprehensive, though not the closest friend, is listening to our talk," he welcomes the reader to an insider's take on a world he has closely observed. The narrator-reader intimacy pivots on its limited nature: it is curated, tasteful, and selective. While Hawthorne strives for a "true relation with his audience," he "keep[s] the inmost Me behind its veil," thus not "violating either the reader's rights or his own" (*SL* 7). The word "rights" should be understood to mean *privacy,* for, as Kristie Hamilton points out, the nineteenth-century sketch becomes key to communicating and developing modern ideas of privacy: the author projects—and helps create—an audience that has both leisure to read and need for companionship in that solitary time.[26] In other words, the narrative closeness between sketcher and reader should not be marred by either the narrator's overexposure or the reader's discomfort. The thoughtful, limited presentation of private information validates the authenticity of the piece and contributes to the pleasure of reading it.

Exemplary in formal terms, "The Custom-House" also relies on the sketch's relation to fragmentation and incompletion. Indeed, despite the piece's reception as a tell-all, Hawthorne maintains that the sketch cannot and does not fully express his experience in the customhouse—"A better book than I shall ever write was there" in the customhouse, he says. As a result, Hawthorne muses, "At some further day, it may be, I shall remember a few scattered fragments and broken paragraphs, and write them down, and find the letters turn to gold upon the page" (*SL* 30). Even as he modestly dismisses the efforts of "The Custom-House," he reinforces the aesthetic of the sketch. It is not a *full* or *whole* account that dazzles the reader. It is "the scattered fragments and broken paragraphs" that, with their ability to express the essence of the past, will "turn to gold upon the page." The sketch supplies bits and pieces and expects the reader to work to see connections, fill spaces, and finish images. The project thus becomes collaborative. Arguably acknowledging the debt his novels owe to the antebellum sketch, Hawthorne makes this point in *The Marble Faun* (1860) when he says that the "first sketch," with its "imperfections," is "suggestive, and sets the imagination to work; whereas the finished picture, if a good one, leaves the spectator nothing to do and if bad, confuses, stupefies, disenchants and disheartens him."[27] Although Hawthorne is discussing a portfolio of pencil drawings, Hamilton argues that the passage "ascribes a specific sort of aesthetic force to sketches" as a literary genre.[28] The sketch, made in haste to capture a fleeting idea, finds its worth and beauty—its golden nature—in its pointed suggestion.

The formal evocation of truth in "The Custom-House" did more than make the sketch pleasurable to read. As Hawthorne tells us in his sketch's second paragraph, it also offered "proofs of the authenticity of" the tale (the genre term Hawthorne uses for "The Scarlet Letter") that followed it (*SL* 8). A detailed history of the genesis of Hester Prynne's story comes some pages after this initial assurance, but there too Hawthorne highlights the truth that the sketch lends to the tale. Finding the scarlet letter along with "several foolscap sheets, containing many particulars respecting the life and conversion of one Hester Prynne," the narrator assures the reader that "the main facts of" Hester's history "are authorized and *authenticated* by the document of Mr. Surveyor Pue" (*SL* 27; my emphasis). Hawthorne is insistent, perhaps even anxious, about expressing the factual basis of Hester's story: "The original papers, together with the scarlet letter itself,—a most curious relic,—are still in my possession, and shall be freely exhibited to whomsoever, induced by the great interest of the narrative, may desire a sight of them" (*SL* 27). As Lawrence Buell remarks, the "aesthetic priorities" of the antebellum United States encouraged "the incorporation of an 'authentic' documentary base into any fictionalized treatment of regional materials."[29] The sketch's association with truth both reflected and enabled this antebellum wish to sincerely represent the world as white Americans experienced it.

Despite his desire for truth, Hawthorne does not want to be limited to reporting facts. Hence he emphasizes that this truth is suggestive, not exhaustive. He acknowledges, "I have allowed myself . . . nearly or altogether as much license as if the facts had been entirely of my own invention. What I contend for is the authenticity of the outline" (SL 27). The sketch's acceptance of the fragmentary and partial, seen in the mention of "the outline," enables the claim for veracity at the heart of an obviously fictional tale. It also provides plenty of space for the artistic invention Hawthorne tells us has taken place. In other words, pairing "The Custom-House" and "The Scarlet Letter" allows for a formal having your cake and eating it too: the truth of the sketch vouches for the core authenticity of the tale. In this light, Hawthorne's famous theorization of a "neutral territory . . . where the Actual and the Imaginary may meet, and each imbue itself with the nature of the other" not only formulates the tenets of Romanticism but also identifies the thematic importance of The Scarlet Letter's bipartite structure—and, indeed, the general utility of the sketch genre for antebellum novels (SL 29).

Hawthorne's sketch and tale complement each other in other ways too. Within The Scarlet Letter, the sketch's acceptance of the incomplete balances a tale that focuses single-mindedly on its subject and thus exemplifies Poe's "unity of effect."[30] Hawthorne worried in a letter to Fields, "Keeping so close to its point as the tale does, and diversified no otherwise than by turning different sides of the same dark idea to the reader's eye, it will weary very many people, and disgust some."[31] Hawthorne understood the novel's central formal principle—an exciting, developing, and adequately complicated plot—and was rightly concerned that that his tale did not have it.[32] Concerned about how his tale would read, Hawthorne continued in his letter to Fields: "Is it safe, then, to stake the fate of the book entirely on this one chance? A hunter loads his gun with a bullet and several buck-shot; and, following his sagacious example, it was my purpose to conjoin the one long story with half a dozen shorter ones; so that, failing to kill the public outright with my biggest and heaviest lump of lead, I might have other chances with the smaller bits, individually and in the aggregate."[33] When Fields discouraged such a collection, Hawthorne offered a compromise, a two-part work—a sketch and a tale.[34] Perhaps Hawthorne felt his fears about genre justified when in 1854 the *North American Review* criticized his plots as "seldom well devised or skillfully developed" and sometimes "too simple to excite curiosity and attract interest."[35] The implication was that Hawthorne's plots fell short of what was expected in a novel. Yet Hawthorne surely recognized that this simplicity of plot, this unity of effect, allowed for a profound exploration of Hester's character. Reviewers acknowledged this fact too; *The Scarlet Letter* was praised for its characterization of a complex and recognizably human figure. In 1850 a *Knickerbocker* review commended *The Scarlet Letter*'s "study of character, in which the human heart is anatomized," and the *Literary World* lauded its "subtle knowledge of character in its secret springs and outer manifestations."[36] In other words, the tight focus of "The Scarlet Letter" had artistic advantages, ones set off by the more loosely focused "Custom-House." Together Hawthorne's sketch and tale create a literary product adequately compelling and varied. It was also most certainly of the 1850s. While Hawthorne does not directly comment on slavery or women's rights, Hester's story engages with both debates and thus illustrates the falseness of Puritan hagiography. In the City on the Hill, juridical power is held by a small coterie of patriarchs who push racial minorities and women to the fringes of society. (In "The Market-Place," a Native American literally stands with Roger Chillingworth, who has just been redeemed from Native American captivity, at the edge of the crowd gathered to watch Hester's public shaming.) The perversity with which this oligarchy metes out punishment undermines Puritan spiritual authority and suggests a timely comparison: like Ham, Hester is permanently branded for a past sin. Yet unlike Ham's descendants, Hester's daughter, Pearl, is ultimately able to escape her mother's crime for a free, happy life. Through its study of a complicated woman whose desires transgress sexual and social mores, *The Scarlet Letter* revises reverential beginning stories. It questions the relationship between the governed and the governing as well as the nature of justice, punishment, and stigma.

My argument about the bipartite structure of *The Scarlet Letter* recognizes what Hawthorne's contemporaries knew well. Responding to the sketch's claim to truth, Whig publications, which had condoned Hawthorne's political removal from the customhouse, attacked the taste and realism of his introduction. The *Salem Register* accused Hawthorne of being "venomous, malignant and unaccountable" in his portraits and indicted Hawthorne's observational skills: "Even where the writer seems to praise, the picture is so overdrawn as to appear intended for caricature."[37] Many others accepted the "general accuracy" (as an unapologetic Hawthorne called it in the preface to the book's second edition) of the sketch (*SL* 5), and the scandal surrounding it certainly helped sales of the work. The *Albany Daily State Register* and the *Philadelphia Cummings' Evening Telegraphic Bulletin* accepted the truth of the introduction in another way; in summarizing the book for their readers, they reported that Hawthorne told the story of a relic he had *actually* found in the customhouse.[38] Other contemporaries more explicitly recognized the bifurcated structure of *The Scarlet Letter.* On March 30, 1850, the *Portland Transcript* praised the "sketch" and the "story" within the volume, asserting that the "work will give its author a high place among our writers."[39] On the same day, the *Literary World* identified two Hawthornes within the book, the one who wrote "little cabinet pictures exquisitely painted" like various Hawthorne sketches, and the one who "represent[s] the old gloomy historic era in the microcosm and eternity of the individual" familiar from "such tales as the Minister's Black Veil." The reviewer concluded that the result is particularly American: "Our literature has given to the world no truer product of the American soil, though of a peculiar culture, than Nathaniel Hawthorne."[40] American readers wanted natural stories that felt true, and they wanted such accounts to be exciting and relevant to a country preoccupied by existential political questions. In pairing a sketch and a tale to respond to this desire, Hawthorne used short fiction to transcend, not transgress, the formal requirements of the novel. The sketch supplied authenticity rooted in a highly specific American location (the customhouse in Salem, Massachusetts) and narrative persona (the restrained but gossipy Hawthorne). Furthermore, its position next to "The Scarlet Letter" provided the book with variation not inherent in the closely plotted tale, and it offered a timely pivot away from the dying culture of beginnings. Hawthorne was not the first to link a sketch and a tale— the popularity of the titular phrase "tales and sketches" belies such an idea. But some part of the genius of *The Scarlet Letter* is how these short fiction forms work together. While it traffics in techniques that generate feelings of authenticity, "The Custom-House" has a fiction—that of the invented surveyor Pue's imagined scarlet letter—at its heart. Similarly, while it employs grand symbols, the feature taken by many to be the defining quality of the antebellum tale, "The Scarlet Letter" relies on the truth of its customhouse origin. This structural complexity reflects the competing desires present as the culture of beginnings ended, a moment in which Hawthorne uses a longer prose work, a novel, to explore how the Puritan past impacts the psychology, actions, and beliefs of nineteenth-century Americans. As he would reiterate in *The House of the Seven Gables,* Hawthorne concludes in *The Scarlet Letter* that we are constrained by historic sins for which we can never sufficiently atone. After all, Hester's scarlet A may stand for both Adultery and Able, but it may also stand for American.

Moby-Dick: The Truth under the Whale's Tale

The year after *The Scarlet Letter* came out, Herman Melville published his magnum opus and dedicated it to the tale and sketch writer Nathaniel Hawthorne. While *Moby-Dick* did not sell as well as *The Scarlet Letter,* it similarly placed a tale on a foundation of sketches, leading to a contemporary complaint about the "double character" of a book, where one part was "statements of absolute fact" and one part was "romantic fictions."[41] Although the *Literary World* disapproved of Melville's genre mixing, the facts presented in his sketches worked to authenticate the romantic whale hunt and the Calvinist logic of the ending. Validating his fiction through a protodocumentary stance was a familiar tack for Melville, even though he had not previously written sketches and tales celebrating American origins. Melville had used his experience sailing as a hired hand for the truthful foundation of his earlier novels *Typee* (1846) and *Omoo* (1847). *Typee,* in particular, was sensational (and thus better selling) because it gave the impression of being an actual account of Melville's life among cannibalistic South Seas natives.[42] As Melville sardonically wrote to Hawthorne about the narrator in *Typee,* "To go down to posterity is bad enough, any way; but to go down as a 'man who lived among the cannibals'!"[43] Following the literary success of *Typee* and *Omoo,* Melville initially intended that an uneasy relationship to autobiography be part of *Moby-Dick's* attraction. When he addressed prospective English publisher Richard Bentley in July of 1850, he called his novel "a romance of adventure, founded upon certain wild legends in the Southern Sperm Whale Fisheries, and illustrated by the author's own personal experience, of two years & more, as harpooner."[44] At that date Melville had probably not yet focused his novel on Ahab's monomaniacal quest, and he exaggerated his own experience (he may never have served as a harpooner and certainly did not for two full years) so as to credit his story with a factual basis. By the time that Ahab had become the heart of the book, however, Melville had moved away from that claim, instead calling his novel a series of "chapters and essays" ostensibly to make a separation between the more and less fictive aspects of *Moby-Dick*.[45] In an attempt to move beyond the adventure novels he had written before, Melville abandoned autobiography in *Moby-Dick* in favor of the truth of the sketch.

Ishmael's digressions work as sketches in a number of ways. Most obviously, Ishmael is an observant traveler who invites us into his world. As he says when entering the inn where he meets Queequeg: "Let us scrape the ice from our frosted feet, and see what sort of place this 'Spouter' may be."[46] Indeed, Ishmael encourages our participation from the first line of the first chapter: "Call me Ishmael" (*Moby-Dick* 18). This friendly injunction establishes a readerly intimacy—we are on a first-name basis, after all—with the persona who will share his experiences and knowledge. Immediately after this famous opening, Ishmael explains the sketches to come: "As every one knows, mediation and water are wedded for ever" (*Moby-Dick* 19). This warning indicates that the novel will be characterized not by plot—that which antebellum reviewers thought to be the central formal principle of the novel—but rather by the musings common to sketches. As we all know, the advisory is accurate. No plot occurs in the first chapter (Ishmael merely presents his resolution to go to sea), and the only rapidly plotted section of the novel is the three-day chase that composes the novel's final three chapters. Though billed as Ishmael's leisurely musings, the sketches within *Moby-Dick* showcase Melville's extensive research and proclaim their relevance to the Ahab story line. From descriptions of the types of whales to the habits of whales and the methods of killing them, this "informational ballast," to borrow James Barbour's term, offers a foundation of truth to Moby Dick's extraordinary malevolence.[47] In "The Affidavit" (chapter 45), Ishmael acknowledges that the sketches are supposed to ground his story: "Without some hints touching the plain facts, historical and otherwise, of the fishery, [landsmen] might scout at Moby Dick as a monstrous fable" (*Moby-Dick* 172). For *Moby-Dick* to be successful, Ishmael needs to cultivate the authenticity inherent in the genre of the sketch. This truth can then validate the extraordinary events aboard the *Pequod*.

The fragmented sketch aesthetic is prominent within the novel as well and actually appears even before the first chapter. The prefatory extracts supplied by a sub-sublibrarian offer a disjointed, gentle trajectory from a powerful and mythic Leviathan to a flesh-and-blood monster, awful in its malignity. These short quotations, these fragments, move us from the beginning of time to the mid-nineteenth century, from Genesis to Owen Chase (1797–1869), and give us the essence of the whale and, by extension, of Moby Dick. Later in the book, chapters like "Cetology" (chapter 32) foreground how many incomplete pieces can give a sense of a whole. "I promise nothing complete; because any human thing supposed to be complete, must for that very reason infallibly be faulty," says Ishmael as he prepares to explain the classification of whales (*Moby-Dick* 116). "Standing thus unfinished" at the end of the chapter, Ishmael's lengthy taxonomy proves insufficient (*Moby-Dick* 125). But Ishmael's recognition of that incompletion illustrates the ambition of Melville's literary project, "for small erections may be finished by their first architects; grand ones, true ones, ever leave the copestone to posterity. God keep me from ever completing anything. This whole book is but a draught—nay, but the draught of a draught" (*Moby-Dick* 125). Through Ishmael, Melville tells us that *Moby-Dick*'s artistry comes from an unfinished quality created as the narrator stitches together bits. The result is a glimpse of the awing immensity of a whale and the inexpressible experience of chasing Moby Dick.

What we can guess about *Moby-Dick*'s composition indicates that Melville, after writing "chapters and essays" separately, linked the two, hoping that, as "The Custom-House" does in *The Scarlet Letter*, the sketches served to balance the tight focus of Ahab's story. Building on decades of speculation, Barbour postulates three distinct periods of *Moby-Dick*'s composition: "the original story of the whale fisheries, which was mostly done by August 1850; the cetological chapters that were added to the narrative in the remaining months of 1850; and the revision begun early in 1851 under the influence of Shakespeare."[48] This time line means that the sketch and sketch-like chapters are not just formally differentiated from the story of Ahab (that which Barbour and others like Harrison Hayford believe took shape in the third and last period of composition) but also temporally separated from the white whale. While Ahab's obsession with, three-day hunt of, and predestined death by Moby Dick necessitate the tale's "unity of effect," the included sketches offset this single-minded drive and make the book's tale and narrator more trustworthy.[49] That the whale, whose eyes are "divided . . . by many cubic feet of solid head," sees "one distinct picture on this side, and another distinct picture on that side" makes this duality not just formal but also thematic (*Moby-Dick* 262).

Moby-Dick strove to be American through its very topic selection: whaling, which "provided raw materials for the chief lighting and lubricating products of the day," was the fifth-most profitable US industry in the nineteenth century.[50] The center of the worldwide whale trade was the United States. The formerly Puritan New Bedford, Massachusetts, from which Ishmael departs, was said to be the richest city in the country because of this fact. And American whaling was at its height in the early 1850s when *Moby-Dick* was published.[51] Moreover, Ishmael's close friendship with Queequeg offers a radical view on interracial friendships and coexistence that was necessarily political. It was also personal after Melville's father-in-law, Lemuel Shaw, chief justice of the Massachusetts Supreme Judicial Court, upheld the legality of the Fugitive Slave Law in the commonwealth shortly before *Moby-Dick*'s publication.[52] Although originally afraid of Queequeg and his cannibalism, Ishmael comes to realize that Queequeg is his "own inseparable twin brother." When the two of them are tied together with a monkey-rope—Queequeg down in the sea on the whale carcass, Ishmael aboard the *Pequod* keeping Queequeg from drowning or being smashed between whale and ship—Ishmael muses about the life metaphor the situation provides: "I saw that this situation of mine was the precise situation of every mortal that breathes; only, in most cases, he, one way or other, has this Siamese connexion with a plurality of other mortals" (*Moby-Dick* 255). This collaboration between Ishmael and Queequeg provides a model for forging alliances outside of one's ethnic group and offers a dire warning about the indelible linkages between white and nonwhite. On the monkey-rope, Ishmael is in danger because Queequeg is in danger: their fates are literally entwined. After all, it is Queequeg's handiwork, a coffin life buoy, that ultimately saves Ishmael when Moby Dick staves in the *Pequod*.

Setting out a program for the American writer in his 1850 review of Hawthorne's *Mosses from an Old Manse*, Melville says: "You must have plenty of sea-room to tell the Truth in; especially, when it seems to have an aspect of newness, as America did in 1492."[53] For Melville, the most potent American beginning is not the act of a president or a Pilgrim, but that of an explorer. Columbus represents discovery and power, rather than republicanism and piety, and the invocation of 1492 shows Melville's commitment to a spacious canvas on which to paint the ship of state. The year 1492 with the tide of European colonization and destruction that followed was an apropos reference immediately after the Mexican-American War that had netted more than 500,000 square miles of territory for the United States. As a result of this expanding frontier, Congress was forced to determine which parcels would become states and which would allow slavery, and the resulting fraught compromises led directly to civil war. Gesturing to the risk and the promise of believing oneself in control over a dominion, Melville's enormous novel obscures as much as it shows in its quest to tell a national story. Melville lamented, "Truth is forced to fly like a scared white doe in the woodlands; and only by cunning glimpses will she reveal herself . . .— even though it be covertly, and by snatches."[54] That the truth of the white doe is revealed in cunning glimpses and covert glances affirms the aesthetic of the sketch: it is the incomplete, fragmented, and less polished work that says something authentic and American. Moreover, this "white doe" and the aforementioned "sea-room" are oddly reflective of the then in-process *Moby-Dick*. They reveal the germ of a novel that relies on the sketch to let its truth (about the meaning of whiteness) be revealed "covertly, and by snatches."

Uncle Tom's Cabin: Sketches of Slavery

Years before *Moby-Dick*, Harriet Beecher Stowe's *The Mayflower* (1843) offered, as the subtitle puts it, "sketches of scenes and characters among the descendants of the Pilgrims." Though these sketches are pleasant enough, it was *Uncle Tom's Cabin or, Life among the Lowly* (1851–52) and her anger about slavery that captured the zeitgeist. More successful than either *Moby-Dick* or *The Scarlet Letter, Uncle Tom's Cabin* sold better than any other book written in the nineteenth century precisely because it addressed the question of slavery. On the first day it was in print, readers bought more than 3,000 books, and the printer went through 120 editions and 300,000 copies within the first year.[55] Given that multiple people may well have read each copy and it was immediately translated into many other languages, the novel's circulation is hard to exaggerate. At the end of the nineteenth century, one of Stowe's sons asserted that *Uncle Tom's Cabin* achieved such popularity because people "understand pictures better than words."[56] His comment reflects that Stowe wrote *Uncle Tom's Cabin* as a series of true, albeit fictionalized, "sketches," a word she herself used in the novel's preface.[57] An 1856 *Putnam's* review also recognized Stowe's debt to short fiction when it criticized *Uncle Tom's Cabin* and Stowe's second novel *Dred* as not "stories in the proper sense of the term; that is, they have no plot which begins, and develops and culminates. . . . Both of Mrs. Stowe's novels are a series of sketches."[58] Nineteenth-century readers liked this fact.

Stowe brought particular attention to her debt to the sketch when republishing *Uncle Tom's Cabin* in volume form with a preface, but she considered the story to made of sketches even when it was serialized in the *National Era* between June 5, 1851, and April 1, 1852. In a letter offering the then-unfinished work to Gamaliel Bailey, editor of the abolitionist *Era*, Stowe wrote that her account would be "a series of sketches which give the lights and shadows of the 'patriarchal institution,' written either from observation, incidents which have occurred in the sphere of my personal knowledge, or in the knowledge of my friends."[59] Telling Bailey that *Uncle Tom's Cabin* would be based on personal experience and knowledge, Stowe, who had not traveled further south than Kentucky, asserted the truthful nature of her depictions. Truth, of course, was critical to an abolitionist work intended to have political impact, as Stowe's was. Enraged by the passage of the Fugitive Slave Act, which required northerners to remand fugitives or face jail time and fines and thus disallowed them from thinking of slavery as a southern problem, Stowe wanted to fashion an effective and accurate attack on slavery. This hoped-for authenticity went hand in hand with the visual quality of the sketch. Stowe explained to Bailey that she was simply "a painter" invested in making "the most lifelike and graphic" descriptions possible because, she asserted, "There is no arguing with *pictures,* and everyone is impressed by them, whether they mean to be or not."[60] When a picture is successful at capturing the essence of a person or moment, it vouches for its own authenticity: if it looks true, the logic runs, it must be true. Such skillfully drawn verbal and visual images also communicate their artistic worth. Indeed, antebellum reviewers believed that to be high art, novels must supply "pictures of life."[61] The visual qualities of the sketch articulate and make memorable the moral universe Stowe outlines and forces the reader to feel its relevance and power. Uncle Tom himself demonstrates the possibility of such visual reading by navigating his Bible with "certain way-marks and guide-boards of Tom's own invention." These "bold, strong marks and dashes, with pen and ink" make it possible for Tom to "in a moment seize upon his favorite passages, without the labor of spelling out what lay between them." But more than just serving as navigational aids to biblical passages, these marks marry the message of God with the situation under which Tom made the mark. For Tom has annotated his Bible over many years as others, usually his master's children, read to him. The marks thus conjure "some old home scene," complete with "some past enjoyment." In other words, Tom is a visual reader whose ability to see pictures forms unity between his past and future lives. As he sits reading on the steamship that carries him further from Shelby's plantation, "his Bible seemed to him all of this life that remained, as well as the promise of a future one" (UTC 132). Tom shows the power of writing images that conjure spiritual and moral feeling, which of course is the aim of a sentimentalist text like Stowe's.

Because she was writing to an antebellum audience, Stowe's pictures of life included references to the Founding Fathers who had been so thoroughly celebrated and detailed in the previous decades. Unlike the historical fiction that I discuss in the preceding chapters, however, Stowe offers mere glimpses of these beginnings figures, pointing to the fragmentation and alteration of the culture of beginnings forced by politics around slavery. At the opening of the novel, we learn that a hand-colored "portrait of General Washington" hangs on the wall of the novel's eponymous cabin: Uncle Tom and Aunt Chloe recognize Washington's greatness and are devoted Americans (UTC 19). But in denominating him a general rather than the president, Stowe makes clear that she and her characters do not celebrate Washington for a presidency during which he held slaves; they celebrate him as a revolutionary leader who fought for the liberty and freedom that they lack. A later reference to Jefferson is similarly suggestive. After seeing his nephew beat a slave, little Eva's father comments sarcastically to his brother Alfred: "All men are born free and equal!" Alfred dismisses the phrasing as "one of Tom Jefferson's pieces of French sentiment and humbug" (UTC 245). The allusion is, of course, to the Declaration of Independence, that foundational American document, whose preamble states a truth increasingly understood to be irreconcilable with keeping fellow humans in bondage. Given that premise, the document that created the United States becomes, for Alfred, un-American and irrelevant—it becomes French humbug.[62] The blasphemy of this statement is supposed to underline Stowe's point that, since the beginning premise of the United States is incompatible with chattel slavery, slavery must end.

By and large, contemporary reviewers focused on the political content of Stowe's novel. Abolitionists praised it (though a number condemned her support of colonization), while southern apologists attacked it. Some reviewers, however, ventured comments on the artistry of the novel that went beyond compliments for or censure of Stowe's characters; among these was George Sand, the nonconforming and fiercely intelligent French author. In 1852, Sand praised the unfinished and fragmentary quality of *Uncle Tom's Cabin*—its "badly constructed" nature—by focusing on the laudable "type[s]" and "portrait[s]" Stowe draws, and noting "that in paintings of manners and characters, there was never too much [verbosity] where every stroke of the pencil [is] in its place." Sand adds, "Mrs. Stowe is all instinct, and for that reason she appears at first not to have talent."[63] Stowe's story, in other words, works like a sketch: it displays essence and truth through its less polished—its incomplete—presentation. Much as Hawthorne says a sketch should, *Uncle Tom's Cabin* makes the spontaneity of its composition felt, and its urgency and earnestness invite readerly trust and readerly participation. In this light, Stowe's famous injunction that the reader *"feel right"* becomes not just the calling card of sentimental fiction but an extension of the sketch's aesthetic (*UTC* 404; emphasis in original). Stowe has provided the narrative gestures; the reader must supply the finishing polish and the emotion as when "those that are not seen in this romance, but of which only three words are spoken by their desolate mothers" are conjured as "little black and white angels, in which every woman recognises the object of her love" (*UTC* 404). The sketch's acceptance of the incomplete and fragmentary becomes the political strength of *Uncle Tom's Cabin*.

The publishing history of *Uncle Tom's Cabin* helped make the novel into a series of sketches. Because Stowe wrote and Bailey published the story section by section, *Uncle Tom's Cabin* consists of many pieces with individual integrity that work together to form a coherent (if episodic) whole. As Susan Belasco Smith notes, these scenes or sketches create many small resolutions, appropriate to a work where each chapter or group of chapters might stand alone in a newspaper.[64] For example, chapter 7, "The Mother's Struggle," one of the most famous moments in the novel, does not have a cliffhanger. Instead of closing with Eliza's clutching her son and jumping down the riverbank onto the ice floes, the chapter ends with the pursuers' reflections upon her successful traverse of the violent water. Eliza's escape works so well as a resolution that Stowe actually rewinds her narrative in the opening sentence of the subsequent chapter: "Eliza made her desperate retreat across the river just in the dusk of twilight" (*UTC* 56). Here Stowe not only reminds her readers, who may have had a time lapse between story installments, what has happened but also momentarily re-creates the suspense of Eliza's hurried flight. She ties one chapter, one sketch, to another, fully aware that they are discrete links in a longer chain. Importantly, though she made some alterations while preparing the manuscript for publication as a two-volume novel, Stowe did not change the redundancies caused by serialization. The aesthetic of wedded sketches was central to *Uncle Tom's Cabin*.

By underlining the visual quality of Stowe's prose, the hundreds of drawings depicting moments within the novel also attest to the connection between *Uncle Tom's Cabin* and the sketch.[65] For the first American edition of the novel, Hammatt Billings made six full-page engravings and one small imprint on the title page despite the fact, as Jo-Ann Morgan reports, that "illustrations were usually not found in antebellum fiction, especially that of a first-time novelist."[66] When the book proved amazingly successful, Billings did over one hundred additional engravings for a more expensive edition. On the other side of the Atlantic, George Cruikshank, notable for being Charles Dickens's illustrator, did wood engravings for an 1852 British edition of *Uncle Tom's Cabin*. Also within the novel's first year of publication, three dramatic versions of the story appeared, each with its own set of playbills, posters, and other visuals.[67] While time-consuming engravings do not have the same aesthetic as a visual sketch, their production testifies to how antebellum Americans had a profoundly visual relationship to Stowe's novel. Contemporary artists made literal the genre analogy—that the verbal sketch was like a visual sketch—at the heart of Stowe's series of sketches.

For Stowe, the most important formal aspect of the sketch remained its associations with truth: "The personal appearance of Eliza, the character ascribed to her, are sketches drawn from life," Stowe assures us in her

"Concluding Remarks" (*UTC* 400). Stowe was writing an exposé of slavery, and when southerners and slavery advocates attacked her novel as false and exaggerated, she produced *A Key to Uncle Tom's Cabin* (1853), a book that provided evidence supporting her depiction of slavery. As Stowe wrote: *Uncle Tom's Cabin* "more, perhaps, than any other work of fiction that ever was written, has been a collection and arrangement of real incidents,—of actions really performed, of words and expressions really uttered,—grouped together with reference to a general result." Strident, Stowe maintained that her novel was "a mosaic of facts."[68] As *A Key to Uncle Tom's Cabin* makes obvious, Stowe felt very strongly about the truth—and her readers' belief in that truth—of *Uncle Tom's Cabin*. The novel sketched life.[69]

Clotel, or the Sketch and Tale Make the First African American Novel in Three Parts: Part 1

Across the Atlantic, another American was employing sketches to write an abolitionist novel, one now recognized as the first published African American novel.[70] Yet because he was black, William Wells Brown's relation to sketch and tale writing—and to the culture of beginnings—was quite different than Hawthorne's, Melville's, or Stowe's. In the sections that follow I explore how and why Brown adopts the position of a sketch writer and what that reveals about the culture of beginnings and the white fictive ethnicity it conjured. Let us start part way through Brown's *Clotel; or, The President's Daughter,* a novel frequently compared by reviewers to *Uncle Tom's Cabin,* when Pompey, the enslaved functionary of a slave trader named James Walker, appears. Brown draws Pompey as a minstrel character: a "genewine artekil," Pompey has a "low stature, round face, and, like most of his race, had a set of teeth, which for whiteness and beauty could not be surpassed" as well as "eyes large, lips thick, and hair short and woolly."[71] "Pomp," as his master calls him, behaves in a way that corresponds with this racist description. Calling himself a "gentman" and speaking in heavy dialect, Pompey prepares other slaves for market. "Den you must have off dem dare whiskers of yours, an when you get to Orleans you must grease dat face and make it look shiney," Pompey instructs one older slave (*Clotel* 66, 67). Although Pompey claims to be no "contefit," he clearly is exactly that (*Clotel* 66). He is a copy of a racist stereotype, one winkingly included in an abolitionist novel precisely because it was a comfortable, legible social type for white readers on both sides of the Atlantic. That the vain Pompey is a fictionalized version of Brown himself (who was, when enslaved, leased to a slave trader named James Walker to work as a functionary) suggests Brown's full acceptance that stereotypes were a critical, if fraught, mode for fashioning an African American presence in a literary tradition that presented itself as wholly white.

Pompey is a path into a work that might well be considered a great American novel, one that, like *The Scarlet Letter, Moby-Dick,* and *Uncle Tom's Cabin,* was possibly stereotyped.[72] While stereotyped plates of *Clotel,* if indeed they were made, would have reflected the books Brown sold or expected to sell as he traveled and lectured, they must also call to mind the racist characters like Pompey. Indeed Jonathan Senchyne argues that the technology of stereotyping underscores how stereotypes, both in the sense of printing technology and in the sense of reductive racial caricatures, were central to midcentury US print culture.[73] We can see such figures in the other three great American novels that I have discussed. Hawthorne reports that the town green often saw whippings of "an idle and lurking Indian, whom the white man's fire-water had made riotous" (*SL* 37). Ishmael initially judges Queequeg as a cannibal and savage and, as Samuel Otter has argued, Melville's fixation on Queequeg's dark body maps uncomfortably onto nineteenth-century fascinations with racial ethnography.[74] Stowe shades her story with colorism, making the lighter-skinned characters smarter and the darker-skinned characters more simpleminded. Brown, who read widely, possibly examined all three of these novels.[75] He certainly knew how people of color were depicted in print, for he frequently quotes or borrows such material from newspapers, magazines, and other sources. Guided by the circulating genre models and character types, Brown thus wove racial stereotypes, most particularly the "tragic mulatta," into a novel built from a sketch and a tale. Even as the stereotypes in books and periodicals degraded people of color and bolstered the slave system, writing books printed from stereotyped plates and salted with stereotyped characters brought Brown mobility, social opportunity, and income. In fact, Brown traveled to England with the plates of *The Narrative of the Life of William Wells Brown, a Fugitive Slave* (1847 in the United States) because he saw the easy reprinting of his writing as critical to his economic self-sufficiency.[76]

While he may have used stereotyped plates for both works, the narrator of *Clotel* is very different from that of Brown's *Narrative.* Imitating

Washington Irving's rhetorical stance, Brown becomes an objective and observant guide through the workings of slavery in the autobiographical "Sketch of the Author's Life" that begins *Clotel*.[77] This opening provides the foundation for the fictional story "Clotel," in which Brown tells the harrowing experiences of Thomas Jefferson's biracial daughters and granddaughters. Like *The Scarlet Letter,* Brown's novel is thus a joined sketch and tale. Yet, while Hawthorne chose the structure for reasons of balance, Brown was determined to use genres recognized by white audiences to dismantle false binaries and stab at the heart of the culture of beginnings. By showing that black characters can pass as white and white characters can be mistaken for black, Brown's bipartite novel mixes the authenticity of the sketch and the transport of the tale to illuminate that the founding promise of the United States—symbolized by Jefferson's words that all men are created equal, which serves as the novel's epigraph—was fictional for African Americans.[78] His novel reveals that unified stories from the culture of beginnings ignored, to quote Toni Morrison quoting Herman Melville, "the power of blackness" that animated, even if by strenuous efforts to ignore its presence, US literature.[79] For Brown, then, there was not a northern and southern story but a black and a white story, which tell an authentic tale of the United States only in concert.

Within *Clotel,* Brown dramatizes the US origin by means of two founding ships, one carrying white pilgrims and the other black slaves. While the *Mayflower* "with it servants of the living God, their wives and little ones, hastening to lay the foundations of nations" is skimming across the water to North America, "a low rakish ship" is also "hastening from the tropics, solitary and alone" with "the first cargo of slaves on their way to Jamestown, Virginia." These two ships represent mirrored beginnings, one pure in its religious mission of self-governance and self-sufficiency, the other rank with greed and stolen labor. And Brown says, these two ships, sailing on the same day, symbolize American genealogy, for each is "a parent, one of the prosperous, labour-honouring, law-sustaining institutions of the North; the other the mother of slavery, idleness, lynch-law, ignorance, unpaid labour, poverty, and dueling, despotism, the ceaseless swing of the whip, and the peculiar institutions of the South" (*Clotel* 184). These two ships symbolize the genealogical beginnings of white and black Americans, and their simultaneity—even if not historically accurate—frustrates efforts to privilege Puritans fathers at the expense of obscuring the foundational existence of slavery and the presence of enslaved peoples in the United States.[80] *Clotel,* with its sketch about slavery and tale about the progeny of a Founding Father, enacts this double story by telling of the lives of black people whose ancestors, actual or spiritual, arrived on that ship to Jamestown. These twinned origins, encapsulated in a twinned sketch and tale, expose the falsity of America as a white republic. William Andrews has famously argued that writing brought a level of increasing freedom to African American authors. As they incorporated more novelistic techniques into their autobiographies, these black authors became ever more free. *Clotel* shows, however, that the journey from slave narrative to novel was not direct: it passed through the sketch and the tale, which proved essential to Brown's creation of a narrative self qualified to write fiction. Short fiction liberates Brown from the constraints of black autobiography, begins the tradition of the African American novel, and provides a shattering critique of beginning stories and the racial exclusion they relied upon.

Part 2: The Black Sketch-Writer

Brown's life story was living proof that liberty was not equally granted to all born in the United States. At age ten, Brown heard the "cries of his mother, while being flogged by the Negro driver for being a few minutes behind the other hands in reaching the field" (*Clotel* 2). At age twelve, he was leased out to the "horse-racer, cock-fighter, gambler" and "inveterate drunkard" Mr. Freeland from whom Brown fled, only to be tracked by "the Negro dogs," dragged home, "tied up in the smoke-house, and whipped until Freeland was satisfied, and then smoked with tobacco stems" (*Clotel* 3). Later Brown was leased to James Walker, the slave trader, who collected slaves in and around St. Louis and brought them south to the New Orleans market. On one journey down the Mississippi River, Brown, who was responsible for chaining and prodding the slave gang, watched a woman who had been "taken from her husband and children, and having no desire to live without them, in the agony of her soul jumped overboard and drowned herself" (*Clotel* 5). Having survived three trips with Walker, Brown saw his sister sold to a man as a concubine and was himself, though the nephew of his owner, sold to a steamboat captain named Enoch Price. It was from Price's boat that Brown finally successfully escaped, disembarking in Cincinnati,

Ohio, on January 1, 1834, and traveling at night in frigid weather without food or an overcoat. Exhausted, ill, and desperate, Brown approached a passerby in a "broad-brimmed hat and a long coat"—a Quaker by the name of Wells Brown who nursed William back to health, renamed him, and sent him north to Cleveland (*Clotel* 21). There Brown taught himself to read and write, worked as a barber and on a boat, got married, conducted fugitives on the Underground Railroad, and began to lecture first on temperance and then on abolition. Tucked in the introductory sketch, all these autobiographical details provide evidence for the story that follows, as if Brown has published his version of a *Key to Uncle Tom's Cabin* along with his *Uncle Tom's Cabin*.[81]

But more than communicating his biography, which was available elsewhere, Brown's sketch provided a framework through which Brown could win the trust of a white readership outside of the limits of the slave narrative. To explain how, I must first describe the ways that Brown's autobiographical sketch draws on the tradition of slave narratives. Although called a "sketch" on the title page, within the volume the piece is labeled "Narrative of the Life and Escape of William Wells Brown," which clearly gestures back to Brown's literary origins. *The Narrative of William Wells Brown*, Brown's first book, went through ten thousand copies and was into its third edition by 1848. Along with selling well and generating income, the manuscript had been his means of entry to the Massachusetts Anti-Slavery Society. The society's corresponding secretary, Edmund Quincy, a Boston Brahmin and abolitionist editor, wrote an endorsement that appeared at the beginning of Brown's *Narrative*, following Brown's portrait and signature and assuring that Brown was real, that his character was trustworthy, and that his story was true.[82] Such testimonials, portraits, and signatures are standard framing devices (paratexts) for slave narratives, carefully calculated to demonstrate the literacy and civilization of the black author for a suspicious white readership. While they intend to assure the narrative's impact, these paratexts also serve, as Beth McCoy has argued, as "an indirect white supremacy, different from the brutality against which white abolitionists fought but one that interferes with the fugitive writer's authorial primacy nonetheless."[83] Through this prefatory material, black authors were shunted into a "reportorial, objective, fact-oriented mode" in which their reliability and truth was foregrounded as always in question.[84] Correspondingly, when an abolitionist praised Brown's *Narrative* for its "simplicity and ingenuous-ness," he affirmed that those were the central desired qualities.[85]

Five years later, Brown was ready to escape this "discursive terrain" (Dwight McBride's term to refer to the codes, language, expectations, and beliefs that preexist and predetermine the telling of African American auto-biography) and embrace the obviously literary but still authentic and true.[86] Brown supplants the paratexts of the slave narrative in *Clotel* by crafting himself as a gentleman sketcher. In lieu of the image of Brown that had in-troduced his *Narrative,* then, *Clotel* features a frontispiece of the eponymous heroine leaping from a bridge to her death in the Potomac River. With this illustration, Brown signals that his imagination, not his body, qualifies him to tell a story. So too in place of a testimony by someone like Edmund Quincy, Brown offers a number of evaluations of his literary skill at the end—not the beginning—of his autobiographical sketch. Rather than as-suring the reader of Brown's truthfulness and thereby reminding readers that Brown's authorship is restricted and compromised, these reviews of Brown's *Three Years in Europe; or, Places I Have Seen and People I Have Met* (1852), the first sketch collection by an African American, emphasize his skill at sketch writing.[87] With praise of a book that is "both in intellect and in style a superior performance," these reviewing venues, many of which ran compliments about Irving's *Sketch Book* thirty-odd years earlier, accept Brown as an *author* as well as a black man. When Brown interpolates these reviews into his autobiographical sketch, he fashions a specifically literary self. He becomes a sketch writer—and thus a novel writer—by evoking and embracing the rhetorical conventions that Irving made famous.

Like Geoffrey Crayon, Brown is an outsider, inviting the reader into the world he is exploring. Instead of narrating in the first person as he does in his *Narrative,* then, Brown flips between first-person and third-person narration and positions himself as both editor and character of the auto-biographical sketch that begins *Clotel.* Even as the authenticity of his story relies on his having experienced slavery's horrors, his authority as an au-thor is contingent on the protodocumentary sensibility of the sketch. The shifting rhetorical stance on his life allows him both to claim the imme-diacy of recounting his experiences while enslaved and to show his abil-ity to reflect on the significance of those experiences. When, for example, Brown and his mother are captured on an escape attempt, Brown quotes his earlier first-person account: "William's mother looked him in the face, and burst into tears. 'A cold chill ran over me,' says he, 'and such a sensation I never experienced before, and I trust I never shall again'" (*Clotel* 14). This eruption of sentiment is framed by dispassionate reporting on how the slave catchers read the handbill offering $200 for William's and his mother's capture, and how William's mother is subsequently sold down the river. So too when William (the character) sees a gang of whites murder an enslaved person in the water and then abandon his body on the shore until the trash cart comes around, Brown (the narrator) expresses his horror in understated tones: "During the whole night [William's] mind was occupied with what he had seen" (*Clotel* 11). The effect is to force contemplation of these foul acts onto the reader while retaining an almost scholarly distance from the event. With this objectivity, Brown removes himself from the immediate action of the story and fashions a familiarity and intimacy between sketcher and reader. Guided by Brown the sketcher, the projected white reader can cross the color line and understand, if incompletely, the slave's perspective for powerful and effective results.[88]

The figure of the sketch writer gives us a new and productive way to think about Brown, who has again and again—by William Andrews, Robert S. Levine, Ann duCille, Paul Gilmore, John Ernest, and others—been classified as a trickster figure. Contemporary reviewers praised the novel in language related to the sketch genre. Picking up on the authentic and visual nature of the sketch, *Tait's Edinburgh Magazine* commended the work, which "abounds in the delineation of actual *scenes* as striking and as appalling as any in the romance of Mrs. Stowe, and is a *remarkable and truthful illustration* of the horrors of the slave system."[89] Similarly, the *Critic*, a London magazine, affirmed, "There is truth of nature in his powerful pictures."[90] Referencing the protodocumentary stance that had come to be associated with the sketch, *Tait's* also underlined Brown's authority as "an eye-witness of the events described," and the *British Mother's Magazine* understood *Clotel* as "statements of fact."[91] By becoming a sketch writer, Brown replaced Edmund Quincy; he made himself a literary author whose objectivity and imagination validated the worth and truth of his story about Clotel.[92] The well-developed formal features of short fiction provided a vehicle for Brown's literary freedom. They allowed him to overcome the restrictions of the slave narrative genre and subvert the identity presumptions of authorship. He may have been in England and legally a fugitive slave, but by means of the sketch and the tale, Brown became an American novelist.

While it is necessary to differentiate between the sketch and the slave narrative, it is worth acknowledging that the form of the sketch for Brown and his reviewers would have been related to both incidents and narratives. The episodic nature of "incidents," as in Harriet Jacobs's *Incidents in the Life of a Slave Girl* (1861), threads together various moments that are more fleshed out rather than delineating each moment in a life equally or giving an easy teleological narrative. Associated more with the stories of slave women, the genre term "incidents" emphasizes the fractured nature of the telling, suggesting that even more horrible events cannot be retold. Although the term places more emphasis on forward plot movement, "narratives" by male slaves like Brown and Douglass similarly incorporated strategic omission. Most famously, of course, Frederick Douglass's *Narrative of the Life of Frederick Douglass* (1845) neglects to reveal exactly how Douglass escapes from slavery, even though that act is the apex of what we might call the book's adventure story line. Such exclusions were often different for women since the projected reader's prudery necessitated that events that might offend a women's sensibility, like sexual assault, be referenced obliquely, if at all. Even as the term "incidents" conjures up a more staid story than "narrative"—Jacobs is literally kept still as a captive in an attic for seven years—both link sketched moments and events together in a manner similar to the biographical sketches popular in periodicals and collections from the 1820s to the 1850s.[93] Together, incidents, narratives, and sketches emphasized the necessity of evoking true pictures of slavery, a reality evident on the abolitionist lecture circuit, where Brown and others frequently tied visuals to lectures to increase their efficacy. In fact, during the winter of 1852–53, immediately before the composition of *Clotel*, Brown commissioned a series of magic lantern slides depicting scenes from *Uncle Tom's Cabin* to accompany his "illuminated" presentations on the novel. Even earlier, Brown had arrived in Europe with sketches done by US artists for a huge panorama about slavery that he planned to have made up in England.[94] By late October of 1850, Brown had arranged for the completion of twenty-four panels, each probably thirty feet wide and six to nine feet tall.[95] In a printed catalog that accompanied the panorama, Brown called his images a "series of sketches of beautiful and interesting American scenery, as well as of many touching incidents in the lives of Slaves."[96] Although not speaking of a written work, Brown's phrasing shows a close relationship between sketches and incidents, and the central importance of visualizations for abolition. Even after Brown declared that "slavery never can be represented," he was embracing strategies for depicting the institution.[97] His solution was using the incompleteness of the sketch to gesture toward a world of horrors beyond the page—to represent a truth without detailing its fullness.[98]

Part 3: A Tale of Disjunction

As I have said, Brown's autobiographical sketch serves as the foundation for a fictional story built of tales. In composing this "Romance of American Slavery," as the second part of the novel was subtitled in an 1860–61 republication, Brown worked off of two tales he had previously published: the opening auction scene of Clotel (before a slave named Ellen Carter), and the closing reunion of the two lovers (Mary, Clotel's daughter, and George Green) in France.[99] More significantly, chapter 4, "The Quadroon's Home," not only feels as if it could be extracted to stand on its own, like Melville's "Town Ho's Tale," but also borrows heavily from a stand-alone tale, "The Quadroons," by Lydia Maria Child, which Brown perfunctorily credits in his conclusion.[100] Indeed, this tale seems to have been the genesis for Brown's novel and forms the major outline of Clotel's story: a phenotypically white but legally black woman is purchased by a man with whom she lives as a wife. They have a beloved daughter together, but soon the husband realizes that his political ambitions will be aided by a marriage to the only child of a prominent society member. To do this, he estranges himself from his first family until it is discovered that he has an unlawful daughter who is also technically a slave. In Child's story, the first, though not legal, wife dies of a broken heart (whereas Clotel, her counterpart in Brown's novel, is sold), but in both tales, the daughter is taken as a domestic slave in the husband's white family. Hinging on this story line, which builds to Clotel's failed rescue of her daughter and subsequent suicide, the fictional part of Brown's novel is actually an elongated and padded tale, with a number of passages directly lifted from Child. This provenance gives *Clotel* an uncertain and uncomfortable status. Despite being recognized as the first African American novel, Clotel's story is simultaneously a white author's and a black author's. Like Clotel herself, who had both a white and a black parent, the story becomes racially ambiguous. Given that Brown writes like an urbane sketcher and borrows Child's tale, *Clotel* is phenotypically white.

And yet, because of Brown's descent, as the title page acknowledgment of his status as a "fugitive slave" makes clear, it reads as black.[101]

Since others have discussed the moral risk of Brown's copious plagiarism (which goes well beyond what he takes from Child), what is most relevant here is how the resulting mixed text frustrates smooth and absorptive reading in *Clotel* and how the textual disruptions become a dominant aesthetic.[102] The seams between Brown's writing and his lifted texts often come with notable shifts in prose and diction. In chapter 4, "The Negro Chase," for example, Brown inserts an account of dogs chasing enslaved people that is more empathetic to dog than human—because the original article was about dogs chasing *robbers*, not slaves. Hence, the reader moves from "the slaves went into the swamps, with the hope that the dogs when put on their scent would be unable to follow them through the water" (Brown's words) to "here these faithful animals, *swimming* nearly all the time, followed the zigzag course, the tortuous twisting and windings of these two fugitives" (the words of "Hunting Robbers with Bloodhounds" from the *Utica Daily Observer*) (*Clotel* 74; emphasis in original).[103] The emphasis on the swimming, the description of the dogs' fidelity, and the focus on the difficulty of the terrain all lend sympathy to the dogs chasing the fugitives rather than the fugitives themselves. Yet surely Brown's concern lay with the humans, not the animals. The anecdote does end with a derisive mention of a "mob" and a "Lynch court" and then an inserted (and set off with quotation marks) newspaper account of a brutal lynching in Natchez (*Clotel* 76).[104] As Geoffrey Sanborn argues, such frequent unmasked shifts in register push the reader into a place of "incessant re-beginning," one that requires a constant reacquaintance with the narrative voice.[105] By changing styles, dictions, and vantages without notice, Brown demonstrates the fragility of stories, which inevitably derive meaning from their surroundings. He forces his reader to reevaluate the narrator and to reinterrogate the narrative context again and again; he thus teaches tools for challenging the singular and hegemonic nature of beginning stories. For readers in the 1850s acutely aware of their historical contingency, this fractured prose style would have resonated with competing views of the past and of the United States. It helps make Brown's novel, to use Lara Langer Cohen's words, "a counterhistory, an intervention that unearths the events suppressed by the official record."[106]

Notably, this counterhistory draws heavily on news sources, like the newspaper story about the Natchez lynching.[107] Along with providing factual basis, these interpolated texts recall how short fiction gained authenticity through its collocation with news stories. What the report of the Harvard College commencement did for "Peter Rugg, the Missing Man" in the pages of the *New-England Galaxy* (as I explained in the introduction of this book), newspaper articles, advertisements, sale bills, sermons, and more do for *Clotel*. They make the novel feel of the real world. For example, Brown includes a notice placed by James W. Hall for "well trained, and known throughout the parish" "Negro Dogs" that will be set to work for "five dollars per day for hunting the trails, whether the negro is caught or not," and "for taking a negro, twenty-five dollars, and no charge made for hunting" (*Clotel* 73). No doubt readers would still have been able to contact the said Hall and arrange his dogs' services upon the publication of *Clotel*. Starting with the real actions of a real president, *Clotel* communicates that its fiction speaks to regular practices and daily events in the United States. From the autobiographical sketch onward, the novel offers a story that uses fiction to speak truth precisely because, as John Ernest has argued, blacks had to write in a metahistorical mode since what was accepted as history was hostile to blackness.[108] Brown's inclusion of the ads for hunting dogs also underscores how the printed materials that capture African Americans, both physically as salable goods and figuratively as stereotypes, bolster slavery as a system. Along with advertising dogs for a chase, newspapers printed notices of fugitives, complete with descriptions and reward terms, and communicated the times and conditions for slave sales. It makes some sense that print would be critical to the maintenance of slavery given that the printed word relies on a rude black/white dialectic, with the black marks being made legible by the whiteness of the paper. Print thus not only communicated the information necessary to uphold chattel slavery but also, according to Jonathan Senchyne, "model[ed] how whiteness is to be seen while unseen, providing the structural backdrop against which marks or types become legible."[109] *Clotel* thus takes the association between short fiction and timeliness to a logical extreme: in some sense, Brown fashions a novel that is a periodical, with news stories, advertisements, sketches, and tales that expose the biases of the reporting in the United States. Recognizing that abolition is a centrally textual endeavor—a battle fought through lectures, mailings, slave narratives, petitions, and poems—Brown arms *Clotel* to reframe and defang the print culture that underpinned slavery. Seeking to change the definition of Americanness, he writes a book about

enslaved folks that embraces all registers of print and that textually demonstrates a redefined *e pluribus unum.*

The story also offers multiplicity in its plot, which starts when Thomas
Jefferson's two daughters by the enslaved female Currer (who is based on
Sally Hemings, Martha Jefferson's enslaved half-sister, who bore four of Jefferson's children) are sold at auction to pay off Jefferson's debts. All three
women, Currer, Althesa, and Clotel, are phenotypically white, though Currer is identified as half African American and her daughters are one-fourth
African American. Clotel's daughter, Mary, and Althesa's daughters, Jane
and Ellen, are even lighter skinned. Of the six biracial, phenotypically white
enslaved women that the novel focuses on, only one, Mary, ends happily.
The rest, in keeping with the "tragic mulatta" trope (which Brown was the
first to employ in African American letters) meet untimely and unhappy
deaths. Currer dies of yellow fever, Althesa and Jane die of broken hearts,
and Ellen and Clotel kill themselves. As family bonds are broken by slavery's machinations, the central absence of Thomas Jefferson, the Founding Father, and the legal legitimacy his fatherhood should confer become
more and more significant. Jefferson's relations with Currer—Brown never
specifies them as sexual assault, though surely Currer lacks the ability to
refuse the man who owns her—and his subsequent denial of paternity are
emblematic of a larger erasure of the African American presence in the
national story. As Russ Castronovo has argued, in telling the story of
the Jefferson daughters, Brown foregrounds previously hidden lines
of descent that challenge monumental accounts of American beginnings.[110]
As soon as the novel starts, Currer and her two daughters are separated
from each other, leaving the narrator three (and soon more) narrative
lines to jump between in a structure that recalls the fractured aesthetic
of a sketch sequence. When Jefferson's unrecognized granddaughters are
born, Brown's fiction starts shifting between *six* different main characters
and a surrounding cast of both black and white figures, who often steal
the limelight from Jefferson's progeny. Twentieth-century critics saw this
proliferation of narrative lines in *Clotel* as evidence of Brown's poor command of the novel form. But far from being artistic failure, this multiplicity,
in which stories start and then quickly stop, uses short fiction aesthetics
to communicate the abrupt and permanent dislocation of the enslaved
families torn asunder by sale, death, gift, and other trade, and it articulates
the consequences of these ruptures for the relationship between African

Americans and the culture of beginnings.[111] With the calculated destruction of black genealogies through the slave trade, African Americans like Clotel and her mother, sister, daughters, and nieces are denied both father and Founding Father: each generation suffers from the death or abandonment of white men, reenacting Jefferson's original desertion of the family, and all are unprotected by basic American liberties.[112] In a world where slave status is determined matrilineally and patronymics are refused, the legal acknowledgment of fatherhood is the purview of whiteness. Brown himself proves this rule. Although a descendant of Stephen Hopkins, a signatory to the Mayflower Compact, through his father George W. Higgins, Brown escaped from slavery with no last name, no relationship to his absent father, and no civil rights. In imagining the lives of Jefferson's descendants and in identifying Jefferson as their father, Brown works against the telling of beginning stories that erase people of color and inserts African Americans in the projection of the American people.[113]

In a novel that is both sketch and tale, both fact and fiction, both self-authored and plagiarized, it is perhaps unsurprising that many internal characters refuse stable identification. Like Jefferson's daughters and granddaughters, who are phenotypically white and legally black, many minor characters challenge the surety of racial classifications in the United States. Daniel Webster, the Massachusetts senator who in 1820 had been lauded for his bicentenary speech at Plymouth Rock before using Puritan ancestors to justify his support for the Compromise of 1850, is almost refused a hotel on Cape Cod because the landlord seems "woefully to mistake the dark features of the traveler as he sat back in the corner of the carriage" and believes Webster to be "a *coloured man*" (*Clotel* 174; emphasis in original). Thomas Corwin, Webster's fellow senator and future secretary of the Treasury, is similarly misread as a black man at a "dining saloon." Brown dubs Corwin, who would later sponsor a constitutional amendment to protect slavery and prevent civil war, "one of the blackest white men in the United States." Using newspaper accounts to underscore the truth of his story, Brown also records the kidnapping into slavery of Salome Miller, a free German white woman: "This, reader, is no fiction; if you think so, look over the files of the New Orleans newspapers of the years 1845–46, and you will see there reports of the trial" (*Clotel* 174). On the other side of the racial binary, a major plot point involves Clotel's dressing as a Spanish gentleman—swapping both her race and her gender—to escape from slavery with the dark-skinned William, another of Brown's fictionalized alter egos, on a steamship, where she successfully fools all the crew and passengers. Despite being trained to observe well, a newspaper reporter on the same boat sees "an apparently handsome young man, with black hair and eyes, and of a darkness of complexion that betokened Spanish extraction" when he looks at Clotel (*Clotel* 171). Later Clotel's daughter, Mary, saves her lover, George Green, from execution by swapping clothes with him so he can slip out of the jail as a light-skinned woman. Especially in aggregate, these moments illustrate the instability of legally regulated identity categories—particularly racial distinctions—in the United States. Landlords, fellow diners, prison guards, steamboat captains, newspaper men, and the general public are all incapable of consistently and reliably recognizing someone's race, a fact that undermines the lynchpin of social ordering in the United States.[114]

One cannot not even certainly know one's own race, for in *Clotel* race is not an internal Freudian truth. Indeed Althesa's daughters, Jane and Ellen, are not aware that their mother has African ancestry until after both parents die, and creditors realize that their father neglected to manumit his wife and children. Jane and Ellen are thus effectively made black by the discovery of their mother's bill of sale. Perhaps even more damning is an anecdote Brown includes wherein race is determined not by descent but by self-declaration. According to a New Orleanian newspaper, "A white man, named Buddington, a teller in the Canal Bank" married "the Negro daughter of one of the wealthiest merchants. Buddington, before he could be married, was obliged to swear that he had Negro blood in his veins, and to do this he made an incision in his arm, and put some of her blood in the cut" (*Clotel* 182). To marry and gain his wife's generous dowry, the man makes himself black by sharing her blood. The act takes the one-drop theory of racial purity (upheld in the Supreme Court case *Plessy v. Ferguson*, 1896) to a logical extreme, and it upends the foundational and, in the 1850s, legal idea that slavery and race are about genealogy. Together these stories recognize the presence of racial categories while draining them of any certain signification.

Both through its many racially ambiguous characters and by means of its fractured story, "Clotel" creates an overarching feeling of risk and uncertainty. Clotel's death exemplifies these ideas while also clearly articulating their national significance. In the novel's most famous scene, Clotel runs down the Long Bridge, a bridge whose construction was authorized by President Jefferson, between Washington, DC, and Arlington, Virginia, toward the estate "occupied by that distinguished relative and descendant of the immortal Washington, Mr. George W. Curtis" when she is surrounded by slave catchers (*Clotel* 216).[115] In "plain sight of the President's house and the capital of the Union, which should be an evidence wherever it should be known, of the unconquerable love of liberty the heart may inherit," Clotel "vault[s] over the railings of the bridge, and [sinks] for ever beneath the waves of the river" (*Clotel* 217, 218). Clotel's death, halfway across a bridge in the nation's capital, symbolizes the national rejection of African Americans. Although the daughter of a president, Clotel is jailed in Washington, awaiting transportation back to her master in New Orleans and permanent separation from her daughter. The drastically different condition between Clotel and George Curtis, both descendants of presidents, underscores the empty American promise of liberty.[116] That three Virginians stop Clotel's escape and thus catalyze her death makes this criticism all the more pointed: the Founding Fathers of Virginia secured their own freedoms by chaining others, and their sons continue to do the same. Clotel jumps midbridge, neither in DC or in Virginia, after she has been separated from all of her family, and her body vanishes in the river's foamy water. The liminality and danger of being black are crystalized in this sentimental death, a death that illustrates a national incoherence and a lack of safe spaces for African Americans. These feelings of disunity become Brown's "unity of effect," that defining mark of the tale according to Poe. Rendered in a frontispiece engraving that shows two opposed groups of white men with a black woman dying between them, this moment expresses the crisis—a lethal one—that is slavery.

Within *Clotel* it is the light-colored women who suffer most from slavery and its sexual exploitation. If we accept Geoffrey Sanborn's postulation that these light-skinned women characters conjure "a special kind of time: the time before it is too late" within the novel, then we can see how Brown's novel also offers a version of the narrative dynamism that Irving first linked to the tale form.[117] As each successive generation of Jeffersonian daughters is born, we as readers must worry about their inevitable future of sale and assault. The novel thus stretches forward in time even as it replays the central scene with little variation for five of the six light-skinned black women characters. Our concern and this double temporality hinge on the widespread knowledge, then and now, of what beautiful biracial enslaved women were valued for—concubinage. Even more than light-skinned men like Brown (who were the products of such unions), phenotypically white but enslaved women represented the rape power that undergirded American chattel slavery. For the reader, these women, born of white fathers and damned to be used by white sons, function recursively. We hope they will not be assaulted, but we know they will be, thus having daughters who begin the cycle again. Currer's story is Clotel's, and Althesa's story is Jane's story. Mary, who is essentially bought as a wife by a Frenchman who helps her escape, also enacts a (less violent) version of this narrative. Her life ends differently only because she is in Europe, passing as white. The evocation of "time before it is too late" brings a second potentially, and almost always refused plot, into play, an echo of the double-plotting in "The Legend of Sleepy Hollow" and "Rip Van Winkle." Whereas in Irving's tales narrative dynamism marked the tale genre as lively and playful, in *Clotel* the genre of the tale is morbid and tense. It presents the dangers of slavery refracted through the American expectations of security and freedom. As Mary shows, whatever hope there is for African Americans lies in escaping such an American story.

As Brown dramatizes with his image of the Plymouth-bound and Jamestown-bound ships, the nation's original sin is slavery. Recognition of that truth displaces accepted origin stories and requires radical reframing of American beginnings. Formally, Brown's novel communicates this point by building on the sketch and the tale, shifting the familiar white modes of storytelling to give voice to African Americans. His characters embody and exceed racial stereotypes, much like Brown, with his use of stereotyped plates, both enacted and exceeded the modes of narrative practiced by the likes of Hawthorne, Melville, and Stowe. Distributing books both at lectures and by means of a web of abolitionists rather than through periodical subscription networks or bookseller's stores, Brown offers a counterpoint to the patterns that I have explored in the previous chapters and reminds us that I have traced one important tradition, not explored all of the activities and characteristics of literary writing in the United States between 1819 and 1853. Moreover, Brown's arrival on the scene provides a connection point between the vital heritage of antebellum African American letters and what by 1853 was the dying culture of beginnings. If Hawthorne's, Melville's, and Stowe's novels demonstrated that the conditions that had made sketches and tales about US origins were waning, Brown's clever repurposing of white sketch writing and tale spinning showed that the ongoing relevance of these two genres lay in their ability to represent new historical realities and to accommodate new literary needs—to be subsumed into what we would now call the novel and the modern short story.[118]

The Foundational Sin and Subtext

Precisely because they had become so culturally legible and so useful for beginning stories, the sketch and the tale formed the basis of four important midcentury novels over three years. As they transmogrified into longer texts, these genres indexed a turn away from singular stories of beginnings that celebrated white founders while winking at the injustices endured by people of color. My discussion of these four great American novels provides the opportunity to underscore that the presence of non-whites was always a subtext in the culture of beginnings. Irving's transatlantic crossing can read as a flipped Middle Passage, making his chosen east-to-west journey and his privileged tourism an inverse of the forced, violent relocation of African peoples. Everywhere Irving goes, this under-story tells us, his reception and ideas are predicated on the privilege of his whiteness, and they even become a form of antiblackness. In Hale's fourth sketch of American character, the granddaughter of a woman with very "black eyes" and that granddaughter's lover, Mr. Freeman, request stories about the American Revolution.[119] Precisely because the freedom of African Americans is not addressed, precisely because they are not *free men* like Freeman, Hale's tale moves uncomfortably around the question of who can earn liberty through revolution. Meanwhile Sedgwick denominates her description of a gift book heroine as a "bill of particulars," mercantile language that reminds us that white men like the girl's soon-to-be southern father-in-law consider African American women to be purchasable property.[120] So too in Sedgwick's "Modern Chivalry," Perdita, the main character, is enslaved on an American plantation close to Washington, DC, and then ends up in an Antiguan mansion staffed by enslaved people during the American Revolution and the height of the West Indies sugar trade. While Sedgwick mentions Perdita's "soft blue eyes and fair round cheeks," Perdita's enslavement, her mother's absence, her lack of surname, her forced silence, her father's evident wealth, and her husband's Caribbean governorship are all indicative that she, like Clotel, might have African ancestry resulting from a rape of a black woman by a white man.[121] In Hawthorne's *Twice-Told Tales,* "The Wedding-Knell" tells a gothic story of two old lovers united at a funereal marriage. What is most frightening about the event is the arrival of "a dark procession" with "another, and another pair, as aged, as black" as the first (*TTT* 45). That these figures remind the lady of her youth in which she was married to a cruel "southern gentleman" who "carried her to Charlestown," suggests that the real horror of the scene is not the ghosts but the evidence of the innumerable deaths of African Americans, a people who form an existential threat to the republic of whiteness represented by white marriage (*TTT* 39). So too, as I argued in chapter 5, Poe's detective Dupin embodies racial difference by contrasting white reason with black atavism. In sum, the sketches and tales discussed in the previous chapters contain, to use Toni Morrison's words, "a subtext that either sabotages the surface text's expressed intentions or escapes them through a language that mystifies what it cannot bring itself to articulate but still attempts to register."[122] The presence of African Americans was critical to beginning stories because only by ignoring enslaved and free black people could these authors craft a white fictive ethnicity through glorifying stories of the US past. In other words, in the culture of beginnings, the projection of a white American people relied on antiblackness. Tensions over slavery in which regional affiliations trumped interest in unifying origins made that elision less tenable and made the sketch and the tale less useful as short fiction genres.

This is the end of a book on beginnings. Queequeg, who ships aboard a boat named after a tribe (the Pequot) decimated by the Puritans, has become "George Washington cannibalistically developed," and Thomas Jefferson's biracial daughters have taken center stage (*Moby-Dick* 55). I have illuminated how early nineteenth-century writers used short fiction to depict American beginnings because of a confluence of forces. After the War of 1812, orators argued that the United States had a worthwhile culture and history, and readers wanted distinctly American literature. Authors turned to the sketch and the tale because their appearances in periodicals gave them a feeling of authenticity and currency, because the aesthetic of brevity helped magnify the importance of beginnings, and because shorter works were easier to publish. While the United States would not sign an international copyright agreement until 1891, publishing had become a profession by the midcentury, and houses like Ticknor and Fields were making good money with increasingly longer works of American literature.[123] Indeed, using short fiction became a particularly American solution to crafting authentic novels in the 1850s because the genre had been so well established and articulated in the culture of beginnings. Even so, while nineteenth-century readers, publishers, and authors came to recognize the cultural use of the novel, they did not disdain short fiction. In fact, Hawthorne, Melville, Stowe, Brown, Irving, Hale, and Sedgwick continued to write and publish sketches and tales in the 1850s.[124] (Poe died in 1849.) Moreover, in the decades following *The Scarlet Letter, Moby-Dick, Uncle Tom's Cabin,* and *Clotel,* the protodocumentary stance of the sketch arguably came to inform the realism of postbellum works, including the regional stories that rely on a knowing urbane observer. So too the arguments realists Henry James and William Dean Howells made against the multiplot novel in favor of a single, driven story recall Poe's definition of the tale. In multiple ways, then, American narrative beginnings lie in short fiction: when trying to professionalize American letters, early nineteenth-century authors wrote many sketches and tales that celebrate American origins and conjure a fictive white ethnicity. Hawthorne, Melville, Stowe, and Brown used the sketch and the tale to form the skeleton of their seminal midcentury novels and complicate singular origin stories. And the sketch and the tale anticipated the aesthetic debates and racialized national projections relevant for years to come.

❖ NOTES ❖

INTRODUCTION

1. "The Annuals," *New-York Mirror: A Weekly Gazette of Literature and the Fine Arts* (December 24, 1836): 207. The reviewer is praising the *Token and Atlantic Souvenir*, which is the gift book resulting from the merger of the *Token* and the *Atlantic Souvenir*. Both annuals were known and respected for their American material.

2. Given that most modern readers would identify a piece under one hundred pages as a novella or a piece of short fiction, Davidson's reliance on the term "novel" reinforces easy critical presumptions about the greater worth of anything labeled with that genre term. Cathy N. Davidson, *Revolution and the Word: The Rise of the Novel in America* (New York: Oxford University Press, 2004), 78.

3. M. M. Bakhtin, "Discourse in the Novel," in *The Dialogic Imagination: Four Essays*, trans. Michael Holquist and Caryl Emerson (Austin: University of Texas Press, 1981), 261, 263.

4. Ralph Waldo Emerson was not enthusiastic about the idea of the country as a miscellany. In his journals he once lamented, "Alas for America as I must so often say, the ungirt, the diffuse, the profuse, procumbent, one wide ground juniper, out of which no cedar, no oak will rear up a mast to the clouds! it all runs to leaves, to suckers, to tendrils, to miscellany." Emerson concluded that because it was a miscellany, "America is formless, has no terrible & no beautiful condensation." Ralph Waldo Emerson, *Emerson in His Journals*, ed. Joel Porte (Cambridge, MA: Harvard University Press, 1982), 372.

5. See Trish Loughran, *The Republic in Print: Print Culture in the Age of U.S. Nation Building, 1770–1870* (New York: Columbia University Press, 2007).

6. Alexis de Tocqueville, *Democracy in America,* trans. Henry Reeve, 4th ed. (Philadelphia: J. and H. G. Langley, 1841), 2:62.

7. The *Oxford English Dictionary*'s first cited usage for "short story" is from 1877.

8. Robert F. Marler, "From Tale to Short Story: The Emergence of a New Genre in the 1850's," *American Literature* 46, no. 2 (May 1974): 156.

9. Michelle R. Sizemore, *American Enchantment: Rituals of the People in the Post-Revolutionary World* (New York: Oxford University Press, 2017), 123, 115, 27.

10. Tim Killick, *British Short Fiction in the Early Nineteenth Century: The Rise of the Tale* (Burlington, VT: Ashgate, 2008), 22. Worth noting is that modern critics may still avoid "sketch" and "tale" because the terms gained pejorative associations in the twentieth century—they were recognized as unsophisticated precursors to the *modern short story* or simplistic, uninteresting, shrimpy cousins of the novel. Robert Marler, for example, contends that the tale's pedantic "tendency towards allegory" makes it a rude precursor to the modern short story (154). Marler, "From Tale to Short Story." For an overview of the inclination to dismiss short fiction, see Mary Louise Pratt, "The Short Story: The Long and the Short of It," in *The New Short Story Theories*, ed. Charles E. May (Athens: Ohio University Press, 1994), 91–113.

11. Sketches and tales did sometimes overlap. For example, James Lawson's collection of *Tales and Sketches, by a Cosmopolite* (1830) frequently frames oral tales with sketch-like introductions and conclusions. In "The Clyde" the narrator describes the atmospheric conditions around the river before relating a tale told him by a fellow traveler. When this "tale," as the narrator calls it, is done, he dismisses the storyteller and returns to his sketch-like descriptions of scenery, ending the piece reminiscing over beautiful "scenes," that frequent synonym of the sketch. This mixing of the tale's fantasy and the sketch's observation results in a protodocumentary view on an imaginative and history-rich world. It is an authentic poise that does national work. As Lawrence Buell tells us, "fluidity" between sketch and tale "is to be expected from a milieu that valued the didactic, the utilitarian, and the exposition of native culture." Furthermore, as I discuss later in the introduction, it is worth remembering than any effort to define a genre will capture the major characteristics of that genre form rather than fully defining the exact qualities of every example that we might classify as of that genre. In other words, genre definitions provide identificatory guidelines rather than absolutes. James Lawson, *Tales and Sketches, by a Cosmopolite* (New York: E. Bliss, 1830), 29, 37. Lawrence Buell, *New*

England Literary Culture from Revolution through Renaissance (New York: Cambridge University Press, 1986), 296–97.

12. According to *The Oxford English Dictionary,* the term "sketch," used to refer to a short description or narrative, was in use by 1668, and the term "tale" was used even earlier.

13. Edgar Allan Poe, "Review: *Twice-Told Tales* by Nathaniel Hawthorne," *Graham's Lady's and Gentleman's Magazine* (May 1842): 2.

14. Anne Thackeray Ritchie cites the working title to *Our Village* in her introduction to *Our Village* (London: Macmillan, 1893), xxv.

15. Edward W. Said, *Beginnings: Intention and Method* (New York: Columbia University Press, 1985), 5.

16. Nathaniel Hawthorne, "The Devil in the Manuscript," *New-England Magazine* (November 1835): 341.

17. Ibid., 345.

18. Etienne Balibar, "The Nation Form: History and Ideology," in *Race Critical Theories: Text and Context,* ed. Philomena Essed and David Theo Goldberg (Malden, MA: Blackwell, 2002), 224.

19. Although I have denominated it the culture of beginnings, I am not the first to notice the American fixation on the past in the nineteenth century. The past forty years has seen much work on historical fiction, a form of beginning stories, and a handful of monographs focused on US beginnings, including Russ Castronovo's *Fathering the Nation* and Terence Martin's *Parables of Possibility.* Martin, who focuses on ideal beginnings in American literature, articulates how negatives become positive as writers of various stripes from the nineteenth and twentieth centuries define their own world through contrast with their invented utopias. Castronovo investigates how "patriarchal lineage administered a national narrative through the deployment of dates, biographies, memorials, and patriotic rituals" and how various authors resisted and revised powerful stories of descent through the idea of parricide. Russ Castronovo, *Fathering the Nation: American Genealogies of Slavery and Freedom* (Berkeley: University of California Press, 1995), 5. Terence Martin, *Parables of Possibility: The American Need for Beginnings* (New York: Columbia University Press, 1995).

20. While some of the pieces that depicted the US past during these years were longer, like James Fenimore Cooper's *The Spy* (1821), many more were short.

21. Richard Strier, "How Formalism Became a Dirty Word and Why We Can't Do without It," in *Renaissance Literature and Its Formal Engagements,* ed. Mark David Rasmussen (New York: Palgrave, 2002), 211.

22. Partha Chatterjee, "Anderson's Utopia," *Diacritics: A Review of Contemporary Criticism* 29, no. 4 (1999): 128–34; Homi K Bhabha, "DissemiNation: Time, Narrative, and the Margins of the Modern Nation," in *Nation and Narration*, ed. Homi Bhabha (London: Routledge, 1990), 291–322.

23. Qtd. in Martin, *Parables of Possibility*, 3.

24. Qtd. in Arthur H. Shaffer, *The Politics of History: Writing the History of the American Revolution, 1783–1815* (New Brunswick, NJ: Transaction, 2009), 32.

25. Abiel Holmes, *American Annals, or, A Chronological History of America, From Its Discovery in 1492 to 1806,* (London: Sherwood, Neely, and Jones, 1813), 1:iii.

26. Homi K. Bhabha, "Introduction: Narrating the Nation," in *Nation and Narration*, ed. Homi Bhabha (London: Routledge, 1990), 1.

27. John R. Herbert, "The Map That Named America: Library Acquires 1507 Waldseemüller Map of the World," Library of Congress, September 2003, http://www.loc.gov/loc/lcib/0309/maps.html.

28. James W. Barker, "Forefather's Day," in *Encyclopedia of American Holidays and National Days,* ed. Len Travers (Westport, CT: Greenwood, 2006), 449; Daniel Webster, *The Great Speeches and Orations of Daniel Webster,* ed. Edwin Percy Whipple (Boston: Little, Brown, 1886), 25.

29. While celebrations like Forefathers' Days and the Fourth of July began in the eighteenth century, they took on new import after the War of 1812, when the passage of years had made the past more remote and the recent conflict put nationalistic language into wide circulation. Early notable historians like David Ramsay and Jeremy Belknap had lived the history about which they wrote, but later historians had inherited an extant nation. "With a mixture of grief, pleasure, and pity," John Adams noted a shift away from personal recollection as early as 1816, when he wrote that the "young gentlemen of genius" giving orations to commemorate the Boston Massacre were "describing scenes they never saw, and descanting on feelings they never felt." Their speeches, he continued, "are infinitely more indicative of the feelings of the moment than of the feelings that produced the Revolution." The July 4, 1826, deaths of both John Adams and Thomas Jefferson, the second and third US presidents, only further underlined that the American Revolution was no longer a present memory. Ten years later, James Madison, architect of the Constitution and last of the Founding Fathers, died too. Because the actors had passed away, the moment was ripe for history-in-fiction and fiction-in-history. John Adams, *The Works of John Adams, Second President of the United States,* ed.

Charles Francis Adams and Charles Doe (Boston: Little, Brown, 1856), 10:203, 204.

30. Cotton Mather's magisterial history of America, *Magnalia Christi Americana*, complete with fawning biographies of Bradford and Winthrop, was reprinted in 1820; Nathaniel Morton's *New-Englands Memoriall*, a Plymouth history with an account of the first Thanksgiving written by William Bradford's nephew, was reprinted in 1826; and John Winthrop's private journal was first printed in a complete form in 1825. So too the Massachusetts Historical Society published the never-before-seen *A Model of Christian Charity*, the location of Winthrop's claim that Boston would be a City on the Hill, in 1838. It fast became, along with the Mayflower Compact, what Joseph Conforti calls "regional scripture." Still, the printing continued, with texts like Alexander Young's two edited collections of primary documents on the founding of Plymouth Plantation and the Massachusetts Bay Colony in the 1840s. Joseph A. Conforti, *Imagining New England: Explorations of Regional Identity from the Pilgrims to the Mid-Twentieth Century* (Chapel Hill: University of North Carolina Press, 2001), 194.

31. Henry Inman, who was commissioned by Congress to paint Daniel Boone, died in 1846 before doing much more than a few studies of the subject. His student William Henry Powell took over the commission in 1847 and painted *Discovery of the Mississippi by De Soto*—a new subject but still a moment celebrating American expansion (by claiming a Spanish explorer).

32. Ralph Waldo Emerson, "Nature," in *Essays & Poems*, ed. Joel Porte, Harold Bloom, and Paul Kane (New York: Library of America, 1996), 7.

33. David James Kiracofe, "The Jamestown Jubilees: 'State Patriotism' and Virginia Identity in the Early Nineteenth Century," *Virginia Magazine of History and Biography* 110, no. 1 (2002): 36.

34. Robert Hughes, *American Visions: The Epic History of Art in America* (New York: Knopf, 1997), 176.

35. Ibid., 179.

36. Along with featuring a fictional tribe (perhaps Cooper meant Mohegan), Cooper's novel supports the cynical interpretation that the best Mohican is actually Hawkeye, the white man. As a "man without a cross" (i.e., with no mixed blood), Hawkeye can take the useful tracking skills and cultural knowledge and transport it to white America as Chingachgook and Uncas die.

37. John Neal, "Late American Books," *Blackwood's Edinburgh Magazine* 18, no. 104 (September 1825): 316.

38. Ibid., 317.
39. Rufus Choate, *Addresses and Orations of Rufus Choate* (Boston: Little, Brown, 1878), 1–2.
40. Ibid., 7.
41. Hayden White argues that nineteenth-century historians become anxious about literature exactly because of the proximity between the two disciplines and the manner in which readers receive literature as true. He paints with a wide brush, talking generally about the nineteenth century. In fact, though his identification of proximity is apt, there is more nuance than he represents. See Hayden V. White, *The Fiction of Narrative: Essays on History, Literature, and Theory, 1957–2007,* ed. Robert Doran (Baltimore: Johns Hopkins University Press, 2010), 187–202.
42. Ibid., 14.
43. Qtd. in Brian Richardson, *Narrative Beginnings: Theories and Practices,* Frontiers of Narrative (Lincoln: University of Nebraska Press, 2008), 7.
44. Between Said and Richardson's edited collection is A. D. Nuttall's *Openings: Narrative Beginnings from the Epic to the Novel* (1992), offering a more taxonomic treatment of openings, those first words of a literary work. Although he pursues a division between "natural" beginnings (*David Copperfield*'s "I am born") and "formal" beginnings (the in medias res of *The Aeneid*) in a highly canonical selection of literary works, he concludes "The field of real openings is too rich for my scheme" and dismantles his own thesis in the book's final chapter. A. D. Nuttall, *Openings: Narrative Beginnings from the Epic to the Novel* (Oxford: Clarendon, 1992), 246.
45. Said, *Beginnings*, 41.
46. Sarah Hardy, "The Short Story: Approaches to the Problem," *Style* 27, no. 3 (1993): 325.
47. Bhabha, "Introduction," 2.
48. Because international copyright protections did not exist in the United States, printers could and did sell European works for the cost of production plus a small profit in what Meredith McGill has dubbed the culture of reprinting. The original writer got no recompense, and often one work would exist in many different formats put out by many different printers competing for buyers at different price points. As a result, literature from established and new European authors was cheap and ubiquitous, and the percentage of American works that hit best-seller status only finally became greater in the 1850s, when writers like Nathaniel Hawthorne and Harriet Beecher Stowe transported short fiction techniques into their

successful novels *The Scarlet Letter* and *Uncle Tom's Cabin*. Authors did not see these conditions as aberrant but rather as ordinary, even when, like Catharine Sedgwick, they advocated for stronger copyright laws. And in that ordinariness, they saw the utility of shorter prose forms. Meredith L. McGill, *American Literature and the Culture of Reprinting, 1834–1853* (Philadelphia: University of Pennsylvania Press, 2007).

49. Cooper really is an exception to early nineteenth-century trends in novels because he writes multiple, long successful novels.

50. See Frank Luther Mott, *Golden Multitudes: The Story of Best Sellers in the United States* (New York: Macmillan, 1947), 305. Mott defines best-seller status as selling a number of copies equal to or greater than 1 percent of the population according to the census that starts that decade, 1810 in this case. Notably, he is interested in overarching sales rather than in sales in the year of publication. His measurement, then, is an imperfect one of popularity over time that reflects the impossibility of finding exact circulation numbers for many of these texts.

51. See ibid., 305–7.

52. John Austin, "United States, 1780–1850," in *The Novel*, ed. Franco Moretti (Princeton, NJ: Princeton University Press, 2006), 1:457.

53. Washington Irving, *The Sketch Book* (London: John Miller and John Murray, 1820), 2:417.

54. Following Leon Jackson's excellent *The Business of Letters*, we must acknowledge that before midcentury, there are many literary economies, not just that of bound-volume sales or magazine publications. I, however, focus on volumes and periodicals. Leon Jackson, *The Business of Letters: Authorial Economies in Antebellum America* (Stanford, CA: Stanford University Press, 2008).

55. There are terms other than "sketch" and "tale" in use. Most, however, seem to be synonyms for or close relatives of these two forms. For example, pencillings (N. P. Willis's "Pencillings by the Way" in the *New York Mirror*, 1833–35, and later collected in volume form), crayon sketches (Albert Pike's "Crayon-Sketches and Journeyings" in the *Boston Pearl and Literary Gazette*, 1834), and charcoal sketches (Joseph C. Neal's *Charcoal Sketches, or Scenes in a Metropolis* [Philadelphia: Carey and Hart, 1838]) are all actually sketches. "Scenes" seems to be, if not a synonym, then a closely related idea similarly pivoting on a visual metaphor as if the author is drawing with words (e.g., anonymous, *Scenes and Thoughts in Europe* [New York: Wiley and Putnam, 1846]). I would further suggest that the term "legend" often means "tale" as it does in Washington Irving's

"The Legend of Sleepy Hollow," a piece that Irving calls a "tale" in its preface.

56. Wai-chee Dimock, *Through Other Continents: American Literature across Deep Time* (Princeton, NJ: Princeton University Press, 2009), 74–75.

57. Ibid., 74.

58. Mary Russell Mitford, *Our Village*, ed. Anne Thackeray Ritchie (New York: Macmillan, 1893), 169, 169–70, 33. Amanpal Garcha notes the importance of the moment when the narrator watches ice-skating in *From Sketch to Novel: The Development of Victorian Fiction* (New York: Cambridge University Press, 2009).

59. Authors like Mary Mitford, Washington Irving, Nathaniel Hawthorne, and Herman Melville create this observational stance through "repose" (a word that Poe uses to describe Hawthorne's sketches in his famous 1842 review of *Twice-Told Tales*)—a sort of urbane posture. Importantly, though, not all sketch writers were upper-class observers. Indeed, Kristie Hamilton celebrates the accessibility of the nineteenth-century sketch to women and other nonelites. Though Irving made his narrator a gentleman sketcher, in the wake of great success of *The Sketch Book*, women writers and middle-class writers increasingly utilized the form in the United States. Kristie Hamilton, *America's Sketchbook: The Cultural Life of a Nineteenth-Century Genre* (Athens: Ohio University Press, 1998).

60. Richard C. Sha, *The Visual and Verbal Sketch in British Romanticism* (Philadelphia: University of Pennsylvania Press, 1998), 5.

61. John Armstrong, *Sketches: Or Essays on Various Subjects* (London: A. Millar, 1758), vi–vii; Sha, *The Visual and Verbal Sketch*, 5.

62. As James Kirke Paulding shows, authenticity was a preoccupation for early nineteenth-century writers. Decades (and a civil war) before realism, Paulding, an early American writer intent on fashioning a distinct American literature, argued that American authors should derive their literature from "real life." By wrapping truth into fiction, he thought, American writers would have something new to say rather than just imitating European writers and ideas. Paulding emphasized the importance of authenticity for compelling cultural production: "Real life is fraught with adventures, to which the wildest fictions scarcely afford a parallel; and it has this special advantage over its rival, that these events, however extraordinary, can always be traced to motives, actions and passions, arising out of circumstances no way unnatural, and partaking of no impossible or supernatural agency" (24). As the 1820 essay later titled "National Literature" makes clear, Paulding believed that the "real" United States

with its history, its people, and its landscape, was the key to writing truly American letters. Along with this more general call for American authors to write about American life, many cultural figures specifically requested historical fiction, stories that animated key events and figures from the US past. See James Kirk Paulding, "National Literature," in *American Literature, American Culture,* ed. Gordon Hutner (New York: Oxford University Press, 1999), 24–25.

63. Frank Luther Mott, *A History of American Magazines, 1741–1850* (Cambridge, MA: Belknap Press of Harvard University Press, 1957), 1:392–93.

64. "Review: *The Token,* for 1829," *Yankee and Boston Literary Gazette* (November 12, 1828): 46–47.

65. William Austin, "Some Account of Peter Rugg," *New-England Galaxy* (September 10, 1824): 3.

66. The ad is on the same page as (and to the right side of) William Austin, "Arrival of Mr. Peter Rugg in Boston," *New-England Galaxy* (January 19, 1827): 3.

67. "Peter Rugg" is referenced in many nineteenth-century pieces including Barnacle, "Selling a Justice," *Spirit of the Times, a Chronicle of the Turf, Agriculture, Field Sports, Literature, and the Stage* (February 10, 1849): 1, which is reprinted in the *Huntress* (March 3, 1849); Eliza Leslie, "Leonilla Lynmore, Part IV," *Godey's Lady's Book* (October 1841): 180–84; and "A Literary Bell on Its Travels," *Maine Farmer: An Agricultural Journal and Family Newspaper* (August 19, 1852): 2. The variety of these publications suggests that many different readerships, from middle-class women to sport-loving men and farmers, knew of Peter Rugg. A January 5, 1827, announcement in the *New-England Galaxy* indicates that the story was also published in volume form (with other stories and poems) and offered by Benjamin Davenport for seventy-five cents. The book was called *The Literary Gem, or Legend and Lyrics.* Louise Imogen Guiney's poetic adaptation made it into the 1891 Christmas edition of *Scribner's,* and the story was reprinted toward century end by, among other periodicals, *Current Literature* (New York, November 1888) and the *Maine Farmer* (Augusta, June 26, 1890).

68. Qtd. in Thomas Wentworth Higginson, "A Precursor to Hawthorne," *Independent* (March 29, 1888): 1.

69. See Peter Rugg, "Some Account of the Family of Notions," *New-England Galaxy* (October 29, 1831): 2; and "Letter to the Editor," *New-England Galaxy* (November 24, 1826): 3.

70. Terramorsi writes, "So convincing was Austin's depiction of Rugg's fictional exploits, that the tale [was] mistaken for fact by many of its initial

readers, several of whom wrote to the *New-England Galaxy* soon after the first part of 'Peter Rugg' appeared in 1824 and demanded to know more of Rugg's whereabouts." Bernard Terramorsi, "'Peter Rugg, the Missing Man,' or The Eclipsing Revolution: An Essay on the Supernatural," Université de la Réunion, O.R.A.C.L.E., July 30, 2018, http://oracle-reunion .pagesperso-orange.fr/documents/peter_rugg_the_missing_man _the_eclipsing_revolut.html. Also see Sizemore, *American Enchantment*, 223n51, where she accepts that readers thought Peter Rugg was fact.

71. Joseph T. Buckingham, "Things in General," *New-England Galaxy* (September 10, 1824): 3.

72. Austin, "Some Account of Peter Rugg," 3.

73. Sizemore writes that Peter Rugg "disappears at the moment of the Revolution, only to return years later." Sizemore, *American Enchantment*, 143.

74. Jeffrey Insko, "The Prehistory of Posthistoricism," in *The Limits of Literary Historicism*, ed. Allen Dunn and Thomas F. Haddox, Tennessee Studies in Literature (Knoxville: University of Tennessee Press, 2011), 110.

75. Henry David Thoreau, "Civil Disobedience," in *Walden and Other Writings*, ed. Brooks Atkinson (New York: Modern Library, 2000), 671.

76. Frederick Douglass, "What to the Slave Is the Fourth of July?" in *My Bondage and My Freedom* (New York: Miller, Orton and Mulligan, 1855), 441.

77. Webster, *The Great Speeches and Orations of Daniel Webster*, 605, 617.

78. Ibid., 621.

1. DUELING TEMPORALITIES IN IRVING'S BEST-SELLING *SKETCH BOOK*

1. Van Winkle published the first American edition of *The Sketch Book* over fifteen months between 1819 and 1820, and he printed the first number of the second edition in 1819; the rest of the numbers appeared in 1820. Van Winkle printed numbers 1 and 2 of a third edition in 1822; he brought out number 3 in 1823. No other numbers of that edition appear to have been printed. In 1824, Van Winkle then printed a two-volume version of *The Sketch Book*, based on the two-volume version of *The Sketch Book* that had appeared in London.

2. See Gordon S. Wood, *Empire of Liberty: A History of the Early Republic, 1789–1815* (New York: Oxford University Press, 2009), 666.

3. See Meredith L. McGill, *American Literature and the Culture of Reprinting, 1834–1853* (Philadelphia: University of Pennsylvania Press, 2007). Irving himself, who set a high price for his *Sketch Book* and urged American readers to support American authors, had earlier reprinted the writings

by Lord Byron, Walter Scott, and others that his brother and his friends shipped across the Atlantic while he was editor of the *Analectic Magazine* (1812–14).

4. Sydney Smith, "ART. III. Statistical Annals of the United States of America." *Edinburgh Review, or Critical Journal* 33, no. 65 (January 1820): 79.

5. In the "Advertisement" that was printed at the beginning of the first British edition and that continued to introduce *The Sketch Book* until it was replaced by the "Preface to the Revised Edition" in 1848, Irving wrote, "The author is aware of the austerity with which the writings of his countrymen have hitherto been treated by British critics" (1:v–vi). Irving dates this "Advertisement" February 1820, a month after Smith's taunt. Washington Irving, *The Sketch Book of Geoffrey Crayon, Gent.* 2 vols. (London: John Miller and John Murray, 1820). Hereafter cited in text as Miller-Murray *SB*. A copy of the Miller-Murray two-volume English edition of *The Sketch Book* is held in Houghton Library, Harvard University.

6. Paul Giles, *Transatlantic Insurrections: British Culture and the Formation of American Literature, 1730–1860* (Philadelphia: University of Pennsylvania Press, 2001), 2.

7. *The Sketch Book* professes to be an account of European travels, but it functions as a record of mostly British scenes. In his "Author's Account of Himself," Geoffrey Crayon indicates that England is representative of Europe. As the ironic Crayon says, "The comparative importance and swelling magnitude of many English travelers among us; who, I was assured, were very little people in their own country" demonstrates that "the great men of Europe" are superior to "degenerated" Americans (1: 8–9). This early statement shows how Crayon and the text frequently jump from Europe to Britain, the latter representing the most meaningful part of the former. Washington Irving, *The Sketch Book of Geoffrey Crayon, Gent.* (New York: C. S. Van Winkle). Hereafter cited in text as Van Winkle *SB* with volume or issue number, a colon, and then the page number(s). Contemporary readers were ready to accept and even magnify this synecdoche; noting that Irving was "anxious to visit Europe," the London *Monthly Review* moved quickly to chauvinistic praise: "Great Britain might well be the object of peculiar attraction" (198). See "Art. XII. The Sketch Book of Geoffrey Crayon, Gent.," *Monthly Review, or, Literary Journal* (October 1820): 196–206. Of the twenty-eight pieces within the original Van Winkle *Sketch Book*, twenty-one are sketches set in Britain or about Britons, including "The Voyage" (which ends with Crayon's arrival in England), "Roscoe," "English Writers on America," "Rural Life in England," "The

Art of Book-Making," "A Royal Poet" (about the Scottish King James, which starts with a visit to Windsor Castle), "The Country Church," "The Widow and Her Son," "The Boar's Head Tavern," "The Mutability of Literature," "Rural Funerals," "Westminster Abbey," "Christmas," "The Stage Coach," "Christmas Eve," "Christmas Day," "The Christmas Dinner," "Little Britain," "Stratford-on-Avon," "John Bull," "The Pride of the Village," and "The Angler" (which starts with mention of New York but quickly shifts focus to Wales). "The Wife," which features Crayon as a character, is set in some unnamed countryside easily presumed to be Britain. Of the three remaining sketches, "The Broken Heart" features the daughter of an Irish barrister; "The Inn Kitchen," which serves as an introduction for the only tale not told by Diedrich Knickerbocker, takes place in the Netherlands; and the first sketch of the collection, "The Author's Account of Himself" is set in no specific locale but includes Crayon's recollections of exploring the Catskills and his projections of explorations in England. The three pieces within the 1819–20 American edition not accounted for above are all tales: "Rip Van Winkle," "The Legend of Sleepy Hollow," and "The Spectre Bridegroom." The sketches, "A Sunday in London" and "London Antiques," are added for the 1848 author revised edition and are thus not tabulated here, though obviously both take place in London. The "Prospectus," a prefatory statement in the first three American editions, takes place nowhere and is not counted as a sketch or a tale; I have also not separately classified the short "Post Script," which is a brief addendum to "The Legend of Sleepy Hollow."

8. "Art. V.: *The Sketch Book of Geoffrey Crayon*," *Edinburgh Monthly Review* (later *Blackwood's*) (September 1820): 306.

9. Qtd. in Jeffrey Rubin-Dorsky, *Adrift in the Old World: The Psychological Pilgrimage of Washington Irving* (Chicago: University of Chicago Press, 1988), 267–68; emphasis in original.

10. "Art. V.: *The Sketch Book of Geoffrey Crayon*," 304, qtd. in Edward Everett, "ART. X.—Bracebridge Hall," *North American Review* (July 1, 1822): 213.

11. John Gibson Lockhart, "On the Writings of Charles Brockden Brown and Washington Irving," *Blackwood's Edinburgh Magazine* (February 1820): 559.

12. "Art. V.: *The Sketch Book of Geoffrey Crayon*," 304.

13. "French Tribute to American Literature," *Columbian Star* (April 27, 1822): 4; emphasis in original.

14. "Review: *The Sketch Book*," *New-England Galaxy* (August 6, 1819): 171.

15. See Frank Luther Mott, *Golden Multitudes: The Story of Best Sellers in the United States* (New York: Macmillan, 1947).

16. Murray printed one thousand copies of the second volume of the first edition, and Springer says that Murray went through at least six editions by 1824. See Haskell Springer, introduction to *The Sketch Book of Geoffrey Crayon, Gent.*, in *The Complete Works of Washington Irving*, ed. Haskell S. Springer (Boston: Twayne, 1978), 8:xix, xx.

17. See "From the Scotsman. Review: Bracebridge Hall," *Calcutta Journal of Politics and General Literature* (November 23, 1822): 310.

18. Burdened by mounting legal costs and aware of the material depreciation of his stake in Irving's writing, Murray eventually sold the copyrights to Bohn at a cut rate and accepted the losses. For Irving's letters to Murray about the case against Bohn, see Ben Harris McClary, ed., *Washington Irving and the House of Murray: Geoffrey Crayon Charms the British, 1817–1856* (Knoxville: University of Tennessee Press, 1969), 193–97.

19. Qtd. in ibid., 196.

20. Remarkably, despite the fact that Irving distinguishes between sketch and tale, and despite the fact that nineteenth-century critics acknowledged the presence of two genres, critics like Ray B. West Jr. have insisted that *The Sketch Book* contains only sketches. Surprisingly, other admirable critics like Paul Giles and Joseph Rezek have not commented upon the genre divide in *The Sketch Book*. See Ray B. West, *The Short Story in America, 1900–1950* (Chicago: H. Regnery, 1952), 4.

21. See Kristie Hamilton, *America's Sketchbook: The Cultural Life of a Nineteenth-Century Genre* (Athens: Ohio University Press, 1998).

22. On the idea of communicating essence over polish, see Sha, *The Visual and Verbal Sketch in British Romanticism* (Philadelphia: University of Pennsylvania Press, 1998), 5.

23. Hamilton, *America's Sketchbook*, 9. Kristie Hamilton and Amanpal Garcha both link this feeling of haste and incompletion to the fragmentariness of modernity. As the economy shifted from agrarian to market-based, social groups and community rituals were upset and reformed. Sketches helped make sense of these massive changes and the technologies—trains, steam-powered presses, and more—that accompanied them. See Amanpal Garcha, *From Sketch to Novel: The Development of Victorian Fiction* (New York: Cambridge University Press, 2009).

24. See Hamilton, *America's Sketchbook*, 8–32.

25. Because this chapter is interested in *The Sketch Book* at its moment of creation, all quotations, will come from C. S. Van Winkle's 1819–20

printing (Shaw-Shoemaker 48355 and held at the American Antiquarian Society) or Murray-Miller's first English edition, cited above in note 5.

26. In later years, Irving, lauded for his essayistic style, was often called the American Addison (Joseph Addison and Richard Steele wrote most of the *Spectator*). Moreover, according to George Haven Putnam, by 1917 *The Sketch Book* had "been translated into almost every European tongue, and for many years it served, and still serves, in France, in Germany, and in Italy as a model of English style and as a text-book from which students are taught their English. In this latter role, it took, to a considerable extent, the place of *The Spectator*." Irving was not only compared to Addison; he eventually replaced him as an exemplum of style. Such praise resulted from the fact that nineteenth-century readers understood Irving's pseudonymous narrator Geoffrey Crayon to be a consummate sketch writer. See George Haven Putnam, "Irving," in *A Century of Commentary on the Works of Washington Irving, 1860–1974*, edited by Andrew B. Myers (Tarrytown, NY: Sleepy Hollow Restorations, 1976), 122.

27. "Review: *The Sketch Book of Geoffrey Crayon, Gent.*," *Literary Gazette* (April 8, 1820): 228.

28. "Review: *The Sketch Book*," *New-England Galaxy*, 171.

29. Brian Jay Jones, *Washington Irving: An American Original* (New York: Arcade, 2008) 5.

30. Elisa Tamarkin, *Anglophilia: Deference, Devotion, and Antebellum America* (Chicago: University of Chicago Press, 2008), xxv.

31. Richard Henry Dana Sr., "ART. XVII.—The Sketch Book," *North American Review* (Sept. 1819): 349.

32. Washington Irving, *The Letters of Washington Irving to Henry Brevoort*, ed. George S. Hellman (New York: Putnam, 1915), 2:106–7.

33. See Eliza, "The Sketch Book, No. II," *Ladies' Literary Cabinet, Being a Reposition of Miscellaneous Literary Production* (August 7, 1819): 101–2; "Review: *The Sketch Book of Geoffrey Crayon, Gent.* First Five Numbers," *Western Review and Miscellaneous Magazine, a Monthly Publication* (May 1820): 244–54; and Dana, "ART. XVII.—The Sketch Book."

34. Irving funded the first volume of the English edition and thus had less money and incentive to revise. When the printer John Miller went bankrupt, John Murray bought up the remaining stock and brought out the second, much more revised, volume. It is important to note that Irving did make changes to other pieces for the English *Sketch Book* See Joseph Rezek, *London and the Making of Provincial Literature: Aesthetics and the*

Transatlantic Book Trade, 1800–1850 (Philadelphia: University of Pennsylvania Press, 2015) 104–12.

35. Springer, introduction, xxix.

36. Although Irving presented *A History of New York* as disinterested, it worked as an allegory of contemporary politics. The Dutchman William the Testy, for example, was understood to be an unflattering version of Thomas Jefferson. The book is relevant for our day and age too: because of Diedrich Knickerbocker, New York's professional basketball team is the Knicks. For a discussion of Thomas Jefferson and William the Testy, see Nancy B. Black and Michael L. Black, introduction to *A History of New York*, by Washington Irving (Boston: Twayne, 1984), xxvi–xxvii.

37. For example, though Leslie Fiedler reads the tale as a straightforward account of a magical sleep which seems to "suggest that escape from the shrew can only be dreamed, not lived," he positions Rip at the origin of a long tradition of American men rejecting American women and civilization to light out for the territory ahead (343). Put another way, despite his endorsement of the more obvious (if less plausible) chain of events, Fiedler's influential thesis can explain and support the tale's second story line. If the American hero really wants to escape domestic responsibility, wouldn't he abandon his wife? See Fiedler, *Love and Death in the American Novel* (New York: Stein and Day, 1966). For another discussion of the misogyny of the tale see Judith Fetterley, *The Resisting Reader: A Feminist Approach to American Fiction* (Bloomington: Indiana University Press, 1978), 3.

38. Jeffrey Insko, "Diedrich Knickerbocker, Regular Bred Historian," *Early American Literature* 43, no. 3 (2008): 623. Also see Lloyd Pratt, *Archives of American Time: Literature and Modernity in the Nineteenth Century* (Philadelphia: University of Pennsylvania Press, 2010); Rezek, *London and the Making of Provincial Literature*; and Michelle R. Sizemore, *American Enchantment: Rituals of the People in the Post-Revolutionary World* (New York: Oxford University Press, 2017).

39. James N. Green, "Chapter 2: The Book Trades in the New Nation. Part 1, The Rise of Book Publishing," in *The History of the Book in America: An Extensive Republic. Print, Culture, and Society in the New Nation, 1790–1840* (Chapel Hill: University of North Carolina Press, 2010), 2:108.

40. In a review of the second volume, the *British Critic* writes: "We do not remember having seen any notice in his former volume of an intention to give the public a continuation of it; but the success which attended his first appearance before the British public has probably emboldened him." The

Literary Gazette, and Journal of the Belles Lettres and the *Literary Chronicle, and Weekly Review* were two other British periodicals that reviewed the first volume thinking it was a complete work. See "Art. VI. *The Sketch Book of Geoffrey Cray, Gent.* Vol. 2." *British Critic* (November 1820): 514–15.

41. "ART.III—*The Sketch Book of Geoffrey Crayon, Gent.*" *Quarterly Review* (April 1821): 58.
42. Dana, "ART. XVII.—The Sketch Book," 349; emphasis in original.
43. Everett, "ART. X.—Bracebridge Hall," 213, 215.
44. "[From the *Eclectic Review.*—London] 2. *The Sketch Book of Geoffrey Crayon, Gent.*," *Literary and Scientific Repository, and Critical Review* (June 1, 1820): 192, 193, 192. NB: this American magazine reprinted the British review.
45. When the *British Critic* does in 1820, its purpose is to set up a comment about "John Bull," the sketch that follows "Philip": "Neither of these [Native American sketches] appeared to us as possessing much point; but the next 'Sketch' possesses unusual merit. The subject of it is the English national character." "Art. VI. *The Sketch Book of Geoffrey Cray, Gent.* Vol. 2," 520.
46. Laura J. Murray, "The Aesthetic of Dispossession: Washington Irving and Ideologies of (De)Colonization in the Early Republic," *American Literary History* 8, no. 2 (July 1, 1996): 214; Rezek, *London and the Making of Provincial Literature,* 107.
47. Both Native American sketches are decidedly sketches and are marked as such. Just as the five Christmas sketches that appear earlier in volume 2 are governed by a single interior title page, these two sketches are joined under the title "Traits of Indian Character." That heading, though properly the title of only the first piece, communicates that both are classic character sketches, committed to detailing the "character and habits of the North American savage" (Miller-Murray SB 2:213). While the first sketch muses more variously on the bravery and nobility of the Native American, "Philip" focuses mostly on King Philip, or Metacomet, the leader of the Pequots. Still, Irving (and the narrator does seem more like Irving and less like Crayon) wants to weigh the evidence of surviving accounts rather than transport the reader through plotting. Eschewing any meaningful personal details, Irving illustrates the behavior of one wronged historical figure to give a sense of an entire population, one largely absent from seventeenth-century Euro-American records.
48. Washington Irving, "Traits of Indian Character," *Analectic Magazine* (February 1814): 145.
49. Murray, "Aesthetic of Dispossession," 214.

50. Dana, "ART. XVII.—*The Sketch Book*," 350.

51. Richard V. McLamore, "The Dutchman in the Attic: Claiming an Inheritance in *The Sketch Book of Geoffrey Crayon*," *American Literature* 72, no. 1 (2000): 34; Harriet Martineau, "'Miss Sedgwick's Works.' The *Westminster Review*," in *Catharine Maria Sedgwick: Critical Perspectives*, ed. Lucinda L. Damon-Bach and Victoria Clements (Boston: Northeastern University Press, 2003), 155.

52. James Fenimore Cooper was also inspired by *The Sketch Book* and imitated Irving's model of publication with *The Spy*. (Cooper later secured publication of *The Pioneers* [1823] with John Murray in England through Irving's help.)

53. Matthews, like most of the other critics mentioned here, is using "short story" to include early nineteenth-century tales. Brander Matthews, "'The Philosophy of the Short-Story,'" *Lippincott's Magazine of Popular Literature and Science* (October 1, 1885): 371.

54. Walter A. Reichart, *Washington Irving and Germany* (Ann Arbor: University of Michigan Press, 1957), 292.

55. William Peden, *The American Short Story: Front Line in the National Defense of Literature* (Boston: Houghton Mifflin, 1964), 1.

56. Frank O'Connor, *The Lonely Voice: A Study of the Short Story* (New York: Harper and Row, 1985), 41.

57. Barbara Korte, *The Short Story in Britain: A Historical Sketch and Anthology* (Tubingen, Germany: A. Francke Verlag Tubingen und Basel, 2003), 7. Maugham qtd. in Korte, 8.

58. There are other examples of the equation between the United States and the short story. T. O. Beachcroft contends that short fiction is American not just because of its origin but also because of its mid-twentieth-century status: "The short story is not an art that has flourished in Britain, but whether this is because brevity, point and form are not qualities that are natural to English writers of fiction or whether because the outlet has not been sufficiently favourable to encourage good writers to employ their gifts in this medium, I do not know. The fact remains that during the last fifty years more good stories have been written by American citizens than British subjects" (232). Though Beachcroft finds the reasons unclear, he is willing to accept the association between the United States and the short story. According to Ian Reid an explanation for what Reid calls the "virtually negligible" nineteenth-century English production of short stories lies in the different demographic conditions of Britain and America: "The short story found its province more often than not among small groups of

working men, especially in those many areas of the American continent which by the early nineteenth century had come to consist of regional settlements still lacking social cohesion" (29). In *The Lonely Voice*, Frank O'Connor includes Russia with the United States when lamenting British short story production: "For some reason Czarist Russia and modern America seemed to be able to produce both great novels and great short stories, while England, which might be called without exaggeration the homeland of the novel, showed up badly when it came to the short story" (19). As indicated by his title, O'Connor believes that one of the major reasons for the "superiority of the American short story . . . is that America is largely populated by submerged population groups" (41). In other words, those who write short stories best speak with voices that are "lonely" or disempowered; O'Connor is interested in twentieth-century writers, but one can see how the argument could apply to an early nineteenth-century American attempting to write in the face of British dismissal of American ability. See O'Connor, *Lonely Voice*; Ian Reid, *The Short Story* (London: Methuen, 1977); and T. O. Beachcroft, *The Modest Art: A Survey of the Short Story in English* (New York: Oxford University Press, 1968).

59. Such an argument is evident as early as Matthews's 1885 article (expanded into a 1901 book); Matthews writes, "There is in the United States a demand for Short-stories which does not exist in Great Britain, or at any rate not in the same degree. The Short-story is of very great importance to the American magazine. But in the British magazine the serial Novel is the one thing of consequence, and all else is termed 'padding'" (370). In 2003, Barbara Korte noted, "America provided (and continues to provide) British writers with publishing opportunities in periodicals when such possibilities in Britain were scarce" (9). See Matthews, "The Philosophy of the Short-Story," and Korte, *Short Story in Britain*.

60. Charles Dudley Warner, "From 'Last Years: The Character of His Literature,'" in *A Century of Commentary on the Works of Washington Irving, 1860–1974*, ed. Andrew B. Myers (Tarrytown, NY: Sleepy Hollow Restorations, 1976), 42.

61. Barrett Wendell, "From 'Washington Irving,'" in *A Century of Commentary on the Works of Washington Irving, 1860–1974*, ed. Andrew B. Myers (Tarrytown, NY: Sleepy Hollow Restorations, 1976), 101.

62. Fred Lewis Pattee, *The Development of the American Short Story: An Historical Survey* (New York: Harper and Bros., 1923), 139, 142.

63. Arthur Voss, *The American Short Story: A Critical Survey* (Norman: University of Oklahoma Press, 1973), 6.

2. BIDING TIME IN HALE'S *LADIES' MAGAZINE*

1. Phillis Wheatley might seem like an exception to this statement, but Wheatley's 1773 book of poems was published in London because the Wheatleys could not muster a subscription list in the United States. Wheatley's work and her life are not written about in any meaningful way in the United States until Margaretta Matilda Odell's 1834 *Memoir and Poems of Phillis Wheatley*, which provides most of what we know about Wheatley's life. Even so, Wheatley is not figured as a founding mother of US letters until late in the twentieth century.

2. Theodore D. Gottlieb, *The Origin and Evolution of the Betsy Ross Flag, Legend or Tradition* (Newark, NJ, 1938), 6.

3. Patricia Okker, *Our Sister Editors: Sarah J. Hale and the Tradition of Nineteenth-Century American Women Editors* (Athens: University of Georgia Press, 1995), 86–87.

4. This account would seem to be true, but the facts of Hale's education are poorly documented outside Hale's own various autobiographical sketches. See Nicole Tonkovich, *Domesticity with a Difference: The Nonfiction of Catharine Beecher, Sarah J. Hale, Fanny Fern, and Margaret Fuller* (Jackson: University Press of Mississippi, 1997), 28.

5. Isabelle Webb Entrikin, "Sarah Josepha Hale and *Godey's Lady's Book*" (PhD diss., University of Pennsylvania, 1946), 7.

6. Over the course of nine years, Hale renames the magazine twice: it goes from the *Ladies' Magazine* to the *Ladies' Magazine and Literary Gazette* (1830) to the *American Ladies' Magazine* (1834). The final title change, made because there was a British *Ladies' Magazine*, indicates that while Hale strove to produce a national periodical, she did so with an eye firmly on what was happening in the United Kingdom.

7. Olive Woolley Burt's 1960 book *First Woman Editor: Sarah J. Hale* incorrectly denominates Hale the first woman editor. As Patricia Okker and others have shown, that honor likely goes to either Susanna Haswell Rowson, who wrote for and may have edited the *Boston Weekly Magazine* in 1802, or to Mary Clarke Carr, who started editing the Philadelphia *Intellectual Regale; or, Ladies' Tea-Tray* in 1814. And even earlier there are examples of women editing newspapers, such as Elizabeth Timothy, who inherited the editorship of the *South Carolina Gazette* after her husband died in 1738. Even if Burt's title is untrue, the sentiment is right, for the

number of female editors remained small into the early nineteenth century, and Sarah Hale stands out for both her long-standing success and her massive influence. She was the first truly consequential US woman editor. Okker, *Our Sister Editors*, 7.

8. Nancy Woloch's *Women and the American Experience* (New York: Knopf, 1984) also contains a short chapter on Hale.

9. Lawrence Martin's articles are an exception, though at moments his tone too feels patronizing, as in the following sentence: "Since she was a woman abounding in vitality the editorial task and the guidance of five children still left her with large parcels of time and energy to be expended in further writing and miscellaneous bustle." Lawrence Martin, "The Genesis of *Godey's Lady's Book*," *New England Quarterly* 1, no. 1 (January 1, 1928): 61.

10. Frank Luther Mott, *A History of American Magazines, 1741–1850* (Cambridge, MA: Belknap Press of Harvard University Press, 1957), 587.

11. Okker cites this date in *Our Sister Editors*, 82. Sarah Josepha Hale, *Liberia, or, Mr. Peyton's Experiments*, Slavery and Anti-Slavery: A Transnational Archive (New York: Harper and Bros, 1853), iv.

12. Beverly A. Peterson, "Mrs. Hale on Mrs. Stowe and Slavery," *American Periodicals* 8 (1998): 30–44.

13. Hale does reprint part of an article calling for the formation of "female emancipation societies," with an introduction about how public political action on slavery "would not, we think, be in perfectly in accordance with woman's character." Sarah Josepha Hale, "An Appeal to the Ladies of the United States," *Ladies' Magazine* (November 1829): 516.

14. In Boston in 1828 these competitors, which would have targeted an Anglo-American audience through reprinted British magazine text, included the *Portfolio*, the *Ladies' Mirror*, the *Young Ladies' Journal*, the *Ladies' Album*, and the *Bower of Taste*. See Martin, "The Genesis of *Godey's Lady's Book*," 41–42.

15. Sarah Josepha Hale, "Introduction," *Ladies' Magazine* (January 1828): 3, 1–2.

16. George B. Forgie, *Patricide in the House Divided: A Psychological Interpretation of Lincoln and His Age* (New York: W. W. Norton, 1979), 14.

17. The most common exception would be because one of the partners had a fertility issue. In 1820, there were 52.8 births per 1,000 white people per annum; in 2000, there were 13.9, numbers that illustrate the high early nineteenth-century birthrate. Michael Haines, "Fertility and Mortality in the United States," EH.net, March 19, 2008, http://eh.net/encyclopedia/fertility-and-mortality-in-the-united-states/.

18. Hale places this sketch second in her volume of *Sketches of American Character* (1829) although it comes in April (i.e., fourth) in the magazine.

19. Sarah Josepha Hale, "Sketches of American Character No. IV: The Soldier of the Revolution," *Ladies' Magazine* (April 1828): 150.

20. Ibid., 151.

21. Arthur H. Shaffer, *The Politics of History: Writing the History of the American Revolution, 1783–1815* (New Brunswick, NJ: Transaction, 2009). The term "nationness" is borrowed from Homi K. Bhabha, "Introduction: Narrating the Nation," in *Nation and Narration*, ed. Homi K. Bhabha (London: Routledge, 1990), 2.

22. Sarah Josepha Hale, "Sketches of American Character No. I: Walter Wilson," *Ladies' Magazine* (January 1828): 7.

23. Ibid., 15.

24. The piece has a byline of "J.," which could well be Sarah *Josepha* Hale, who used a range of bylines to mask how much of the magazine she herself penned. J., "Musings of an Invalid. No. I. Reading," *Ladies' Magazine and Literary Gazette* (June 1833): 241.

25. Ibid.

26. Hale, "The Soldier of the Revolution," 152.

27. Shirley Samuels, introduction to *The Culture of Sentiment: Race, Gender, and Sentimentality in Nineteenth-Century America*, ed. Shirley Samuels (New York: Oxford University Press, 1992), 3.

28. Qtd. in Laurel Thatcher Ulrich, *The Age of Homespun: Objects and Stories in the Creation of an American Myth* (New York: Knopf, 2001), 180.

29. Qtd. in ibid., 183–84.

30. Elaine Scarry, *Resisting Representation* (New York: Oxford University Press, 1994), 65.

31. Hannah Arendt, "The Public and the Private Realm," in *The Portable Hannah Arendt*, ed. Peter R. Baehr (New York: Penguin Books, 2003), 189.

32. Sarah Josepha Hale, "Sketches of American Character No. X. The Apparition," *Ladies' Magazine* (October 1828): 444. Emphasis in original.

33. Sarah Josepha Hale, "Sketches of American Character No. V. The Village Schoolmistress," *Ladies' Magazine* (May 1828): 205.

34. Teresa De Lauretis, *Alice Doesn't: Feminism, Semiotics, Cinema* (London: Macmillan, 1984).

35. According to the reviewer, "The subject matter of this number is chiefly original, and although not so well calculated to prove entertaining, it is intimately connected with the interests of that portion of society to whom the work is chiefly devoted. Essays on Education, however, when very

long are not generally interesting, and might we speak our free opinions, an occasional fictitious narrative, would not deteriorate from the value of this periodical." "The *Ladies' Magazine*," *Philadelphia Album and Ladies Literary Gazette* (January 30, 1828): 277.

36. Sarah Josepha Hale, "Sketches of American Character No. VII. The Belle and the Bleu," *Ladies' Magazine* (July 1828): 307.

37. Sarah Josepha Hale, "Sketches of American Character No. XII. A Winter in the Country," *Ladies' Magazine* (December 1828): 535. Note that this page is actually improperly paginated as page 435.

38. Sarah Josepha Hale, "Sketches of American Character No. IX. Prejudices," *Ladies' Magazine* (September 1828): 404.

39. Hilary M. Schor, "The Make-Believe of a Middle: On (Not) Knowing Where You Are in Daniel Deronda," in *Narrative Middles: Navigating the Nineteenth-Century British Novel,* ed. Caroline Levine and Mario Ortiz-Robles, Theory and Interpretation of Narrative (Columbus: Ohio State University Press, 2011), 51.

40. Qtd. in Caroline Levine and Mario Ortiz-Robles, introduction to *Narrative Middles: Navigating the Nineteenth-Century British Novel,* ed. Caroline Levine and Mario Ortiz-Robles, Theory and Interpretation of Narrative (Columbus: Ohio State University Press, 2011), 8.

41. "Female Education," *Western Review and Miscellaneous Magazine, a Monthly Publication* (February 1821): 47.

42. From the *Boston Spectator,* April 28, 1827. Qtd. in Entrikin, "Sarah Josepha Hale," 13.

43. Sarah Josepha Hale, *Northwood* (New York: H. Long and Brother, 1852), v.

44. From the *Ledger,* May 8, 1869. Qtd. in Tonkovich, *Domesticity with a Difference,* 37–38.

45. Qtd. in Rev. D. W. Clark, "Literary Women of America—Sarah Josepha Hale," *Ladies' Repository: A Monthly Periodical, Devoted to Literature, Arts, and Religion* (April 1855): 196.

46. Ibid.

47. Hale, "The Village Schoolmistress," 207, 208.

48. Woloch, *Women and the American Experience,* 99.

49. Sarah Josepha Hale, "The Fatherless and Widows' Society, Boston," *Ladies' Magazine* (January 1828): 48.

50. Woloch, *Women and the American Experience,* 105.

51. Hale, "The Village Schoolmistress," 210.

52. Abigail Adams, "Letter from Abigail Adams to John Adams, 31 March–5 April 1776," *Adams Family Papers,* http://www.masshist.org/digitaladams/.

53. Sarah Josepha Hale, *Three Hours; or, The Vigil of Love: And Other Poems* (Philadelphia: Carey and Hart, 1848), viii.

54. "Many, indeed most of the Pilgrim Fathers were from families of high respectability in their own country; and there were some from among the best nobility of English." Hale, *Three Hours*, 64n4.

55. Ibid., 66.

56. Paul Ricoeur, *Time and Narrative* (Chicago: University of Chicago Press, 1984), 1:52.

57. Sarah Josepha Hale, "Sketches of American Character No. XI. William Forbes," *Ladies' Magazine* (November 1828): 501, 502. Emphasis in original.

58. Ibid., 489.

59. Ibid., 500.

60. Hale, "The Village Schoolmistress," 215.

61. Woloch, *Women and the American Experience*, 104.

62. Hale, "William Forbes," 501.

63. Ibid., 503.

64. Frank Kelleter talks about recursivity as a normal part of serial narratives, which must necessarily go back and reinterpret past events to accommodate more recent developments. See Frank Kelleter, *Media of Serial Narrative*, Theory and Interpretation of Narrative (Columbus: Ohio State University Press, 2017), 16–18.

65. Rita Felski, *Uses of Literature*, Blackwell Manifestos (Malden, MA: Blackwell, 2008), 25.

66. These are all states where the magazine's paper wrappers listed agents. See Woloch, *Women and the American Experience*, 100, for the number of subscribers.

67. Sarah Josepha Hale, "The *Ladies' Magazine*," *Ladies' Magazine and Literary Gazette* (December 1832): 576.

68. Exact numbers are impossible to know, but we can conjecture about the circulation. Woloch, *Women and the American Experience*, 106.

69. Hale, "William Forbes," 501.

70. Sarah Josepha Hale, "What Can Women Do?" *American Ladies' Magazine* (May 1834): 216.

71. Ibid., 215.

72. Abigail Adams, "Letter from Abigail Adams to John Adams, 31 March–5 April 1776."

73. I am not suggesting that a narrative is inherently gendered or sexed but rather that certain narrative techniques are traditionally associated with male or female authors.

74. Mary Kelley, *Private Woman, Public Stage: Literary Domesticity in Nineteenth-Century America* (New York: Oxford University Press, 1984), 10.
75. Hale, "Prejudices," 393.
76. Hale, "Walter Wilson," 8.
77. Kristie Hamilton, *America's Sketchbook: The Cultural Life of a Nineteenth-Century Genre* (Athens: Ohio University Press, 1998), 18.
78. Sarah Josepha Hale, "Sketches of American Character No. II. Ann Ellsworth." *Ladies' Magazine* (February 1828): 63.
79. Ibid., 64.
80. Kelleter, *Media of Serial Narrative*, 13.
81. Ibid.
82. Hale, "Introduction," 2.
83. As Mary Kelley has shown, many middle- and upper-class white women in the late eighteenth and early nineteenth centuries, including Sarah Hale, spoke passionately about their intellectual relationship with reading and books. Indeed, "The intense yearning for books manifest in the letters, commonplace books, journals, and diaries" that Kelley studied "registers the sustained and sustaining role that reading played in the lives of these women." Reading served as intellectual fodder, available increasingly to a wide population. Mary Kelley, "Crafting Subjectivities: Women, Reading, and Self-Imagining," in *Reading Women: Literacy, Authorship, and Culture in the Atlantic World, 1500–1800,* ed. Heidi Brayman Hackel and Catherine E. Kelly (Philadelphia: University of Pennsylvania Press, 2008), 64.
84. Okker gets these numbers from John Tebbel and Lee Soltow and Edward Stevens. See Okker, *Our Sister Editors,* 110–11.
85. Woloch, *Women and the American Experience,* 100. Only one US magazine started before 1845 has continued, uninterrupted, until the present day, the *New England Journal of Medicine,* which commenced in 1812. (The *Saturday Evening Post* was started in 1821, but died in 1969 and was rebooted in 1971.) Sammye Johnson and Patricia Prijatel, *Magazine from Cover to Cover,* 3rd ed. (New York: Oxford University Press, 2013), 68.
86. Sarah Josepha Hale, "Contributors to the *Ladies' Magazine,*" *American Ladies' Magazine* (January 1834): 48.
87. The paper wrapper of the May 1828 issue advertised the magazine as "contain[ing] about fifty pages of original matter, printed on fine paper, and new and elegant type."
88. In the year-end editorial to volume 5, Hale asserted that her magazine deserved continued patronage because it was "useful" to "our countrywomen," both because it advocated for women's causes (particularly

women's education) and because it published and paid "many of our best female writers." Hale, "The *Ladies' Magazine*," 576.

89. Incidentally, retooling and republishing articles as chapters in a monograph is standard practice in academic writing.

90. Hale wrote of *Fanshawe*: "We must therefore briefly recommend the book to all those who wish to encourage the talents of our own writers. But do not depend on obtaining it for perusal from a circulating library, or from a friend. Purchase it, reader." Sarah Josepha Hale, "Literary Notices: *Fanshawe*," *Ladies' Magazine* (November 1828): 526.

91. Sarah Josepha Hale, "To Our Friends," *American Ladies' Magazine* (December 1834): 576.

92. Hale took over editing duties from 1834 to 1836, when the magazine folded.

93. Daniel Webster, *An Address Delivered at the Completion of the Bunker Hill Monument, June 17, 1843* (Boston: Tappan and Dennet, 1843), 4.

94. Lawrence Martin, "Women Fought at Bunker Hill," *New England Quarterly* 8, no. 4 (December 1935): 467–79.

3. NONSYNCHRONOUS SYNCHRONICITY IN SEDGWICK'S GIFT BOOK STORIES

1. Note that because a literary annual is published the fall before its date, the date given is not the date of publication. For example, the *Token* of 1831 was published on August 30, 1830.

2. Qtd. in Katherine D. Harris, "Feminizing the Textual Body: Female Readers Consuming the Literary Annual," *Papers of the Bibliographical Society of America* 99, no. 4 (December 2005): 582. Also see Katherine D. Harris, *Forget Me Not: The Rise of the British Literary Annual, 1823–1835* (Athens: Ohio University Press, 2015), 122, where she lists the contents of the final part of the 1823 *Forget Me Not*, including a "Historical Chronicle for 1822." Note that Ackermann borrowed the idea from what he had seen in Germany.

3. Catharine Maria Sedgwick, "A Reminiscence of Federalism," in *The Token and Atlantic Souvenir: A Christmas and New Year's Present, 1834*, ed. Samuel G. Goodrich (Boston: Charles Bowen, 1834), 103. The *Token* of 1830 contains both an engraving and a poem called "Greek Lovers." Sedgwick's story "A Reminiscence of Federalism" appeared in the *Token* for 1834, a year that would see the Tappan Riot, four nights of antiabolitionist violence in New York City, and antiabolitionist riots in Philadelphia. The following year saw the Snow Riot in Washington, DC, which targeted

abolitionists and free blacks and quickly devolved into a lynch mob, as well as an antiabolitionist riot in Boston in which a crowd dragged William Lloyd Garrison, editor of the *Liberator*, through the streets at the end of a rope. Before this Boston riot, the US abolitionist-poet John Greenleaf Whittier and British abolitionist George Thompson were stoned (but not killed) in Concord, New Hampshire.

4. Lucinda L. Damon-Bach and Victoria Clements, introduction to *Catharine Maria Sedgwick: Critical Perspectives,* ed. Lucinda L. Damon-Bach and Victoria Clements (Boston: Northeastern University Press, 2003), xxvi. It was through Sedgwick's efforts in 1850 that Herman Melville and Nathaniel Hawthorne first met.

5. For the argument that Hawthorne's rosebush references *A New-England Tale,* see Carolyn Karcher, "Catharine Maria Sedgwick in Literary History," in *Catharine Maria Sedgwick: Critical Perspectives,* ed. Lucinda L. Damon-Bach and Victoria Clements (Boston: Northeastern University Press, 2003), 12. Poe's praise is quoted in Karcher, "Sedgwick in Literary History," 9.

6. Qtd. in Mary Kelley, *Private Woman, Public Stage: Literary Domesticity in Nineteenth-Century America* (New York: Oxford University Press, 1984), 67.

7. Sedgwick, "A Reminiscence of Federalism," 132–33.

8. Catharine Maria Sedgwick, "Modern Chivalry," in *The Atlantic Souvenir, a Christmas and New Year's Offering. 1827* (Philadelphia: Carey and Lea, 1827), 43.

9. Ibid., 19.

10. The narratorial "I" is identified as "C.——." That, coupled with her acknowledgment of a having a senator for a father and of being descended from Federalist royalty clearly indicate we should identify the narrator with Sedgwick herself.

11. The *Euterpeiad* reflected that "the Souvenir has certainly the advantage of the Token: A day in New-York, Giles Heatherby, and the Story of Shay's War, make up a considerable part of the contents of the volume; The Adventurer, Mary Dyre, and the New-England Village, are the counterbalancing American tales of the Token." "Mary Dyre" and "The Story of Shay's War" were both Sedgwick's. "The Boston Token," *Euterpeiad; an Album of Music, Poetry & Prose* (December 15, 1830): 155.

12. "Art. IX.—The Annuals," *North American Review* (January 1834): 198.

13. Ralph Thompson, *American Literary Annuals & Gift Books, 1825–1865* (New York: H. W. Wilson, 1936), 50.

14. Ibid., 11.

15. These numbers come from ibid., 7.

16. Ibid., 21, 22.

17. A wonderful review of the *Token* of 1829 speculates about "The Journey of Truth," a poem included in that volume: "Anonymous; but I shall lay it to Miss Sedgwick. Let her deny it if she dares: I do not know that she ever wrote a word of rhyme in her life; but whether she did or not, she is the author of these." Along with its amusement value, the comment shows that Sedgwick was known for her submissions to literary annuals. It is doubtful that the poem was actually Sedgwick's. "Review: *The Token*, for 1829," *Yankee and Boston Literary Gazette* (November 12, 1828): 48.

18. Thompson, *American Literary Annuals,* 9.

19. For a graph of the number of gift books and literary annuals between 1826 and 1865, see ibid., 167.

20. Mark Twain, *Adventures of Huckleberry Finn,* ed. Victor Fischer and Lin Salamo (Berkeley: University of California Press, 2001), 137.

21. Qtd. in Alexandra Urakova, "'The Purloined Letter' in the Gift Book: Reading Poe in a Contemporary Context," *Nineteenth-Century Literature* 64, no. 3 (December 2009): 332.

22. Anna Reading, "From *The Social Inheritance of the Holocaust: Gender Culture and Memory,*" in *Theories of Memory: A Reader,* ed. Michael Rossington and Anne Whitehead (Baltimore: Johns Hopkins University Press, 2007), 221–22.

23. "Boston Token," 155. Both the *Token* and the *Atlantic Souvenir* did include the occasional translation of a European poem or an engraving of a European painting, but since the translation and engraving would be done by an American, editors and reviewers saw no inconsistency.

24. Catharine Maria Sedgwick, "Mary Dyre," in *The Token and Atlantic Souvenir: A Christmas and New Year's Present. 1831,* ed. Samuel G. Goodrich (Boston: Gray and Bowen, 1831), 294.

25. James Emmett Ryan, *Imaginary Friends: Representing Quakers in American Culture, 1650–1950* (Madison: University of Wisconsin Press, 2009), 97.

26. William Sewel, *The History of the Rise, Increase, and Progress of the Christian People Called Quakers,* 4th ed., (London: James Phillips and Son, 1799), 1:385.

27. Sedgwick, "Mary Dyre," 300.

28. Ibid., 304.

29. Ibid., 312.

30. "Introduction. Addressed to the Ladies," in *The Offering: A Christmas and New Year's Present* (Philadelphia: Thomas T. Ash, 1834), 8.

31. The text block on the *Token* is 10.8 cm by 16 cm.

32. "The Boston Token," 155, emphases mine.

33. Rita Felski, *Doing Time: Feminist Theory and Postmodern Culture,* Cultural Front (New York: New York University Press, 2000), 3.

34. Sedgwick, "Mary Dyre," 303; emphasis in original.

35. In her 1844 *Tales and Sketches, Second Series,* Sedgwick returned to the by-line of "the Author of 'Hope Leslie,' 'Home,' 'Letters from Abroad,' &c., &c."

36. Meredith L. McGill, *American Literature and the Culture of Reprinting* (Philadelphia: University of Pennsylvania Press, 2007), 24. Longer works were more clearly viewed as an author's property even if that author was anonymous. Moreover, publishers and authors were more likely to register copyright on a longer work or volume. In fact, when *Godey's Lady's Book* and *Graham's Magazine* began copyrighting their contents in 1845, they were the first magazines to do so. Frank Luther Mott, *A History of American Magazines, 1741–1850* (Cambridge, MA: Belknap Press of Harvard University Press, 1957), 503.

37. Even as reviewers referred to Catharine Sedgwick as "Miss Sedgwick," the honorific "Miss" was an infrequent one for early nineteenth-century female authors to have as a byline. Sedgwick did have two sisters-in-law who started publishing as Mrs. Sedgwicks around the time when Catharine Sedgwick's byline first appears in annuals; that fact may well have encouraged publishers to distinguish Catharine with a "Miss." Eliza Leslie is sometimes credited as "Miss Leslie," as in the *Atlantic Souvenir* of 1831, and in the *Offering* of 1834, both "Miss Sedgwick" and "Mrs. Sedgwick" have credited pieces. When the poet Hannah Flagg Gould, who published in many of the same annuals as Sedgwick, was credited, however, she was "H. F. Gould," though she too remained unmarried her whole life. Frances Smith Foster points out that throughout the century, African American women were customarily called "Mrs." in person and on paper even if like Harriet Jacobs, they had not ever been married. Frances Smith Foster, email message to author, July 5, 2012.

38. Melissa J. Homestead, email message to author, July 10, 2012.

39. Samuel G. Goodrich, preface to *The Token and Atlantic Souvenir: A Christmas and New Year's Present. 1831,* ed. Samuel G. Goodrich (Boston: Gray and Bowen, 1831), v. The one letter that does exist from Sedgwick to Goodrich, an 1831 missive shortly after when the byline first appeared, suggests that she thought of herself with that name when speaking in the formal third person. "Miss Sedgwick informs Mr. Goodrich," she wrote. Homestead, email message to author.

40. Catharine Maria Sedgwick, "The Catholic Iroquois," in *The Atlantic Souvenir; a Christmas and New Year's Offering. 1826* (Philadelphia: Carey and Lea, 1826), 83.

41. Ibid., 102.

42. Catharine Maria Sedgwick, "St. Catharine's Eve," in *The Token and Atlantic Souvenir: A Christmas and New Year's Present. 1835* (Boston: Charles Bowen, 1835), 14.

43. Although Sedgwick does not give these details, Philip originally asked for annulment based on nonconsummation *per maleficium,* meaning essentially that Queen Isemburg bewitched him with impotence.

44. Lauren Berlant, *The Female Complaint: The Unfinished Business of Sentimentality in American Culture* (Durham, NC: Duke University Press, 2008), vii.

45. Catharine Maria Sedgwick, "The Country Cousin," in *The Token; a Christmas and New Year's Present. 1830,* ed. Samuel G. Goodrich (Boston: Carter and Hendee, 1830), 192.

46. Ibid., 162.

47. Susan K. Harris, "The Limits of Authority: Catharine Maria Sedgwick and the Politics of Resistance," in *Catharine Maria Sedgwick: Critical Perspectives,* ed. Lucinda L. Damon-Bach and Victoria Clements (Boston: Northeastern University Press, 2003), 274.

48. Sedgwick, "The Country Cousin," 156. Robyn Warhol has argued that, by midcentury, the earnest direct address had become marked as particularly female in the United States and United Kingdom, but even before it became a mainstay of sentimental novels like Harriet Beecher Stowe's *Uncle Tom's Cabin,* the narrative strategy gave women an ability to address a public audience without violating the social mores that prohibited women from public speaking. Robyn Warhol-Down, *Gendered Interventions: Narrative Discourse in the Victorian Novel* (New Brunswick, NJ: Rutgers University Press, 1989), vii.

49. Catharine Maria Sedgwick, "Old Maids," in *The Offering: A Christmas and New Year's Present* (Philadelphia: Thomas T. Ash, 1834), 33.

50. Ibid., 44.

51. Ibid., 46.

52. Harriet Martineau, "'Miss Sedgwick's Works.' The *Westminster Review,*" in *Catharine Maria Sedgwick: Critical Perspectives,* ed. Lucinda L. Damon-Bach and Victoria Clements (Boston: Northeastern University Press, 2003), 155.

53. One editor remarked about the *Token* of 1835, "Considering that this beautiful Annual is designed especially for a holiday gift, its appearance

in September must be considered early; but it comes in good season, let it make its advent when it may." "Literary Notices: Book Table. The Token for 1835," *New-York Mirror: A Weekly Gazette of Literature and the Fine Arts* (October 4, 1834): 110.

54. "Editors' Table: The Annuals and Gift-Books for 1842," *Iris; or, Literary Messenger* (October 1841): 572.

55. Sarah Josepha Hale, "Literary Notices: Annuals and Poems," *Ladies' Magazine and Literary Gazette* (December 1830): 572.

56. Karcher, "Sedgwick in Literary History," 10; Charlene Avallone, "The 'Art' of Conversation," in *Catharine Maria Sedgwick: Critical Perspectives,* ed. Lucinda L. Damon-Bach and Victoria Clements (Boston: Northeastern University Press, 2003), 192–203; Lucinda L. Damon-Bach and Victoria Clements, introduction, xxvii. Susan K. Harris notes that Sedgwick's *A New England Tale* distributes "its message among a varied cast of minor characters" in *Nineteenth-Century American Women's Novels: Interpretative Strategies* (New York: Cambridge University Press, 1990), 50.

57. "*Southern Literary Messenger.* Review of Tales and Sketches," in *Catharine Maria Sedgwick: Critical Perspectives,* ed. Lucinda L. Damon-Bach and Victoria Clements (Boston: Northeastern University Press, 2003), 156.

58. This same *Token* also includes an engraved version of a painting in which Cora is kneeling before Telemund in a scene from Cooper's *The Last of the Mohicans.* The figures are so small in the engraving that it becomes almost a generic bit of American scenery.

59. Qtd. in Thompson, *American Literary Annuals & Gift Books,* 37.

60. Ibid., 40.

61. In literary annuals, steel engravings were the dominant tool, though "wood engraving succeeded copper plates as the chief medium for good-quality book illustration during the first decade of the century and . . . retain their position until satisfactory photographic blocks became freely available around 1890." Philip Gaskell, *A New Introduction to Bibliography* (New York: Oak Knoll, 1995), 266.

62. The *Atlantic Souvenir* paid about 20 percent of its production cost for engravings and less than 10 percent for its literary material according to Thompson, *American Literary Annuals & Gift Books,* 42.

63. E. L., "The Souvenir," in *Affection's Gift* of 1832, 55, qtd. in Thompson, *American Literary Annuals & Gift Books,* 2.

64. In 1829 John Neal's *Yankee and Boston Literary Gazette* took two weeks each to review the *Atlantic Souvenir* 1829 and then the *Token* of 1829, giving each item a short paragraph response.

65. "Review: *The Atlantic Souvenir* . . . 1829," *Yankee and Boston Literary Gazette* (November 19, 1828): 1.

66. Okker points out that there are multiple products that hinge on variety and were marked as female in the nineteenth century, including flowers, the quilt, the scrapbook, and ladies' magazines. See Patricia Okker, *Our Sister Editors: Sarah J. Hale and the Tradition of Nineteenth-Century American Women Editors* (Athens: University of Georgia Press, 1995), 32.

67. Catharine Maria Sedgwick, "Romance in Real Life," in *The Legendary, Consisting of Original Pieces, Principally Illustrative of American History, Scenery, and Manners,* ed. Nathaniel Parker Willis, (Boston: Samuel G. Goodrich, 1828), 1:126.

68. Edward Said distinguishes between *origin* and *beginning*, wherein the first is more passive "X *is the origin of* Y," while the second is more active, "The beginning A *leads to* B" (6). Later he illustrates the difference in this way: "*author* (origin) and *beginning intention* (purpose and interpretation)" (174). Edward W. Said, *Beginnings: Intention and Method* (New York: Columbia University Press, 1985).

69. Sedgwick, "Romance in Real Life," 161.

70. Catharine Maria Sedgwick, "The Story of Shay's War," in *The Atlantic Souvenir for 1831* (Philadelphia: Carey and Lea, 1831), 295.

4. THE CHRONICLE, THE RECKONING, AND HAWTHORNE'S PURITAN TALES

1. This request is reflected in a letter from Carey, Lea and Blanchard to Theodore Sedgwick. "July 28, 1835 Letter from Carey, Lea & Blanchard to Theodore Sedgwick," July 28, 1835, Historical Society of Pennsylvania. I am indebted to Melissa for generously sharing a transcription of this and other letters.

2. John Austin, "The Collection as Literary Form: Sedgwick's *Tales and Sketches* of 1835," in *Catharine Maria Sedgwick: Critical Perspectives,* ed. Lucinda L. Damon-Bach and Victoria Clements (Boston: Northeastern University Press, 2003), 168.

3. Like Sedgwick, Hawthorne published a number of sketches and tales—thirty-three over his career—in literary annuals, twenty-seven of those in the Boston-based *Token.* See Bradford A. Booth, "Taste in the Annuals," *American Literature* 14, no. 3 (November 1942): 301; and Ralph Thompson, *American Literary Annuals & Gift Books, 1825–1865* (New York: H. W. Wilson, 1936), 68.

4. *Twice-Told Tales* was printed in 1837 (1,000 copies at $1 each), 1841 (a two-volume expanded collection, 1,500 copies at $2.25 for each set), 1851 (2,000 copies at $1.50 for each of two volumes), 1852 (title page says 1853; 500 copies at $1.50 for each of two volumes), and 1853 (500 copies at $1.50 for each of two volumes). Mott's "best seller" status indicates that Hawthorne's collection continued to sell. Frank Luther Mott, *A History of American Magazines, 1741–1850* (Cambridge, MA: Belknap Press of Harvard University Press, 1957). It still sells today, in fact.

5. Another way of saying the same thing is that, since the *sjuzhet* (the representation and manipulation of story events in a narrative) often deviates from the *fabula* (the actual chronological story happenings of a narrative), the disclosure that requires, encourages, or allows a reader to (re)conceptualize a chronologically prior happening does not have to be in the final paragraphs of a text.

6. Matthew P. Brown, *The Pilgrim and the Bee: Reading Rituals and Book Culture in Early New England* (Philadelphia: University of Pennsylvania Press, 2007).

7. Puritanism is both an imprecise and necessary term. In essence, Puritanism was a particularly intense form of Reformed Protestantism. Originally a term of abuse for nonconformist clergy within the Elizabethan church, "Puritan" came to refer to a broader movement by the seventeenth century. See John Coffey and Paul C. H. Lim, introduction to *The Cambridge Companion to Puritanism*, ed. John Coffey and Paul Chang-Ha Lim (Cambridge: Cambridge University Press, 2008), 1–7.

8. Paul Ricoeur and Frank Kermode discuss this temporal paradox with different emphasis and by different terms. According to Ricoeur the episodic or chronological aspect of time aligns with standard definitions of plot that emphasize the succession of events—the "then . . . and then . . . and then . . ." structure of stories—while the configurational or recollective aspect highlights the way in which readers comprehend narratives retrospectively as a single "thought" or "theme." Frank Kermode, following John Marks and Oscar Cullmann and working from biblical Greek, cites *kairos*, "passing time," and *chronos*, "a point in time filled with significance, charged with a meaning derived from its relation to the end," as divergent and dialectical modes of time. He, however, uses these terms more flexibly and broadly than I use "chronicle" and "reckoning." See Paul Ricoeur, "Narrative Time," in *Narrative Dynamics: Essays on Plot, Time, Closure, and Frames*, ed. Brian Richardson, Theory and Interpretation of Narrative (Columbus: Ohio State University Press, 2002), 35–46; and

Frank Kermode, *The Sense of an Ending: Studies in the Theory of Fiction,* The Mary Flexner Lectures, 1965 (New York: Oxford University Press, 1967), 47.

9. Emphasizing the chronicling aspects of Puritan life, the Geneva Bible, a version endorsed by Calvin and brought over on the Mayflower, was the first English-language Bible to divide the scripture into numbered verses.

10. Dewey D. Wallace Jr., "Puritan Polemical Divinity and Doctrinal Controversy," in *The Cambridge Companion to Puritanism,* ed. John Coffey and Paul Chang-Ha Lim (Cambridge: Cambridge University Press, 2008), 214.

11. This chapter focuses on the first volume of *Twice-Told Tales* (1837), though there are many connections between the first and second volumes of that name (published together in 1842). Most obviously, Hawthorne includes a Puritan history-tale, "Endicott and the Red Cross," within the second volume.

12. Nathaniel Hawthorne, *Twice-Told Tales* (Boston: American Stationers, 1837), 194. Hereafter cited in text as *TTT.*

13. Rufus Choate, *Addresses and Orations of Rufus Choate* (Boston: Little, Brown, 1878), 2.

14. In the sketch "The Sister Years," Hawthorne actually does use the terms "chronicle" and "reckoning." There the narrator depicts the personification of the outgoing year as holding a bound volume that the narrator calls "her own biography," and that the year calls "her Book of Chronicles"; the collection is "neither more nor less than the Salem Gazette for 1838," a catalog of periodicals that emphasize the onward plod of chronology. Though the text is the memory book that the outgoing year will take with her to Father Time, the narrator prohibits the books of Chronicles from being the ultimate account of humanity, for the old year "in the company of Time and all her kindred, must hereafter hold a reckoning with Mankind." In the end, time will move backward, reevaluating the petty cares of humanity and its forward-moving world. Originally published as an eight-page supplement to the *Salem Gazette,* this sketch appears in volume 2 of *Twice-Told Tales* (1842). Nathaniel Hawthorne, *Twice-Told Tales* (New York: Modern Library, 2001), 262, 266.

15. It is worth acknowledging here that it is impossible to equate history with the chronicle. History always includes interpretations, whether it is a personal history or a national history. Fact and events only exist—"breathe," Hawthorne said—when they are placed in a narrative, which inevitably involves explaining the relationship among phenomena and curating the data. History and story, in other words, are necessarily reckonings,

no matter how closely to the historical event a writer produces those narratives. In truth, there can be no pure chronicle because such records are always ex post facto. Yet the dyad retains its meaning because a writer's job—at least one trying to write fiction with a sense of realism—is to conjure the sensation of an actor within a story world. And actors most certainly react to events in the present moment with the assumption that their choices have impact. Re-creating that sense is the basis of mimesis.

16. Millicent Bell, *Hawthorne and the Real: Bicentennial Essays* (Columbus: Ohio State University Press, 2005), 14.

17. Increase Mather, "Predestination and Human Exertions," in *The Puritans: A Sourcebook of Their Writings,* ed. Perry Miller and Thomas Herbert Johnson, rev. ed. (New York: Harper and Row, 1963), 1:335–36.

18. Ibid., 336.

19. Wallace, "Puritan Polemical Divinity," 217.

20. Sargent Bush Jr., *The Writings of Thomas Hooker: Spiritual Adventure in Two Worlds* (Madison: University of Wisconsin Press, 1980), 98.

21. Ibid., 159.

22. Ibid., 148.

23. Qtd. in ibid., 157; emphasis in original.

24. Qtd. in ibid., 162.

25. Ibid., 166.

26. Qtd. in Perry Miller, *Nature's Nation* (Cambridge, MA: Harvard University Press, 1967), 61.

27. Ibid., 71.

28. Hooker's *Application of Redemption* was endorsed and published in England in 1657. See Miller, *Nature's Nation,* 70.

29. Ibid., 70.

30. Sketches include "Sunday at Home," "Little Annie's Ramble," "A Rill from the Town-Pump," "Sights from a Steeple," and "The Vision of the Fountain." ("The Toll-Gatherer's Day," another sketch, was added to the volume in 1842.) Fantasy tales include "The Wedding Knell," "Mr. Higginbotham's Catastrophe," "David Swan: A Fantasy," "The Hollow of the Three Hills," "Fancy Show Box: A Morality," and "Dr. Heidegger's Experiment." Two other tales, "The Great Carbuncle: A Mystery of the White Mountains" and "Wakefield," are tales but fall somewhat between the designations of history and fantasy. Both of them have narrators who reference the historicity of the legend that inspires the tale and then proceed to demonstratively create a fantastical version of that legend.

31. Nathaniel Hawthorne, *The Works of Nathaniel Hawthorne* (New York: Houghton Mifflin, 1883), 12:227.

32. G. Harrison Orians, "The Angel of Hadley in Fiction: A Study of the Sources of Hawthorne's 'The Grey Champion,'" *American Literature* 4, no. 3 (November 1932): 257–69.

33. The narrator mentions that included in the gathered crowd are Puritan "veterans of King Philip's war who had burnt villages and slaughtered young and old, with pious fierceness, while the godly souls throughout the land were helping them with prayer" (*TTT* 13). Within this sentence, neither Puritan fighting nor Puritan prayer is admirable. Similarly, though Endicott is the villain in "The May-Pole of Merry Mount," a tale discussed below, the final sentence of "Endicott and the Red Cross" (in volume 2) underlines his position as patriotic hero: "We look back through the mist of ages, and recognize in the rending of the Red Cross from New England's banner, the first omen of that deliverance which our fathers consummated, after the bones of the stern Puritan had lain more than a century in the dust." Hawthorne, *Twice-Told Tales*, Modern Library, 345.

34. Gary Richard Thompson, *The Art of Authorial Presence: Hawthorne's Provincial Tales* (Durham, NC: Duke University Press, 1993), 86; Frederick C. Crews, *The Sins of the Fathers: Hawthorne's Psychological Themes* (Berkeley: University of California Press, 1989), 40.

35. Peter Brooks, *Reading for the Plot: Design and Intention in Narrative* (Oxford: Oxford University Press, 1984), 23.

36. Philip Ranlet lays out part of the rebellion's schedule, which included an hour-by-hour time table of significant people's captures and various sites' securing. See Philip Ranlet, *Enemies of the Bay Colony: Puritan Massachusetts and Its Foes*, 2nd ed. (Lanham, MD: University Press of America, 2006), 139.

37. Julian Hawthorne, *Nathaniel Hawthorne and His Wife: A Biography* (Boston: Houghton, Mifflin, and Company, 1884), 1:142.

38. "The Gray Champion," which originally appeared in the January 1835 issue of the *New-England Magazine,* identified itself as "by the author of 'The Gentle Boy,'" but "The Gentle Boy," which was first published (with two other tales by Hawthorne) in the *Token* of 1832 carried no byline, likely both to mask that Hawthorne had written three pieces for the annual and because Hawthorne had no notable reputation at that point. Hawthorne also wrote three pieces for the *Token* of 1836, for which he was paid forty-six dollars. See Wayne Allen Jones, "Hawthorne's First Published Review," *American Literature* 48, no. 4 (January 1977): 494.

39. Lawrence Buell, *New England Literary Culture from Revolution through Renaissance* (New York: Cambridge University Press, 1986), 196.

40. Michael Davitt Bell, *Hawthorne and the Historical Romance of New England* (Princeton, NJ: Princeton University Press, 1971), 108.

41. For a list of the changes from *Token* "Gentle Boy" to *Twice-Told Tales* "Gentle Boy," see James McIntosh, "Hawthorne's Revisions of 'The Gentle Boy,'" in *Nathaniel Hawthorne's Tales: Authoritative Texts, Backgrounds, Criticism*, ed. James McIntosh (New York: W. W. Norton, 1987), 262–64; and Seymour L. Gross, "Hawthorne's Revision of 'The Gentle Boy,'" *American Literature* 26, no. 2 (May 1954): 196–208.

42. Gross, "Hawthorne's Revision of 'The Gentle Boy,'" 196.

43. Nathaniel Hawthorne, "The Gentle Boy," in *The Token and Atlantic Souvenir: A Christmas and New Year's Present. 1832* (Boston: Gray and Bowen, 1831), 194, 195.

44. Ibid., 240.

45. Hawthorne's charge card at the Salem Athenaeum shows that over a third of his considerable reading was in history, politics, and biography between 1828 and 1850, a span that includes the composition of all of the pieces in *Twice-Told Tales* (Kesselring 8). He read contemporary accounts, like George Bancroft's *History of the United States* (the first volume of which presented the Puritans as the origin of the United States), canonized histories like William Sewel's *The History of the Rise, Increase, and Progress of the Christian People Called Quakers* (which Sedgwick had challenged in her "Mary Dyre"), and primary sources like those in the boxes that Hawthorne borrowed from the Massachusetts Historical Society. Marion Louise Kesselring, *Hawthorne's Reading, 1828–1850: A Transcription and Identification of Titles Recorded in the Charge-Books of the Salem Athenaeum* (New York: New York Public Library, 1949).

46. In his famed review of the second volume of *Twice-Told Tales*, Poe suggested that the cause of the veil is a sexual transgression, "a crime of dark dye, (having reference to the 'young lady')." Edgar Allan Poe, "Review: *Twice-Told Tales* by Nathaniel Hawthorne," *Graham's Lady's and Gentleman's Magazine* (May 1842): 299.

47. Qtd. in Ranlet, *Enemies of the Bay Colony*, 10.

48. Simon P. Newman points out that liberty poles, common symbols of freedom and common gathering places for political demonstrations in revolutionary and early national America, function as a version of the maypole. Through this historical association, Endicott's destruction of the maypole becomes positively anti-American, aligned with, for example, the

Tories and Redcoats who, between June of 1766 and February of 1770, chopped down no fewer than five New York City liberty poles. Simon P. Newman, *Parades and the Politics of the Street: Festive Culture in the Early American Republic* (Philadelphia: University of Pennsylvania Press, 2010), 25.

49. My treatment of this tale considers opposing narrative temporalities rather than themes or characters. As Michelle Sizemore has helpfully summarized, most criticism has plumbed the opposition of "some version of the pleasure principle versus the reality principle, whether in the realm of religion (paganism vs. Calvinism), the social (carnival vs. prudery), the political (Royalists vs. Roundheads), or the aesthetic (art vs. utility)." Michelle R. Sizemore, *American Enchantment: Rituals of the People in the Post-Revolutionary World* (New York: Oxford University Press, 2017), 18.

50. After Calvin's death, there is some disagreement among Puritans about exactly when double predestination comes into being. On one hand, supralapsarian Puritans believed that predestination meant that God's reprobation of the damned preceded and determined both Creation and the Fall. On the other hand, infralapsarian Puritans believed that predestination came after God's decree allowed the Fall. In other words, supralapsarians thought that Eve was damned to eat the apple, while infralapsarians thought that God *allowed* Eve to be tempted, knowing full well that she would fall. Once again, the difference is the existence of free will in a divinely controlled and ordered world. In both cases, God controls the world, but in one Eve chooses her preordained Fall. Some notable Puritans, including William Ames and, in New England, Samuel Willard, were supralapsarians, but the various Puritan confessions of faith including the Westminster Confession of Faith were infralapsarian. See Dewey D. Wallace Jr., "Predestination," in *Puritans and Puritanism in Europe and America: A Comprehensive Encyclopedia*, ed. Francis J. Bremer and Tom Webster, 2 vols. (Santa Barbara, CA: ABC-CLIO, 2006), 2:491.

51. Neal Frank Doubleday, *Hawthorne's Early Tales: A Critical Study* (Durham, NC: Duke University Press, 1972), 97.

52. Nathaniel Hawthorne, *Grandfather's Chair: A History for Youth* (Chicago: Belford, Clarke, 1840), 4.

53. Ibid., 28. Both Grandfather and Hawthorne share Judge Hathorne as an ancestor.

54. Ibid., 11. The final section of *Grandfather's Chair*, "The Liberty Tree," details the run-up to the War of Independence and ends with the 1794

election of Samuel Adams as governor of Massachusetts. Underscoring the relationship of the end to the beginning, Grandfather says: "I have told you what a distinguished patriot he was, and how much he resembled the stern old Puritans. Could the ancient freemen of Massachusetts who lived in the days of the first charter have arisen from their graves, they would probably have voted for Samuel Adams to be governor" (218).

55. Lea Bertani Vozar Newman cites these two readings in *A Reader's Guide to the Short Stories of Nathaniel Hawthorne* (Boston: G. K. Hall, 1979), 255.

56. Hawthorne's journal records an idea for a tale that displays a similar anxiety about controlling one's creation. In an entry for October 25, 1835 (an entry edited by Sophia Hawthorne), Hawthorne writes: "A person to be writing a tale, and to find that it shapes itself against his intentions; that the characters act otherwise that he thought; that unforeseen events occur; and a catastrophe comes which he strives in vain to avert. It might shadow forth his own fate,—he having made himself one of the personages." Nathaniel Hawthorne, *Passages from the American Note-Books,* vol. 9 of *The Complete Works of Nathaniel Hawthorne,* ed. George Parsons Lathrop (Boston: Houghton, Mifflin, 1886), 28.

57. Poe, "Review: *Twice-Told Tales,*" 299–300.

58. George Eliot, *Middlemarch,* ed. David Carroll, Oxford World Classics (New York: Oxford University Press, 1996), 261.

59. Nathaniel Hawthorne, *Twice-Told Tales,* Modern Library, 234. Underlining his attention to beginnings, Hawthorne starts the second volume of *Twice-Told Tales* with four stories about Anglo-American tensions in revolutionary Boston. In "Legends of the Province-House," the narrator goes to the Province House, a Boston pub that was the former abode of Royal governors, for stories that tell of various interactions between those loyal to the British Crown and those clamoring for independence. In the first "Legends" tale, Sir William Howe, the British commander at the Battle of Bunker Hill, asks of the apparitions that appear at his party, "A procession of the regicide judges of King Charles, the martyr?" (*TTT* Modern Library, 191). Another guest identifies the various Puritan ghosts as the seventeenth-century founders of the Bay Colony; though none is the Angel of Hadley, their posthumous appearance to chide a British officer over the city's occupation makes them much like Hawthorne's Gray Champion. In sum, both volumes of *Twice-Told Tales* open with explicit considerations of American beginnings.

60. Ibid.

61. Poe, "Review: *Twice-Told Tales,*" 298.

62. Charles F. Hoffman, "Review," in *Nathaniel Hawthorne: Critical Assessments*, ed. Brian Harding (Mountfield, East Sussex: Helm Information, 1995), 1:80.

63. Henry Wadsworth Longfellow, "Review," in *Nathaniel Hawthorne: Critical Assessments*, ed. Brian Harding, 4 vols., (Mountfield, East Sussex: Helm Information, 1995), 1:66.

64. Elizabeth Palmer Peabody, "Review," in *Nathaniel Hawthorne: Critical Assessments*, ed. Brian Harding (Mountfield, East Sussex: Helm Information, 1995), 1:74–75.

65. Tegg's *Twice Told Tales* includes, in order, "Footprints on the Sea Shore," "Fancy's Show Box," "The White Old Maid," "A Rill from the Town Pump," "The Hollow of the Three Hills," "Mr. Higginbotham's Catastrophe," "The Haunted Mind," "The Prophetic Pictures," "The Ambitious Guest," "Chippings with a Chisel," "Wakefield," "Sunday at Home," "The Threefold Destiny," "David Swan," "The Vision of the Fountain," "Little Annie's Ramble," "The Lily's Quest," "Snow Flakes," "Edward Fane's Rosebud," "Sights from a Steeple," "Lady Eleanore's Mantle," "Dr. Heidegger's Experiment," "Night Sketches, Beneath an Umbrella," "The Toll Gatherer's Day," and "The Great Carbuncle." See Nathaniel Hawthorne, *Twice Told Tales* (London: William Tegg, 1850).

66. *Little Annie's Ramble: And Other Tales* contains, in order, "Little Annie's Ramble," "The Hollow of the Three Hills," "The Vision of the Fountain," "Dr. Heidegger's Experiment," "The Gentle Boy," "The Toll-Gatherer's Day," "The Haunted Mind," "The Village Uncle," "The Ambitious Guest," "The Seven Vagabonds," "The White Old Maid," "The Shaker Bridal," "Endicott and the Red Cross," and "Chippings with a Chisel." See Nathaniel Hawthorne, *Little Annie's Ramble: And Other Tales* (Halifax: Milner and Sowerby, 1853).

67. Nathaniel Hawthorne, *Our Old Home, and English Note-Books*, Riverside ed., vol. 7 of *The Complete Works of Nathaniel Hawthorne* (Boston: Houghton, Mifflin, 1887), 16.

68. Puritans do serve as background to lesser or greater degrees in many of Hawthorne's novels; they also make an appearance in the sketch "Main-Street," which was supposed to be part of a collection which would have contained a shorter "The Scarlet Letter" but was published in *The Snow-Image and Other Twice-Told Tales* (1852). See chapter 6 for an explanation of the history of *The Scarlet Letter*.

69. A recent example of this tendency: in her excellent monograph, Sizemore incorrectly says that Hawthorne wrote "endlessly" about Puritans. Sizemore, *American Enchantment*, 18.

5. BEGINNING DETECTION WITH POE'S MARY/MARIE

1. Edgar Allan Poe, "Critical Notices: Traits of American Life," *Southern Literary Messenger* (December 1835): 67.

2. Sarah Josepha Hale, "Literary Notices: Al Aaraaf, Tamerlane, &c., by Edgar Allan Poe," *Ladies' Magazine and Literary Gazette* (January 1830): 47.

3. Nathaniel Hawthorne to Edgar Allan Poe, June 17, 1846, Edgar Allan Poe Society of Baltimore, https://www.eapoe.org/misc/letters/t4606170 .htm.

4. This endorsement, an excerpt from a letter, was printed in the "Advertisements" for *Tales of the Grotesque and Arabesque,* vol. 2. See Edgar Allan Poe, *Tales of the Grotesque and Arabesque* (Philadelphia: Lea and Blanchard, 1840): 2:i.

5. Poe would not have used the word "detective" because, as the *OED* indicates, it was coined after Poe's tales were published. The adjective first appears in 1843, the noun in 1850.

6. The excerpts are often verbatim, and the original sources have been identified by William K. Wimsatt. T. O. Mabbott also offers source material in his extensive annotations of the tale. Both critics believed that Poe had made up one of the newspaper accounts, but Richard Kopley has recently discovered the source for the excerpt that discusses the sailor's rudderless boat. See Richard Kopley, *Edgar Allan Poe and the Dupin Mysteries,* (New York: Palgrave Macmillan, 2008), 48–49; Mabbott's notes following Edgar Allan Poe, "The Mystery of Marie Rogêt," in *Tales and Sketches,* ed. Thomas Ollive Mabbott, Eleanor D. Kewer, and Maureen Cobb Mabbott (Urbana: University of Illinois Press, 2000), 2:778–84; and William Kurtz Wimsatt Jr., "Poe and the Mystery of Mary Rogers," *PMLA* 56, no. 1 (March 1941): 230–48.

7. Dorothy L. Sayers, introduction to *The Omnibus of Crime,* ed. Dorothy L. Sayers (New York: Payson and Clarke, 1929), 18.

8. Leonard Dinnerstein and David M. Reimers, *Ethnic Americans: A History of Immigration,* 5th ed. (New York: Columbia University Press, 2009), 36.

9. Amy Gilman Srebnick, *The Mysterious Death of Mary Rogers: Sex and Culture in Nineteenth-Century New York,* Studies in the History of Sexuality (New York: Oxford University Press, 1995), 6.

10. Philadelphia experienced five antiblack riots between 1834 and 1849. See Eric Ledell Smith, "The End of Black Voting Rights in Pennsylvania: African Americans and the Pennsylvania Constitutional Convention of 1837–1838," *Pennsylvania History: A Journal of Mid-Atlantic Studies* 65, no. 3 (1998): 284.

11. Edgar Allan Poe, "The Literati of New York City.—No. III," *Godey's Magazine and Lady's Book* (July 1846): 13; emphasis in original.

12. Edgar Allan Poe, "The Murders in the Rue Morgue," *Graham's Lady's and Gentleman's Magazine* (April 1841): 173.

13. Ed White, "The Ourang-Outang Situation," *College Literature* 30, no. 3 (July 29, 2003): 88–108.

14. Ibid.

15. Poe, "The Murders in the Rue Morgue," 178.

16. Elise Lemire, "'The Murders in the Rue Morgue': Amalgamation Discourses and the Race Riots of 1838 in Poe's Philadelphia," in *Romancing the Shadow: Poe and Race,* ed. J. Gerald Kennedy and Liliane Weissberg (New York: Oxford University Press, 2001), 178. For more on Poe and Cuvier, see Lindon Barrett, "Presence of Mind: Detection and Racialization in 'The Murders in the Rue Morgue,'" in *Romancing the Shadow: Poe and Race,* ed. J. Gerald Kennedy and Liliane Weissberg (New York: Oxford University Press, 2001), 157–76.

17. Barrett, "Presence of Mind," 171.

18. Ibid.

19. Leonard Cassuto makes this assertion, following Richard Kopley's surmise. Leonard Cassuto, "Poe the Crime Writer: Historicizing 'The Murders in the Rue Morgue,'" in *Approaches to Teaching Poe's Prose and Poetry,* ed. Jeffrey Andrew Weinstock and Tony Magistrale (New York: Modern Language Association, 2008), 36.

20. Qtd. in Lemire, "Amalgamation Discourses," 183.

21. Samuel Otter says that between ten thousand and thirty thousand bystanders watched the building burn while firefighters did nothing to try and put the fire out. (They did wet down nearby buildings to stop the fire from spreading.) Some accounts had the mob cheering when the roof fell in. Samuel Otter, *Philadelphia Stories: America's Literature of Race and Freedom* (New York: Oxford University Press, 2010), 135. Relatedly, Ed White in "The Ourang-Outang Situation" argues that "Murders" should be understood as dramatizing the fear and paranoia around slave insurrections.

22. Otter, *Philadelphia Stories,* 8.

23. Teresa A. Goddu, *Gothic America: Narrative, History, and Nation* (New York: Columbia University Press, 1997), 2.

24. Mark Seltzer, *True Crime: Observations on Violence and Modernity* (New York: Routledge, 2007).

25. Bennett had done something similar in April of 1836 when a young woman was murdered in a brothel. Sensing the promise of this story, Bennett took

it upon himself to investigate the crime, visit the brothel, and defend an accused clerk. He was a detective in the service of increased sales—during coverage of the event, his circulation soared from five thousand to fifteen thousand a day. Jean Folkerts, Dwight L. Teeter, and Edward Caudill, *Voices of a Nation: A History of Mass Media in the United States*, 5th ed. (Boston: Pearson/Allyn and Bacon, 2009), 118.

26. Srebnick has a wonderful overview of Mary Rogers's death in the first chapter of *The Mysterious Death of Mary Rogers*. In a later chapter on Poe's story, Srebnick argues that Poe's "'Marie' has even superseded the 'real' or historical Mary, just as Poe's recreation of the events (if not his solution to the crime) has infused all subsequent accounts of the Rogers death. . . . Poe's achievement was considerable; not only did he invent the narrative framework through which we see the Mary Rogers story, he structured the way in which we associate violent death with urban life as an event of intellectual rather than emotional engagement, and as a mystery predicated on complex, but always depersonalized, male/female relations." Srebnick, *The Mysterious Death of Mary Rogers*, 110.

27. Edgar Allan Poe, "The Mystery of Marie Rogêt," *Ladies' Companion, a Monthly Magazine; Devoted to Literature and the Fine Arts* (November 1842): 20. Part 1 of "The Mystery of Marie Rogêt" is hereafter cited in text as *MR1*. For the bulk of this chapter, I will quote and refer to the story originally published in Snowden's *Ladies' Companion* in three installments: November and December 1842 and January of 1843. Because the serialization is relevant, I have cited the various parts: *MR1* denotes the first serialized section of "Marie Rogêt"; *MR2*, the second; and *MR3*, the third. The changes Poe makes to later versions of the tale will be treated below. Citations for parts 2 and 3 of the story are as follows: Edgar Allan Poe, "The Mystery of Marie Rogêt," *Ladies' Companion, a Monthly Magazine; Devoted to Literature and the Fine Arts* (December 1842): 93–99; and Poe, "The Mystery of Marie Rogêt," *Ladies' Companion, a Monthly Magazine; Devoted to Literature and the Fine Arts* (February 1843): 162–67.

28. Despite their reputation for sensationalism, these penny papers pushed American journalism forward. Bennett hired correspondents, arranged a ship news service, covered court news, and experimented with illustrations. Many of these were firsts that moved newspapers away from the cut-and-paste norms of so-called scissors editors. In "Literati of New York," Poe said about the New York *Sun*'s invention of the penny paper: "The consequences of the scheme, in their influence on the whole newspaper business of the country, and through this business on the interests of the country at

large, are probably beyond all calculation." The *Sun* and the *Herald* were rivals—and both successful. The very first notice of Mary Rogers's disappearance was in the *Sun* in the form of a missing persons notice placed by Mary's fiancé. Edgar Allan Poe, "Richard Adams Lock," in unpublished manuscript book entitled "Literary America," 1848, Edgar Allan Poe Society of Baltimore, https://www.eapoe.org/works/misc/litamlra.htm, 94.

29. Srebnick, *The Mysterious Death of Mary Rogers*. See also Karen Halttunen, *Murder Most Foul: The Killer and the American Gothic Imagination* (Cambridge, MA: Harvard University Press, 1998).

30. David M. Henkin, *City Reading: Written Words and Public Spaces in Antebellum New York* (New York: Columbia University Press, 1998), 15.

31. Poe, "The Murders in the Rue Morgue," 168.

32. Despite their being tales, Poe's detective stories borrow much from the sketch tradition. Most obviously, the story hinges on the excellent observation of Dupin, who reveals a place and a moment to the reader as he exposes who did it and how. Just as importantly, the narrator, Dupin's unnamed American friend, declares his "design" to be the "depicting of [the] character" of the impressive detective (*MR1* 15). Because the sidekick's job is to retell what the detective reveals, not to catalyze action or to solve the crime, the narrative can be understood as a character sketch. The visual language—"depicting"—encourages us to treat the piece as a portrait (a triptych, if we take all three tales into account) of a truly great mind. Long unplotted and sketch-like sections, such as the introduction on checkers, whist, and chess in "Murders" and the many interpolated newspaper accounts in "Marie Rôget," illustrate just how well Dupin can see information and understand clues. Moreover, as do *The Scarlet Letter, Moby-Dick,* and *Uncle Tom's Cabin* some years later, these stories mobilize the sense of "truth" associated with the sketch. The detective works to uncover what *really* happened—in "Mary Rôget" that revelation was supposed to be the Parisian truth of New Yorker Mary Roger's death.

33. Dana Brand, *The Spectator and the City in Nineteenth-Century American Literature* (New York: Cambridge University Press, 1991), 99.

34. Poe, "The Murders in the Rue Morgue," 173.

35. Qtd. in Brand, *The Spectator and the City,* 77.

36. Nathaniel Parker Willis, a notable nineteenth-century sketch writer and acquaintance of Poe, had started his career by writing London sketches for the *New York Mirror*—pieces later collected in the successful *Pencillings by the Way* (1835). By 1840, though, Willis had turned his attention to his home city. The number of New York sketch collections—including

E. Porter Belden's *New York: Past, Present, and Future* (1849), George G. Foster's *New York in Slices* (1849), Joel H. Ross's *What I Saw in New-York* (1851), and Cornelius Matthews's *A Pen-and-Ink Panorama of New York City* (1853)—showed that others agreed.

37. Poe's choice of Paris may reference a source of inspiration for his creation of Dupin. Vidocq, a French ex-convict who became the first popularly known detective-like figure—he easily passed among criminals and then supplied information and suspects to the highest bidder—published a memoir of his investigations in 1828. (It was translated into English by 1829, and Poe mentions Vidocq in "The Murders in the Rue Morgue.") Detective historians A. E. Murch and Howard Haycraft believe Vidocq's narrative is an important moment in the development of the genre because it presents the first detective-like figure in writing; still, the memoir does not offer clues leading up to a revelation of the crime and hence is not structured like detective fiction. See Howard Haycraft, *Murder for Pleasure: The Life and Times of the Detective Story* (New York: Biblo and Tannen, 1968); and A. E. Murch, *The Development of the Detective Novel* (New York: Greenwood, 1968).

38. The Barrière de Roule is also called the Barrière de Ternes and is where the present-day Ternes metro is.

39. Qtd. in Dinnerstein and Reimers, *Ethnic Americans*, 40.

40. According to the editors of *The Papers of Benjamin Franklin*, who supply the whole essay, the quotation I have provided was actually not included when the piece was published in *Gentleman's Magazine*. Benjamin Franklin, "Observations Concerning the Increase of Mankind," in *The Papers of Benjamin Franklin*, ed. Leonard Woods Labaree, vol. 4, *July 1, 1750, through June 30, 1753* (New Haven, CT: Yale University Press, 1961), 234.

41. Nancy Harrowitz and Ed White have both argued that "Murders" and the invention of detective fiction (to use Harrowitz's language) "invokes some specific historical tensions of America in the early 1840s." Here I extend that argument to "Marie Rogêt." Nancy Harrowitz, "Criminality and Poe's Orangutan: The Question of Race in Detection," in *Agnostics: Arenas of Creative Contest*, ed. Janet Lungstrum and Elizabeth Sauer (Albany: SUNY Press, 1997), 182; White, "The Ourang-Outang Situation."

42. Tzvetan Todorov, "The Typology of Detective Fiction," in *The Poetics of Prose* (Ithaca, NY: Cornell University Press, 1977), 42–52.

43. Arthur Conan Doyle, "The Problem of Thor Bridge," in *Sherlock Holmes: The Complete Novels and Stories*, ed. Loren D. Estleman (New York: Bantam Dell, 1986), 2:628–29.

44. Qtd. in John Evangelist Walsh, *Poe the Detective: The Curious Circumstances behind "The Murder of Marie Roget"* (New Brunswick, NJ: Rutgers University Press, 1968), 19.

45. It is important to remember that while Mary Rogers was real, she became infamous through a series of textual installments. To most people in New York, then, she too was a story.

46. Edgar Allan Poe, *The Brevities: Pinakidia, Marginalia, Fifty Suggestions, and Other Works,* vol. 2 of *The Collected Writings of Edgar Allan Poe,* ed. Burton R. Pollin (New York: Gordian, 1985), 508; emphasis in original.

47. The denouement appeared after a month-long gap during which, John Walsh argues, Poe could have traveled to New York (where Snowden's was published) from Philadelphia (where he lived) to amend his manuscript. Poe's pride in his ability to solve puzzles makes plausible the supposition that he held and altered the story's finale, but there is no definite evidence for the theory. Walsh, *Poe the Detective.*

48. With about 80 deleted and some 150 added words, the tale shifts from a firm accusation of the sailor to a possible endorsement of an accident. For an excellent and visual depiction of the three significant deletions and some twelve important additions in Poe's story see Walsh, *Poe the Detective,* 69–70.

49. In a letter to his friend George Eveleth. Edgar Allan Poe, *The Collected Letters of Edgar Allan Poe,* ed. John Ward Ostrom, Burton Ralph Pollin, and Jeffrey A. Savoye, 3rd ed. (Staten Island, NY: Gordian, 2008), 1:641; emphasis in original.

50. Edgar Allan Poe, "A Few Words on Secret Writing," *Graham's Lady's and Gentleman's Magazine* (July 1, 1841): 34; emphasis in original.

51. Poe, *The Collected Letters,* 1:293.

52. Ibid., 340; emphasis in original.

53. Edgar Allan Poe, "Review: *Barnaby Rudge* by Charles Dickens," *Graham's Lady's and Gentleman's Magazine* (May 1842): 3.

54. Terence Whalen, "Average Racism: Poe, Slavery, and the Wages of Literary Nationalism," in *Romancing the Shadow: Poe and Race,* ed. J. Gerald Kennedy and Liliane Weissberg (New York: Oxford University Press, 2001), 4. Teresa Goddu writes about Poe's use of "conventions of slavery and race," which she argues are a product of the marketplace that Poe cleverly deploys (94). See Teresa A. Goddu, "Poe, Sensationalism, and Slavery," in *The Cambridge Companion to Edgar Allan Poe,* ed. Kevin J. Hayes (Cambridge: Cambridge University Press, 2002), 92–112.

55. For an example, see Wimsatt, "Poe and the Mystery of Mary Rogers," 247.

56. Henry David Thoreau, "Civil Disobedience," in *Walden and Other Writings*, ed. Brooks Atkinson (New York: Modern Library, 2000), 671.

57. William Walker, *The War in Nicaragua* (New York: S. H. Goetzel, 1860), 271–72.

58. Kopley, *Edgar Allan Poe and the Dupin Mysteries*, 2.

59. Haycraft, *Murder for Pleasure*, 313.

60. Neil Harris further suggests that the interest in revealing secrets that characterizes detective fiction was a particular feature of the antebellum (and abolitionist) North; the South, because it had a vested interest in maintaining slavery, was much more hostile to revelations or exposures. Decoding and demasking is, Harris suggests, integral to the healthy maintenance of a democracy, and antebellum audiences appreciated aesthetic treatments of that principle. Neil Harris, *Humbug: The Art of P. T. Barnum* (Boston: Little, Brown, 1973).

61. Jon Thompson, *Fiction, Crime, and Empire: Clues to Modernity and Postmodernism* (Urbana: University of Illinois Press, 1993), 44.

62. Ibid., 45.

63. Poe, *The Collected Letters*, 1:595.

64. Leland S. Person, "Cruising (Perversely) for Context: Poe and Murder, Women and Apes," in *Poe and the Remapping of Antebellum Print Culture*, ed. J. Gerald Kennedy and Jerome McGann (Baton Rouge: Louisiana State University Press, 2012), 144.

65. Poe, "Review: *Twice-Told Tales*," 1.

66. Ibid., 1–2; emphasis in original.

67. Edward J. O'Brien, "Extract from *The Advance of the American Short Story*," in *Edgar Allan Poe: Critical Assessments*, ed. Graham Clarke, Helm Information Critical Assessments of Writers in English (Mountfield, East Sussex: Helm Information, 1991), 3:283.

68. Poe, "Review: *Twice-Told Tales*," 2.

6. THE SHORT FICTION SKELETON OF THE GREAT AMERICAN NOVEL

1. I have tallied the titles Bell lists in his bibliography. See Michael Davitt Bell, *Hawthorne and the Historical Romance of New England* (Princeton, NJ: Princeton University Press, 1971).

2. Elizabeth Barrett Browning, *The Complete Works of Mrs. E. B. Browning*, ed. Charlotte Porter and Helen A. Clarke (New York: Fred DeFau, 1900), 3:168. The poem is first published in *The Liberty Bell* and sold at the Anti-Slavery Bazaar of 1848.

3. Ibid., 169.

4. Wendell Phillips, *Speeches, Lectures and Letters, 2nd Series* (Boston: Lee and Shepard, 1891), 308.

5. William Wells Brown, ed., *The Anti-Slavery Harp: A Collection of Songs for Anti-Slavery Meetings* (Boston: Bela Marsh, 1848), 23.

6. Eliza Lee Follen, *The Liberty Cap* (Boston: Leonard C. Bowles, 1846), 13–14.

7. Mary Henderson Eastman, *Aunt Phillis's Cabin; or, Southern Life as It Is* (Philadelphia: Lippincott, Grambo, 1852), 74, 75.

8. J. Thorton Randolph [Charles Jacobs Peterson], *The Cabin and Parlor; or Slaves and Masters* (Philadelphia: T. B. Peterson, 1852), 5.

9. For Buell, *The Scarlet Letter* enacts the "script" or model of story frequently adapted, often contrary to the original author's intentions. *Uncle Tom's Cabin* follows a different script, that of the family drama riven by social and racial divisions and inequities. And *Moby-Dick* is a mega-novel with a large group of characters who show, in small form (here, in the "ship of state"), the challenges of democracy itself. The final script is the "up-from" story exemplified by Benjamin Franklin's *Autobiography*. See Lawrence Buell, *The Dream of the Great American Novel* (Cambridge, MA: Harvard University Press, 2014).

10. *Clotel* is a family epic, much like *Uncle Tom's Cabin*. It arguably also has the thread of the up-from script, the fourth script that Buell identifies for great American novels. Obviously, any slave narrative that depicts a journey to freedom is a story of rising up from degradation to liberty.

11. Nina Baym, *Novels, Readers, and Reviewers: Responses to Fiction in Antebellum America* (Ithaca, NY: Cornell University Press, 1984), 245.

12. Ibid., 160.

13. Kristie Hamilton, *America's Sketchbook: The Cultural Life of a Nineteenth-Century Genre* (Athens: Ohio University Press, 1998), 35–63.

14. Ibid., 2.

15. Ibid., 8.

16. Michael Winship, *American Literary Publishing in the Mid-Nineteenth Century: The Business of Ticknor and Fields* (New York: Cambridge University Press, 1995), 55.

17. "The Custom-House" still retains a mention of "Main-Street," a sketch that Hawthorne wanted to publish in his projected collection (*Scarlet Letter* 26). See chapter 4, note 68, above for more on "Main-Street" and note 19, this chapter, below for a citation of *The Scarlet Letter*.

18. James Thomas Fields, *Yesterdays with Authors* (Boston: James R. Osgood, 1872), 51.

19. Nathaniel Hawthorne, *The Scarlet Letter and Other Writings: Authoritative Texts, Contexts, Criticism*, ed. Leland S. Person, Norton Critical Edition (New York: W. W. Norton, 2005), 8. Hereafter cited in text as *SL*.

20. Goodrich's numbers are cited in Eugene Exman, *The Brothers Harper: A Unique Publishing Partnership and Its Impact upon the Cultural Life of America from 1817 to 1853* (New York: Harper and Row, 1965), 326.

21. When the offices of the Harper Brothers, Melville's publisher, burned down in 1853, the firm lost a whopping $1,500,000 worth of property. See Charles Allan Madison, *Book Publishing in America* (New York: McGraw-Hill, 1966), 27. Perhaps even more indicative of the relative strength of the midcentury literary market is that the Harpers were able to recover quickly from the disaster.

22. Philip Gaskell, *A New Introduction to Bibliography* (New York: Oak Knoll, 1995), 205. Stereotyping and electrotyping differ in the method by which the plate is created, but they both result in a metal plate of type.

23. Ticknor and Fields (actually Ticknor, Reed and Fields in 1850) start spending more dollars (that form a smaller percentage of their firm's total production cost) on stereotyping from 1852 on. See Winship, *American Literary Publishing*, 146.

24. Gaskell, *A New Introduction to Bibliography*, 201.

25. After quickly selling two full editions of twenty-five hundred copies each, *The Scarlet Letter* was stereotyped in late 1850 for a third edition (*SL* xv). All other editions produced during Hawthorne's lifetime were printed from those plates. Similarly, *Uncle Tom's Cabin* was stereotyped in 1852 for its second edition, after the first printing sold more than half of the five-thousand-book run in a single day. Melville, possibly because he was unsure if he was going to publish with the Harper brothers, went ahead and contracted Robert Craighead to stereotype *Moby-Dick* (Hayford and Tanselle 662). The Harpers then paid Craighead and used the plates for the 2,915 copies of the first printing (Hayford and Tanselle 686). (Harpers intended a three-thousand-book print run, but the paper ran short [Exman 296].) Unfortunately for Melville, the book did not sell well. Nonetheless, the 1853 Harper fire destroyed some stock, and the slow trickle of sales justified three more small print runs of the book (all from the stereotype plates that Craighead made) in 1855, 1863, and 1871 (Hayford and Tanselle 688). By 1887 no new copies of *Moby-Dick* remained to be sold, and the book was out of print for the last four years of Melville's life (Hayford and Tanselle 689). See Harrison Hayford and G. Thomas Tanselle, "Historical Note," in *Moby-Dick, or, The Whale*, vol. 6 of *The Writings of Herman*

Melville, ed. Harrison Hayford and G. Thomas Tanselle (Chicago: New-berry Library, 1988), 581–762; and Exman, *The Brothers Harper.*

26. Hamilton, *America's Sketchbook,* 9.

27. Nathaniel Hawthorne, "The Marble Faun," in *The Hawthorne Treasury: Complete Novels and Selected Tales of Nathaniel Hawthorne,* ed. Norman Holmes Pearson (New York: Modern Library, 1999), 1190.

28. Kristie Hamilton, "Hawthorne, Modernity, and the Literary Sketch," in *The Cambridge Companion to Nathaniel Hawthorne,* ed. Richard H. Mill-ington (New York: Cambridge University Press, 2004), 100.

29. Lawrence Buell, *New England Literary Culture from Revolution through Re-naissance* (New York: Cambridge University Press, 1986), 297.

30. Poe, "Review: *Twice-Told Tales,*" 298.

31. Nathaniel Hawthorne, *The Letters, 1843–1853,* in *The Centenary Edition of the Works of Nathaniel Hawthorne,* ed. Thomas Woodson, L. Neal Smith, and Norman Holmes Pearson (Athens: Ohio State University Press, 1985), 16:307.

32. Contemporary reviewers carefully evaluated the plot of novels and made clear that plot was the feature separating long and short fiction. Baym, *Novels, Readers, and Reviewers,* 81.

33. Hawthorne, *The Letters,* 16:307.

34. Though the divide between *novel* and *romance* has influenced much criti-cal discussion of antebellum texts, Baym convincingly shows that *romance* was employed as a synonym for *novel* by antebellum reviewers, who did not have a general acceptance of *romance* as a genre category. Indeed, many reviewers rejected Hawthorne's distinction between the two terms. See Baym, *Novels, Readers, and Reviewers,* 226–35.

35. Qtd. in ibid., 78.

36. Qtd. in ibid., 95.

37. "From the *Salem Register,* 21 March 1850, 2:1–2," in *The Critical Response to Nathaniel Hawthorne's "The Scarlet Letter,"* ed. Gary Scharnhorst, Critical Responses in Arts and Letters (New York: Greenwood, 1992), 2:16.

38. The Norton Critical Edition of *The Scarlet Letter* feels the need to footnote Hawthorne's mention of an actual scarlet letter in surveyor Pue's papers by saying, "There is no evidence that the scarlet letter of these papers ever existed outside Hawthorne's imagination" (*SL* 27).

39. "'Book Notices,' *Portland Transcript,* 30 March 1850, p. 3.," in *The Critical Response to Nathaniel Hawthorne's "The Scarlet Letter,"* ed. Gary Scharn-horst, Critical Responses in Arts and Letters (New York: Greenwood, 1992), 2:24.

40. "'Nathaniel Hawthorne,' *Literary World*, 30 March 1850, Pp. 323–325," in *The Critical Response to Nathaniel Hawthorne's "The Scarlet Letter,"* ed. Gary Scharnhorst, Critical Responses in Arts and Letters (New York: Greenwood, 1992), 2:21, 23.

41. Qtd. in Baym, *Novels, Readers, and Reviewers,* 67.

42. For more about antebellum perception of Melville's earlier novels as true, see James L. Machor, *Reading Fiction in Antebellum America: Informed Response and Reception Histories, 1820–1865* (Baltimore: Johns Hopkins University Press, 2011), especially 145–65.

43. Herman Melville, *The Letters of Herman Melville* (New Haven, CT: Yale University Press, 1960), 130.

44. Ibid., 109.

45. Ibid., 132.

46. Herman Melville, *Moby-Dick,* ed. Harrison Hayford and Hershel Parker, 2nd ed. (New York: W. W. Norton, 2002), 25. Hereafter cited in text.

47. James Barbour, "'All My Books Are Botches': Melville's Struggle with *The Whale,"* in *Writing the American Classics,* ed. Tom Quirk and James Barbour (Chapel Hill: University of North Carolina Press, 1990), 30.

48. See ibid., 40. Hershel Parker and Harrison Hayford note that when he dates specific chapters, Barbour relies on some biographical specifics now known to be incorrect. Still, Parker and Hayford do not dispute the grand claims of Barbour's argument, and many scholars accept the notion of "three *Moby-Dicks.*" See Melville, *Moby-Dick,* 697n.

49. The publishing history of *Moby-Dick* arguably displays that the novel has discrete parts akin to pieces of short fiction. As a means of advertising *Moby-Dick,* the Harper brothers printed "The Town-Ho's Story" separately in the October 1851 issue of *Harper's Magazine.* Though it carried a footnote indicating the piece was "from 'The Whale' . . . the title of a new work by Mr. Melville, in the press of Harper and Brothers," it stood alone as a coherent tale. Herman Melville, "The Town-Ho's Story," *Harper's New Monthly Magazine* (October 1851): 658.

50. See Lance E. Davis, Robert E. Gallman, and Karin Gleiter, *In Pursuit of Leviathan: Technology, Institutions, Productivity, and Profits in American Whaling, 1816–1906* (Chicago: University of Chicago Press, 1997), 4.

51. Hunting declined slightly as the 1850s wore on and then dropped off drastically after 1860. See ibid., 131.

52. It is possible to read Ahab's obsessive search for the white whale as an allegory of the single-minded and unethical search for African Americans (fugitive or not) after the passage of the Fugitive Slave Act.

53. Herman Melville, "Hawthorne and His Mosses," in *Moby-Dick*, ed. Harrison Hayford and Hershel Parker, 2nd ed. (New York: W. W. Norton, 2002), 525.

54. Ibid., 523.

55. Elizabeth Ammons, introduction to *Harriet Beecher Stowe's Uncle Tom's Cabin: A Casebook*, ed. Elizabeth Ammons (New York: Oxford University Press, 2007), 8.

56. Qtd. in Ammons, introduction, 8.

57. Harriet Beecher Stowe, *Uncle Tom's Cabin: Authoritative Text, Backgrounds and Contexts, Criticism*, ed. Elizabeth Ammons, 2nd ed. (New York: W. W. Norton, 2010), vii. Hereafter cited in text as *UTC*.

58. "American Literature and Reprints," *Putnam's Monthly Magazine of American Literature, Science, and Art* 8, no. 47 (November 1856): 537.

59. Qtd. in E. Bruce Kirkham, *The Building of Uncle Tom's Cabin* (Knoxville: University of Tennessee Press, 1977), 66.

60. Qtd. in ibid., 66–67; emphasis in original.

61. Baym, *Novels, Readers, and Reviewers*, 273.

62. Importantly, Stowe does not have the slave owner argue that slaves have no souls as some slavery apologists did.

63. This version of Sand's review was reprinted in *The National Era* from a translation done by the *New York Evening Post*, demonstrating that Sand's words circulated in the United States despite first appearing in a French newspaper. George Sand, "George Sand and Uncle Tom," *National Era* (January 27, 1853), http://utc.iath.virginia.edu/notices/noar01awt.html.

64. Susan Belasco Smith, "Serialization and the Nature of Uncle Tom's Cabin," in *Periodical Literature in Nineteenth-Century America*, by Kenneth M. Price and Susan Belasco Smith (Charlottesville: University Press of Virginia, 1995), 69–89.

65. For the illustrations from various editions of *Uncle Tom's Cabin*, see the University of Virginia's wonderful online resource at utc.iath.virginia.edu/uncletom/illustra/52illf.html.

66. Jo-Ann Morgan, *Uncle Tom's Cabin as Visual Culture* (Columbia: University of Missouri Press, 2007), 2.

67. Ironically, the ease with which *Uncle Tom's Cabin* translated from verbal into visual images helped shift the meaning of the story Stowe wrote. By the turn of the century, artists had refashioned Tom from strong and virile to old and servile. Posing the angelic Eva with a grandfatherly—not strapping—Tom eliminated any potential sexual energy between black man and white girl even while it violated Stowe's original intention. Images

were used to make and unmake the radical message of *Uncle Tom's Cabin*. For more detail on this transition, see Morgan, *Uncle Tom's Cabin as Visual Culture*, 20–63.

68. Harriet Beecher Stowe, *A Key to Uncle Tom's Cabin: Presenting the Original Facts and Documents upon Which the Story Is Founded, Together with Corroborative Statements Verifying the Truth of the Work* (St. Clair Shores, MI: Scholarly, 1977), 5.

69. Sarah Hale followed Stowe's example in associating her 1837 novel *Northwood* (which disdains but defends slavery) with sketches when she republished it in 1852 as a direct response to *Uncle Tom's Cabin*. Hale dropped the previous subtitle "A New England Tale" instead substituting "Showing the True Character of Both" to emphasize that her novel provided some revelation of the authentic qualities of northerners and southerners—in short, character sketches. (Unlike in her *Ladies' Magazine* sketches, in *Northwood* Hale recognizes the all-important regional divide. There is no longer one version of "American" character to be drawn.) As Hale writes in the 1852 preface to the novel, "Fiction derives its chief worth from the truths it teaches." Once again, the sketch is working to fashion authentic-feeling mid-century fiction. Sarah Josepha Hale, *Northwood* (New York: H. Long and Brother, 1852), iv.

70. Brown's is accepted as the first African American novel, but Frederick Douglass's "The Heroic Slave" is accepted as the first piece of published African American fiction. (Douglass's story appears by March 1853, while Brown's novel comes later, in December of that year.) Worth noting is that Douglass's 1853 story, like Brown's, is based in truth and similarly attacks the culture of beginnings: the slave Madison Washington, whose name recalls two Virginian slaveholding Founding Fathers, leads a successful slave rebellion in Douglass's story as he did in real life. Moreover, Douglass's story traffics in the sketch's aesthetic of the incomplete: "Glimpses of this great character are all that can now be presented," he tells the reader. Frederick Douglass, "The Heroic Slave," in *Autographs for Freedom*, ed. Julia Griffiths (Cleveland: John P. Jewett and Company, 1853), 175.

71. William Wells Brown, *Clotel; or, The President's Daughter: A Narrative of Slave Life in the United States* (London: Partridge and Oakey, 1853), 66. Hereafter cited in text.

72. Philip Gaskell notes that "it is usually difficult to tell whether a particular book has been printed from type or plates," and the copy of *Clotel* (1853) held physically in the Bodleian gives no certain indication that it was printed from letter press or from plates. The collation is unremarkable

(A^4 B-Q8 R^4 [S]^6), and while pages like 68 display more inking on the bottom line of text, it is not a definitive indication that battered plates were in use. I have found no advertisements or other records that confirm the book is stereotyped, but Brown was familiar with the technology before 1853 and would seem likely to have preferred it since it gave him the ability to put out new editions when he had sold out his current stock. He did something similar with his *Narrative*. Gaskell, *New Introduction to Bibliography*, 204. My thanks to Jo Maddocks, rare books assistant curator at the Weston Library (part of the Bodleian Library) for help with evaluating *Clotel*.

73. Jonathan Senchyne, "Bottles of Ink and Reams of Paper: *Clotel*, Racialization, and the Material Culture of Print," in *Early African American Print Culture*, ed. Lara Langer Cohen and Jordan Alexander Stein (Philadelphia: University of Pennsylvania Press, 2012), 140–58. Brown's novel was first published in England, albeit with the stated purpose of influencing the United States. Like Irving, Brown was looking both cisatlantically and transatlantically, but Brown's novel would take another edition with substantial changes, including the removal of the autobiographic sketch, before it saw real circulation in the United States. Still, the community of abolitionists were undoubtedly aware of the 1853 edition, which Brown sent to friends back in the States and which received mention in US abolitionist newspapers. Brown even announced the publication to a US audience by means of a letter to William Lloyd Garrison, editor of the *Liberator*.

74. Samuel Otter, *Melville's Anatomies* (Berkeley: University of California Press, 1999), 101–71.

75. Christopher Mulvey intriguingly compares the full-length description of Clotel on the auction block to Hester Prynne in the marketplace. See Christopher Mulvey, "The Fugitive Self and the New World of the North: William Wells Brown's Discovery of America," in *The Black Columbiad: Defining Moments in African American Literature and Culture*, ed. Werner Sollors and Maria Diedrich (Cambridge, MA: Harvard University Press, 1994), 104.

76. Senchyne, "Bottles of Ink," 140–42.

77. Brown plagiarizes Irving's "The Art of Book-Making" (which itself is a condemnation of plagiarism) in his *Three Years in Europe*, so it is indisputable that he is familiar with the text. See Geoffrey Sanborn, *Plagiarama! William Wells Brown and the Aesthetic of Attractions* (New York: Columbia University Press, 2015), 28.

78. In a pamphlet for his panorama (discussed below), Brown gave the following epigraph on the title page: "FICTION: 'We hold these truths to be self-evident; that all men are created equal: that they are endowed by their Creator with certain inalienable rights, and that among these are LIFE, LIBERTY, and the PURSUIT OF HAPPINESS.'—*Declaration of American Independence* FACT: 'They touch our country, and their shackles fall.'—Cowper." Qtd. in Sergio Costola, "William Wells Brown's Panoramic Views," *Journal of American Drama and Theatre* 24, no. 2 (Spring 2012): 23.

79. Toni Morrison, *Playing in the Dark: Whiteness and the Literary Imagination* (Cambridge, MA: Harvard University Press, 1992), 37.

80. Clearly in this binary Native Americans are ignored.

81. Ezra Greenspan concludes that Brown "absorbed a crucial lesson from Stowe's . . . combination of . . . *Uncle Tom's Cabin* and *A Key to Uncle Tom's Cabin*," and one contemporary reviewer made the corollary point: "The narrative of 'Clotel' might almost serve as a key to 'Uncle Tom's Cabin.'" Ezra Greenspan, *William Wells Brown: An African American Life* (New York: W. W. Norton, 2014), 298; "*Clotel; or, the President's Daughter*: A Narrative of Slave Life in the United States," *Tait's Edinburg Magazine* (January 1854): 58.

82. As it happens, Brown's image would have been familiar to abolitionist readers since the engraving was done by the same artist who had done Douglass's portrait for *The Narrative of the Life of Frederick Douglass* (1845).

83. Beth A. McCoy, "Race and the (Para)Textual Condition," in *The Broadview Reader in Book History*, ed. Michelle Levy and Tom Mole (Tonawanda, NY: Broadview, 2015), 201.

84. William L. Andrews, *To Tell a Free Story: The First Century of Afro-American Autobiography, 1760–1865* (Urbana: University of Illinois Press, 1986), 110.

85. Qtd. in ibid., 108.

86. Dwight A. McBride, *Impossible Witnesses: Truth, Abolitionism, and Slave Testimony* (New York: New York University Press, 2001).

87. Although it is much more complete in *Clotel*, Brown's move away from the authorizing conventions of the slave narrative begins with *Three Years in Europe*. *Three Years* borrows directly from the tradition of Geoffrey Crayon even from its subtitle, which references a sketch collection by Nathaniel Parker Willis, likely the US author most associated with sketches after Irving. Similarly, Brown's preface, in which he asks his readers "with no little diffidence . . . kindly to remember, that the author was a slave in one of the Southern States of America," recalls Irving's London *Sketch*

Book, in which he apologizes for the "deficiencies [that] are increased by a diffidence arising from his peculiar situation" of "writing in a strange land." And yet Brown still relied on the paratextual features of the slave narrative for his 1852 sketch book. *Three Years* started, like Brown's *Narrative*, with an engraved portrait of Brown above his signature, and on the cover was embossed a supplicating slave, the oldest icon of the transatlantic antislavery movement. Moreover, Brown's collection begins with a short biography written by a notable white abolitionist, William Farmer, who in recounting Brown's life testifies to the truth of Brown's story and qualifies his authorship. Although it is the first sketch collection by an African American, Brown's book arises out of the genre traditions of the slave narrative. Brown is more a "fugitive tourist," to borrow Charles Baraw's term, than a gentleman sketcher. William Wells Brown, *Three Years in Europe; or, Places I Have Seen and People I Have Met* (London: Charles Gilpin, 1852), xxxii; Washington Irving, *The Sketch Book of Geoffrey Crayon, Gent.* (London: John Miller and John Murray, 1820), 2:418. See also Charles Baraw, "William Wells Brown, 'Three Years in Europe,' and Fugitive Tourism," *African American Review* 44, no. 3 (2011): 453–70.

88. Baraw makes a similar point about *Three Years*. See Baraw, "William Wells Brown, 'Three Years in Europe,' and Fugitive Tourism," 454.

89. "*Clotel; or, the President's Daughter*," *Tait's Edinburg Magazine*, 58; my emphasis.

90. "Fiction," *Critic* 12, no. 304 (December 1, 1853): 625.

91. Ibid.; "Notices of Books," *British Mothers' Magazine* (January 1, 1854): 21.

92. That the sketch had the feeling of truth is not to say that it was true. Critics have noted how Brown's telling of his life changes from account to account and how Brown has multiple moments in his *Narrative* where he artfully lies. In his discussion of Brown's *Narrative*, Andrews distinguishes between "truth" and "*my* truth," the latter of which may be a lie that has the feeling of authenticity. See Andrews, *To Tell a Free Story*, 164–66.

93. Sketches, particularly biographical sketches, also would have had relation to the biographical retellings in "accounts" as in Thomas Anderson's *Interesting Account of Thomas Anderson, a Slave, Taken from His Own Lips* (1854).

94. Greenspan, *William Wells Brown*, 242.

95. Ibid., 244.

96. Qtd. in ibid., 242–43. For a description of the images in the panorama, see Costola, "William Wells Brown's Panoramic Views," 25–31.

97. Qtd. in Greenspan, *William Wells Brown*, 166.

98. According to Mary Ganster, "Fragmentation, which might manifest in anachronism of inconsistent plot chronology, is a discursive strategy through which African American rhetorical performers (preachers, poets, novelists, orators) both make and mask potentially dangerous arguments that challenge authority." See Mary Ganster, "Fact, Fiction, and the Industry of Violence: Newspapers and Advertisements in Clotel," *African American Review* 48, no. 4 (December 9, 2015): 437.

99. Greenspan, *William Wells Brown*, 290.

100. Child's tale plays the largest role in the first version of *Clotel*. In the 1853 *Clotel*, unmarked passages from Child's story appear in chapters 4, 8, 19, and 23. In *Miralda; or, the Beautiful Quadroon, a Romance of American Slavery, Founded on Fact* (1860–61) and *Clotelle; a Tale of the Southern States* (1864), both of which are altered versions of the 1853 *Clotel*, the borrowings decrease from 1,960 words in four chapters to 36 words in just one chapter (though we are missing the first six chapters of *Miralda*). As Geoffrey Sanborn has shown, the amount of plagiarism from all sources declines in subsequent versions of Brown's novel from 23 percent in *Clotel* to 10 percent, 8 percent, and 6 percent for, respectively, *Miralda*; *Clotelle: A Tale of the Southern States*; and *Clotelle; or The Colored Heroine* (1867). As these numbers indicate, all of these versions are significantly different, even going so far as to change the heroine's name. Borrowing from at least 120 sources, Brown's 1853 story becomes a telescoping one that joins disparate texts through time and offers multiple readings and contexts for the same set of words. Sanborn, *Plagiarama!*, 135–38, 14. J. Noel Heermance identifies a number of chapters that he thinks stand on their own, calling chapter 23 "a short story all in itself" (166). J. Noel Heermance, *William Wells Brown and Clotelle: A Portrait of the Artist in the First Negro Novel* (Hamden, CT: Archon Books, 1969).

101. For a related discussion of "the disciplinary uses of authorial racial identity in critical practice," see Holly Jackson's discussion of Emma Dunham Kelly, who was initially believed to be African American but who is now thought to have been white (732). Holly Jackson, "Identifying Emma Dunham Kelley: Rethinking Race and Authorship," *PMLA* 122, no. 3 (2007): 728–41.

102. To be sure, there were risks in plagiarizing. Douglass once obliquely accused Brown of doing so with distinct disapproval, and it seems likely that Douglass's opinion of Brown was impacted by his realization of Brown's plagiarism. Geoffrey Sanborn gives the most extensive discussion of Brown's plagiarism, but Robert Levine, Ezra Greenspan, John Ernest,

and others treat it. Lara Langer Cohen has a succinct description of the two major critical understandings of his plagiarism in "Notes from the State of Saint Domingue: The Practice of Citation in Clotel," in *Early African American Print Culture*, ed. Lara Langer Cohen and Jordan Alexander Stein (Philadelphia: University of Pennsylvania Press, 2012), 166–67.

103. Although he does not speak about this passage directly, Geoffrey Sanborn identified the source of this borrowing. See his appendixes A and B in *Plagiarama!*.

104. Heermance identified this moment as when Brown lets go of his message and becomes "the completely emancipated Ariel artist, pursuing a subject and point of view simply because it intrigues him" (*William Wells Brown and Clotelle*, 169). That Heermance—without knowing the passage was plagiarized—recognizes the register shift and identifies Brown as a different type of narrator supports my argument.

105. Sanborn, *Plagiarama!*, 16.

106. Cohen, "Notes from the State of Saint Domingue," 174.

107. When Heermance declares Brown "more interesting in documenting a broadside against slavery than he was in writing a novel" in his *William Wells Brown and Clotelle*, he chastises Brown for importing other texts, without appreciating how doing so gestures to the tradition of short fiction (162). Brown is not just writing a novel; he is writing a novel from sketches and tales. One might also make the obvious connection between Brown's intertextual novel and Theodore Weld's *American Slavery as It Is: Testimony of a Thousand Witnesses* (1839), which compiled documentary evidence framed by small amounts of interpretation and discussion of slavery in a sort of printed scrapbook. Heermance, *William Wells Brown and Clotel*.

108. John Ernest, *Liberation Historiography: African American Writers and the Challenge of History, 1794–1861* (Chapel Hill: University of North Carolina Press, 2004).

109. Senchyne, "Bottles of Ink," 142.

110. Russ Castronovo, "Radical Configurations of History in the Era of American Slavery," *American Literature* 65, no. 3 (September 1993): 527–29.

111. M. Giulia Fabi makes a very similar argument; see M. Giulia Fabi, introduction to *Clotel; or, The President's Daughter*, by William Wells Brown, edited by Giulia M. Fabi (New York: Penguin Books, 2004), xvii. So too does Lara Langer Cohen, "Notes from the State of Saint Domingue," 166. As Charles Baraw puts it about *Three Years in Europe* in his "William Wells

Brown, 'Three Years in Europe,' and Fugitive Tourism": "The jarring contrasts and frequent absence of transitions in Brown's writing function as verbal correlatives of the disruptive anomalies that Brown sought to generate in all of his efforts to represent slavery" (461).

112. Tess Chakkalakal reads the novel as being about risks arising from black women's inability to access legal marriage protections. See Tess Chakkalakal, *Novel Bondage: Slavery, Marriage, and Freedom in Nineteenth-Century America* (Urbana: University of Illinois Press, 2011).

113. Brown would have been responding to the stories and ideas of his own moment, but it is worth noting, as Ann duCille has shown, that there remains great resistance to the idea of Jefferson fathering biracial children to this day, despite the fact that the evidence is incontrovertible. DuCille shows that the scholarly establishment (dominated by whites) dismissed the stories and evidence in the African American community for decades and decades and only came around to accepting the idea that Jefferson and Hemings had children together as a result of a DNA test in 1998. Even with this shift in the winds, the Thomas Jefferson Heritage Society, which was formed explicitly to dispute claims that Jefferson fathered children with Sally Hemings, is still active today. Ann duCille, "Where in the World Is William Wells Brown? Thomas Jefferson, Sally Hemings, and the DNA of African-American Literary History," *American Literary History* 12, no. 3 (2000): 443–62.

114. This racial fluidity is embodied in Joseph Jenkins, a multitalented man Brown observes in London and writes a later sketch about. Although denominated an "African Genius" in the table of contents of *The American Fugitive in Europe*, a revised and expanded version of *Three Years in Europe*, Brown describes Jenkins as "a good-looking man, neither black nor white," who sells bills, sings hymns, acts on the stage, preaches sermons, plays in a band, and sweeps streets to make his living. In mastering so many skills, Jenkins, in some sense, overcomes racial classifications. His genius is to exceed the narrow definition of blackness thrust upon him when he is kidnapped into slavery in Africa. William Wells Brown, *The American Fugitive in Europe: Sketches of Places and People Abroad* (John P. Jewett, 1855), 268.

115. As Holly Jackson has shown, the dramatic moment of Clotel's suicide by means of a jump off the Long Bridge that crosses the Potomac River embodies the inevitable destruction that comes to be closely associated with the "tragic mulatta." This harrowing scene started as an account in the *New York Evangelist* in September 1842 and proliferated thereafter

in newspaper reprintings (such as in the *Herald of Freedom* and in *Prisoner's Friend*), poems (by Sarah J. Clarke and John Kemble Lasky), and addresses (by Frederick Douglass). All these uses of a scene originally witnessed by New York congressman Seth M. Gates occurred in the years before Brown immortalized Clotel's jump from the Long Bridge, but other versions continued to appear even after the Civil War. Both Frances E. W. Harper's *Iola Leroy* (1892) and Pauline Hopkins's *Hagar's Daughter* (1901–2) include the scene. See Holly Jackson, "Another Long Bridge: Reproduction and Reversion in *Hagar's Daughter*," in *Early African American Print Culture*, ed. Lara Langer Cohen and Jordan Alexander Stein (Philadelphia: University of Pennsylvania Press, 2012), 192.

116. Washington had no natural children, but his adopted son (actually Martha's grandson by her first marriage) George Washington Parker Custis is clearly whom Brown references. Incidentally, Custis's daughter would later marry Robert E. Lee, forging a direct familial connection between Washington as American origin and the Confederacy.

117. Sanborn, *Plagiarama!*, 94.

118. Supporting the idea that these strategies were particular to the early 1850s is that no subsequent edition or version of Brown's novel contains the introductory autobiographical sketch. See note 101, chapter 6, above, for a short explanation of the many different versions of the novel.

119. Sarah Josepha Hale, "Sketches of American Character No. IV: The Soldier of the Revolution," *Ladies' Magazine* (April 1828): 154.

120. Catharine Maria Sedgwick, "A Reminiscence of Federalism," in *The Token and Atlantic Souvenir: A Christmas and New Year's Present, 1834*, ed. Samuel G. Goodrich (Boston: Charles Bowen, 1834), 109.

121. Catharine Maria Sedgwick, "Modern Chivalry," in *The Atlantic Souvenir, a Christmas and New Year's Offering. 1827* (Philadelphia: Carey and Lea, 1827), 7.

122. Morrison, *Playing in the Dark*, 66.

123. John Austin shows that the average length of literary works was growing at this moment. See John Austin, "United States, 1780–1850," in *The Novel*, ed. Franco Moretti (Princeton, NJ: Princeton University Press, 2006), 1:461.

124. Hawthorne's *The Snow-Image, and Other Twice-Told Tales* was published in 1852, and Melville's "Bartleby, the Scrivener" appeared in 1853. Likewise, Melville serialized "The Encantadas" in 1854 and later published these linked sketches in *The Piazza Tales* (1856). Though she turned her attention to another novel after *Uncle Tom's Cabin*, Stowe penned multiple

series of travel sketches after her explosion onto the world stage. William Wells Brown published an expanded version of his sketch book as *The American Fugitive in Europe: Sketches of Places and People Abroad* (1854) and wrote copious historical works with biographical sketches after the war. Washington Irving's *Wolfert's Roost* (1855) contained pieces by Geoffrey Crayon and Diedrich Knickerbocker; Catharine Sedgwick contributed short fiction to various magazines in the 1850s, including *Harper's Monthly Magazine*, *Putnam's Monthly*, and *Sartain's Union Magazine*, and Hale continued to write for and edit *Godey's* until 1877, when it was sold to Frank Munsey.

❖ BIBLIOGRAPHY ❖

"A Literary Bell on Its Travels." *Maine Farmer: An Agricultural Journal and Family Newspaper* (August 19, 1852): 2.

Adams, Abigail. "Letter from Abigail Adams to John Adams, 31 March–5 April 1776." Adams Family Papers. http://www.masshist.org/digitaladams /archive/doc?id=L17760331aa&bc=%2Fdigitaladams%2Farchive%2F browse%2Fletters_1774_1777.php.

Adams, John. *The Works of John Adams, Second President of the United States.* Edited by Charles Francis Adams and Charles Doe. Vol. 10. Boston: Little, Brown, 1856.

"American Literature and Reprints." *Putnam's Monthly Magazine of American Literature, Science, and Art* (November 1856): 536–52.

Ammons, Elizabeth. Introduction to *Harriet Beecher Stowe's Uncle Tom's Cabin: A Casebook*, 3–14. Edited by Elizabeth Ammons. New York: Oxford University Press, 2007.

Anderson, Benedict R. O'G. *Imagined Communities: Reflections on the Origin and Spread of Nationalism.* Rev. ed. New York: Verso, 2006.

Anderson, Thomas. *Interesting Account of Thomas Anderson, A Slave.* Edited by J. P. Clark. N.p: n.p., 1854.

Andrews, William L. *To Tell a Free Story: The First Century of Afro-American Autobiography, 1760–1865.* Urbana: University of Illinois Press, 1986.

"The Annuals." *New-York Mirror: A Weekly Gazette of Literature and the Fine Arts* (December 24, 1836): 207.

Arendt, Hannah. "The Public and the Private Realm." In *The Portable Hannah Arendt*, edited by Peter R. Baehr, 182–230. New York: Penguin Books, 2003.

Armstrong, John. *Sketches: Or Essays on Various Subjects.* London: A. Millar, 1758.

"ART.III—*The Sketch Book of Geoffrey Crayon, Gent.*" *Quarterly Review* (April 1821): 69–80.

"Art. V.: *The Sketch Book of Geoffrey Crayon.*" *Edinburgh Monthly Review* (September 1820): 303–35.

"Art. VI. *The Sketch Book of Geoffrey Cray, Gent.* Vol. 2." *British Critic* (November 1820): 514–25.

"Art. IX.—The Annuals." *North American Review* (January 1834): 198–209.

"Art. XII. *The Sketch Book of Geoffrey Crayon, Gent.*" *Monthly Review, or, Literary Journal* (October 1820): 196–206.

Austin, John. "The Collection as Literary Form: Sedgwick's *Tales and Sketches* of 1835." In *Catharine Maria Sedgwick: Critical Perspectives,* edited by Lucinda L. Damon-Bach and Victoria Clements, 158–70. Boston: Northeastern University Press, 2003.

———. "United States, 1780–1850." In *The Novel,* edited by Franco Moretti, 1:455–65. Princeton, NJ: Princeton University Press, 2006.

Austin, William. "Arrival of Mr. Peter Rugg in Boston." *New-England Galaxy* (January 19, 1827): 3.

———. "Some Account of Peter Rugg." *New-England Galaxy* (September 10, 1824): 2–3.

———. "Some Further Account of Peter Rugg the Missing Man Late of Boston, New-England." *New-England Galaxy* (September 1, 1826): 2–3.

Avallone, Charlene. "The 'Art' of Conversation." In *Catharine Maria Sedgwick: Critical Perspectives,* edited by Lucinda L. Damon-Bach and Victoria Clements, 192–203. Boston: Northeastern University Press, 2003.

Bakhtin, M. M. "Discourse in the Novel." In *The Dialogic Imagination: Four Essays,* translated by Michael Holquist and Caryl Emerson, 259–422. Austin: University of Texas Press, 1981.

Balibar, Etienne. "The Nation Form: History and Ideology." In *Race Critical Theories: Text and Context,* edited by Philomena Essed and David Theo Goldberg, 220–30. Malden, MA: Blackwell, 2002.

Bancroft, George. *A History of the United States: From the Discovery of the American Continent.* 15th ed. Boston: Little, Brown, 1853.

Baraw, Charles. "William Wells Brown, 'Three Years in Europe,' and Fugitive Tourism." *African American Review* 44, no. 3 (2011): 453–70.

Barbour, James. "'All My Books Are Botches': Melville's Struggle with *The Whale.*" In *Writing the American Classics,* edited by Tom Quirk and James Barbour, 25–52. Chapel Hill: University of North Carolina Press, 1990.

Barker, James W. "Forefather's Day." In *Encyclopedia of American Holidays and National Days,* edited by Len Travers, 491–503. Westport, CT: Greenwood, 2006.

Barnacle. "Selling a Justice." *Spirit of the Times, a Chronicle of the Turf, Agriculture, Field Sports, Literature, and the Stage* (February 10, 1849): 1.

Barrett, Lindon. "Presence of Mind: Detection and Racialization in 'The Murders in the Rue Morgue.'" In *Romancing the Shadow: Poe and Race,* edited by J. Gerald Kennedy and Liliane Weissberg, 157–76. New York: Oxford University Press, 2001.

Baym, Nina. *Novels, Readers, and Reviewers: Responses to Fiction in Antebellum America.* Ithaca, NY: Cornell University Press, 1984.

Beachcroft, T. O. *The Modest Art: A Survey of the Short Story in English.* New York: Oxford University Press, 1968.

Belden, E. Porter. *New York: Past, Present, and Future.* New York: G. P. Putnam, 1849.

Bell, Michael Davitt. *Hawthorne and the Historical Romance of New England.* Princeton, NJ: Princeton University Press, 1971.

Bell, Millicent. *Hawthorne and the Real: Bicentennial Essays.* Columbus: Ohio State University Press, 2005.

Berlant, Lauren. *The Female Complaint: The Unfinished Business of Sentimentality in American Culture.* Durham, NC: Duke University Press, 2008.

Bhabha, Homi K. "DissemiNation: Time, Narrative, and the Margins of the Modern Nation." In *Nation and Narration,* edited by Homi Bhabha, 291–322. London: Routledge, 1990.

———. "Introduction: Narrating the Nation." In *Nation and Narration,* edited by Homi Bhabha, 1–7. London: Routledge, 1990.

Black, Nancy B., and Michael L. Black. Introduction to *A History of New York,* by Washington Irving, xv–lxvii. Boston: Twayne, 1984.

"'Book Notices,' *Portland Transcript,* 30 March 1850, p. 3." In *The Critical Response to Nathaniel Hawthorne's "The Scarlet Letter,"* edited by Gary Scharnhorst, 2:24. Critical Responses in Arts and Letters. New York: Greenwood, 1992.

Booth, Bradford A. "Taste in the Annuals." *American Literature* 14, no. 3 (November 1942): 299–302.

"The Boston Token." *Euterpeiad; an Album of Music, Poetry & Prose* (December 15, 1830): 155.

Brand, Dana. *The Spectator and the City in Nineteenth-Century American Literature.* New York: Cambridge University Press, 1991.

Brooks, Peter. *Reading for the Plot: Design and Intention in Narrative.* Oxford: Oxford University Press, 1984.

Brown, Matthew P. *The Pilgrim and the Bee: Reading Rituals and Book Culture in Early New England.* Philadelphia: University of Pennsylvania Press, 2007.

Brown, William Wells. *The American Fugitive in Europe: Sketches of Places and People Abroad.* John P. Jewett, 1855.

——, ed. *The Anti-Slavery Harp: A Collection of Songs for Anti-Slavery Meetings.* Boston: Bela Marsh, 1848.

——. *Clotel; or, The President's Daughter: A Narrative of Slave Life in the United States.* London: Partridge and Oakey, 1853.

——. *Three Years in Europe; or, Places I Have Seen and People I Have Met.* London: Charles Gilpin, 1852.

Browning, Elizabeth Barrett. *The Complete Works of Mrs. E. B. Browning.* Edited by Charlotte Porter and Helen A. Clarke. Vol. 3. New York: Fred DeFau, 1900.

Buckingham, Joseph T. "Things in General." *New-England Galaxy* (September 10, 1824): 3.

Buell, Lawrence. *The Dream of the Great American Novel.* Cambridge, MA: Harvard University Press, 2014.

——. *New England Literary Culture from Revolution through Renaissance.* New York: Cambridge University Press, 1986.

Burt, Olive Woolley. *First Woman Editor: Sarah J. Hale.* New York: Julian Messner, 1960.

Bush, Sargent, Jr. *The Writings of Thomas Hooker: Spiritual Adventure in Two Worlds.* Madison: University of Wisconsin Press, 1980.

Cassuto, Leonard. "Poe the Crime Writer: Historicizing 'The Murders in the Rue Morgue.'" In *Approaches to Teaching Poe's Prose and Poetry,* edited by Jeffrey Andrew Weinstock and Tony Magistrale, 33–38. New York: Modern Language Association, 2008.

Castronovo, Russ. *Fathering the Nation: American Genealogies of Slavery and Freedom.* Berkeley: University of California Press, 1995.

Castronovo, Russ. "Radical Configurations of History in the Era of American Slavery." *American Literature,* 65, no. 3 (September 1993): 523–47.

Chakkalakal, Tess. *Novel Bondage: Slavery, Marriage, and Freedom in Nineteenth-Century America.* Urbana: University of Illinois Press, 2011.

Chatterjee, Partha. "Anderson's Utopia." *Diacritics: A Review of Contemporary Criticism* 29, no. 4 (1999): 128–34.

Choate, Rufus. *Addresses and Orations of Rufus Choate.* Boston: Little, Brown, 1878.

Clark, Rev. D. W. "Literary Women of America—Sarah Josepha Hale." *Ladies' Repository: A Monthly Periodical, Devoted to Literature, Arts, and Religion,* April 1855, 193–97.

"*Clotel; or, the President's Daughter*: A Narrative of Slave Life in the United States." *Tait's Edinburg Magazine* (January 1854): 58–59.

Coffey, John, and Paul C. H. Lim. Introduction to *The Cambridge Companion to Puritanism,* 1–15. Edited by John Coffey and Paul Chang-Ha Lim. Cambridge: Cambridge University Press, 2008.

Cohen, Lara Langer. "Notes from the State of Saint Domingue: The Practice of Citation in Clotel." In *Early African American Print Culture*, edited by Lara Langer Cohen and Jordan Alexander Stein, 161–77. Philadelphia: University of Pennsylvania Press, 2012.

Cohen, Michael C. *The Social Lives of Poems in Nineteenth-Century America*. Philadelphia: University of Pennsylvania Press, 2015.

Conforti, Joseph A. *Imagining New England: Explorations of Regional Identity from the Pilgrims to the Mid-Twentieth Century*. Chapel Hill: University of North Carolina Press, 2001.

Cooper, James Fenimore. *The Wept of Wish-ton-wish*. Philadelphia: Carey and Lea, 1829.

Costola, Sergio. "William Wells Brown's Panoramic Views." *Journal of American Drama and Theatre* 24, no. 2 (Spring 2012): 13–31.

Crèvecoeur, J. Hector St. John. *Letters from an American Farmer*. London: Davies and Davis, 1782.

Crews, Frederick C. *The Sins of the Fathers: Hawthorne's Psychological Themes*. Berkeley: University of California Press, 1989.

Damon-Bach, Lucinda L., and Victoria Clements. Introduction to *Catharine Maria Sedgwick: Critical Perspectives*, xxi–xxxi. Edited by Lucinda L. Damon-Bach and Victoria Clements. Boston: Northeastern University Press, 2003.

Dana, Richard Henry, Sr. "ART. XVII.—The Sketch Book." *North American Review* 9, no. 25 (September 1819): 322.

Davidson, Cathy N. *Revolution and the Word: The Rise of the Novel in America*. New York: Oxford University Press, 2004.

Davis, Lance E., Robert E. Gallman, and Karin Gleiter. *In Pursuit of Leviathan: Technology, Institutions, Productivity, and Profits in American Whaling, 1816–1906*. Chicago: University of Chicago Press, 1997.

De Lauretis, Teresa. *Alice Doesn't: Feminism, Semiotics, Cinema*. London: Macmillan, 1984.

Dimock, Wai-chee. *Through Other Continents: American Literature across Deep Time*. Princeton, NJ: Princeton University Press, 2009.

Dinnerstein, Leonard, and David M. Reimers. *Ethnic Americans: A History of Immigration*. 5th ed. New York: Columbia University Press, 2009.

Doubleday, Neal Frank. *Hawthorne's Early Tales: A Critical Study*. Durham, NC: Duke University Press, 1972.

Douglass, Frederick. "The Heroic Slave." In *Autographs for Freedom*, edited by Julia Griffiths, 174–239. Cleveland: John P. Jewett, 1853.

Douglass, Frederick. *The Narrative of the Life of Frederick Douglass*. Boston: Anti-Slavery Office, 1845.

———. "What to the Slave Is the Fourth of July?" In *My Bondage and My Freedom,* 441–45. New York: Miller, Orton and Mulligan, 1855.

Doyle, Arthur Conan. "The Problem of Thor Bridge." In *Sherlock Holmes: The Complete Novels and Stories,* edited by Loren D. Estleman, 2:626–52. New York: Bantam Dell, 1986.

DuCille, Ann. "Where in the World Is William Wells Brown? Thomas Jefferson, Sally Hemings, and the DNA of African-American Literary History." *American Literary History* 12, no. 3 (2000): 443–62.

Eastman, Mary Henderson. *Aunt Phillis's Cabin; or, Southern Life as It Is.* Philadelphia: Lippincott, Grambo, 1852.

"Edgar Allan Poe: Review of the Works of the Late Edgar Allan Poe." *Southern Literary Messenger* 16, no. 3 (March 1850): 172–88.

"Editors' Table: The Annuals and Gift-Books for 1842." *Iris; or, Literary Messenger* (October 1841): 572–75.

Eliot, George. *Middlemarch.* Edited by David Carroll. Oxford World Classics. New York: Oxford University Press, 1996.

Eliot, T. S. *To Criticize the Critic, and Other Writings.* Edited by Elizabeth Bishop. New York: Farrar, Straus and Giroux, 1965.

Eliza. "The Sketch Book, No. II." *Ladies' Literary Cabinet, Being a Reposition of Miscellaneous Literary Production* (August 7, 1819): 101–2.

Emerson, Ralph Waldo. *Emerson in His Journals.* Edited by Joel Porte. Cambridge, MA: Harvard University Press, 1982.

———. "Nature." In *Essays & Poems,* edited by Joel Porte, Harold Bloom, and Paul Kane, 3–49. New York: Library of America, 1996.

Entrikin, Isabelle Webb. "Sarah Josepha Hale and *Godey's Lady's Book.*" PhD diss., University of Pennsylvania, 1946.

Ernest, John. *Liberation Historiography: African American Writers and the Challenge of History, 1794–1861.* Chapel Hill: University of North Carolina Press, 2004.

Everett, Edward. "ART. X.—Bracebridge Hall." *North American Review* (July 1, 1822): 204–24.

Exman, Eugene. *The Brothers Harper: A Unique Publishing Partnership and Its Impact upon the Cultural Life of America from 1817 to 1853.* New York: Harper and Row, 1965.

Fabi, M. Giulia. Introduction to *Clotel; or, The President's Daughter,* by William Wells Brown, vii–xxviii. Edited by Giulia M. Fabi. New York: Penguin Books, 2004.

Felski, Rita. *Doing Time: Feminist Theory and Postmodern Culture.* Cultural Front. New York: New York University Press, 2000.

———. *Uses of Literature*. Blackwell Manifestos. Malden, MA: Blackwell, 2008.

"Female Education." *Western Review and Miscellaneous Magazine, a Monthly Publication* (February 1821): 47–55.

Fetterley, Judith. *The Resisting Reader: A Feminist Approach to American Fiction*. Bloomington: Indiana University Press, 1978.

"Fiction." *Critic* 12, no. 304 (December 1, 1853): 625–26.

Fiedler, Leslie A. *Love and Death in the American Novel*. Rev. ed. New York: Stein and Day, 1966.

Fields, James Thomas. *Yesterdays with Authors*. Boston: James R. Osgood, 1872.

Finley, Ruth E. *The Lady of Godey's, Sarah Josepha Hale*. Philadelphia: J. B. Lippincott Company, 1931.

Folkerts, Jean, Dwight L. Teeter, and Edward Caudill. *Voices of a Nation: A History of Mass Media in the United States*. 5th ed. Boston: Pearson/Allyn and Bacon, 2009.

Follen, Eliza Lee. *The Liberty Cap*. Boston: Leonard C. Bowles, 1846.

Forgie, George B. *Patricide in the House Divided: A Psychological Interpretation of Lincoln and His Age*. New York: W. W. Norton, 1979.

Foster, George G. *New York in Slices*. New York: W. F. Burgess, 1849.

Franklin, Benjamin. "Observations Concerning the Increase of Mankind." In *The Papers of Benjamin Franklin*, edited by Leonard Woods Labaree, vol. 4, *July 1, 1750, through June 30, 1753*, 225–34. New Haven, CT: Yale University Press, 1961.

Freeman, Elizabeth. *Time Binds: Queer Temporalities, Queer Histories*. Perverse Modernities. Durham, NC: Duke University Press, 2010.

"French Tribute to American Literature." *Columbian Star* (April 27, 1822): 4.

"[From the *Eclectic Review*.—London] 2. The Sketch Book of Geoffrey Crayon, Gent." *Literary and Scientific Repository, and Critical Review* (June 1, 1820): 192–96.

"From the *Salem Register*, 21 March 1850, 2:1–2." In *The Critical Response to Nathaniel Hawthorne's "The Scarlet Letter,"* edited by Gary Scharnhorst, 2:13–17. Critical Responses in Arts and Letters. New York: Greenwood, 1992.

"From the *Scotsman*. Review: Bracebridge Hall." *Calcutta Journal of Politics and General Literature* (November 23, 1822): 310.

Ganster, Mary. "Fact, Fiction, and the Industry of Violence: Newspapers and Advertisements in Clotel." *African American Review* 48, no. 4 (December 9, 2015): 431–44.

Garcha, Amanpal. *From Sketch to Novel: The Development of Victorian Fiction*. New York: Cambridge University Press, 2009.

Gaskell, Philip. *A New Introduction to Bibliography*. New York: Oak Knoll, 1995.

Giles, Paul. *Transatlantic Insurrections: British Culture and the Formation of American Literature, 1730–1860.* Philadelphia: University of Pennsylvania Press, 2001.

Goddu, Teresa A. *Gothic America: Narrative, History, and Nation.* New York: Columbia University Press, 1997.

——. "Poe, Sensationalism, and Slavery." In *The Cambridge Companion to Edgar Allan Poe,* edited by Kevin J. Hayes, 92–112. Cambridge: Cambridge University Press, 2002.

Goodrich, Samuel G. Preface to *The Token and Atlantic Souvenir: A Christmas and New Year's Present. 1831,* v–vi. Edited by Samuel G. Goodrich. Boston: Gray and Bowen, 1831.

Gottlieb, Theodore D. *The Origin and Evolution of the Betsy Ross Flag, Legend or Tradition.* Newark, NJ, 1938.

Green, James N. "Chapter 2: The Book Trades in the New Nation. Part 1, The Rise of Book Publishing." In *The History of the Book in America: An Extensive Republic. Print, Culture, and Society in the New Nation, 1790–1840,* 2:75–127. Edited by Robert A. Gross and Mary Kelley. Chapel Hill: University of North Carolina Press, 2010.

Greenspan, Ezra. *William Wells Brown: An African American Life.* New York: W. W. Norton, 2014.

Gross, Seymour L. "Hawthorne's Revision of 'The Gentle Boy.'" *American Literature* 26, no. 2 (May 1954): 196–208.

Haines, Michael. "Fertility and Mortality in the United States." EH.net, March 19, 2008. http://eh.net/encyclopedia/fertility-and-mortality-in-the -united-states/.

Hale, Sarah Josepha. "An Appeal to the Ladies of the United States." *Ladies' Magazine* (November 1829): 515–17.

——. "Contributors to the *Ladies' Magazine.*" *American Ladies' Magazine* (January 1834): 48.

——. "Introduction." *Ladies' Magazine* (January 1828): 1–4.

——. *Liberia, or, Mr. Peyton's Experiments.* Slavery and Anti-Slavery: A Transnational Archive. New York: Harper and Bros., 1853.

——. "Literary Notices: Al Aaraaf, Tamerlane, &c., by Edgar A. Poe." *Ladies' Magazine and Literary Gazette* (January 1830): 47.

——. "Literary Notices: Annuals and Poems." *Ladies' Magazine and Literary Gazette* (December 1830): 571–78.

——. "Literary Notices: *Fanshawe.*" *Ladies' Magazine* (November 1828): 526–27.

——. *Northwood.* 2nd ed. New York: H. Long and Brother, 1852.

——. *Sketches of American Character.* Boston: Putnam and Hunt, 1829.

——. "Sketches of American Character No. I: Walter Wilson." *Ladies' Magazine* (January 1828): 5–16.

——. "Sketches of American Character No. II. Ann Ellsworth." *Ladies' Magazine* (February 1828): 53–65.

——. "Sketches of American Character No. IV: The Soldier of the Revolution." *Ladies' Magazine* (April 1828): 149–64.

——. "Sketches of American Character No. V. The Village Schoolmistress." *Ladies' Magazine* (May 1828): 202–19.

——. "Sketches of American Character No. VII. The Belle and the Bleu." *Ladies' Magazine* (July 1828): 297–308.

——. "Sketches of American Character No. IX. Prejudices." *Ladies' Magazine* (September 1828): 392–404.

——. "Sketches of American Character No. X. The Apparition." *Ladies' Magazine* (October 1828): 441–53.

——. "Sketches of American Character No. XI. William Forbes." *Ladies' Magazine* (November 1828): 489–504.

——. "Sketches of American Character No. XII. A Winter in the Country." *Ladies' Magazine* (December 1828): 535–55.

——. "The Fatherless and Widows' Society, Boston." *Ladies' Magazine* (January 1828): 48.

——. "The *Ladies' Magazine*." *Ladies' Magazine and Literary Gazette* (December 1832): 576.

——. *Three Hours; or, The Vigil of Love: And Other Poems*. Philadelphia: Carey and Hart, 1848.

——. "To Our Friends." *American Ladies' Magazine* (December 1834): 576.

——. "What Can Women Do?" *American Ladies' Magazine* (May 1834): 215–16.

Halttunen, Karen. *Murder Most Foul: The Killer and the American Gothic Imagination*. Cambridge, MA: Harvard University Press, 1998.

Hamilton, Kristie. *America's Sketchbook: The Cultural Life of a Nineteenth-Century Genre*. Athens: Ohio University Press, 1998.

——. "Hawthorne, Modernity, and the Literary Sketch." In *The Cambridge Companion to Nathaniel Hawthorne*, edited by Richard H. Millington, 99–120. New York: Cambridge University Press, 2004.

Hardy, Sarah. "The Short Story: Approaches to the Problem." *Style* 27, no. 3 (1993): 325–26.

Harris, Katherine D. "Feminizing the Textual Body: Female Readers Consuming the Literary Annual." *Papers of the Bibliographical Society of America* 99, no. 4 (December 2005): 573–622.

———. *Forget Me Not: The Rise of the British Literary Annual, 1823–1835*. Athens: Ohio University Press, 2015.

Harris, Neil. *Humbug: The Art of P. T. Barnum*. Boston: Little, Brown, 1973.

Harris, Susan K. "The Limits of Authority: Catharine Maria Sedgwick and the Politics of Resistance." In *Catharine Maria Sedgwick: Critical Perspectives*, edited by Lucinda L. Damon-Bach and Victoria Clements, 272–85. Boston: Northeastern University Press, 2003.

———. *Nineteenth-Century American Women's Novels: Interpretative Strategies*. New York: Cambridge University Press, 1990.

Harrowitz, Nancy. "Criminality and Poe's Orangutan: The Question of Race in Detection." In *Agnostics: Arenas of Creative Contest*, edited by Janet Lungstrum and Elizabeth Sauer, 177–95. Albany: SUNY Press, 1997.

Hawthorne, Julian. *Nathaniel Hawthorne and His Wife: A Biography*. Vol. 1. Boston: Houghton, Mifflin, 1884.

Hawthorne, Nathaniel. "The Devil in the Manuscript." *New-England Magazine* (November 1835): 340–46.

———. "The Gentle Boy." In *The Token and Atlantic Souvenir: A Christmas and New Year's Present, 1832*, edited by Samuel Goodrich and George S. Hilliard, 193–240. Boston: Gray and Bowen, 1832.

———. *Grandfather's Chair: A History for Youth*. Chicago: Belford, Clarke, 1840.

———. Letter to Edgar Allan Poe, June 17, 1846. Edgar Allan Poe Society of Baltimore. https://www.eapoe.org/misc/letters/t4606170.htm.

———. *Little Annie's Ramble: And Other Tales*. Halifax: Milner and Sowerby, 1853.

———. "The Marble Faun." In *The Hawthorne Treasury: Complete Novels and Selected Tales of Nathaniel Hawthorne*, edited by Norman Holmes Pearson, 1097–1409. New York: Modern Library, 1999.

———. *Mosses from an Old Manse*. New York: Wiley and Putnam, 1846.

———. *Our Old Home, and English Note-Books*. Vol. 7 of *The Complete Works of Nathaniel Hawthorne*, Riverside ed., edited by George Parsons Lathrop. Boston: Houghton, Mifflin, 1887.

———. *The Letters, 1843–1853*. Vol. 16 of *The Centenary Edition of the Works of Nathaniel Hawthorne*, edited by Thomas Woodson, L. Neal Smith, and Norman Holmes Pearson. Columbus: Ohio State University Press, 1985.

———. *Passages from the American Note-Books*. Vol. 9 of *The Complete Works of Nathaniel Hawthorne*, edited by George Parsons Lathrop. Boston: Houghton, Mifflin, 1886.

———. *The Scarlet Letter and Other Writings: Authoritative Texts, Contexts, Criticism*. Edited by Leland S. Person. Norton Critical Edition. New York: W. W. Norton, 2005.

——. *The Snow-Image and Other Twice-Told Tales*. Boston: Ticknor, Reed, and Fields, 1852.

——. *Twice-Told Tales*. Boston: American Stationers, 1837.

——. *Twice Told Tales*. London: William Tegg, 1850.

——. *Twice-Told Tales*. New York: Modern Library, 2001.

——. *The Works of Nathaniel Hawthorne*. Edited by George Parsons Lathrop. Vol. 12. Boston: Houghton Mifflin, 1883.

Haycraft, Howard. *Murder for Pleasure: The Life and Times of the Detective Story*. New York: Biblo and Tannen, 1968.

Hayford, Harrison. "Unnecessary Duplicates: A Key to the Writing of Moby-Dick." In *Hawthorne and His Mosses*, 2nd ed., edited by Harrison Hayford and Hershel Parker, 674–96. New York: Norton, 2002.

Hayford, Harrison, and G. Thomas Tanselle. "Historical Note." In *Moby-Dick, or, The Whale*, vol. 6 of *The Writings of Herman Melville*, edited by Harrison Hayford and G. Thomas Tanselle, 581–762. Chicago: Newberry Library, 1988.

Heermance, J. Noel. *William Wells Brown and Clotelle: A Portrait of the Artist in the First Negro Novel*. Hamden, CT: Archon Books, 1969.

Henkin, David M. *City Reading: Written Words and Public Spaces in Antebellum New York*. New York: Columbia University Press, 1998.

Herbert, John R. "The Map That Named America: Library Acquires 1507 Waldseemüller Map of the World." Library of Congress, September 2003. http://www.loc.gov/loc/lcib/0309/maps.html.

Herring, James, and James Barton Longacre. *The National Portrait Gallery of Distinguished Americans*. New York: Bancroft, 1834. http://archive.org/details/nationalportrait01herr3.

Higginson, Thomas Wentworth. "A Precursor to Hawthorne." *Independent* (March 29, 1888): 1.

Hoffman, Charles F. "Review." In *Nathaniel Hawthorne: Critical Assessments*, edited by Brian Harding, 1:68–80. Mountfield, East Sussex: Helm Information, 1995.

Holmes, Abiel. *American Annals, or, A Chronological History of America, From Its Discovery in 1492 to 1806*. Vol. 1. London: Sherwood, Neely, and Jones, 1813.

Hughes, Robert. *American Visions: The Epic History of Art in America*. New York: Knopf, 1997.

Insko, Jeffrey. "Diedrich Knickerbocker, Regular Bred Historian." *Early American Literature* 43, no. 3 (2008): 605–41.

——. "The Prehistory of Posthistoricism." In *The Limits of Literary Historicism*, edited by Allen Dunn and Thomas F. Haddox, 105–23. Tennessee Studies in Literature. Knoxville: University of Tennessee Press, 2011.

"Introduction. Addressed to the Ladies." In *The Offering: A Christmas and New Year's Present*, 7–8. Philadelphia: Thomas T. Ash, 1834.

Irving, Washington. *Chronicles of Wolfert's Roost and Other Papers*. Edinburgh: Thomas Constable, 1855.

——. *The Letters of Washington Irving to Henry Brevoort*. Edited by George S. Hellman. Vol. 2. New York, Putnam, 1915.

——. "Philip of Pokanoket." *Analectic Magazine* (June 1814): 502–15.

——. *The Sketch Book of Geoffrey Crayon, Gent.* 2 vols. London: John Miller and John Murray, 1820.

——. *The Sketch Book of Geoffrey Crayon, Gent.* New York: C. S. Van Winkle, 1819–20.

——. "Traits of Indian Character." *Analectic Magazine* (February 1814): 145–56.

J. "Musings of an Invalid. No. I. Reading." *Ladies' Magazine and Literary Gazette* (June 1833): 241–45.

Jackson, Holly. "Another Long Bridge: Reproduction and Reversion in *Hagar's Daughter*." In *Early African American Print Culture*, edited by Lara Langer Cohen and Jordan Alexander Stein, 192–202. Philadelphia: University of Pennsylvania Press, 2012.

——. "Identifying Emma Dunham Kelley: Rethinking Race and Authorship." *PMLA* 122, no. 3 (2007): 728–41.

Jackson, Leon. *The Business of Letters: Authorial Economies in Antebellum America*. Stanford, CA: Stanford University Press, 2008.

Jacobs, Harriet. *Incidents in the Life of a Slave Girl*. Boston: published for Harriet Jacobs, 1861.

Johnson, Sammye, and Patricia Prijatel. *Magazine from Cover to Cover*. 3rd ed. New York: Oxford University Press, 2013.

Jones, Brian Jay. *Washington Irving: An American Original*. New York: Arcade, 2008.

Jones, Wayne Allen. "Hawthorne's First Published Review." *American Literature* 48, no. 4 (January 1977): 492–500.

"July 28, 1835 Letter from Carey, Lea & Blanchard to Theodore Sedgwick." July 28, 1835. Historical Society of Pennsylvania.

Karcher, Carolyn. "Catharine Maria Sedgwick in Literary History." In *Catharine Maria Sedgwick: Critical Perspectives*, edited by Lucinda L. Damon-Bach and Victoria Clements, 5–16. Boston: Northeastern University Press, 2003.

Kelleter, Frank. *Media of Serial Narrative*. Theory and Interpretation of Narrative. Columbus: Ohio State University Press, 2017.

Kelley, Mary. "Crafting Subjectivities: Women, Reading, and Self-Imagining." In *Reading Women: Literacy, Authorship, and Culture in the Atlantic World, 1500–1800,* edited by Heidi Brayman Hackel and Catherine E. Kelly, 51–71. Philadelphia: University of Pennsylvania Press, 2008.

———. *Private Woman, Public Stage: Literary Domesticity in Nineteenth-Century America.* New York: Oxford University Press, 1984.

Kennedy, J. Gerald. "'A Mania for Composition': Poe's Annus Mirabilis and the Violence of Nation-Building." *American Literary History* 17, no. 1 (2005): 1–35.

Kermode, Frank. *The Sense of an Ending: Studies in the Theory of Fiction.* The Mary Flexner Lectures, 1965. New York: Oxford University Press, 1967.

Kesselring, Marion Louise. *Hawthorne's Reading, 1828–1850: A Transcription and Identification of Titles Recorded in the Charge-Books of the Salem Athenaeum.* New York: New York Public Library, 1949.

Killick, Tim. *British Short Fiction in the Early Nineteenth Century: The Rise of the Tale.* Burlington, VT: Ashgate, 2008.

Kiracofe, David James. "The Jamestown Jubilees: 'State Patriotism' and Virginia Identity in the Early Nineteenth Century." *Virginia Magazine of History and Biography* 110, no. 1 (2002): 35–68.

Kirkham, E. Bruce. *The Building of Uncle Tom's Cabin.* Knoxville: University of Tennessee Press, 1977.

Kopley, Richard. *Edgar Allan Poe and the Dupin Mysteries.* New York: Palgrave Macmillan, 2008.

Korte, Barbara. *The Short Story in Britain: A Historical Sketch and Anthology.* Tubingen, Germany: A. Francke Verlag Tubingen und Basel, 2003.

"The *Ladies' Magazine.*" *Philadelphia Album and Ladies Literary Gazette* (January 30, 1828): 277.

Lawson, James. *Tales and Sketches, by a Cosmopolite.* New York: E. Bliss, 1830.

Lemire, Elise. "'The Murders in the Rue Morgue': Amalgamation Discourses and the Race Riots of 1838 in Poe's Philadelphia." In *Romancing the Shadow: Poe and Race,* edited by J. Gerald Kennedy and Liliane Weissberg, 177–224. New York: Oxford University Press, 2001.

Leslie, Eliza. "Leonilla Lynmore, Part IV." *Godey's Lady's Book* (October 1841): 180–84.

"Letter to the Editor." *New-England Galaxy* (November 24, 1826): 3.

Levin, David. *History as Romantic Art: Bancroft, Prescott, Motley, and Parkman.* New York: AMS, 1967.

Levine, Caroline, and Mario Ortiz-Robles. Introduction to *Narrative Middles: Navigating the Nineteenth-Century British Novel,* 1–21. Edited by Caroline

Levine and Mario Ortiz-Robles. *Theory and Interpretation of Narrative.* Columbus: Ohio State University Press, 2011.

Levine, Robert S. *Dislocating Race & Nation: Episodes in Nineteenth-Century American Literary Nationalism.* Chapel Hill: University of North Carolina Press, 2008.

"Literary Notices: Book Table. The Token for 1835." *New-York Mirror: A Weekly Gazette of Literature and the Fine Arts* (October 4, 1834): 110.

Lockhart, John Gibson. "On the Writings of Charles Brockden Brown and Washington Irving." *Blackwood's Edinburgh Magazine,* Sec. 6:35 (February 1820): 554.

Longfellow, Henry Wadsworth. "Review." In *Nathaniel Hawthorne: Critical Assessments,* edited by Brian Harding, 1:64–67. Mountfield, East Sussex: Helm Information, 1995.

Loughran, Trish. *The Republic in Print: Print Culture in the Age of U.S. Nation Building, 1770–1870.* New York: Columbia University Press, 2007.

Machor, James L. *Reading Fiction in Antebellum America: Informed Response and Reception Histories, 1820–1865.* Baltimore: Johns Hopkins University Press, 2011.

Madison, Charles Allan. *Book Publishing in America.* New York: McGraw-Hill, 1966.

Marler, Robert F. "From Tale to Short Story: The Emergence of a New Genre in the 1850's." *American Literature* 46, no. 2 (May 1974): 153–69.

Martin, Lawrence. "The Genesis of *Godey's Lady's Book.*" *New England Quarterly* 1, no. 1 (January 1, 1928): 41–70.

———. "Women Fought at Bunker Hill." *New England Quarterly* 8, no. 4 (December 1935): 467–79.

Martin, Terence. *Parables of Possibility: The American Need for Beginnings.* New York: Columbia University Press, 1995.

Martineau, Harriet. "'Miss Sedgwick's Works.' The *Westminster Review.*" In *Catharine Maria Sedgwick: Critical Perspectives,* edited by Lucinda L. Damon-Bach and Victoria Clements, 155. Boston: Northeastern University Press, 2003.

Mather, Increase. "Predestination and Human Exertions." In *The Puritans: A Sourcebook of Their Writings,* rev. ed., edited by Perry Miller and Thomas Herbert Johnson, 1:335–40. New York: Harper and Row, 1963.

Matthews, Brander. "'The Philosophy of the Short-Story.'" *Lippincott's Magazine of Popular Literature and Science* (October 1, 1885): 366–74.

Matthews, Cornelius. *A Pen-and-Ink Panorama of New York City.* New York: John S. Taylor, 1853.

McBride, Dwight A. *Impossible Witnesses: Truth, Abolitionism, and Slave Testimony.* New York: New York University Press, 2001.

McClary, Ben Harris, ed. *Washington Irving and the House of Murray: Geoffrey Crayon Charms the British, 1817–1856.* Knoxville: University of Tennessee Press, 1969.

McCoy, Beth A. "Race and the (Para)Textual Condition." In *The Broadview Reader in Book History,* edited by Michelle Levy and Tom Mole, 199–211. Tonawanda, NY: Broadview, 2015.

McGill, Meredith L. *American Literature and the Culture of Reprinting, 1834–1853.* Philadelphia: University of Pennsylvania Press, 2007.

McIntosh, James. "Hawthorne's Revisions of 'The Gentle Boy.'" In *Nathaniel Hawthorne's Tales: Authoritative Texts, Backgrounds, Criticism,* edited by James McIntosh, 262–64. New York: W. W. Norton, 1987.

McLamore, Richard V. "The Dutchman in the Attic: Claiming an Inheritance in *The Sketch Book of Geoffrey Crayon.*" *American Literature* 72, no. 1 (2000): 31–57.

Melville, Herman. "Hawthorne and His Mosses." In *Moby-Dick,* 2nd ed., edited by Harrison Hayford and Hershel Parker, 517–32. New York: W. W. Norton, 2002.

———. *The Letters of Herman Melville.* New Haven, CT: Yale University Press, 1960.

———. *Moby-Dick.* 2nd ed. Edited by Harrison Hayford and Hershel Parker. New York: W. W. Norton, 2002.

———. *The Piazza Tales.* New York: Dix and Edwards, 1856.

———. "The Town-Ho's Story." *Harper's New Monthly Magazine* (October 1851): 658–65.

"Melville's Moby Dick; or, The Whale.: Second Notice." *Literary World* (November 22, 1851): 403.

Miller, Perry. *Nature's Nation.* Cambridge, MA: Harvard University Press, 1967.

Mitford, Mary Russell. *Our Village.* Edited by Anne Thackeray Ritchie. New York: Macmillan, 1893.

Mizruchi, Susan L. *The Power of Historical Knowledge: Narrating the Past in Hawthorne, James, and Dreiser.* Princeton, NJ: Princeton University Press, 1988.

Morgan, Jo-Ann. *Uncle Tom's Cabin as Visual Culture.* Columbia: University of Missouri Press, 2007.

Morrison, Toni. *Playing in the Dark: Whiteness and the Literary Imagination.* Cambridge, MA: Harvard University Press, 1992.

Mott, Frank Luther. *Golden Multitudes: The Story of Best Sellers in the United States.* New York: Macmillan, 1947.

——. *A History of American Magazines, 1741–1850.* Vol. 1. Cambridge, MA: Belknap Press of Harvard University Press, 1957.

Mulvey, Christopher. "The Fugitive Self and the New World of the North: William Wells Brown's Discovery of America." In *The Black Columbiad: Defining Moments in African American Literature and Culture,* edited by Werner Sollors and Maria Diedrich, 99–111. Cambridge, MA: Harvard University Press, 1994.

Murch, A. E. *The Development of the Detective Novel.* New York: Greenwood, 1968.

Murray, Laura J. "The Aesthetic of Dispossession: Washington Irving and Ideologies of (De)Colonization in the Early Republic." *American Literary History* 8, no. 2 (July 1, 1996): 205–31.

"'Nathaniel Hawthorne,' *Literary World,* 30 March 1850, Pp. 323–325." In *The Critical Response to Nathaniel Hawthorne's "The Scarlet Letter,"* edited by Gary Scharnhorst, 2:21–23. Critical Responses in Arts and Letters. New York: Greenwood, 1992.

Neal, John. "Late American Books." *Blackwood's Edinburgh Magazine* 18, no. 104 (September 1825): 316–34.

Neal, Joseph C. *Charcoal Sketches, or Scenes in a Metropolis* (Philadelphia: Carey and Hart, 1838).

Newman, Lea Bertani Vozar. *A Reader's Guide to the Short Stories of Nathaniel Hawthorne.* Boston: G. K. Hall, 1979.

Newman, Simon P. *Parades and the Politics of the Street: Festive Culture in the Early American Republic.* Philadelphia: University of Pennsylvania Press, 2010.

"Notices of Books." *British Mothers' Magazine* (January 1, 1854): 20.

Nuttall, A. D. *Openings: Narrative Beginnings from the Epic to the Novel.* Oxford: Clarendon, 1992.

O'Brien, Edward J. "Extract from *The Advance of the American Short Story.*" In *Edgar Allan Poe: Critical Assessments,* edited by Graham Clarke, 3:277–86. Helm Information Critical Assessments of Writers in English. Mountfield, East Sussex: Helm Information, 1991.

O'Connor, Frank. *The Lonely Voice: A Study of the Short Story.* New York: Harper and Row, 1985.

Okker, Patricia. *Our Sister Editors: Sarah J. Hale and the Tradition of Nineteenth-Century American Women Editors.* Athens: University of Georgia Press, 1995.

Otter, Samuel. *Melville's Anatomies.* Berkeley: University of California Press, 1999.

——. *Philadelphia Stories: America's Literature of Race and Freedom.* New York: Oxford University Press, 2010.

Orians, G. Harrison. "The Angel of Hadley in Fiction: A Study of the Sources of Hawthorne's 'The Grey Champion.'" *American Literature* 4, no. 3 (November 1932): 257–69.

Pattee, Fred Lewis. *The Development of the American Short Story: An Historical Survey.* New York: Harper and Bros., 1923.

———. "Edgar Allan Poe." In *Edgar Allan Poe: Critical Assessments,* edited by Graham Clarke, 3:287–309. The Helm Information Critical Assessments of Writers in English. Mountfield, East Sussex: Helm Information, 1991.

Paulding, James Kirk. "National Literature." In *American Literature, American Culture,* edited by Gordon Hutner, 24–25. New York: Oxford University Press, 1999.

Peabody, Elizabeth Palmer. "Review." In *Nathaniel Hawthorne: Critical Assessments,* edited by Brian Harding, 1:71–77. Mountfield, East Sussex: Helm Information, 1995.

Peden, William. *The American Short Story: Front Line in the National Defense of Literature.* Boston: Houghton Mifflin, 1964.

Person, Leland S. "Cruising (Perversely) for Context: Poe and Murder, Women and Apes." In *Poe and the Remapping of Antebellum Print Culture,* edited by J. Gerald Kennedy and Jerome McGann, 143–69. Baton Rouge: Louisiana State University Press, 2012.

Peterson, Beverly A. "Mrs. Hale on Mrs. Stowe and Slavery." *American Periodicals* 8 (1998): 30–44.

Phillips, Wendell. *Speeches, Lectures and Letters, 2nd Series.* Boston: Lee and Shepard, 1891.

Pike, Albert. "Crayon Sketches and Journeyings, Nos. I–III." *Boston Pearl and Literary Gazette* 4 (Nov. 8, 22, 1834; Jan. 10, 1835): 69–70, 88–89, 143.

Poe, Edgar Allan. "Autography." *Southern Literary Messenger* (February 1836): 205–12.

———. *The Brevities: Pinakidia, Marginalia, Fifty Suggestions, and Other Works.* Vol. 2 of *The Collected Writings of Edgar Allan Poe,* edited by Burton R. Pollin. New York: Gordian, 1985.

———. *The Collected Letters of Edgar Allan Poe.* 3rd ed. Edited by John Ward Ostrom, Burton Ralph Pollin, and Jeffrey A. Savoye. Vol. 1. Staten Island, NY: Gordian, 2008.

———. "Critical Notices: Traits of American Life." *Southern Literary Messenger* (December 1835): 67.

———. "A Few Words on Secret Writing." *Graham's Lady's and Gentleman's Magazine* (July 1, 1841): 33–38.

———. "The Literati of New York City.—No. III." *Godey's Magazine and Lady's Book* (July 1846): 13–15.

———. "The Murders in the Rue Morgue." *Graham's Lady's and Gentleman's Magazine* (April 1841): 166–78.

———. "The Mystery of Marie Rogêt." *Ladies' Companion, a Monthly Magazine; Devoted to Literature and the Fine Arts* (November 1842): 15–20.

———. "The Mystery of Marie Rogêt." *Ladies' Companion, a Monthly Magazine; Devoted to Literature and the Fine Arts* (December 1842): 93–99.

———. "The Mystery of Marie Rogêt." *Ladies' Companion, a Monthly Magazine; Devoted to Literature and the Fine Arts* (February 1843): 162–67.

———. "The Mystery of Marie Rogêt." In *Tales and Sketches,* edited by Thomas Ollive Mabbott, Eleanor D. Kewer, and Maureen Cobb Mabbott, 2:715–88. Urbana: University of Illinois Press, 2000.

———. "Review: *Barnaby Rudge* by Charles Dickens." *Graham's Lady's and Gentleman's Magazine* (May 1842): 124–29.

———. "Review: *Twice-Told Tales* by Nathaniel Hawthorne." *Graham's Lady's and Gentleman's Magazine* (May 1842): 298–300.

———. "Richard Adams Lock." In unpublished manuscript book entitled "Literary America," 1848. Edgar Allan Poe Society of Baltimore. https://www.eapoe.org/works/misc/litamlra.htm.

———. *Tales.* New York: Wiley and Putnam, 1845. https://www.eapoe.org/works/editions/talesc.htm.

———. *Tales of the Grotesque and Arabesque.* Vol. 2. Philadelphia: Lea and Blanchard, 1840.

Pratt, Lloyd. *Archives of American Time: Literature and Modernity in the Nineteenth Century.* Philadelphia: University of Pennsylvania Press, 2010.

Pratt, Mary Louise. "The Short Story: The Long and the Short of It." In *The New Short Story Theories,* edited by Charles E. May, 91–113. Athens: Ohio University Press, 1994.

Putnam, George Haven. "Irving." In *A Century of Commentary on the Works of Washington Irving, 1860–1974,* edited by Andrew B. Myers, 118–36. Tarrytown, NY: Sleepy Hollow Restorations, 1976.

Randolph, J. Thorton [Charles Jacobs Peterson]. *The Cabin and Parlor; or Slaves and Masters.* Philadelphia: T. B. Peterson, 1852.

Ranlet, Philip. *Enemies of the Bay Colony: Puritan Massachusetts and Its Foes.* 2nd ed. Lanham, MD: University Press of America, 2006.

Reading, Anna. "From *The Social Inheritance of the Holocaust: Gender Culture and Memory.*" In *Theories of Memory: A Reader,* edited by Michael Rossington and Anne Whitehead, 219–22. Baltimore: Johns Hopkins University Press, 2007.

Reichart, Walter A. *Washington Irving and Germany*. Ann Arbor: University of Michigan Press, 1957.

Reid, Ian. *The Short Story*. London: Methuen, 1977.

"Review: *The Atlantic Souvenir . . .* 1829." *Yankee and Boston Literary Gazette* (November 19, 1828): 1–3.

"Review: *Bracebridge Hall; or the Humorists* by Geoffrey Crayon." *Edinburgh Magazine and Literary Miscellany* (July 1822): 91–96.

"Review: *The Sketch Book*." *New-England Galaxy* (August 6, 1819): 171.

"Review: *The Sketch Book*." *Examiner* (April 16, 1820): 252–53.

"Review: *The Sketch Book of Geoffrey Crayon, Gent*." *Literary Gazette* (April 8, 1820): 228–29.

"Review: *The Sketch Book of Geoffrey Crayon, Gent*. First Five Numbers," *Western Review and Miscellaneous Magazine, a Monthly Publication* (May 1820): 244–54.

"Review: *The Token*, for 1829." *Yankee and Boston Literary Gazette* (November 12, 1828): 46–48.

Rezek, Joseph. *London and the Making of Provincial Literature: Aesthetics and the Transatlantic Book Trade, 1800–1850*. Philadelphia: University of Pennsylvania Press, 2015.

Richardson, Brian. *Narrative Beginnings: Theories and Practices*. Frontiers of Narrative. Lincoln: University of Nebraska Press, 2008.

Ricoeur, Paul. "Narrative Time." In *Narrative Dynamics: Essays on Plot, Time, Closure, and Frames,* edited by Brian Richardson, 35–46. Theory and Interpretation of Narrative. Columbus: Ohio State University Press, 2002.

———. *Time and Narrative*. Vol. 1. Chicago: University of Chicago Press, 1984.

Ritchie, Anne Thackeray. Introduction to *Our Village,* by Mary Russell Mitford, vii–liii. Edited by Anne Thackeray Ritchie. London: Macmillan, 1893.

Romagnolo, Catherine. *Opening Acts: Narrative Beginnings in Twentieth-Century Feminist Fiction*. Frontiers of Narrative. Lincoln: University of Nebraska Press, 2015.

———. "Recessive Origins in Julia Alvarez's *Garcia Girls*: A Feminist Exploration of Narrative Beginnings." In *Narrative Beginnings: Theories and Practices,* edited by Brian Richardson, 149–65. Frontiers of Narrative. Lincoln: University of Nebraska Press, 2008.

Ross, Joel H. *What I Saw in New-York*. Auburn, NY: Derby and Miller, 1851.

Rubin-Dorsky, Jeffrey. *Adrift in the Old World: The Psychological Pilgrimage of Washington Irving*. Chicago: University of Chicago Press, 1988.

Rugg, Peter. "Some Account of the Family of Notions." *New-England Galaxy* (October 29, 1831): 2.

Ryan, James Emmett. *Imaginary Friends: Representing Quakers in American Culture, 1650–1950.* Madison: University of Wisconsin Press, 2009.

Said, Edward W. *Beginnings: Intention and Method.* New York: Columbia University Press, 1985.

Samuels, Shirley. Introduction to *The Culture of Sentiment: Race, Gender, and Sentimentality in Nineteenth-Century America,* 3–8. Edited by Shirley Samuels. New York: Oxford University Press, 1992.

Sanborn, Geoffrey. *Plagiarama! William Wells Brown and the Aesthetic of Attractions.* New York: Columbia University Press, 2015.

Sand, George. "George Sand and Uncle Tom." *National Era* (January 27, 1853). http://utc.iath.virginia.edu/notices/noar01awt.html.

Sayers, Dorothy L. Introduction to *The Omnibus of Crime,* 9–47. Edited by Dorothy L. Sayers. New York: Payson and Clarke, 1929.

Scarry, Elaine. *Resisting Representation.* New York: Oxford University Press, 1994.

Scenes and Thoughts in Europe. New York: Wiley and Putnam, 1846.

Schor, Hilary M. "The Make-Believe of a Middle: On (Not) Knowing Where You Are in Daniel Deronda." In *Narrative Middles: Navigating the Nineteenth-Century British Novel,* edited by Caroline Levine and Mario Ortiz-Robles, 47–74. Theory and Interpretation of Narrative. Columbus: Ohio State University Press, 2011.

Scott, Walter. *Peveril of the Peak.* Edinburgh: Archibald Constable, 1822.

Sedgwick, Catharine Maria. "The Catholic Iroquois." In *The Atlantic Souvenir: A Christmas and New Year's Offering,* 72–103. Philadelphia: Carey and Lea, 1826.

———. "The Country Cousin." In *The Token; A Christmas and New Year's Present.* edited by Samuel G. Goodrich, 153–93. Boston: Carter and Hendee, 1830.

———. "Mary Dyre." In *The Token and Atlantic Souvenir: A Christmas and New Year's Present,* edited by Samuel G. Goodrich, 294–312. Boston: Gray and Bowen, 1831.

———. "Modern Chivalry." In *The Atlantic Souvenir: A Christmas and New Year's Offering,* 5–47. Philadelphia: Carey and Lea, 1827.

———. *A New-England Tale.* New York: E. Bliss and E. White, 1822.

———. "Old Maids." In *The Offering: A Christmas and New Year's Present,* 17–46. Philadelphia: Thomas T. Ash, 1834.

———. *Redwood.* New York: E. Bliss and E. White, 1824.

———. "A Reminiscence of Federalism." In *The Token and Atlantic Souvenir: A Christmas and New Year's Present,* edited by Samuel G. Goodrich, 102–43. Boston: Charles Bowen, 1834.

———. "Romance in Real Life." In *The Legendary, Consisting of Original Pieces, Principally Illustrative of American History, Scenery, and Manners,* edited by Nathaniel Parker Willis, 1:118–61. Boston: Samuel G. Goodrich, 1828.

———. "St. Catharine's Eve." In *The Token and Atlantic Souvenir: A Christmas and New Year's Present,* 7–36. Boston: Charles Bowen, 1835.

———. "The Story of Shay's War." In *The Atlantic Souvenir for 1831,* 281–313. Philadelphia: Carey and Lea, 1831.

———. *Tales and Sketches, Second Series.* New York: Harper and Brothers, 1844.

Seltzer, Mark. *True Crime: Observations on Violence and Modernity.* New York: Routledge, 2007.

Senchyne, Jonathan. "Bottles of Ink and Reams of Paper: *Clotel,* Racialization, and the Material Culture of Print." In *Early African American Print Culture,* edited by Lara Langer Cohen and Jordan Alexander Stein, 140–58. Philadelphia: University of Pennsylvania Press, 2012.

Sewel, William. *The History of the Rise, Increase, and Progress of the Christian People Called Quakers.* 4th ed. Vol. 1. London: James Phillips and Son, 1799.

Sha, Richard C. *The Visual and Verbal Sketch in British Romanticism.* Philadelphia: University of Pennsylvania Press, 1998.

Shaffer, Arthur H. *The Politics of History: Writing the History of the American Revolution, 1783–1815.* New Brunswick, NJ: Transaction, 2009.

Sizemore, Michelle R. *American Enchantment: Rituals of the People in the Post-Revolutionary World.* New York: Oxford University Press, 2017.

———. "'Changing by Enchantment': Temporal Convergence, Early National Comparisons, and Washington Irving's Sketchbook." *Studies in American Fiction* 40, no. 2 (2013): 157–83.

Smith, Eric Ledell. "The End of Black Voting Rights in Pennsylvania: African Americans and the Pennsylvania Constitutional Convention of 1837–1838." *Pennsylvania History: A Journal of Mid-Atlantic Studies* 65, no. 3 (1998): 279–99.

Smith, Susan Belasco. "Serialization and the Nature of Uncle Tom's Cabin." In *Periodical Literature in Nineteenth-Century America,* by Kenneth M. Price and Susan Belasco Smith, 69–89. Charlottesville: University Press of Virginia, 1995.

Smith, Sydney. "ART. III. Statistical Annals of the United States of America." *Edinburgh Review, or Critical Journal* 33, no. 65 (January 1820): 69–80.

"*Southern Literary Messenger*. Review of Tales and Sketches." In *Catharine Maria Sedgwick: Critical Perspectives,* edited by Lucinda L. Damon-Bach and Victoria Clements, 156–57. Boston: Northeastern University Press, 2003.

Springer, Haskell S. Introduction to *The Sketch Book of Geoffrey Crayon, Gent,* xi–xxxii. Edited by Haskell S. Springer. Boston: Twayne, 1978.

Srebnick, Amy Gilman. *The Mysterious Death of Mary Rogers: Sex and Culture in Nineteenth-Century New York.* Studies in the History of Sexuality. New York: Oxford University Press, 1995.

Stowe, Harriet Beecher. *A Key to Uncle Tom's Cabin.* St. Clair Shores, MI: Scholarly, 1977.

——. *Uncle Tom's Cabin: Authoritative Text, Backgrounds and Contexts, Criticism.* 2nd ed. Edited by Elizabeth Ammons. Norton Critical Edition. New York: W. W. Norton, 2010.

Strier, Richard. "How Formalism Became a Dirty Word and Why We Can't Do without It." In *Renaissance Literature and Its Formal Engagements,* edited by Mark David Rasmussen, 207–15. New York: Palgrave, 2002.

Tamarkin, Elisa. *Anglophilia: Deference, Devotion, and Antebellum America.* Chicago: University of Chicago Press, 2008.

Terramorsi, Bernard. "'Peter Rugg, the Missing Man,' or The Eclipsing Revolution: An Essay on the Supernatural." Université de la Réunion. O.R.A.C.L.E., July 30, 2018. http://oracle-reunion.pagesperso-orange.fr/documents /peter_rugg_the_missing_man_the_eclipsing_revolut.html.

Thompson, Gary Richard. *The Art of Authorial Presence: Hawthorne's Provincial Tales.* Durham, NC: Duke University Press, 1993.

Thompson, Jon. *Fiction, Crime, and Empire: Clues to Modernity and Postmodernism.* Urbana: University of Illinois Press, 1993.

Thompson, Ralph. *American Literary Annuals & Gift Books, 1825–1865.* New York: H. W. Wilson, 1936.

Thoreau, Henry David. "Civil Disobedience." In *Walden and Other Writings,* edited by Brooks Atkinson, 665–93. New York: Modern Library, 2000.

Tocqueville, Alexis de. *Democracy in America.* 4th ed. Translated by Henry Reeve. Vol. 2. New York: J. and H. G. Langley, 1841.

Todorov, Tzvetan. "The Typology of Detective Fiction." In *The Poetics of Prose,* 42–52. Ithaca, NY: Cornell University Press, 1977.

Tonkovich, Nicole. *Domesticity with a Difference: The Nonfiction of Catharine Beecher, Sarah J. Hale, Fanny Fern, and Margaret Fuller.* Jackson: University Press of Mississippi, 1997.

Twain, Mark. *Adventures of Huckleberry Finn.* Edited by Victor Fischer and Lin Salamo. Berkeley: University of California Press, 2001.

Ulrich, Laurel Thatcher. *The Age of Homespun: Objects and Stories in the Creation of an American Myth.* New York: Knopf, 2001.

Urakova, Alexandra. "'The Purloined Letter' in the Gift Book: Reading Poe in a Contemporary Context." *Nineteenth-Century Literature* 64, no. 3 (December 2009): 323–46.

Voss, Arthur. *The American Short Story: A Critical Survey.* Norman: University of Oklahoma Press, 1973.

Walker, William. *The War in Nicaragua.* New York: S. H. Goetzel, 1860.

Wallace, Dewey D., Jr. "Predestination." In *Puritans and Puritanism in Europe and America: A Comprehensive Encyclopedia,* edited by Francis J. Bremer and Tom Webster, 2:491–93. Santa Barbara, CA: ABC-CLIO, 2006.

———. "Puritan Polemical Divinity and Doctrinal Controversy." In *The Cambridge Companion to Puritanism,* edited by John Coffey and Paul Chang-Ha Lim, 206–22. Cambridge: Cambridge University Press, 2008.

Walsh, John Evangelist. *Poe the Detective: The Curious Circumstances behind "The Murder of Marie Roget."* New Brunswick, NJ: Rutgers University Press, 1968.

Warhol-Down, Robyn. *Gendered Interventions: Narrative Discourse in the Victorian Novel.* New Brunswick, NJ: Rutgers University Press, 1989.

Warner, Charles Dudley. "From 'Last Years: The Character of His Literature.'" In *A Century of Commentary on the Works of Washington Irving, 1860–1974,* edited by Andrew B. Myers, 40–48. Tarrytown, NY: Sleepy Hollow Restorations, 1976.

Webster, Daniel. *An Address Delivered at the Completion of the Bunker Hill Monument, June 17, 1843.* Boston: Tappan and Dennet, 1843.

———. *The Great Speeches and Orations of Daniel Webster.* Edited by Edwin Percy Whipple. Boston: Little, Brown, 1886.

Weinstock, Jeffrey Andrew. "Introduction: The American Gothic." In *The Cambridge Companion to American Gothic,* edited by Jeffrey Andrew Weinstock, 1–12. New York: Cambridge University Press, 2017.

Weissberg, Liliane. "Black, White, and Gold." In *Romancing the Shadow: Poe and Race,* edited by J. Gerald Kennedy and Liliane Weissberg, 127–56. New York: Oxford University Press, 2001.

Weld, Theodore Dwight. *American Slavery as It Is: Testimony of a Thousand Witnesses.* New York: American Anti-Slavery Society, 1839.

Wendell, Barrett. "From 'Washington Irving.'" In *A Century of Commentary on the Works of Washington Irving, 1860–1974,* edited by Andrew B. Myers, 94–102. Tarrytown, NY: Sleepy Hollow Restorations, 1976.

West, Ray Benedict. *The Short Story in America, 1900–1950.* Chicago: H. Regnery, 1952.

Whalen, Terence. "Average Racism: Poe, Slavery, and the Wages of Literary Nationalism." In *Romancing the Shadow: Poe and Race,* edited by J. Gerald Kennedy and Liliane Weissberg, 3–40. New York: Oxford University Press, 2001.

Wheatley, Phillis, and Margaretta Matilda Odell. *Memoir and Poems of Phillis Wheatley, a Native African and a Slave. Dedicated to the Friends of the Africans.* Boston: Geo. W. Light, 1834.

White, Ed. "The Ourang-Outang Situation." *College Literature* 30, no. 3 (July 29, 2003): 88–108.

White, Hayden V. *The Fiction of Narrative: Essays on History, Literature, and Theory, 1957–2007.* Edited by Robert Doran. Baltimore: Johns Hopkins University Press, 2010.

Willis, Nathaniel Parker. *Pencillings by the Way.* 2 vols. Philadelphia: Carey, Lea, and Blanchard, 1836.

Wimsatt, William Kurtz, Jr. "Poe and the Mystery of Mary Rogers." *PMLA* 56, no. 1 (March 1941): 230–48.

Winship, Michael. *American Literary Publishing in the Mid-Nineteenth Century: The Business of Ticknor and Fields.* New York: Cambridge University Press, 1995.

Woloch, Nancy. *Women and the American Experience.* New York: Knopf, 1984.

Wood, Gordon S. *Empire of Liberty: A History of the Early Republic, 1789–1815.* New York: Oxford University Press, 2009.

❖ INDEX ❖

CPSIA information can be obtained
at www.ICGtesting.com
Printed in the USA
LVHW091357190221
679471LV00021B/44